FROM COAST TO FEN: ARCHAEOLOGY IN A DYNAMIC LANDSCAPE

THE ARCHAEOLOGY OF THE TRITON KNOLL
ELECTRICAL SYSTEM, LINCOLNSHIRE

Edited by

CLAIRE CHRISTIE AND JOSHUA T. HOGUE

With contributions by

Laura Bailey, Michael Bamforth, Marina Chorro-Giner, Rebecca Devaney,
Hugh G. Fiske, Val Fryer, Kevin Hayward, Tom Lane, Christine Milton,
Gwladys Montiel, Ian M. Rowlandson, Hannah Russ, Owain Scholma-Mason,
Ruth Shaffrey, Rebecca Sillwood, Maria Stockdale, Zoe Tomlinson, Kate Turner,
Joanna R. Walker, Michael Wallace, and Jane Young

Illustrations by

Tom Watson, Beata Wieczorek-Oleksy, and Marc Zubia-Pons

Oxford & Philadelphia

Published in the United Kingdom in 2025 by
OXBOW BOOKS
81 St Clements, Oxford OX4 1AW

and in the United States by
OXBOW BOOKS
1950 Lawrence Road, Havertown, PA 19083

© Oxbow Books and the individual authors 2025

Paperback Edition: ISBN 979-8-88857-195-8
Digital Edition: ISBN 979-8-88857-196-5 (epub)

A CIP record for this book is available from the British Library

Library of Congress Control Number: 2025935489

All rights reserved. No part of this book may be reproduced or transmitted in any form or by any means, electronic or mechanical including photocopying, recording or by any information storage and retrieval system, without permission from the publisher in writing.

Printed in Malta by Melita Press
Typeset in India by DiTech Publishing Services

For a complete list of Oxbow titles, please contact:

UNITED KINGDOM
Oxbow Books
Telephone (0)1226 734350
Email: oxbow@oxbowbooks.com
www.oxbowbooks.com

UNITED STATES OF AMERICA
Oxbow Books
Telephone (610) 853-9131, Fax (610) 853-9146
Email: queries@casemateacademic.com
www.casemateacademic.com/oxbow

Oxbow Books is part of the Casemate Group

The text was copy edited by Owain Scholma-Mason and Cindy Nelson-Viljoen.

Front cover: Artist's reconstruction of a Roman salt production site (created by Leia Carter)
Back cover: GoPro photo of Structure Complex 2, TAM04

The Publisher's authorised representative in the EU for product safety is Authorised Rep Compliance Ltd., Ground Floor, 71 Lower Baggot Street, Dublin D02 P593, Ireland.
www.arccompliance.com

Contents

List of illustrations	v
List of tables	vii
Acknowledgements	ix

1. Introduction   1
   Claire Christie and Joshua T. Hogue
   - Background to the project   1
   - Landscape Parcels   1
   - Monograph structure   5

2. A changing landscape   9
   Joanna R. Walker and Christine Milton
   - Warming up: Prehistoric coastlines and landscapes   10
   - A dynamic landscape: Middle and late Holocene changes   14
   - The initial onset of wet conditions   18
   - Slowing sea level rise and marine regression   22
   - Renewed expansion of tidal flat areas   23
   - Medieval and post-medieval land reclamation   28
   - Glossary of terms   30

3. Prehistoric landscapes   32
   Claire Christie
   - Mesolithic and Neolithic: Prehistoric patterns   32
   - Bronze Age: Timber and tides   36
   - Late Bronze Age–Iron Age beginnings   42

4. Living near the edge: Settlement and agriculture in the Roman period   46
   Maria Stockdale and Owain Scholma-Mason
   - A Roman agricultural landscape   47
   - Environmental evidence   68
   - Artefactual evidence   82

5. An esteemed resource: Roman saltworking at Triton Knoll   94
   Owain Scholma-Mason and Tom Lane
   - The anatomy of saltmaking   103
   - Triton Knoll and salt production in Lincolnshire   111

6. Inhabiting the Fens: Communities and connections during the Roman period   114
   Owain Scholma-Mason, Maria Stockdale, and Tom Lane
   - *Veni, vidi, colui*: Roman agriculture at Triton Knoll   114
   - Salt of the earth: saltworking at Triton Knoll   122
   - Building connections: Exchange and community   123

7. Medieval and post-medieval rural settlement and industry *Joshua T. Hogue and Maria Stockdale*	130
Medieval field systems and landscape evolution	130
Late medieval and post-medieval industry	139
Artefactual evidence	144
Environmental evidence	158
Conclusion	164
8. Ebbs and flows: The archaeology of Triton Knoll *Owain Scholma-Mason, Joshua T. Hogue, and Claire Christie*	165
Bibliography	168

List of illustrations

Figure 1.1	Route of the Triton Knoll Electrical System	2
Figure 1.2	Triton Knoll Electrical System analysis sites and Landscape Parcels	6
Figure 1.3	Map of principal sites showing key periods and activities	7
Figure 2.1	Map of The Fens showing the major Fen basins in Lincolnshire and the route of the Scheme	10
Figure 2.2	Map of the superficial geology and site locations across the northern half of the Scheme	12
Figure 2.3	Map of the superficial geology and site locations across the southern half of the Scheme	13
Figure 2.4	Diagrammatic maps showing the route of the Scheme and possible coastline throughout the Holocene	17
Figure 2.5	Map of the Scheme showing the extent of marine flooded areas in augered cores at 4000 BC	19
Figure 2.6	Map of the Scheme showing the extent of marine flooded areas in augered cores at 3000 BC	20
Figure 2.7	Map of the Scheme showing the extent of marine flooded areas in augered cores at 2000 BC	23
Figure 2.8	Map of the Scheme showing the extent of marine flooded areas in augered cores at AD 1	25
Figure 2.9	LiDAR map showing the dendritic pattern of roddons around the River Witham, near Boston	26
Figure 3.1	Prehistoric activity identified along the route of the Scheme	33
Figure 3.2	Prehistoric activity identified in the Historic Environment Record (HER) 1 km from the route of the Scheme from SMR01 to SMR10	35
Figure 3.3	East-facing section of Pit 0037, SPE01	36
Figure 3.4	The topographic setting of HDD95 and TAM14	37
Figure 3.5	Southwest facing photograph of the wooden structure in HDD95	38
Figure 3.6	The wooden structure in HDD95 during excavation	38
Figure 3.7	Driven oak pile SF5, Tree 5	40
Figure 3.8	Cross sections of driven piles	41
Figure 3.9	The late Bronze Age socketed axe from TAM14	42
Figure 3.10	Iron Age features at SPE01	43
Figure 3.11	Examples of Iron Age pottery from SPE01	44
Figure 4.1	Roman sites excavated along the route of the Scheme	47
Figure 4.2	Comparative site plans of Roman features at SMR01, SPE01, and SMR04	50
Figure 4.3	Roman features at SPE01 aligned to the crescent-shaped plateau	52
Figure 4.4	The coastal landscape showing the location of the excavated sites and Roman sites identified in the Historic Environment Record (HER) 1 km from the route of the Scheme	53
Figure 4.5	Roman burials at SPE02	54
Figure 4.6	Landscape around Burgh le Marsh showing the location of the excavated sites and Roman sites identified in the Historic Environment Record (HER) 1 km from the route of the Scheme	54
Figure 4.7	The landscape between Sibsey and Bicker Parish showing the location of the excavated sites and Roman sites identified in the Historic Environment Record (HER) 1 km from the route of the Scheme	55
Figure 4.8	Comparative site plans of SPE03, SPE04 and SMR17	56
Figure 4.9	Early Roman phases of SPE03 showing the distribution of key artefacts	57
Figure 4.10	Plans of Structure 12 and 5 at SPE03	58
Figure 4.11	Middle Roman phases of SPE03 (Enclosure 4) showing the distribution of key artefacts	59
Figure 4.12	Middle Roman phases of SPE04	60
Figure 4.13	Late Roman phases of SPE04	62

vi *List of illustrations*

Figure 4.14	Roman phases of SMR17	63
Figure 4.15	The landscape around SMR01/TAM04 showing the location of the excavated sites and Roman sites listed in the Lincolnshire HER (1 km)	64
Figure 4.16	Roman activity at SMR01 and TAM04	65
Figure 4.17	Development of Structure Complex 2	66
Figure 4.18	GoPro photograph of Structure Complex 2	67
Figure 4.19	GoPro photograph of excavated Structures 16 and 17	68
Figure 4.20	Comparative chart of the animal bone assemblages of the Coastal, Lincolnshire Marsh, Fen Edge and Inland Fen Edge Landscape Parcels	70
Figure 4.21	Comparison of untreated and pre-treated analysed charred grain samples	76
Figure 4.22	Results of $\Delta^{13}C$ and $\delta^{15}N$ analysis of charred wheat grain and cattle mandibular bone	77
Figure 4.23	Results of $\delta^{13}C$ analysis of tooth increments	79
Figure 4.24	Results of $\delta^{15}N$ analysis of tooth increments	79
Figure 4.25	Examples of Roman pottery from SPE03 and SPE04	86
Figure 4.26	Pottery stamps from the Fen Edge and Inland Fen Edge	87
Figure 4.27	Fired clay balls from SPE03	92
Figure 5.1	The geography and context of the principal saltern sites identified across the Scheme	95
Figure 5.2	Triton Knoll saltern sites in relation to other known saltern sites recorded in the Historic Environment Record (HER) (1 km)	97
Figure 5.3	Plan of Roman features at SMR05 and SMR07	98
Figure 5.4	Section through Saltern 1 at SMR07 showing deposits of saltern waste and flooding events	99
Figure 5.5	Plan of middle and late Roman features at SMR06	100
Figure 5.6	Plan of middle and late Roman features at SPE02	101
Figure 5.7	Plan of late Roman saltworking features at SPE02	102
Figure 5.8	Examples of key briquetage forms from Lincolnshire Marsh Landscape Parcel	106
Figure 5.9	Base of large grey ware jar (SF002) *in situ* at SMR06	107
Figure 5.10	Timber planks in upper fill of Well 6.26 at SMR06	107
Figure 5.11	Oven 2.19 at SPE02	108
Figure 5.12	Mid-excavation photo of Oven 2.18 with elements of charcoal in fill *in situ*	108
Figure 5.13	Post-excavation photo of Oven 2.18	109
Figure 5.14	Section through Oven 2.18	109
Figure 5.15	Grey ware beaker from Oven 2.18, SPE02	110
Figure 5.16	Examples of Roman pottery from SMR06 and SPE02	112
Figure 6.1	Sites in their Roman landscape context	115
Figure 6.2	Spilsby sandstone Beehive Quern from SPE04	117
Figure 6.3	Topography and layout of SPE03 and SPE04	118
Figure 6.4	Interpretive plan of early–late Roman activity at TAM04	119
Figure 6.5	Pottery vessels with evidence of dairy residue	121
Figure 6.6	Examples of weaving tools from TAM04/SMR01	122
Figure 6.7	The wider Roman context of the Scheme	125
Figure 6.8	Roman find spots identified in the Historic Environment Record (HER) 1 km from the route of the Scheme	127
Figure 7.1	Distribution of key medieval and post-medieval sites across the Scheme	131
Figure 7.2	Sites in relation to the Landscape Parcels	132
Figure 7.3	SMR09 and SMR10 in their landscape and historical context	134
Figure 7.4	SPE01 in its landscape and historical context	135
Figure 7.5	Early medieval (Saxon) archaeological features and other activity at SMR10, Croft End	136
Figure 7.6	Early medieval (Saxon) field boundary at SMR10, Croft End	137
Figure 7.7	Early medieval (Saxon) and medieval archaeological features at SPE01, near Mumby	138
Figure 7.8	SMR17 in its landscape context and historic setting	140
Figure 7.9	Plan of medieval features at SMR17	141
Figure 7.10	Plan of all features at SMR09	142
Figure 7.11	Selected examples of medieval and post-medieval pottery from SMR09	149
Figure 7.12	Iron key and copper alloy awl or stylus	158
Figure 7.13	Iron horseshoe	158
Figure 7.14	Small finds from SMR10	159

List of tables

Table 1.1	Overview of mitigation areas with a summary of the archaeology uncovered	3
Table 1.2	Summary of the archaeological activity within each Landscape Parcel	4
Table 1.3	Chronological periods used within the Landscape Parcel reports and the monograph	5
Table 2.1	Summary table of Holocene conditions in the East and West Fen areas, Lincolnshire	15
Table 2.2	Stickney Moraine onsite vegetation during the middle Neolithic to middle Bronze Age	24
Table 3.1	Summary of lithics by Landscape Parcel, site and lithic type	34
Table 3.2	Details of the dendrochronological samples taken from the timber structure at HDD95	39
Table 3.3	Timber condition scale used in this report	40
Table 4.1	Principal Roman sites recorded across the Scheme	47
Table 4.2	Iron Age and Roman evidence excavated at other locations along the Scheme	48
Table 4.3	Radiocarbon dates from Roman sites across the Scheme	49
Table 4.4	Summary of Roman artefacts from the Coastal Landscape Parcel	53
Table 4.5	Presence/absence of identified taxa for the middle Roman period	72
Table 4.6	Presence/absence of identified taxa for the late Roman period	74
Table 4.7	Archaeobotanical samples subjected to stable isotope analysis	75
Table 4.8	Archaeozoological samples subjected to stable isotope analysis	75
Table 4.9	Summary results for stable isotope analysis of crops samples	78
Table 4.10	Summary results of stable isotope analysis of faunal remains	78
Table 4.11	Quantification of Roman small finds by object type and phase	88
Table 5.1	Overview of salt production sites recorded across the Scheme	96
Table 5.2	Overview of salt production sites recorded across the Scheme	101
Table 5.3	Principal forms of briquetage	104
Table 5.4	Morris's briquetage phases	105
Table 6.1	Summary of economic activities across the Scheme	124
Table 7.1	Pottery from all sites summarised by sherd count, vessel count, weight, and REVE	145
Table 7.2	Pottery summarised by Landscape Parcel and ceramic period with vessel count	146
Table 7.3	Pottery summarised by Codename with full name and date range by sherd count, vessel count, weight, and REVE	146
Table 7.4	Quantification of the animal bone assemblages by site and period	161

Acknowledgements

The works along the Triton Knoll Electrical System were commissioned by J Murphy and Sons Ltd on behalf of Triton Knoll Offshore Wind Farm Ltd. Royal HaskoningDHV and RWE are also thanked for their support and input throughout the excavation and post-excavation stages. Thanks are extended to the Historic Environment Team at Lincolnshire County Council and Boston Borough Council who provided comments and support throughout the project.

The fieldwork was undertaken by multiple teams from Headland Archaeology (UK) Ltd and Allen Archaeology Ltd. The fieldwork undertaken by Allen Archaeology Ltd was managed by Tobin Rayner, and the Headland Archaeology excavations were managed by Candy Hatherley.

The post-excavation analysis was a collaborative programme of work between Headland Archaeology and Allen Archaeology Ltd managed by Claire Christie with Joshua T. Hogue. The original post-excavation assessment reports for Headland Archaeology were authored by Aisling Fitzpatrick-Sinclair, Don Wilson, Genevieve Shaw, Josh Gaunt, and Sam Bithell, whilst those at Allen Archaeology Ltd were authored by Charlotte Tooze. The post-excavation analysis reports were authored by Owain Scholma-Mason, Kim Gaunt, Megan Roberts, Alan Telford, and Maria Stockdale.

Numerous specialists provided contributions to the post-excavation analysis and to this monograph, with Julie Franklin managing the overall programme of finds work and Kate Turner the environmental analysis. The graphics for the post-excavation analysis and publication were managed by Beata Wieczorek-Oleksy, with Marc Zubia-Pons acting as lead illustrator. Additional illustrations were provided by Tom Watson, with Leia Carter completing the reconstruction of the Roman saltern site. The overall archiving process was managed by Charlotte Self, with Amy Koonce completing the physical and digital archive for Headland Archaeology and Yvonne Rose overseeing the archiving for Allen Archaeology Ltd.

The digital archive has been uploaded to the Archaeology Data Service (ADS) (https://doi.org/10.5284/1125918). This digital archive includes the individual Landscape Parcel reports referred to throughout this volume.

1

Introduction

Claire Christie and Joshua T. Hogue

The Triton Knoll Electrical System (henceforth the 'Scheme') extends for over 60 km making landfall at Anderby Creek on the East Lincolnshire Coast (TF5510 7710) before continuing in a south-westerly direction to Bicker in the Borough of Boston (TF1960 3840) (Fig. 1.1). The system connects the Triton Knoll Offshore Wind Farm (TKOWF), *c.* 33 km (20.5 miles) east off the Lincolnshire coast, to the National Grid substation at Bicker Fen, Boston. The Scheme extends through a dynamic landscape that has witnessed significant and complex change with periods of marine transgression, regression and later reclamation. The archaeology uncovered during the evaluation and excavation works along the route and at the substation site reflects this changing landscape. The excavations revealed hints of prehistoric activity, evidence of Roman settlement and saltmaking and provided insights into medieval and post-medieval rural settlement and industry.

This monograph presents an exploration of changing settlement and activity patterns across a dynamic landscape. The excavated sites are considered in detail, supported by finds and environmental analysis, and compared to those across the region. The monograph builds on the rich dataset collected from the Scheme through thematic period-based discussion, elucidating key regional research themes, and contributing to a range of nationally important questions. The monograph is supported by a series of detailed archaeological and specialist reports (grouped into four Landscape Parcels, see below), and a digital archive available on the Archaeological Data Service (ADS) (https://doi.org/10.5284/1125918). The documentary and physical archive have been submitted to the Lincoln Museum.

Background to the project

Beginning in 2018, the initial archaeological work comprised a Historic Environment Impact Assessment informed by the Historic Environment Record (HER), historic map regression, aerial photographic assessment, LiDAR assessment and site walkover survey (RSK 2015). This was followed by a metal detector survey (Allen Archaeology 2018a), a non-intrusive survey (Allen Archaeology 2018b), a geoarchaeological desk-based assessment (Allen Archaeology 2018c) and an archaeological evaluation (Allen Archaeology 2018d). The evaluation works involved the excavation of 350 trial trenches along the entire Scheme, which revealed evidence of prehistoric peat development and finds, Roman settlement and saltmaking, and post-medieval field boundaries (*ibid.*). Further geoarchaeological analysis was undertaken to enable a more detailed understanding of the environmental changes and place the archaeological sites in their landscape context (Allen Archaeology 2019; 2020; 2021a). The results of these works informed the final mitigation strategy. The excavations along the cable route comprised four areas of set-piece excavation (SPE), 18 of strip, map and record (SMR), 27 of targeted archaeological monitoring (TAM) and the monitoring of 148 Horizontal Direct Drilling Sites (HDD Pits) and 50 Joint Bays (Headland Archaeology 2020; Allen Archaeology 2021b). In addition to excavations along the cable route, a further eight areas of SMR and TAM along with the monitoring of 24 HDD Pits and four Joint Bays were conducted at the substation site (Allen Archaeology 2022a).

Landscape Parcels

The monograph is supported by a series of detailed analyses presented as four reports, each focused on a different Landscape Parcel: Coastal, Lincolnshire Marsh, Fen Edge and Inland Fen Edge (Fig. 1.2). These parcels were defined during the post-excavation analysis, representing convenient divisions primarily relating to the modern landscape. The grouping of sites in this way provides a holistic and

Figure 1.1 Route of the Triton Knoll Electrical System

coherent approach to the archaeology and its landscape context, grouping together the results from the different excavation areas (Headland Archaeology 2023; Fig. 1.2, Table 1.2). The preliminary analyses were built upon, and different approaches standardised, through the application of a Scheme-wide methodology for stratigraphic analysis (*ibid.*). A chronological framework for describing the results was adapted from established period divisions as defined in the Regional Research Framework (Knight *et al.* 2012; https://researchframeworks.org/emherf/) and this schema is utilised throughout this volume (Table 1.3).

All radiocarbon dates presented in the text are presented as calibrated dates at 95% confidence (unless otherwise stated) rounded outward to ten years. All dates were calibrated using the internationally agreed terrestrial calibration curve of Reimer *et al.* (2020) and the OxCal v4.4.4 computer programme (Bronk Ramsey 2021).

Coastal Landscape Parcel

The Coastal Landscape Parcel comprised three sites: SMR01, SMR04 and SPE01, located between Anderby and Hogsthorpe on Lincolnshire's east coast (Gaunt and

Table 1.1 Overview of mitigation areas with a summary of the archaeology uncovered

Site	NGR (centred on)	Area (ha)	Summary of results	Report Reference
SPE01	TF 53315 74417	0.57	Prehistoric pit. Iron Age & Roman saltmaking. Roman ditches & 'ladder' enclosure system	HA 2020
SPE02	TF 52684 69195	0.24	Roman salt production site with 3 burials	HA 2020
SPE03	TF 2848 4801	0.85	Roman farmstead	AAL 2021
SPE04	TF 2740 4740	1.55	Roman farmstead	AAL 2021
SMR1	TF53726 75826	0.25	Roman enclosure & ditch. Medieval ditches	HA 2020
SMR2	TF5369 75660	0.34	2 Bronze Age pits & a series of post-medieval ditches	HA 2020
SMR3	TF53726 75826	0.33	A single ditch	HA 2020
SMR4	TF52684 69195	0.094 0.066	Roman ditches	HA 2020
SMR5	TF53157 74244	0.42	Roman salt production site	HA 2020
SMR6	TF52735 69420	0.25	Roman salt production site	HA 2020
SMR7	TF52781 70514	0.15	Roman salt production site	HA 2020
SMR9	TF52310 67980	0.45	Prehistoric pits. Medieval–post-medieval farmstead & brick production site	HA 2020
SMR10	TF52416 67496 TF52418 67554	0.68	Saxon field system	HA 2020
SMR12	TF49651 63879	0.27	Medieval–post-medieval ditches	HA 2020
SMR13	TF48796 63148	0.37	Post-medieval ditches	HA 2020
SMR14a	TF34437 53942	0.23	Undated gullies	HA 2020
SMR14b	TF30303 49465	0.12	Post-medieval–modern activity as evident on historic maps (OS 1888)	HA 2020
SMR16	TF28690 48314	0.21	Undated ditches	HA 2020
SMR17	TF28569 48117		Roman farmstead. Medieval structure	AAL 2021
SMR 8,11, 15	–	–	No archaeology	HA 2020
TAM 1–27	–	–	Limited archaeology uncovered. Results are referenced but do not form focus of further analysis	AAL 2021
HDD 1-148	–	–	Limited archaeology uncovered. Results are referenced but do not form focus of further analysis. HDD24, 26–28, 35 and 95 are of interest	AAL 2021
HDD24	TF 52807 69862 TF 52797 69812	–	Saltern deposits	AAL 2021
HDD26	TF 52622 68972	–	Saltern deposits	AAL 2021
HDD27	TF 52462 68573	–	Saltern deposits	AAL 2021
HDD28	TF 52324 68234 TF 52310 68237	–	Saltern deposits	AAL 2021
HDD35	TF 51796 65596	–	Saltern deposits	AAL 2021
HDD95	TF 34348 53869	–	Bronze Age timber structure	AAL 2021
Joint Bays	–	–	Limited archaeology uncovered. Results are referenced but do not form focus of further analysis	AAL 2021
Joint Bay 5	TF 52754 69455	–	Saltern deposit	AAL 2021

(Continued)

Table 1.1 Overview of mitigation areas with a summary of the archaeology uncovered (Continued)

Site	NGR (centred on)	Area (ha)	Summary of results	Report Reference
Joint Bay 6	TF 52358 67906	–	Late Iron Age–early Roman pottery sherds, fired clay, briquetage & animal bones recovered from alluvium	AAL 2022a
SMR1 (E1)	TF 19118 39915	0.49	Roman farmstead	AAL 2022a
SMR2–4 (E1)	–	–	Limited archaeology uncovered. Results are referenced but do not form focus of further analysis	AAL 2022a
TAM1–3 (E1)	–	–	Limited archaeology uncovered. Results are referenced but do not form focus of further analysis	AAL 2022a
TAM4 (E1)	TF 19265 40090	5.75	Roman farmstead	AAL 2022a
HDD1, 2, 4–7, 10, 13			No archaeology (natural deposits only)	AAL 2022a
Joint Bays 1, 2			No archaeology (natural deposits only)	AAL 2022a

Table 1.2 Summary of the archaeological activity within each Landscape Parcel

Landscape Parcel	Location	Key sites	Summary
Coastal	Anderby	SMR01, SPE01, SMR04	Iron Age & Roman activity
Lincolnshire Marsh	West of Ingoldmells	SMR05, SMR06, SPE02, SMR07	Salt production sites
Fen Edge	Burgh le Marsh – Boston	SMR09, SMR10, HDD95, SMR12, SMR13, SMR14, SMR17, SPE03, SPE04, SMR16	Bronze Age timber structure Roman farmsteads Saxon field system Medieval–post-medieval farmsteads & rural industry
Inland Fen Edge	North of Bicker	SMR01 & TAM4	Roman farmstead including a multiphase structure

Roberts 2024) (Fig. 1.2). Archaeological remains were identified on all three sites, dating from the Iron Age to the post-medieval period. The sites are located within a once-tidal landscape with the site with the greatest concentration of archaeology, SPE01, located on a slight rise. Evidence for later prehistoric saltmaking was identified at SPE01, with briquetage recovered from structures and pits. The use of the site shifted from the Roman period onwards with ditches and boundaries associated with agriculture (Fig. 1.3). Further Roman boundaries were identified at SMR01 to the north and SMR04 to the south. Post-Roman agricultural field systems and boundaries were present in two areas with the alignment of modern and historic boundaries adhering to the orientation of these earlier boundaries.

Lincolnshire Marsh Landscape Parcel

The Lincolnshire Marsh Landscape Parcel comprised four key areas: SMR05, SMR06, SMR07 and SPE02, located between the A52 and Skegness Road (Scholma-Mason 2024) (Fig. 1.2). The archaeology uncovered within the Lincolnshire Marsh Landscape Parcel was centred on salt production (Fig. 1.3). This includes evidence for eight salterns, which form part of a wider spread of Roman salt production within the vicinity. Features relating to all stages of salt production were uncovered, including tanks for the collection of salt water, kilns and hearths used to heat brine and the waste from these processes that was widely recorded in the form of highly visible mounds of briquetage. Associated dating evidence suggests that this activity took place during the mid- to later Roman period, with limited evidence for activity preceding this.

Fen Edge Landscape Parcel

The Fen Edge Landscape Parcel was the most extensive, stretching from Burgh le Marsh in the East Lindsey district to Swineshead Bridge in Boston (Stockdale et al. 2024) (Fig. 1.2). The Landscape Parcel comprised several key sites: SMR09, SMR10, SMR12–14, SMR17, SPE03 (and

Table 1.3 Chronological periods used within the Landscape Parcel reports and the monograph

Database no.	Period	Date Range
1	**Prehistoric**	*c.* **950 kya–AD 43**
2	Palaeolithic	*c.* 950 kya–9500 BC
3	Mesolithic	9500–4000 BC
4	Neolithic	4000–2200 BC
5	**Bronze Age**	**2200–800 BC**
6	Early Bronze Age	2200–1500 BC
7	Middle Bronze Age	1500–1150 BC
8	**Late Bronze Age**	**1150–800 BC**
9	Iron Age	800 BC–AD 43
10	Early Iron Age	800–500 BC
11	Middle Iron Age	500–150 BC
12	Late Iron Age	150 BC–AD 43
13	**Roman**	**AD 43–410**
14	Early Roman	AD 43–100
15	Middle Roman	100–250
16	Late Roman	250–410
17	**Early medieval (Saxon)**	**410–1066**
18	Medieval	1066–1485
19	Post-medieval	1485–1750
20	Modern	1750 to present

SMR16), SPE04 and HDD95. The archaeology uncovered ranges from a possible Bronze Age structure at Northlands (HDD95) to organised Roman agricultural settlements with a large focus on cattle and dairy production around the ancient River Witham in Langrick (SPE03) and Langrick Bridge (SPE04) and further south-west in Amber Hill (SMR17) (Fig. 1.3). Anglo-Saxon field systems were uncovered in Croft End (SMR10), near Burgh le Marsh and also near the town was evidence of later medieval clay extraction, a tradition which grew during the post-medieval period into small-scale brick production (SMR09). Post-medieval field systems were intermittently exposed in the parishes of Sibsey, Frithville and Westville and Langriville.

Inland Fen Edge Landscape Parcel

The Inland Fen Edge Landscape Parcel stretched from Swineshead Bridge to Bicker Fen and comprised two key neighbouring sites, SMR01 and TAM04 (Telford and Stockdale 2024) (Fig. 1.2). A small area in Bicker Fen, along Doubletwelves Drove and Bicker Drove, was targeted revealing archaeological remains indicating an agricultural landscape spanning from the early to the late Roman period (Fig. 1.3). The continuous rebuilding of a wooden structure during the early Roman period may suggest ongoing exploitation of the surrounding landscape (TAM04). Activity continued through the middle Roman period, during which the land appears to have been more stringently managed with enclosures and drainage ditches. This system appears to have been reconfigured during the later Roman period, providing further evidence for continuity in the region. There appears to have been a consistent connection to this place throughout the Roman period.

Monograph structure

This monograph builds upon the Landscape Parcel reports to explore a series of key themes emerging from these. The Landscape Parcel reports are available online via the Archaeology Data Service (ADS). The chapters are authored by key contributors providing greater contextualisation of the results with each focusing on different elements supported by specific specialist contributions. In many cases, sites across different Landscape Parcels are compared to explore the distribution of activities. In others, key sites are focused upon to explore key features and themes in more detail.

A changing landscape

The route of the Triton Knoll Electrical System passes through a distinct landscape which has been subject to dramatic change through the Holocene with periods of marine transgression and regression. This chapter combines the evidence from geology, topography, geoarchaeology, and environmental analysis undertaken at various stages to explore landscape change and the impact of this from prehistory to the present. The geoarchaeological works conducted for the project, including auguring and analysis of organic deposits, allow for an interpretation of the conditions under which deposits formed such as saltmarshes, freshwater fens or marshes, river sediments and ancient land surfaces. This chapter outlines the key phases of landscape change to help understand the distribution of archaeological sites and how interactions have changed over time.

Prehistoric landscape

The excavations revealed limited evidence of earlier prehistoric activity with the Mesolithic and Neolithic evidence comprising pits and artefacts scatters. At SMR09 a single pit containing Neolithic to Bronze Age artefacts was recorded (Fig. 1.3). The distribution of activity reflects the contemporary environmental conditions with activity focused on areas of higher ground. The environmental context continues to be key to understanding the distribution of archaeology in the Bronze Age. The excavation of a timber structure

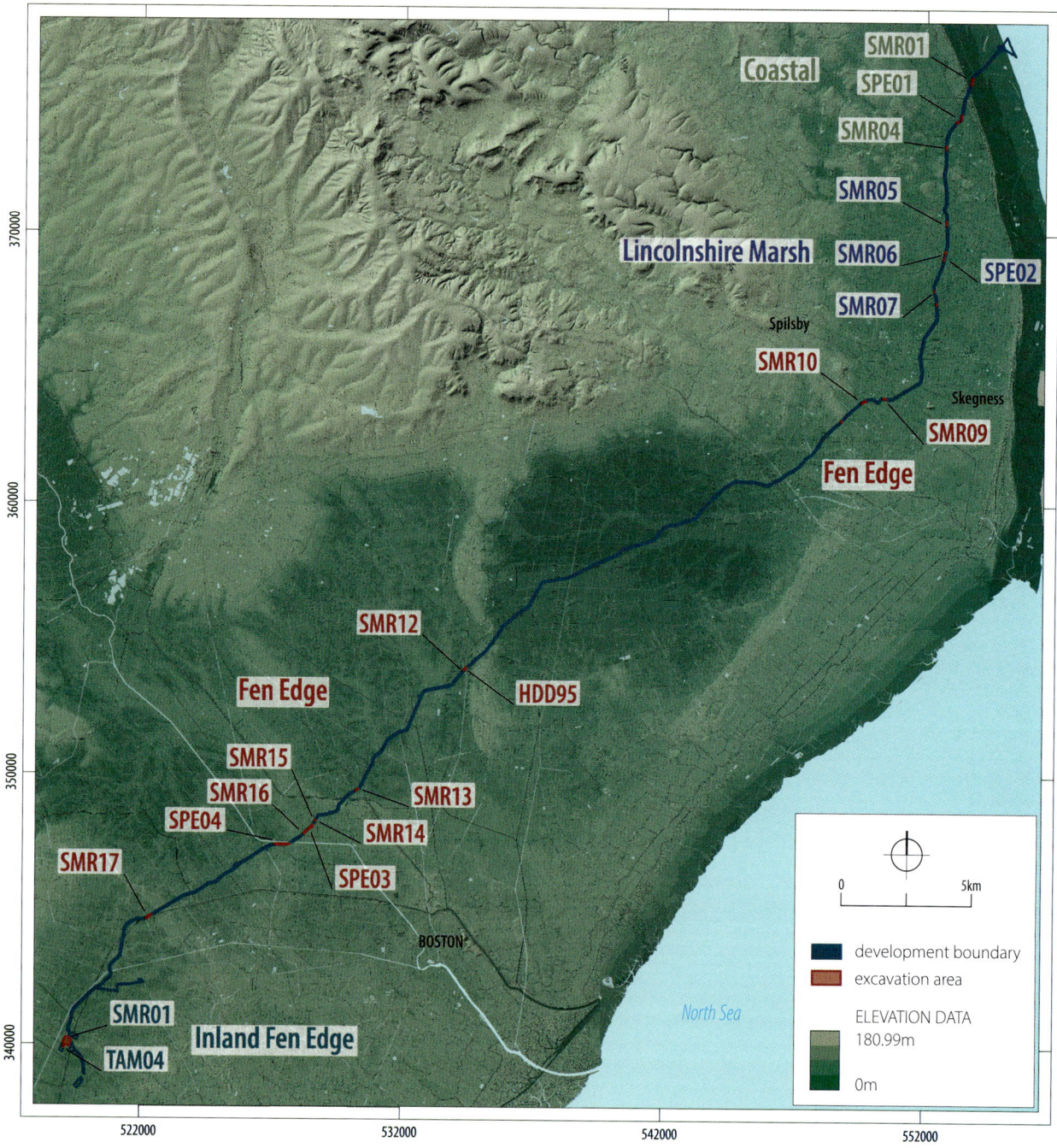

Figure 1.2 Triton Knoll Electrical System analysis sites and Landscape Parcels

at Northlands (HDD95) provides an opportunity to consider local conditions, construction techniques and the purpose of such structures. The structure provides evidence of early efforts to move and live in this constantly changing landscape. From the middle–late Bronze Age there is evidence for the commencement of salt production with features representing early salt production excavated at SPE01 (Fig. 1.3). This activity continued into the Iron Age with the site situated within a landscape with abundant evidence of later Iron Age salt production. The Iron Age witnessed the beginning of more extensively recognised salt production and to a lesser degree settlement which would expand in the Roman period. The initial evidence of these activities is placed in its wider context to introduce themes expanded upon in later chapters.

Living near the edge: settlement and agriculture in the Roman period

The Roman period witnessed an expansion of settlement evidence with activity occurring at varying

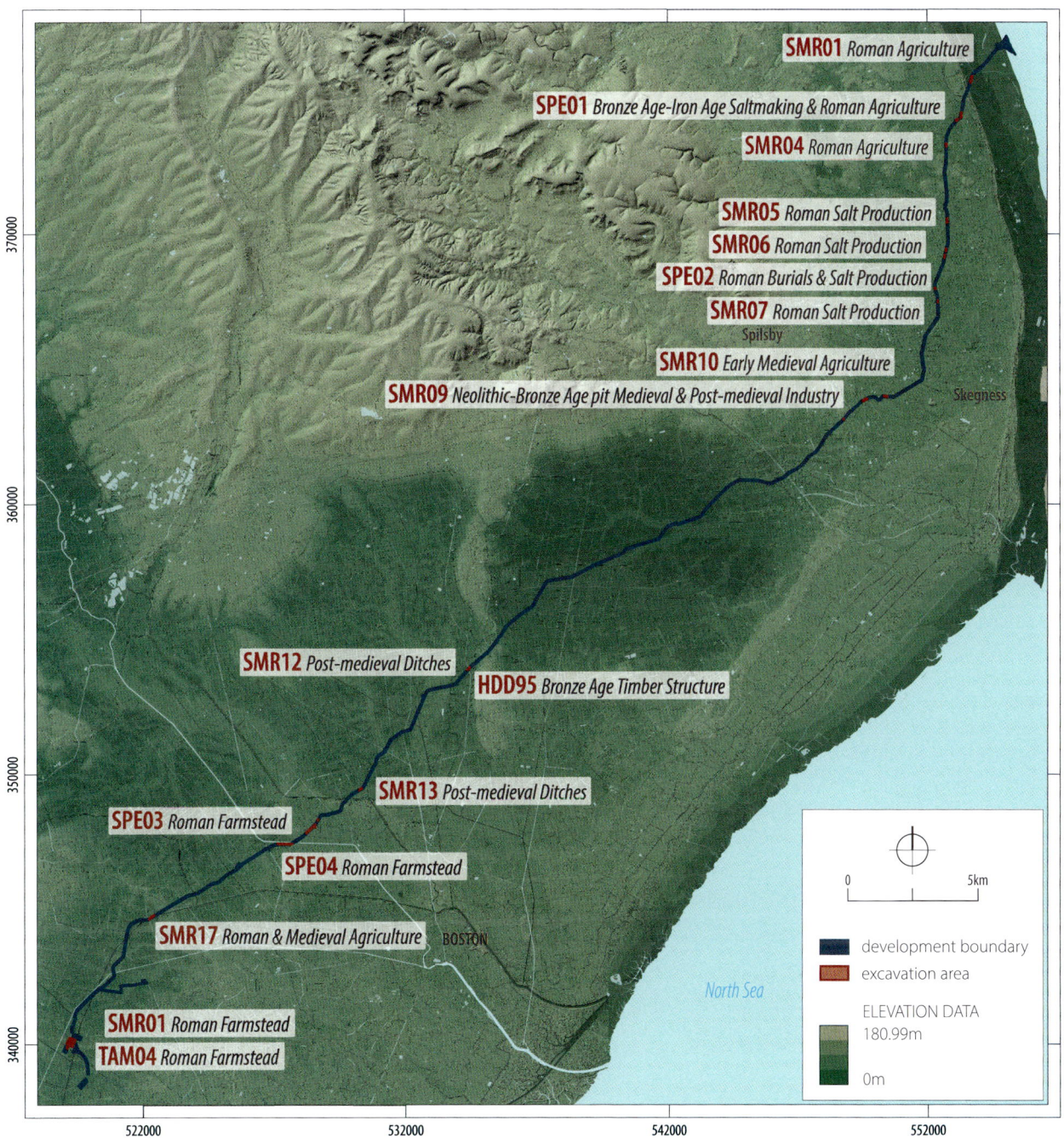

Figure 1.3 Map of principal sites showing key periods and activities

scales across the Scheme (Fig. 1.3). A total of 11 sites were identified and have been grouped into four broad categories: farmsteads, salt production, funerary and agriculture. Agriculture sites encompass those with evidence of agricultural activity in the form of ditches or enclosures but lacking strong evidence for a domestic component. Sites such as these are primarily located to the north of the Scheme while larger farmsteads, such as at SPE03, SPE04 and TAM04/SMR01, are located to the south (Fig. 1.3). In light of this, the excavations across the Scheme provide an opportunity to further explore site morphology, development and distribution within this dynamic region. This chapter provides an overview of all the site types followed by a detailed consideration of the chronological development of key sites, activities and structures before placing the sites in their wider context. This is supported by detailed sections on the environmental and artefactual evidence. The themes highlighted within this chapter are addressed collectively in Chapter 6, with Chapter 5 focusing on saltworking.

An esteemed resource: Roman saltworking at Triton Knoll

Salt was a valuable resource during the Roman period with the Lincolnshire coastline believed to be one of Britain's longest running and most significant areas of production. The four salt production sites excavated at SMR05, SMR06, SMR07 and SPE02 are located on the Lindsey Marshland in an area with considerable evidence of Iron Age and Roman saltmaking. The sites at SMR05 and SMR07 like many other saltern sites in the region were characterised by saltern deposits, whilst at SPE02 and SMR06 a more complex arrangement of salt production features was identified (Fig. 1.3). Importantly, dating evidence from these, including radiocarbon dates, showed that they date to the late Roman period, suggesting that elements of the salt industry in this region persisted beyond its apparent demise in the early Roman period.

Inhabiting the Fens: Communities and connections during the Roman period

This chapter brings together the key themes from Chapters 4 and 5 to explore aspects of settlement and economy across the region. The data from the excavations at Triton Knoll provides a unique opportunity to further explore the Roman use of this area, expanding on previous narratives which have typically focused on aspects of salt production. Drawing on this dataset this chapter explores the nature of arable and pastoral farming across the Scheme. Within this, shifts in the nature of agricultural regimes across the Roman period are highlighted, in particular the evidence for sites placing certain emphasis on key products, such as cereals, dairy and meat. This is complemented by a review of the data for salt production drawing on the narrative outlined in Chapter 5, but also exploring the inter-relationship of this to the agricultural regimes. The final part of this chapter explores the networks in which these sites were engaged, looking at wider connections and trade. Through this, the broader context of the sites is explored and the implications of this on our interpretation of the data from Triton Knoll is outlined.

Medieval–post-medieval rural settlement and industry

This chapter traces the rural settlement of the region through a number of key sites. Evidence of early medieval (Saxon) field systems at Croft End (SMR10), provides a rare opportunity to explore the nature of settlement before the Norman Conquest that has been otherwise largely overlooked. This is contrasted against more substantial evidence of medieval land use identified at extremes of the cable route near Mumby (SPE01) and Amber Hill (SMR17), including that of a small rural farmstead (Fig. 1.3). A rare opportunity to discuss the origins and development of brick manufacture in Lincolnshire is also provided by the excavations at Burgh le Marsh (SMR09), which revealed evidence of clay extraction, structures and kilns associated with the brick production dating to the late medieval and early post-medieval eras.

2

A changing landscape

Joanna R. Walker and Christine Milton

With contributions from Laura Bailey, Val Fryer,
Kate Turner, and Michael Wallace

The route of the Scheme passes through a distinct lowland landscape that has been subject to dramatic change through the Holocene with periods of marine transgression and regression (Fig. 2.1). This chapter combines evidence from the geology, topography, geoarchaeology, environmental, and archaeological analyses undertaken at various stages to explore landscape change and the impact it has had from prehistory to the present. The geoarchaeological works conducted for the project, including augering and analysis of organic deposits, yielded insights into changing environmental conditions under which deposits formed, such as saltmarshes, freshwater fens or marshes, rivers, and ancient land surfaces. These geoarchaeological works comprising multiple stages led by James Rackham, included:

Rackham, J. (2018) *Geoarchaeological Desk-Top Report: Triton Knoll Wind Farm, Onshore Cable Route*. Allen Archaeology Ltd.
Rackham, J. (2019) *Geoarchaeology Stage 3 Auger Survey: For The Triton Knoll Electrical System*. Allen Archaeology Ltd.
Rackham, J. (2020) *Geoarchaeology Stage 4 Coring Report: For The Triton Knoll Electrical System*. Allen Archaeology Ltd.
Rackham, J., Scaife, R. and Langdon, C. (2021) *Geoarchaeological Stage 4 Analysis Report: For The Triton Knoll Electrical Scheme*. Allen Archaeology Ltd.

Rackham's works have highlighted the complexity and discontinuities in sea level changes across the Scheme and the impact these changes had on the landscape and environment, principally from the late Mesolithic to the middle Bronze Age (Rackham 2018; 2019; 2020; Rackham *et al.* 2021). The geoarchaeological auger surveys provided new insight into the topography of the prehistoric landscape, with the caveat that later water channels (estuarine rivers and tidal creeks) may have scoured parts of the prehistoric land surface and that the distances between the auger points is likely to mask changes outside of the studied locations (Rackham *et al.* 2021, 9; see Figs 2.2 and 2.3 for auger locations). The geoarchaeological work contributes to a growing corpus of data from development schemes across Lincolnshire. These data have significant potential to advance our understanding of landscape and environmental change providing an important resource for future research. As such, the reports from Triton Knoll have been made available as part of the Archaeological Data Service (ADS) archive.

The results of the geoarchaeological survey have been incorporated into this chapter primarily when discussing early and middle Holocene landscape change (Mesolithic–Bronze Age) and are referenced throughout. This work forms the foundation of our understanding with the chapter using a variety of sources, including the Fenland Survey publications (Lane 1993; Hall and Coles 1994; Waller 1994; Crowson *et al.* 2000; Lane and Morris 2001; Lane and Trimble 2010), and wider academic discourse (*e.g.* Hallam 1970; Godwin 1978; Brew *et al.* 2000; 2015; Shennan and Andrews 2000; Horton and Shennan 2009; Evans *et al.* 2019; Walker *et al.* 2020; Green 2023a) to explore landscape change across the Scheme. Vegetational history and local environmental changes were also reconstructed through the specialist assessment of sediment and organic deposits from archaeological sites (Headland Archaeology 2020; Fryer and Bailey 2024; Fryer and Turner 2024; Wallace

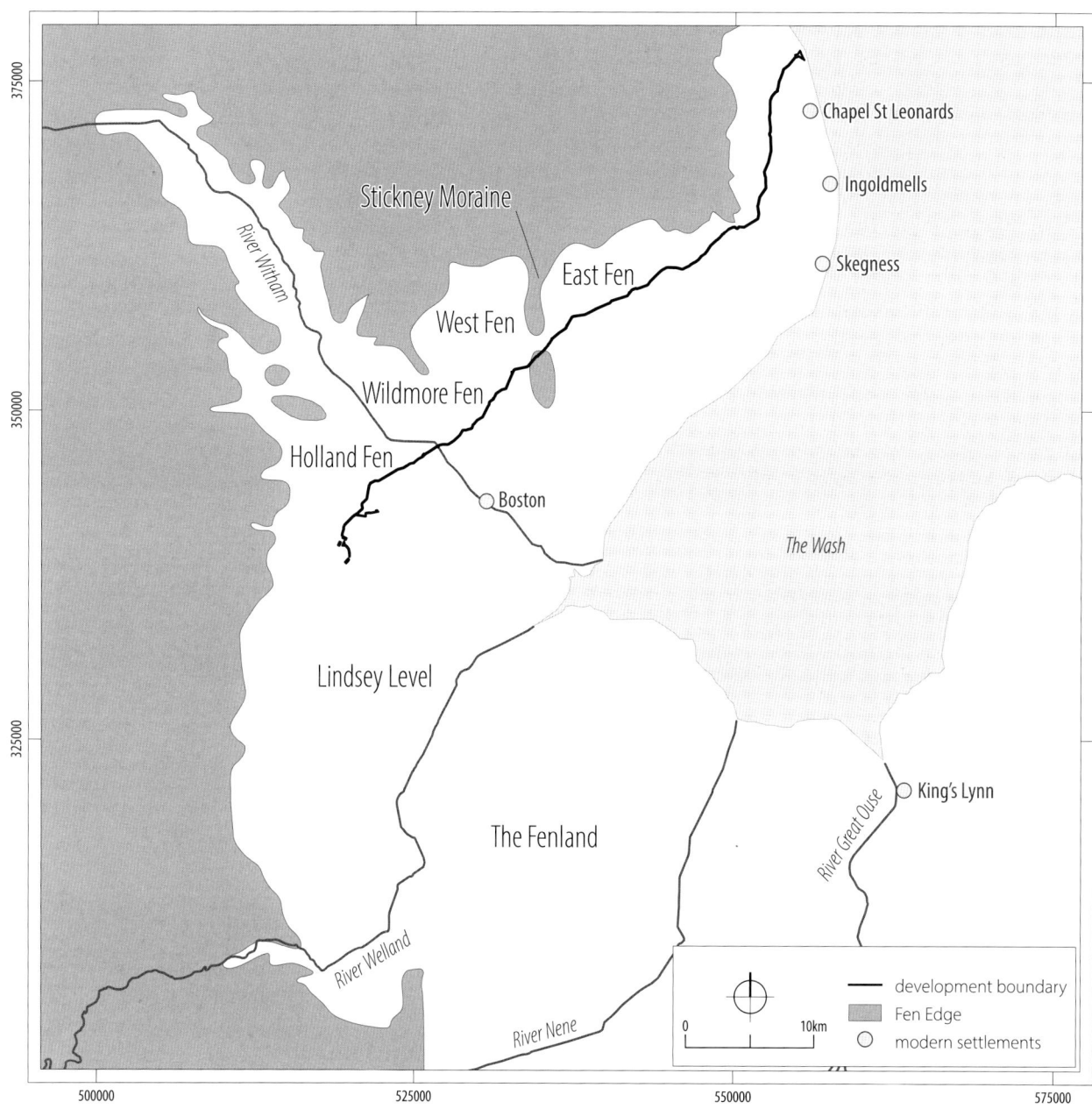

Figure 2.1 Map of the Fens showing the major Fen basins in Lincolnshire and the route of the Scheme

and Fryer 2024) which contained a range of biological remains, preserved pollen, plant and insect macrofossils, wood, and occasionally other invertebrate and vertebrate remains. This multi-proxy study has provided valuable insights into the distribution of archaeological sites within this complex environment and how human-environment interactions may have changed over time.

Warming up: Prehistoric coastlines and landscapes
The bedrock and Pleistocene glaciation

In this part of Lincolnshire the bedrock geology is an easterly dipping succession of uplifted Jurassic and Cretaceous sedimentary rocks, mostly limestones, mudstones, sandstones, and chalks. This is then generally followed by a blanket of glacial till, except in a few places where a river or tidal channel has cut down into the underlying bedrock geology.

In the lowland coastal areas glacial till was created and transported potentially large distances in the last Glacial period (between 115,000 and 14,700 years ago) by ice sheets, and as outwash in glaciofluvial channels (Evans *et al.* 2019). These deposits are present as a superficial geological unit which is widespread across the route area (see mapping of Till and Quaternary Sand & Gravels deposits in Figs 2.2 and 2.3;

NERC 2024). Glacial activity acts as a significant scour across landscapes, largely erasing pre-existing sedimentary sequences, and with them any record of previous human activity. It is for this reason that the till is usually deemed to be the lower limit of relevance for human–environment interactions, although it should be noted that north of the route at Welton-le-Wold several Palaeolithic handaxes have been found in arguably undisturbed deposits beneath the till (Wymer and Straw 1977). Glaciation would have made the landscape far less accessible to humans, with coastal lowland areas in eastern Lincolnshire covered by the onshore incursion of the North Sea Lobe (NSL) of the British–Irish Ice Sheet that occurred *c.* 29,000–14,700 years ago and southern and western areas inundated with glacial lakes; and the more elevated Lincolnshire Wolds left as a periglacial island with a frigid periglacial environment (Evans *et al.* 2019).

Deposited glacial till was found along the Scheme and identified in the hand-augered cores as a chalky till with a generally decalcified upper surface (Rackham *et al.* 2021, 7). The upper surface of the till was variable, and in some locations sandy glaciofluvial deposits of the late Pleistocene were located directly beneath Holocene deposits (*ibid.*, 7). It is likely that the most elevated parts of the till surface may have formed dry islands that were persistently present in the Holocene (*ibid.*, 19). Microtopography such as this and later roddons would have acted to constrain waterflow in an otherwise relatively flat landscape, directing the development of environments and providing a focus for human activity in the late Pleistocene and into the Holocene.

Late Glacial to Mesolithic: The pre-transgressive environment

In the early Holocene (Greenlandian Age), the weathered and decalcified till – where it has not been truncated by later action – was found to have developed a palaeosol, the surface of which represents a prehistoric ground surface (old ground level or 'ogl') (Rackham *et al.* 2021, 7). Soil formation is indicative of a period of landscape stability and across the route the warming Holocene climate saw boreal vegetation of the late Pleistocene succeeded by mixed temperate woodland. Wetland areas were located around rivers and in hollows but these did not appear to be extensive at this time (Rackham *et al.* 2021).

The palaeosol formed during a period of lower relative sea levels, caused by the combination of ongoing melting of glaciers and ice sheets around the globe, as well as the local isostatic rebound of previously glaciated areas in the British Isles (Lambeck 1993). In Lincolnshire, lower relative sea level would have meant that the coastline extended offshore of the modern coastline – possibly by several hundred kilometres, although the exact extent is debated – before this exposed land surface (Doggerland) was slowly inundated from the late Pleistocene into the middle Holocene period (Walker *et al.* 2020; see Fig. 2.4). It has been suggested that parts of the Doggerland archipelago may have persisted until 4000 cal BC, providing shelter for the Lincolnshire coastline from the North Sea as well as further environments that early settlers could exploit (Coles and Hall 1998; Long *et al.* 2000; Shennan *et al.* 2000).

Palaeolithic and early Mesolithic: Late Pleistocene–Holocene

Two of the studied sequences close to the modern coast at the northern end of the route have been used to tell us about the character of the landscape during the early Holocene prior to the marine transgressions (Rackham *et al.* 2021, 58; Fig. 2.2). The first, Profile 02/15, at the northern end of the Scheme near Anderby, had a thin, degraded peat that survived in a shallow stream valley beneath a fluvial or marine deposit. A radiocarbon date of 10,668–10,422 cal BC (10,520±40 BP, Beta-563668) was obtained here for the 81–82 cm unit at the top of the pollen series (*ibid.*, 12, 27). The second sequence, Profile 08/01 at Howlet House, Hogthorpe, was further inland than Profile 02/15, and preserved an early fluvial and alluvial sequence (*ibid.*, 28). The bottom of this sequence corresponds with vegetation patterns found in the Preboreal period, although the radiocarbon date from the basal peat is older, 11,317–11,133 cal BC (11,320±40 BP, Beta-563669; *ibid.*, 12). This sequence is thought to represent a channel in a non-tidal river valley that may have existed before the sea level rose.

Despite the late glacial radiocarbon dates, the pollen in both sequences suggest an early Holocene Preboreal date (early Mesolithic). The pollen evidence indicates that during the late Pleistocene–early Holocene transition the wider Preboreal lowland landscape was largely open, with limited areas of birch woodland and some hazel (Rackham *et al.* 2021, 58). At 08/01 some pine on the higher ground is indicated, with the pollen accumulations giving a date of *c.* 8000–7000 BC with traces of Juniper suggesting that the transition between the late glacial and Holocene occurred at the base of the sequence (*ibid.*, 28–30). More locally to 02/15 there was a freshwater marsh/fen environment fringed by typical fen reed conditions (bur reed and/or reedmace, sedges, water plantain, possibly hemlock, water dropwort, and grass pollen) with some willow on the fringes of this zone (*ibid.*, 27). At Profile 08/01 the valley floor was freshwater marsh with open water lacustrine conditions and willow carr (*ibid.*, 31).

After a possible short hiatus at *c.* 3.40 m, oak and hazel were recorded as colonising the site followed by alder

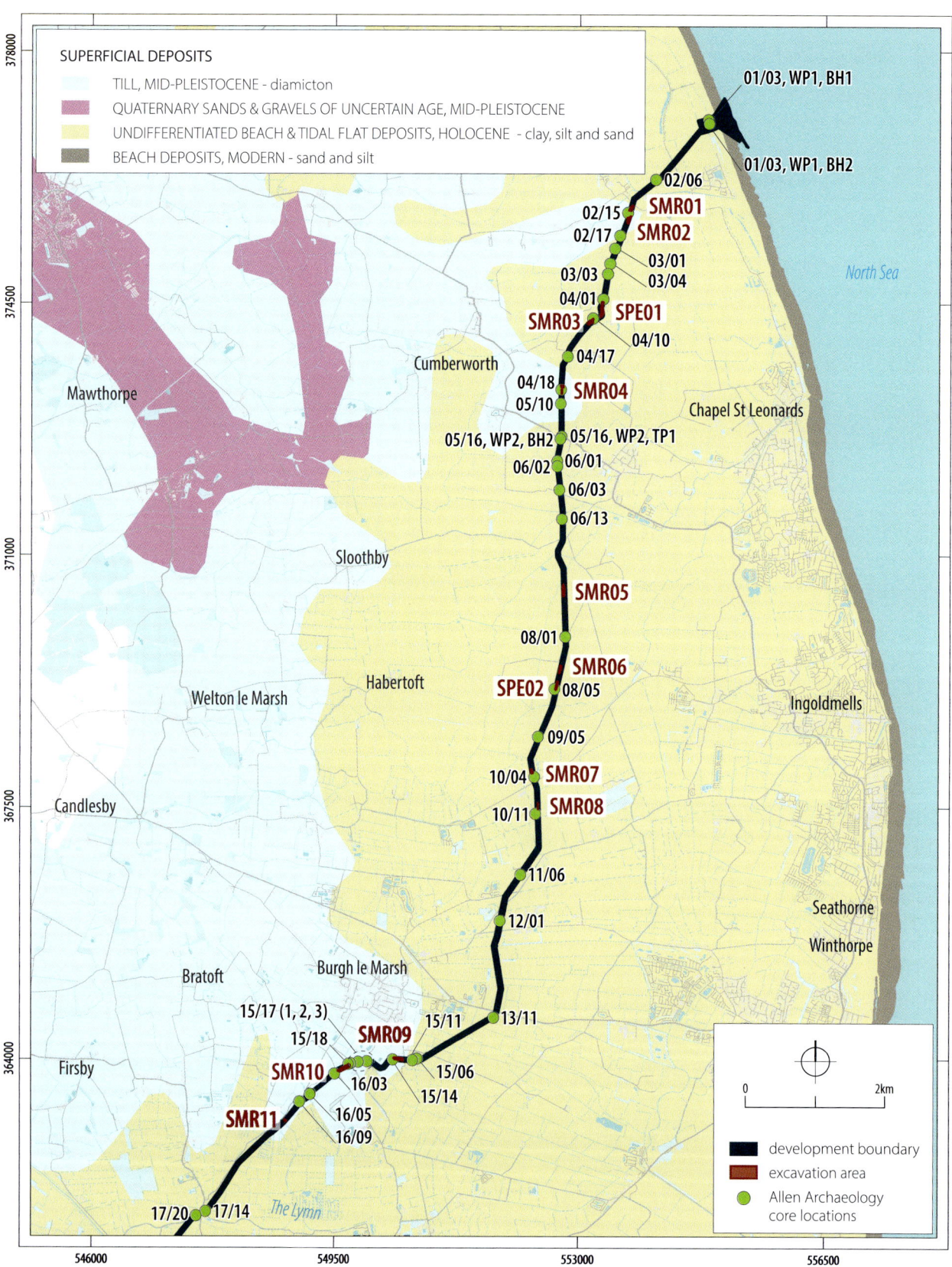

Figure 2.2 Map of the superficial geology and site locations across the northern half of the Scheme (Superficial geology data reproduced from the British Geological Survey under Open Government Licence v3.0; NERC 2024)

2 A changing landscape

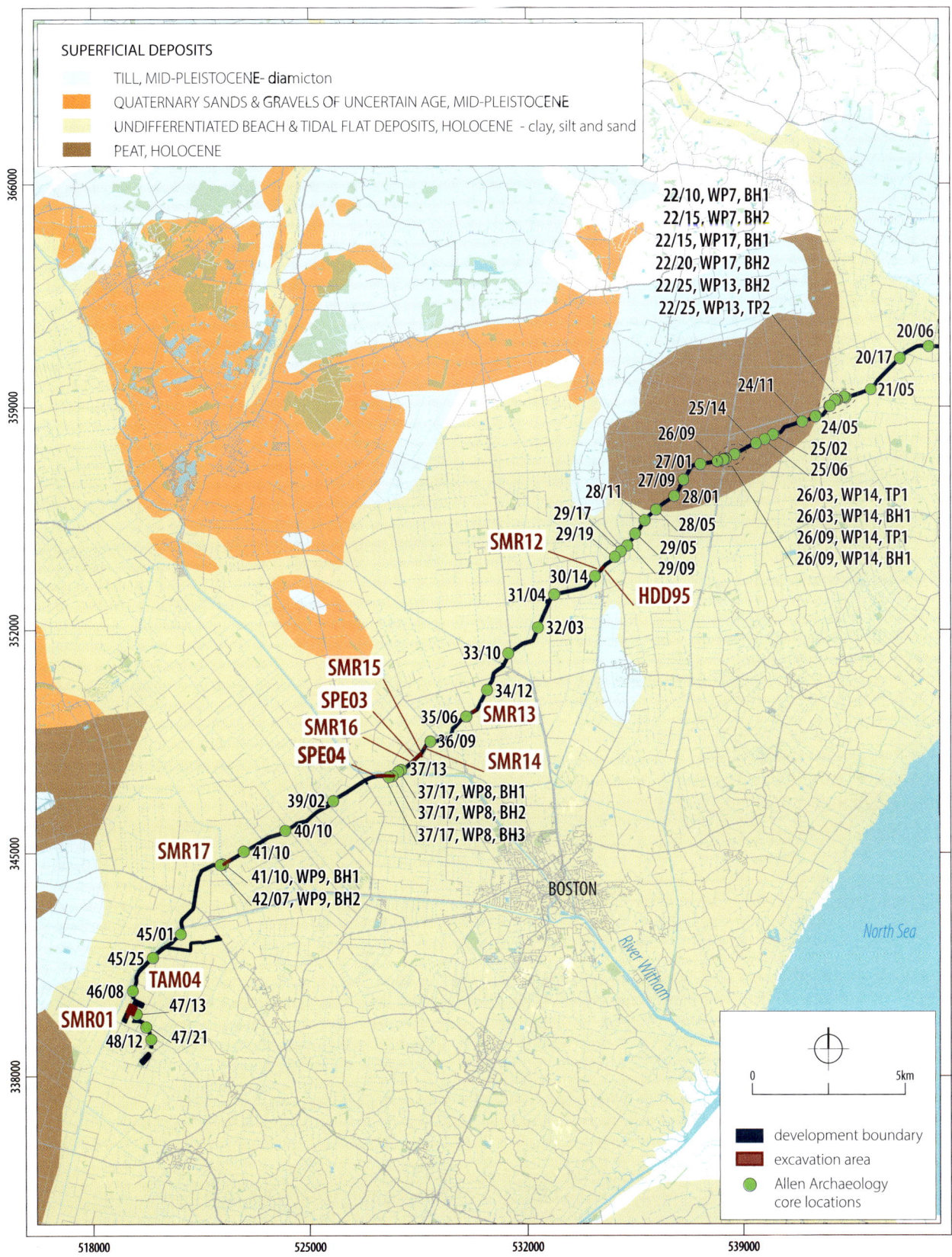

Figure 2.3 Map of the superficial geology and site locations across the southern half of the Scheme (Superficial geology data reproduced from the British Geological Survey under Open Government Licence v3.0; NERC 2024)

and lime; this coincides with a change from clayey silts to peat and probably represents a hiatus in sedimentation and then a stabilisation of the site towards drier conditions (Rackham *et al.* 2021, 30–31, 64). This development of temperate woodland is dated to about 8200 BC and, with a small peak of lime, is seen to continue throughout the middle peats to the upper level, which is dated to about 2200 BC (Neolithic–Bronze Age transition). Significant biogeographical changes, such as the arrival of more competitive tree taxa from their glacial refugia and their subsequent colonisation across Britain, are absent in this profile (Birks 1989). This suggests the absence on the whole of the Boreal period in this sequence despite the date of 8142–7968 cal BC (8920±30 BP, Beta-569336) for the base of the peat (*ibid.*). Physical remnants of these prehistoric temperate forests can be seen today in coastal areas close to the Scheme such as Cleethorpes and Wolla Bank, where, at low tide, submerged forests are exposed on the seashore.

A dynamic landscape: Middle and late Holocene changes

Fluctuating sea levels

The Lincolnshire coastline fluctuated in response to sea level changes during the middle and late Holocene, moving inland as sea level rose (transgression) and seawards as relative sea level fell (regression), bringing with it a suite of environmental changes even far inland of the coast (Waller 1994; Shennan and Andrews 2000; Horton and Shennan 2009, Brew *et al.* 2015). The low relief of the Scheme landscape, with only 10 m of altitude range along the whole 58 km of the cable route (Rackham *et al.* 2021, 57), means that even small changes to relative sea level had the potential to impact the lives of people using the area, both directly through losses and gains of available land and, more indirectly through changes in the wider environment and vegetation.

Waller's (1994) comprehensive analysis of Holocene sediments across the East and West Fens conducted as part of the Fenland Project has formed the basis for much of the environmental reconstruction in the Lincolnshire Fenland area since (see Fig. 2.1 for location of fen basins). In the West Fen, the onset of the Phase 1 marine transgression was radiocarbon dated to the late Neolithic reaching a maximum inland extent *c*. 3600 BP (Waller 1994, 295), with a second period of transgression (Phase 4) occurring in the late Roman–early medieval periods starting in the 4th century AD and likely continuing into the 7th century (Hallam 1970; Waller 1994, 295). In the East Fen basin, the onset of the first transgression (Phase 1) was slightly earlier, occurring in the middle–late Neolithic and reaching a maximum inland extent *c*. 3400 BP (Waller 1994, 319). This was quickly followed by a second phase of transgression beginning after the middle Bronze Age (Phase 2), and a third in the early Iron Age (Phase 3).

A summary of the major transgressions and regressions that affected the East and West Fen areas along the route of the Triton Knoll Electrical System is given in Table 2.1. Evidence of these sea transgression was also found in Rackham's auger survey shown here in relation to LiDAR of the route area in Figures 2.5–2.8 (Rackham *et al.* 2021, figs 17–20). It should be noted that, although this table identifies the major trends in marine transgression and regression, there is spatial and temporal variation of these events seen within each Fen area as a results of local topography (such as roddons).

The typical Holocene stratigraphy above the palaeosol across much of the Scheme is dictated by sea level changes similar to those outlined in Table 2.1, and generally occurs as follows: a basal peat, overlain by silty clays/clayey silts with surviving organics and sometimes organic laminae; then, intercalated peats, overlain by silty clays, silts and fine sands (within fen areas deep peat deposits accumulate prior to drainage) (Waller 1994; Rackham *et al.* 2021, 15–16). The top of the fine sands now forms the modern ploughsoil, but in some areas, such as the East Fen, the ploughsoil incorporates a degraded or lost surface peat.

The later Holocene sedimentary environments

As a result of the middle to late Holocene sea level changes, new types of environments developed across the Scheme replacing the temperate lowland forests that had previously stood in the now coastal areas. These new environments brought with them new challenges and opportunities for early settlers. The formation processes for these environments, and an overview of their conditions is given in the section below.

Peatlands

Basal peats accumulated along the inner margins of the fen basin as groundwater levels rose due to rising sea level in the middle Holocene (Northgrippian Age). The peat formed in saturated conditions, such as fen and carr, where standing water prevented the decomposition of organics. The earliest peats lie well buried by later marine sediments, and progressively higher peats (in Ordnance Datum [OD] terms) formed later with the progressive rise in sea level. Along the cable route of the Scheme the rising sea levels are first reflected in peat formation and then later the deposition of marine silts from as early as 4500 BC, around the Mesolithic–Neolithic transition (Waller 1994; Rackham *et al.* 2021, 16). The area of marine impact and deposition of silts and fine sands then expanded inland over the next three thousand years during the Neolithic and Bronze Ages, with the tidal limit at its maximum reaching as far upstream as Branston in

Table 2.1 *Summary table of Holocene conditions in the East and West Fen areas, Lincolnshire. This table shows the approximate phasing of major marine transgressions and regressions*

Phase	East Fen (east of Stickney Moraine)	West Fen, Wildmore & Swineshead (west of Stickney Moraine)
Post-Glacial/Early Holocene	Across Lincolnshire, there is low relative sea level caused by post-glacial isostatic rebound (Lambeck 1993) & lower global sea levels due to ongoing melting of glaciers (Long *et al.* 2000; Shennan *et al.* 2000). The Doggerland Archipelago also provides coastal storm protection, possibly as late as *c.* 4000 cal BC (Walker *et al.* 2020) allowing palaeosols & mixed temperate forest to develop as temperatures rise in the Holocene	
1 – Neolithic Transgression	Basal peats form as water table rises, before silty/clayey marine deposits are laid: *onset of marine conditions occurs between 3340–2940 & 2310–2135 cal BC, maximum onshore extent at c.* 3400 BP (Waller 1994, 317–319)	Basal peats form as water table rises before silty/clayey marine deposits are laid: *onset of marine conditions occurs between 2575–2320 & 2145–1800 cal BC, maximum onshore extent at c.* 3600 BP (Waller 1994, 295)
Regression	Formation of intercalated peats, freshwater reedswamp & fen: *maximum freshwater seawards regression occurs c.* 3100 BP (Waller 1994, 319)	Between the late Bronze Age & Iron Age, intertidal environments develop across fen areas west of the Stickney moraine
2 – Bronze Age Transgression	Deposition of marine clastic material and inland movement of fens: *onset of marine conditions c.* 1500 cal BC, *maximum onshore extent likely at c.* 2900 BP (Waller 1994, 319)	Phase 2 transgression missing in areas west of Stickney moraine
Regression	Freshwater phase, bog vegetation develops. At Friskney this is dated to *between* 2735±60 & 2385±60 BP (Waller 1994, 319). Roddons from earlier periods are exposed in drying areas	–
3 – Iron Age Transgression	Last widespread marine transgression in East Fen begins in Iron Age: 2480±80 BP/800–410 cal BC at Thorpe Culvert & 540–395 cal BC at Friskney (Waller 1994, 319)	Phase 3 transgression missing in areas west of Stickney moraine
Regression	Sea regresses & deep deposits of peat build-up in the fen. Roddons from earlier periods are exposed in drying areas	In the late Iron Age–early Roman period there is a marine regression & seaward movement of communities into Saltern areas (Hallam 1970)
4 – Late Roman Transgression	Phase 4 transgression missing in the East Fen, peat continues to develop in the Fen keeping pace with sea level rise	Deposition of marine silts in the late Roman and early medieval period: *from c.* 315–395 cal AD (Waller 1994, 295) *to* 7th century AD (Hallam 1970)
Regression	It is possible that peat cutting of 'turves' that later occurs hollows out 'deepes' that appear as the lakes that are described in the Fen from the medieval to modern period (Godwin 1978)	Sea regresses & peats develop in the fen, Phase 1 & Phase 4 roddons are exposed in drier areas
Post-medieval Fen Drainage	Major drainage of East Fen begins in 1806 with the construction of the Hobhole Sluice	Major drainage of West Fen begins in the post-medieval period with the Maud Foster Drain in 1568

the Witham Valley (Gardiner 2021) and marine sediments covering coastal areas (Fig. 2.4).

Following this a relative stabilisation or potentially even a slight regression of sea level in the 1st millennium BC during the late Bronze Age resulted in the slight seaward expansion of peats on the landward side of the East Fen basin (between the Neolithic and Bronze Age marine transgressions; see Table 2.1), with more significant regressions seen across the East and West Fens in the Iron Age (post-Phase 3) (Rackham *et al.* 2021). In the late Roman period a further marine transgression, Phase 4, started flooding the recolonised areas of the West Fen, with another phase of peat formation occurring around the margins of the advancing sea, sealing some young peats with a subsequent period of marine silt and silty clay deposition (Gardiner 2021; Rackham *et al.* 2021). By the Phase 4 transgression the Witham tidal limit was thought to have retreated to Nocton Fen (Gardiner 2021).

Saltmarsh and mudflats

The silty clays that succeeded the basal peats following the initial transgression (Phase 1 from 3340–2940 cal BC; Waller 1994, 317–319) were generally laminated with a very fine sand fraction that was often concentrated within the laminations separating silt laminae (Rackham *et al.* 2021, 7). These sediments were indicative of tidal conditions associated with mudflat and lower saltmarsh environments (Shennan 1994a; 1994b).

As well as these finer sediments, several of the assessed boreholes recorded a coarser sequence of sandy silts, silty sands, laminated sands, and fine sand indicative of more energetic depositional environments associated with the ebb and flow of the daily tides within creeks and channels (Rackham 2019; 2020; Rackham *et al.* 2021). Evidence of such channel activity has been preserved as roddons, with their characteristic dendritic channels easily seen in modern LiDAR imagery.

Roddons

Roddons, the dry raised beds of former watercourses, were a key feature of the estuarine environment and became the focus for human activity from later prehistory onwards (Hayes and Lane 1992; Rackham *et al.* 2021, 61). They are characterised by the fine sands that are deposited within former creeks and estuarine channels and, with even the smaller roddons containing over 5 m of fine sands and laminated sands, there was generally little chance of recovering preserved earlier Holocene sediments from beneath roddons encountered in this landscape (Rackham *et al.* 2021, 8). The roddons form as surrounding peat dries out or is drained, causing the surface elevation of the formerly saturated peaty areas to drop and leaving the roddon sands as areas of higher ground (Waller 1994, 45–46; Smith *et al.* 2010).

Roddons have been a useful tool for identifying the different episodes of marine transgression from LiDAR images. A general overview of the LiDAR imagery for the area shows that the Witham Valley and the East and West Fen are covered with the dendritic drainage systems characteristic of estuarine and intertidal zones. This is clearly reflected in the pattern of roddons visible on the maps, which reflects the infilled channels of the estuarine and intertidal drainage creeks. In the East Fen basin at least two phases of marine transgression can be seen in the dendritic system. An earlier roddon system at a lower OD height can be seen across the whole fen draining eastwards, while a later roddon system with a higher elevation can be seen overlying this and draining southwards towards the Witham.

A relative fall in sea level during the 1st millennium BC led to the coastline moving eastwards and areas of marine sedimentation becoming exposed (Lane and Trimble 2010). Perhaps the most significant archaeological impact of this regression is that the roddons that serve to identify the courses of the large and small prehistoric intertidal channels associated with the early marine transgressions became dry and, over time, raised above the rest of the floodplain. In the case of the major roddons, such as that of the tidal River Witham, they can be as much as 3 km wide, and during the late Iron Age and Roman period these new areas of land were colonised and utilised for agriculture including probable large scale cereal production (Rackham *et al.* 2021, 10). Roddons remained a focus for human activity into the medieval and modern period.

Islands within the marsh

Although most of the sites studied along the Scheme showed evidence of periods of inundation in the various phases of marine transgression, there were some exceptions where, due to their greater elevation, they appear to have remained as islands above surrounding areas of marshy fen since the post-glacial period. These areas are important to highlight as they may have provided opportunities for human exploitation even during transgressive phases.

To the north of the Scheme between SMR01 and SMR05 there are many small hummocks formed of till that rise above 5 m AOD that are likely to have remained as raised ground throughout the various sea transgression phases (NERC 2024; Fig. 2.2). This area also has a high density of Iron Age and Roman salterns (an area or installation for making salt) (Lane and Morris 2001, 7, 405–408).

The Stickney Moraine near SMR12 runs north to south bisecting the East and West Fen north of Boston, reaching a maximum of *c.* 10 m AOD. Most of this ridge likely remained above the marsh throughout the Holocene. The villages of Sibsey, Stickney, and

2 A changing landscape

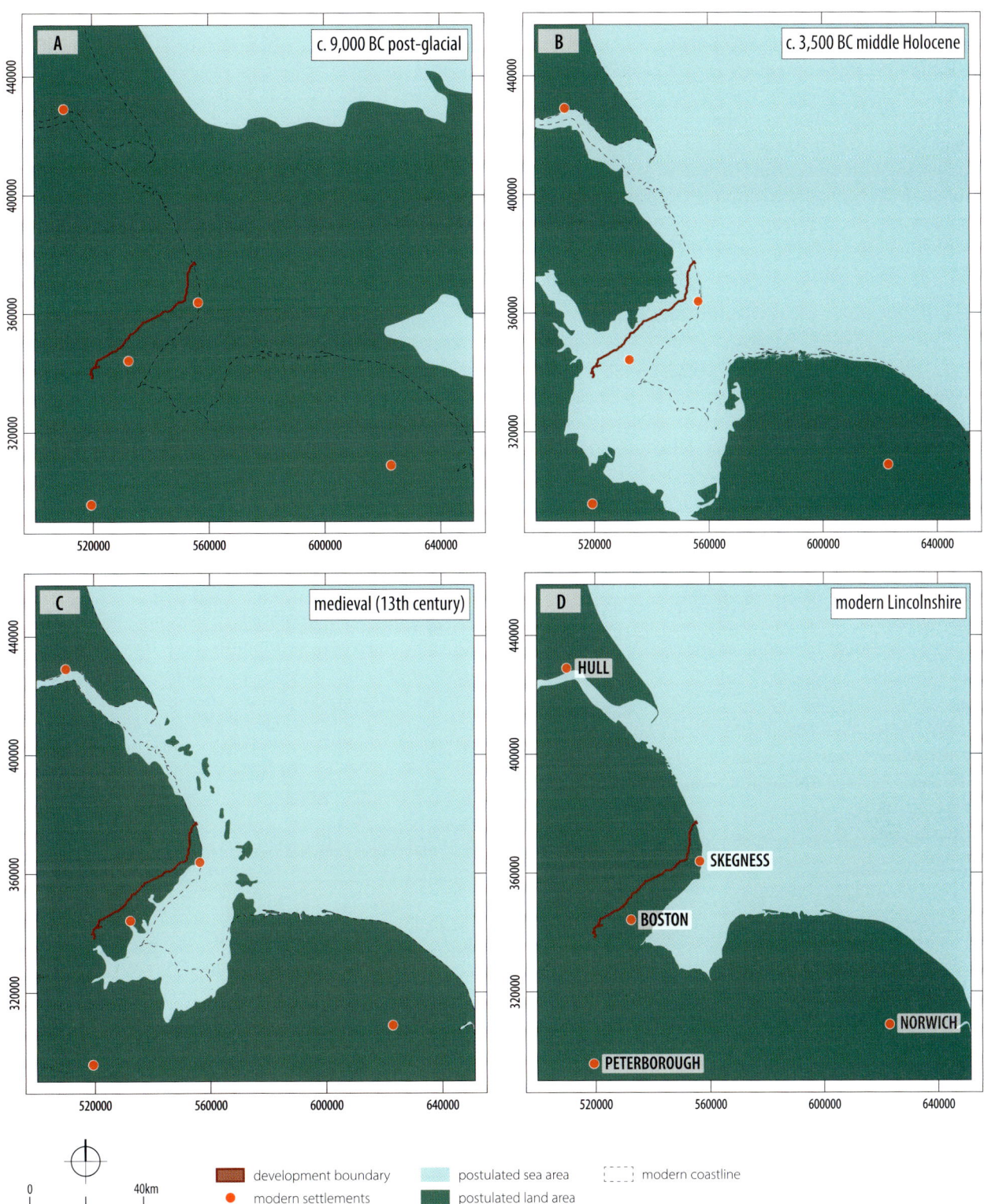

Figure 2.4 Diagrammatic maps showing the route of the Scheme and possible coastline throughout the Holocene: A. c. 9000 BP, post-glacial coastline (based on Walker et al. 2020, fig. 2, 1414); B. c. 3500 BC, Middle Holocene coastline: Phase 1 Marine Transgression (based on Shennan 1988, fig. 1, 146); C. medieval (13th century), coastline prior to drainage (based on Pawley 1984, map two, 70); D. Modern Lincolnshire Coastline

Stickford atop the moraine have produced various artefacts attesting to its long history for human activities spanning the Holocene periods (Lincolnshire County Council 2024).

South of the Witham roddon the Scheme crosses a small outcrop of terrace gravels forming an 'island' of higher ground at Amber Hill. The palaeo-land surface here had an AOD height of 1.29 m and so it is possible that this area may have remained an island during most of the marine transgressive phases (Rackham *et al.* 2021, 10).

The initial onset of wet conditions

The onset of the initial post-glacial marine transgression that occurred during the later Mesolithic and early Neolithic saw the inland spread of fen and carr into areas that were previously forested. Where there was previously mixed temperate forest with lime on the drier ground this was gradually replaced with sedges and reed swamp in low-lying areas, and then tidal environments. These changes, that began at the coastal margins, spread inland and show that initially around 4000 BC the whole route lay within the terrestrial landscape (Rackham *et al.* 2021). Over the next four thousand years 90% of the route was covered by the sea, with the inundation at its peak spreading far inland of the modern coastline to the Fen edge.

Later Mesolithic and Neolithic: Early to middle Holocene

Mapping the marine transgression

The stratigraphic sequence in many of the auger holes along the Scheme shows the prehistoric palaeosol overlain by peat (Rackham 2019; 2020; Rackham *et al.* 2021). Peat can form rapidly under the cool, humid conditions that have been common in the post-glacial British climate, and the onset of peat at a location is indicative of a rise in the ground water table. In the Fens, the rising ground water table has been attributed to rising sea levels pushing back the freshwater and flooding lowland landscapes. These peatlands then became brackish or saline environments where the peat growth failed to keep pace with rising sea level (Rackham *et al.* 2021, 14). The loss of peat can then lead to the rapid loss of the coastal wetland areas as increased wave energy prevents further peat growth and may lead to increased peat erosion or collapse (Chambers *et al.* 2019; Sirianni *et al.* 2023), and the boundary between the basal peats and the overlying clayey silts or clastic marine sediments on the route marked the onset of tidal conditions.

This transition to new saltmarsh and then intertidal clastic sediments was seen as a sharp lithological boundary above the lower peat (Rackham 2019; 2020; Rackham *et al.* 2021, 15). Although the pattern of organic laminae within some of these silts suggests that there was a continued intermittent growth of upper saltmarsh in locations where tidal flooding may have been restricted to occasional high spring tides (Rackham *et al.* 2021, 11).

The wet conditions associated with the development of a fen, fen carr, or alder carr environment therefore indicate the time when the dated location ceased to be easily accessible for human terrestrial activities such as settlement, hunting, and gathering; and the later onset of marine and estuarine conditions when the landscape became almost entirely inaccessible for activities except on areas of higher ground.

Fourteen samples collected from the palaeosol or the bottom of the basal peats at different elevations along the Scheme's cable route were used by Rackham *et al.* (2021, 12–19) to create a chronology for the initiation of waterlogging at different AOD heights along the Scheme. This work suggests that an altitudinal rise in the coastal wetlands of 4.5 m occurred over a period of some 3000 years between the late Mesolithic (when the cable route was almost entirely terrestrial) and the middle Bronze Age, with the landscape becoming waterlogged due to rising sea level at a rate of about 1 m every 700 years, until 90% of the route was inundated by the sea and the coastline retreated far inland (Waller 1994; Shennan and Andrews 2000; Brew *et al.* 2015; Rackham *et al.* 2021, 16, 59). At the peak of the sea transgression only the hillocks in the north, the edge of the Wolds, the highest parts of the Stickney Moraine, and the Witham roddon would have remained above the Mean High Water Spring Tide level (see Fig. 2.3) (Rackham *et al.* 2021, 65). Some of the pollen assessments suggest that these areas of higher ground and 'islands' in the fen may have been settled in the Neolithic, particularly the Stickney Moraine and those in the northern coastal zone, although the human impact on the forest is not seen in the pollen diagrams until the Bronze Age (*ibid.*, 64). The appearance of more open herb fen in the late Mesolithic to early Neolithic at Profile 31/04 in the West Fen near Stickney Moraine is such an example, although there is little evidence for woodland clearance in proximity to the site (*ibid.*, 33; Fig. 2.3).

From forest to fen

EARLY NEOLITHIC

The East Fen was one of the first areas along the Scheme to experience full marine conditions and from the early Neolithic to middle Neolithic the mixed forest in this low-lying basin was gradually replaced with sedges and reed swamp (see Fig. 2.5). The onset of wetter conditions led initially to a gradual expansion of herbs and then species more commonly associated with marine environments (Rackham *et al.* 2021, 58). This inland movement of the coastline is perhaps a little earlier than previously modelled (Brew *et al.* 2000), reflecting the particularly

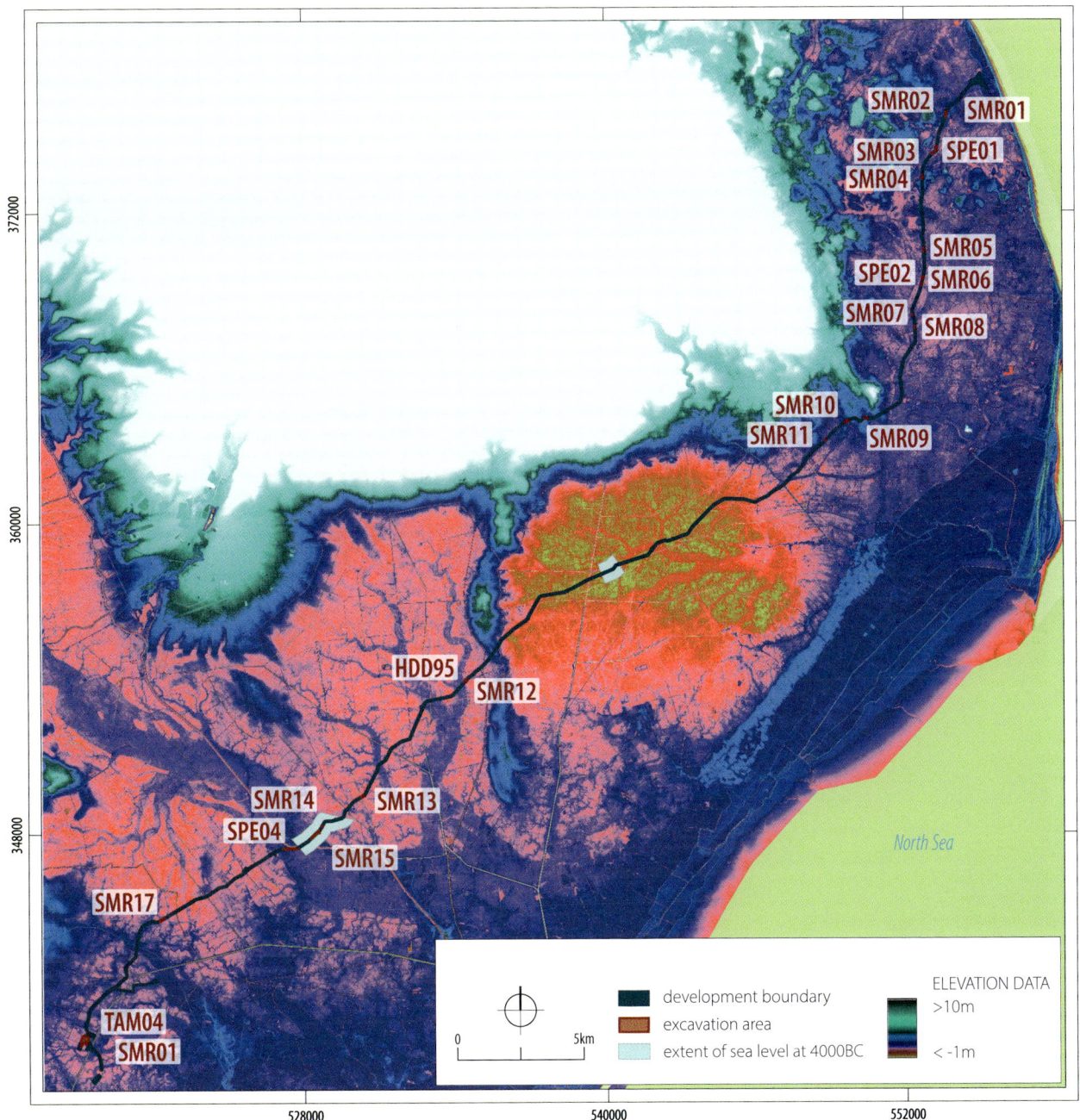

Figure 2.5 Map of the Scheme showing the extent of marine flooded areas in augered cores at 4000 BC (based on Rackham et al. 2021, fig. 17). LiDAR background mapping shows dendritic roddon networks across the route (Environment Agency reproduced under Open Government Licence v3.0; Environment Agency 2024)

low elevation of the old ground level in the East Fen. Some cereal pollen dating to this period was identified but otherwise there is little evidence for deliberate clearance. This is not unusual, as an absence of human settlement in low coastal areas during the early Neolithic period across Britain is well documented (see Sidell and Haughey 2007).

Marine incursion was particularly apparent at Steeping River West (Profile 19/01; Fig. 2.2) and Thorpe Fendykes (Profile 20/06; Fig. 2.3), where the marine incursion is dated to the middle Neolithic (3635–3500 cal BC and 3431–3379 cal BC; 4740±30 BP, Beta-569340), and 3127–3007 cal BC (4440±30 BP, Beta-552739) respectively (Rackham *et al.* 2021, 12). These two profiles are in an area that has sometimes been described as a 'Northern Basin' to the east of the East Fen (Robson 1985; Brew *et al.* 2015; Rackham *et al.* 2021).

At Steeping River West (19/01) this transition was seen as a palaeosol overlain by shallow unit of peat at 89 cm in the auger profile (Rackham 2020, 44). The transition was also associated with a distinct palynological

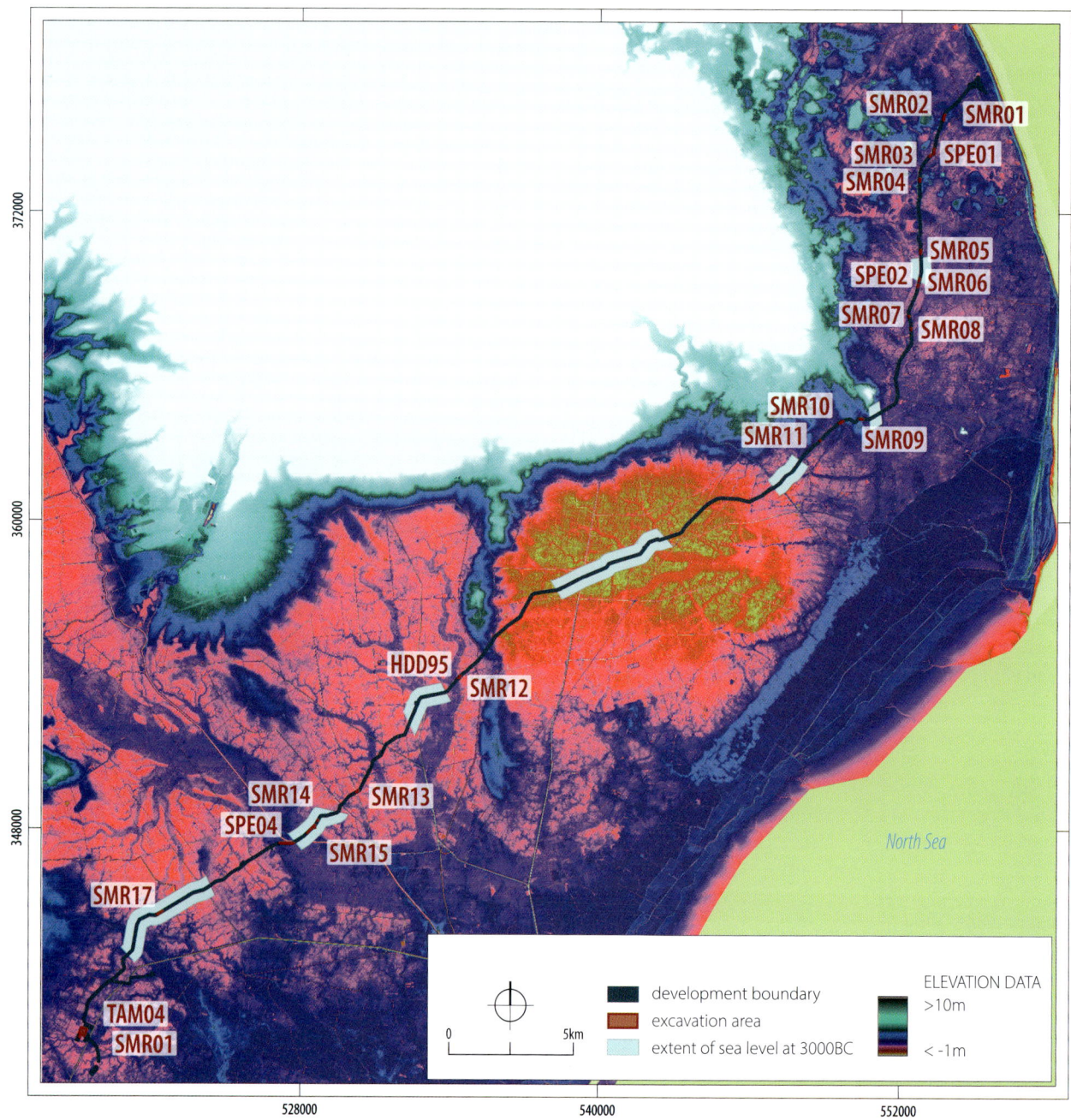

Figure 2.6 Map of the Scheme showing the extent of marine flooded areas in augered cores at 3000 BC (based on Rackham et al. 2021; fig. 18). LiDAR background mapping shows dendritic roddon networks across the route (Environment Agency reproduced under Open Government Licence v3.0; Environment Agency 2024)

change from a tree and shrub dominated pollen mix in the palaeosol indicative of a damp or periodically wet floor habitat, to an environment with an increase in halophytes (goosefoot, orache and samphire, thrift and sea lavender, spurrey and sea plantain) influenced by brackish water conditions in the peat. The presence of thrift pollen is particularly remarkable in the peat unit and suggestive of on-, or very near, site growth of saltmarsh. Overlying the shallow peat (4 cm) laminated bands of organics and silts suggest an upper saltmarsh environment shortly developed (Rackham *et al.* 2021, 38–39).

MIDDLE NEOLITHIC

Marine conditions then extended into the West Fen in the middle Neolithic with the lime dominated woodland here being increasingly dominated by oak then alder, and willow fen expanding in the low wetland area as waterlogging and brackish conditions become prevalent

(Waller and Grant 2012; Rackham *et al.* 2021, 50; Figs 2.5 and 2.6).

The area remained relatively open with some evidence to suggest the presence of pasture, although such areas were probably significantly affected by the arrival of marine conditions which would have limited the potential for this type of environment to develop. South of the Witham Roddon that likely formed during this period, trace cereal pollen was recorded indicating agriculture which, along with a quantity of fire cracked flint from Profile 47/21, is probably the best evidence for human activity in the area (Rackham *et al.* 2021, 20, 61; Fig. 2.3). Lower ground had transitioned to full mudflat conditions by this period but the marine influence was not felt on the higher ground further south (*i.e.* Profile 48/12) until the late Neolithic, and here only as saltmarsh rather than mudflats (Fig. 2.3).

At the southern end of the Scheme, Bicker Fen was one of the later areas to be inundated due to a relatively high early Holocene topography. The sequence at Profile 47/21 is middle Neolithic in date (3381–3335/3501–3431 cal BC; 4600±30 BP, Beta-569344 and 3241–3104/3365–3264 cal BC; 4540±30 BP, Beta-552737) and shows an area in which lime woodland was succeeded by oak dominated woodland with alder and willow carr and freshwater fen in the immediate locality and some grassland pollen (including daisy and buttercup indicating open areas in the wider landscape; Rackham *et al.* 2021, 12, 40). Dandelion and ribwort plantain found here may indicate the presence of pasture in the wider landscape although there are no traces of human activity prior to the first indications of marine influence, which is marked by the slow expansion of Chenopodiaceae and the arrival of sea plantain and sea spurrey (herbaceous coastal vegetation). The initial arrival of marine influence coincided with a decrease in open area (grass) vegetation indicating that these taxa were the first to be impacted (*ibid.*, 40–42).

Nearby at Swineshead (Profile 45/01; Fig. 2.3), the early Holocene palaeosol was overlain by a shallow detrital peat with a middle Neolithic date (3024–2896 cal BC; 4340±30 BP, Beta-552735) that was in turn followed by an upper humic peat deposit (*ibid.*, 45). In the sandy palaeosol present prior to rising water levels, there is evidence of oak woodland occurring locally as well as some indicators of agricultural activity in the sites vicinity due to the presence of cereal-type pollen and species such as ribwort plantain and dandelions (*ibid.*, 45–46). The sandy nature of the paleosol deposit suggests that this was a fluvial floodplain setting, which has been argued to be a favoured location for agricultural activities in the Neolithic period, although it should be noted that there is little physical evidence for human activity at the site beyond pollen already remarked on (Cappers and Raemaekers 2008; Rackham *et al.* 2021, 46). Overlying the palaeosol the detrital peat showed a significant decline in woodland taxa and an increase in halophyte-type herbs indicating the onset of the marine/brackish transition on site. However, this phase was short-lived and is followed by a humic peat containing pollen more indicative of freshwater fen suggestive of the beginning of a period of regression (Rackham *et al.* 2021, 45–46).

LATE NEOLITHIC

On the slightly higher ground to the south of Bicker Fen (Profile 48/22; Fig. 2.3) the increase in marine influence appears to be delayed further still to the middle/late Neolithic (Rackham *et al.* 2021, 63; Fig. 2.6). Despite the later onset of wet conditions the site appears to have followed the typical Neolithic vegetation pattern of increasing oak woodland on a palaeosol, before a transition into peat and then an upward-fining sediment sequence of organic soft clayey silts found to contain halophytic pollen taxa is recorded, and is indicative of the formation of upper saltmarsh at the site (*ibid.*, 43–45). At the northern end of the Scheme, close to the coast at Land Fall, Moggs Eye (Profile 01/03; Fig. 2.2), a palaeosol was identified beneath the peats at a height of 1.65 m AOD. The profile has been radiocarbon dated to the middle to late Neolithic – 2880–2632 cal BC (378–379 cm, 4160±30 BP, Beta-569333) and 2925–2779 cal BC (394–395 cm, 4270±30 BP, Beta-563667) (*ibid.*, 13, table 3), and assessment of the pollen has shown a decrease in lime before a growth of oak-dominated woodland interspersed with some open areas at this time. In the subsequent phase of peat formation, fen and marsh taxa were reduced, and there was an expansion of grasses and cereals in the peat suggestive of some local agricultural activity, perhaps on the nearby higher ground to the west of the auger location (*ibid.*, 63). The stable peat phase is short-lived though, and halophyte taxa were soon recorded in the pollen sequence followed by a transition to organic clastic fine silty clays typical of an upper saltmarsh environment (*ibid.*)

Evidence of early Holocene human occupation?

There is potential evidence of late Mesolithic human activity at Profile 31/04 in the West Fen indicated by a piece of charcoal found at the base of the basal peats dated to 4546–4444 cal BC (524–525 cm, 5650±30 BP, Beta-554253; Rackham *et al.* 2021, 12; Fig. 2.2). Human activity may have occurred within the vicinity of this site into the Neolithic, as a single grain of cereal pollen was also recorded alongside large grasses at this point in the sequence (Rackham *et al.* 2021, 33). The cereal pollen grains from the Neolithic found in the Land Fall (Profile 01/03) and Swineshead (45/01; Figs 2.2 and 2.3) sequences were from distinctly different palaeoenvironments and were widely spaced occurring at either end of the Scheme. These sites help to demonstrate the potential range of different environments being exploited for early agriculture in this landscape. At Land Fall proximity to the coast and the coastal resources may have been the desirable factor in the location, whereas at Swineshead the fluvial floodplain at and its accompanying wetter environs may have appealed.

A single flint found in the palaeosol at Bicker Fen (Profile 47/21; Fig. 2.3) was positively identified as fire-cracked suggestive of human activity in this area and was accompanied by charcoal fragments on a Neolithic land surface (Rackham *et al.* 2021, 20).

Slowing sea level rise and marine regression

Early to middle Bronze Age

Despite hints of early agricultural activity in the pollen sequences, there was very little evidence for any widespread human impact across the Scheme in the form of either deliberate clearances or agriculture before the Bronze Age (Rackham *et al.* 2021, 65). The drier landscape area of the Stickney Moraine and northern coastal zone were the first to show a clear human impact starting in the late Neolithic–early Bronze Age, with more apparent impacts seen by the middle Bronze Age. Palynological evidence suggests that settlement during the Bronze Age was probably concentrated on the peripheral higher and drier areas, while the lowland areas remained inundated and thus relatively unexploitable. This suggests that by the middle Bronze Age the only land available for terrestrial activities would likely be that at +0.5 m AOD or greater elevation, illustrating the impact of sea level rises on the availability of exploitable land (*ibid.*, 16; Fig. 2.7).

Marine regression in the North (Coastal) Basin

At the northern end of the route, the coastal areas showed a regional picture of mixed oak, hazel, and lime woodland dominating the higher ground through to the middle Bronze Age whilst lower areas show decreasing marine influence as regression occurred following the Phase 1 Neolithic marine transgression (Rackham *et al.* 2021, 62). Palynologically, lime/linden is often under-represented in pollen spectra (Andersen 1970; 1973). As such, despite the low quantities recorded it is likely that it was locally dominant in the environment at 01/03 (Land Fall, Moggs Eye) and 08/01 (Howlet House, Hogsthorpe; Fig. 2.2) until the later Neolithic indicating that these sites remained free from brackish incursions to this time (Rackham *et al.* 2021, 28, 46, 62). The subsequent decline in lime is then associated with the transition to saltmarsh when the lime forests retreat further inland away from the coast (*ibid.*, 48).

This transgression sequence is seen in detail at Howlet House, Hogsthorpe, Profile 08/01 where, after a hiatus in sedimentation due to drying out and/or erosion, there are then two phases of brackish marine incursion. Of interest the initial Phase 1 incursion was seen in augered sediments as a change from peat to clayey silts and was bracketed by a pair of radiocarbon dates from the late Neolithic (2296–2052 cal BC; 248–249 cm, 3780±30 BP, Beta-569335), and early Bronze Age (1975–1861 cal BC; 206–207 cm, 3550±30 BP, Beta-552745; Rackham *et al.* 2021, 13, 28–1). Thus it was demonstrated that the Phase 1 period of marine transgression was short-lived at 08/01 and, by the early Bronze Age, peat had begun developing again with an increase in freshwater plants and a short-lived expansion of alder and willow indicative of freshwater fen formation during a period of regression in sea level following Phase 1.

At Hogsthorpe (Profile 06/03; Fig. 2.2) a slightly different sequence was seen, with a paleosol recorded from 2.53–2.44 m dated to the late Neolithic (2151–2017 cal BC; 244–245 cm, 3700±30 BP, Beta-552741), overlain by peat from 2.42–1.84 m dated to the middle Bronze Age (1683–1521 cal BC; 196–184 cm, 3320±30 BP, Beta-569334; Rackham *et al.* 2021, 13, 53). Here there was little evidence of any local marine or marshy environments in the pollen taxa seen in the sequence until the basal peat was laid, which was later than at Profile 08/01. This prolonged dryness may have contributed towards this site being more favoured for agriculture as some pastoral indicators and cereal-type pollen points were identified in this sequence from the late Neolithic. An increase of alder and willow taxa in the Bronze Age alder likely indicates an increase in fen carr into the peat lands or the drier fringes during this time (*ibid.*, 53–54). This dryer northern area of the route can be clearly seen in mapping of marine sediments found in augered cores, where at 2000 BC the area north of SMR05 is still mapped as mostly dry at this time (Fig. 2.7).

Evidence of farming at Stickney Moraine

Stickney Moraine is a prominent topographical feature rising above the surrounding landscape, separating the West Fen and East Fen basins, as seen in Figures 2.1 and 2.9. It seems likely that there were ongoing agricultural activities taking place in the vicinity of the Stickney Moraine from the middle Neolithic into the middle Bronze Age due to the consistent presence of cereal-type pollen grains and pastoral indicators in pollen sequences (Rackham *et al.* 2021, 56). It is also notable that all of the Stickney Moraine sequences showed a level of woodland clearance and open grassland not seen in any of the earlier sequences (Table 2.2). In terms of physical evidence a likely burnt flint piece was recovered from a Bronze Age surface at Profile 28/05 (Fig. 2.3), along with a charcoal deposit which may represent human activity in the vicinity at this time (*ibid.*, 20, 59). Saline influences contemporary with the intercalated peat elsewhere along the Scheme's cable route are not seen to begin until after the middle Bronze Age at Profile 29/05 (Fig. 2.3), where the base of the peat was dated to 1437–1288 cal BC (3110±30 BP, Beta-552743; *ibid.*, 56–57).

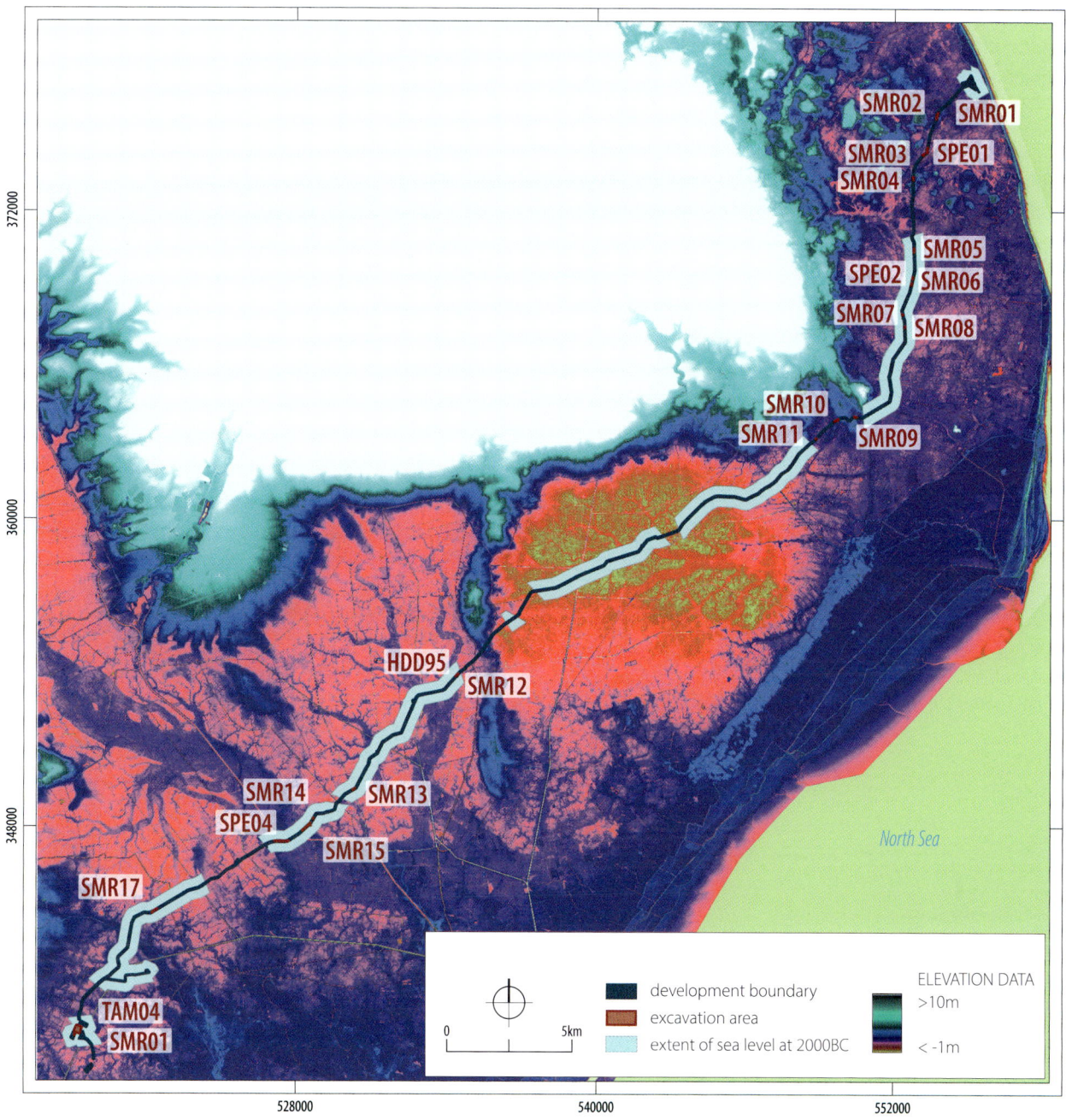

Figure 2.7 Map of the Scheme showing the extent of marine flooded areas in augered cores at 2000 BC (based on Rackham et al. 2021, fig. 19). LiDAR background mapping shows dendritic roddon networks across the route (Environment Agency reproduced under Open Government Licence v3.0; Environment Agency 2024)

Renewed expansion of tidal flat areas

Sedimentological evidence suggests a renewed phase of tidal flat expansion and marine transgression towards the end of the Bronze Age and then again in the late Iron Age and Roman period. These are representative of the Phase 2 and Phase 3 marine transgressions (between c. 2750 and 1500 cal BP; Brew et al. 2000; Shennan and Andrews 2000) and were interspersed with periods of marine regression where colonisation of the fens occurred. Raised roddons that were exposed during the marine regression between Phase 1 and Phase 2 became a major focus for colonisation.

Middle to late Bronze Age

During this period silty clays indicative of saltmarsh environments are recorded in cores across the Scheme. As well as this, laminated deposits of alternate silts and very fine sands were seen in some cores indicating regular

Table 2.2 Stickney Moraine onsite vegetation during the middle Neolithic to middle Bronze Age

Profile	Sample depth (m)	Date	Vegetation	Environment
33/10 (Frithville)	2.47–2.48 (date)	Late Neolithic: 2817–2666 & 2887–2835 cal BC (4180±30 BP, Beta–563672)	Goosefoot, oraches & samphire thrift &/or sea lavender (*Armeria*), sea plantain (*Plantago maritima*), spurrey (*Spergularia*) and probably sea arrow grass (*Triglochin/Potamogeton* type)	Marine/brackish conditions increasing to salt marsh. Then expansion of hazel scrub & willow. Reedswamp throughout
28/05 (Stickney)	0.37–0.50, 0.48–0.49 (date) 0.77–0.78 (date)	Late Neolithic: 2578–2453 cal BC (3980±30 BP, Beta–552741), & middle Bronze Age: 1643–1504 cal BC (3300±30 BP, Beta–569342)	28/05:1 Chenopodiaceae & *Plantago maritima* pollen with *Potamogeton* type (pondweed or alternatively sea arrow grass) plantain & spurrey 28/05:2 Poaceae (grass), reed mace, *Sparganium/Typha angustifolia* type (bur-reed/bulrushes) then alder, willow, sedges and Apiaceae pollen grain (*Oenanthe* type)	Alder decline with increase in halophytes likely to represent saltmarsh. Hiatus & possible erosion then fresh water vegetation of reed swamp which is in turn replaced by fen carr
29/05 (Stickney)	0.18–0.19 (date)	Mid-Bronze Age: 1437–1288 cal BC (3110±30 BP, Beta–552743)	Goosefoot, samphire, oraches, sea plantain, sea lavender &/or thrift decreasing with increasing alder, willow & lesser bulrush &/or bur-reed	Saltmarsh declining & increasing fen carr (alder & willow) vegetation

tidal events in relatively still tidal waters, characteristic of intertidal mudflats (Rackham *et al.* 2021, 11).

In some boreholes between Hogsthorpe and Stickney Moraine these silty clays and laminated deposits were then overlain by intercalated peats. This peat horizon marked a likely regression phase or coastline stabilisation that enabled the development of peat in either brackish or freshwater conditions (*ibid.*, 11). The depth of this peat was not uniform and it has been suggested that much of the undulation could be due to differential compaction of the mineral and organic sediments due to differences in location across the earlier saltmarsh and mudflats (*ibid.*). Few dates are available for these intercalated peat deposits; but they have been dated to the middle Bronze Age (1695–1600 cal BC; 3350±30 BP, Beta-552744 at 18/05B (Tip Lane, Thorpe Culvert), just east of the Steeping River, and 1975–1861 cal BC; 3550±30 BP, Beta-552745 at 08/01 (Howlet House, Hogsthorpe; Rackham *et al.* 2021, 12; table 3) (Fig. 2.2).

Onset of Phase 2 transgression
This period shows more diversity in the background pollen signal than earlier phases, suggesting maturity and diversity in the wider landscape. Oak and hazel woodland are still a major component of the regional landscape at Tip Lane, Thorpe Culvert, just east of the Steeping River in the Northern Basin (Profile 18/05B; Fig. 2.2) towards the end of the Bronze Age. Subsequently a major expansion of sedges and ferns through the peat associated with the alder suggests the development of fen carr woodland. Initial clastic deposits of silty clay and clayey silt with occasional traces of organics were interpreted as saltmarsh and found to show a local dominance of Chenopodiaceae illustrative of the marine influence (Rackham *et al.* 2021, 64).

The East Fen anomaly
Across the Scheme relative sea levels generally rise with the Phase 2 transgression, although there are exceptions, including at the East Fen where peat growth appears to keep pace with the sea level rise across the basin (Rackham *et al.* 2021, 17). This is in contrast to the coastal area north of the East Fen (08/01: Howlet House, Hogsthorpe) where peat from fen carr and reed swamp instead persists through the middle Bronze Age to the Iron Age–Roman transition (*ibid.*, 28, 64).

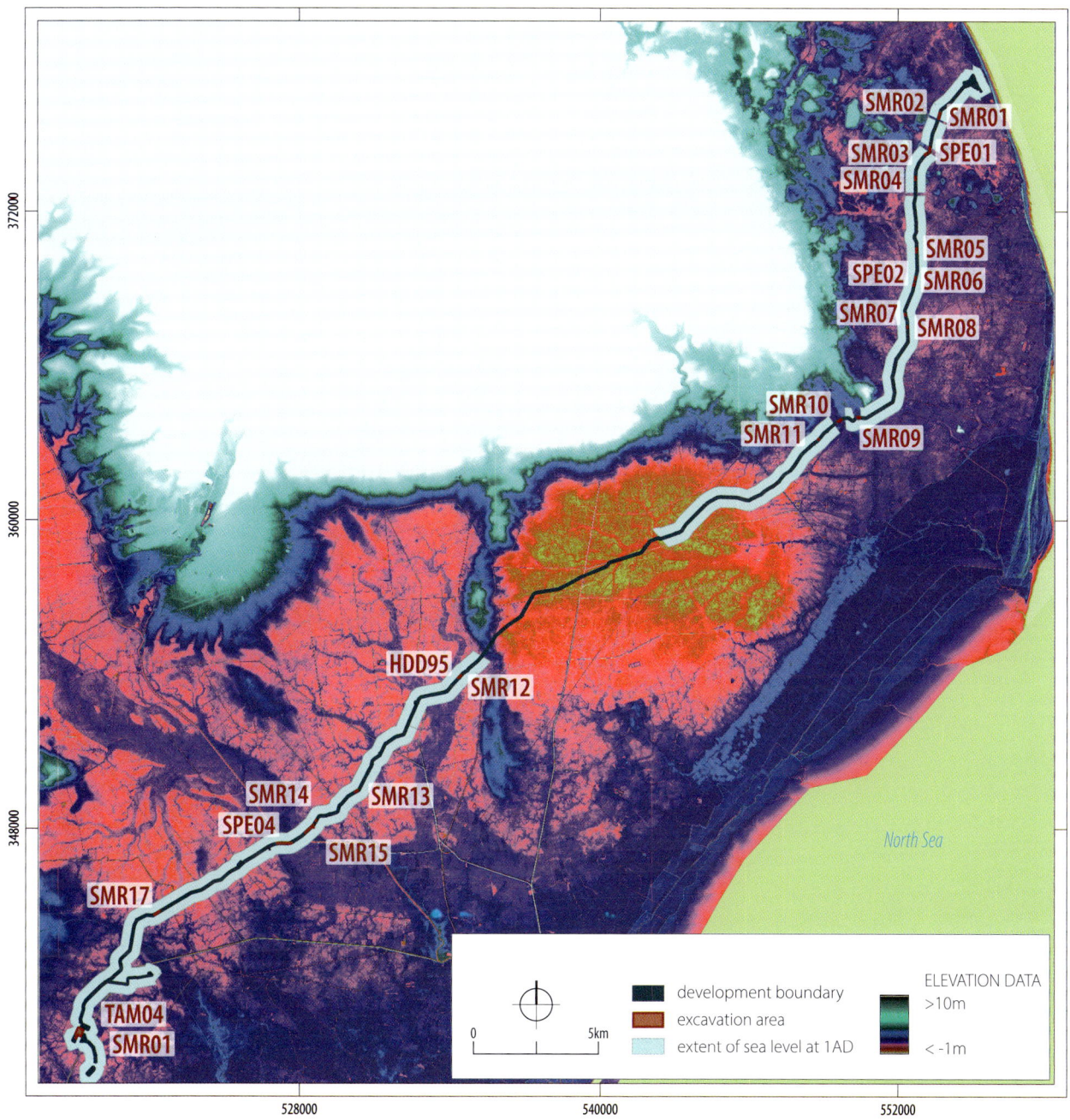

Figure 2.8 Map of the Scheme showing the extent of marine flooded areas in augered cores at AD 1 (based on Rackham et al. 2021; fig. 20). LiDAR background mapping shows dendritic roddon networks across the route (Environment Agency reproduced under Open Government Licence v3.0; Environment Agency 2024)

The East Fen basin is anomalous as it is currently the lowest area along the route, yet it is not filled with marine sediments to the same level as adjacent areas and there is no return to brackish conditions seen after the early Bronze Age seen in the Fen (*ibid.*, 17; see Figs 2.7 and 2.8). The lack of marine sediments deposited on the upper peats suggests that the sea never reached the main East Fen basin during the Phase 2 or later transgressions and the Phase 2 dendritic creek systems that approach the southern and eastern margins of the Fen do not reach the centre of the basin. The absence of later marine sediments therefore implies that peat growth within the East Fen was sufficient to maintain the surface level above the advancing sea, as well as suggesting that several metres of peat have been lost from this area through drainage and agriculture over the last few centuries, likely along with any post-Neolithic archaeology (*ibid.*).

Iron Age

The prehistoric landscape, and particularly the roddons, influenced the development of archaeological sites during the Iron Age and Roman period. Between the Phase 1 and 2

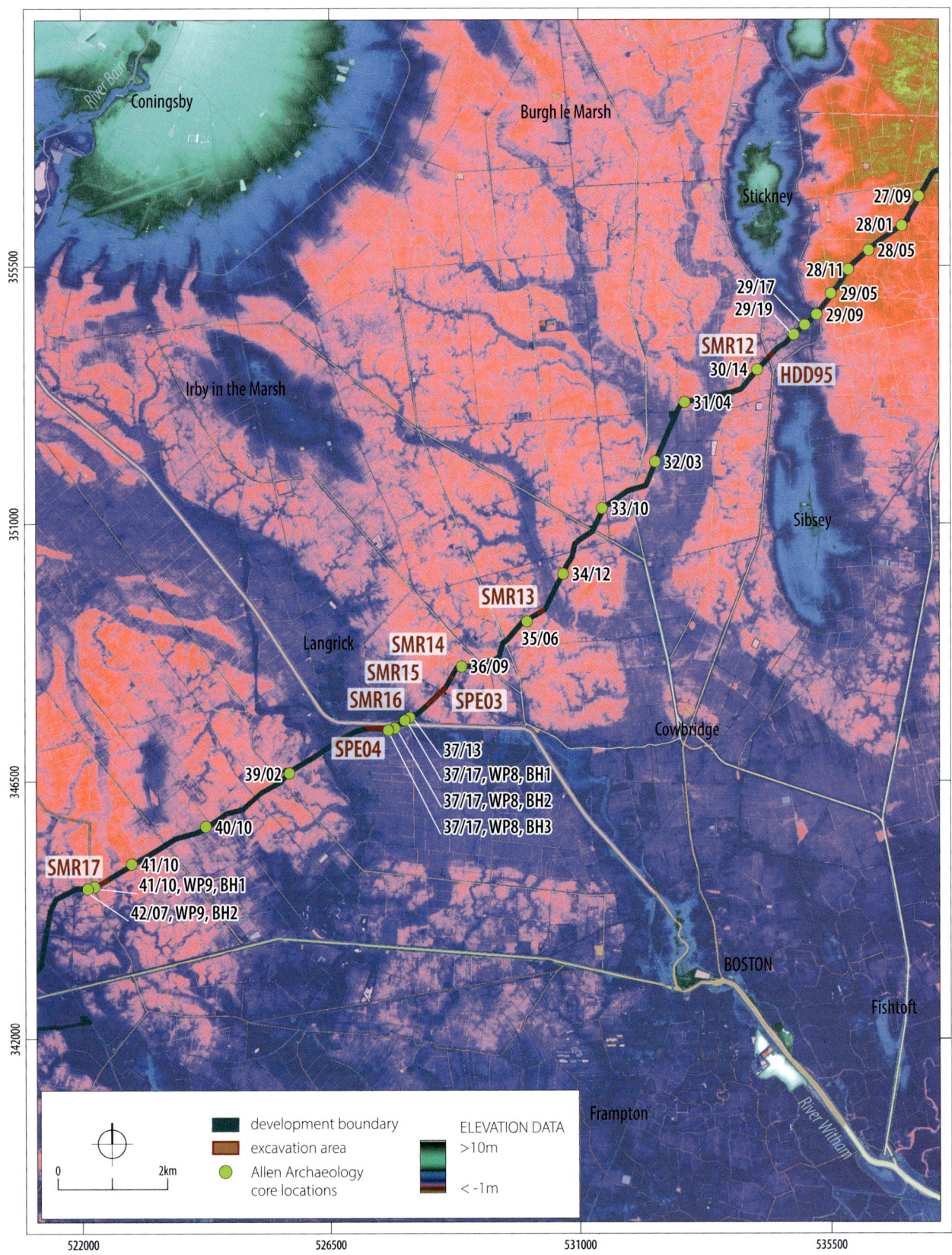

Figure 2.9 LiDAR map showing the dendritic pattern of roddons around the River Witham, near Boston (LiDAR: Environment Agency reproduced under Open Government Licence v3.0; Environment Agency 2024)

transgressions a slight regression in the 1st millennium BC led to the coastline moving eastwards and areas of marine sedimentation becoming exposed (Rackham *et al.* 2021). The most significant archaeological impact of this regression was that the roddons identifying the courses of the large and small prehistoric intertidal channels associated with the Phase 1 transgression became dry and raised above the rest of the floodplain over time. In the case of the major roddons such as that of the tidal River Witham they can be as much as 3 km wide, and during the late Iron Age and Roman period these newly raised areas of land were colonised and utilised for agriculture including probable large-scale cereal production (Headland Archaeology 2020; Rackham *et al.* 2021; Fryer and Bailey 2024; Fryer and Turner 2024; Wallace and Fryer 2024).

Regression and colonisation of the Fens
The intercalated peat deposits that followed the Phase 2 clastic marine sediments showed a dramatic drop in the halophyte elements, with alder pollen indicative of some growth of fen carr woodland on the peat's drier margins (Rackham *et al.* 2021, 61). This marked a transition to a prolonged phase (up to 1700 years in some locations) of reduced brackish influences and saw a reduction in the saltmarsh halophytes and a tendency for the development of a more freshwater habitat as indicated by algal cysts and Zygnemataceae (*ibid.*, 55). Major colonisation of roddons in the Fens began during this period, and there is generally an expansion of grasses and pastoral indicators seen within the late Iron Age sequences (Headland Archaeology 2020; Rackham *et al.* 2021).

The upper surface of the intercalated peats at 18/05B (Tip Lane, Thorpe Culvert; Fig. 2.2) has a Roman date of cal AD 74–226 (1870±30BP, Beta-569338; Rackham *et al.* 2021, 13; table 3). The continuation of this peat sequence through to the Roman period demonstrating the discontinuous and variable impact area of the later marine transgressions. The prolonged regression at this site was accompanied by a major expansion of birch in the upper part of the pollen sequence as the site experienced a prolonged period of drying out and stabilisation during the 1st millennium BC (*ibid.*, 64)

The distribution of Iron Age sites shows that, as marine regression occurred, the landscape was colonised focusing on the raised roddon beds. Indicative of this is the group of salterns that extends around the Burgh le Marsh region (Profiles 07/14 to 12/24), clustered around roddons and creeks, which suggest an extensive area of saltmaking during this period (Lane and Morris 2001; Rackham *et al.* 2021).

Roman period
The River Witham and its roddons
The River Witham appears to have been a particular focus for Roman activity, with the Car Dyke assumed to be cut during this period to connect the Witham to the Nene, and the Foss Dyke created around AD 120 to connect the Witham to the Trent (Simmons 1979). This is the first evidence of the wetland area itself being managed, as the walling of the dykes for navigation purposes would have assisted with the drainage of the Fen (Galloway 2013).

Roddons were still the focus for terrestrial activities during the Roman period, and evidence of roddons associated with the River Witham was found in several locations between SMR12 and SMR 17 to the west of the Stickney Moraine (Fig. 2.3).

Where the Scheme crosses the main Witham roddon it is 1.8 km wide (Rackham *et al.* 2021, 2). The British Geological Survey (BGS 1995) records a significant depth of channel incision by this roddon – over 15 m in places, and in the geoarchaeological survey the base of the tidal channel was reached at –4.23 m AOD in Profile 37/17 WP8 (BH1), yet in Profile 37/17 WP8 (BH2 and BH3) silty sands of the roddon were still being encountered to –7.62 m AOD when the boreholes were terminated (*ibid.*, 10).

It therefore appears that the palaeo-estuarine channel of the Witham has removed all the earlier prehistoric river sediments and adjacent floodplain across the breadth of the roddon at its crossing by the cable route. Although this channel has destroyed the prehistoric landscape, it created a unique landscape, the surface of which was the focus of later activity, with the top of the roddon being colonised at the end of the 1st millennium BC and during the Roman period as the relative sea level fell (Rackham 2019).

The late Roman marine transgression
As the Roman period progressed a fourth marine transgression followed (Phase 4), likely beginning in the middle Roman period, evidence for which is found in the downcutting creeks identified at the northern end of the Scheme in the Coastal area between Anderby Creek and Hogsthorpe, and the Thorpe Culvert and Friskney areas (Waller 1994, 317). The upper intercalated peat is again sealed by clastic sediments in these locations, with clayey silts and fine sands that are often laminated and are indicative of the return to intertidal mudflat conditions; the increased sand content pointing to a more energetic tidal environment. Radiocarbon dating of the upper surface of the intercalated peat dates the return to a transgressive environment and rising relative sea levels at 18/05B (Tip Lane, Thorpe Culvert; Fig. 2.2) to cal AD 74–226 (1870±30 BP, Beta-569338; Rackham *et al.* 2021).

By the late Roman period, the final marine advance had started flooding many of the areas recolonised in the Iron Age and early Roman period leading to the abandonment of many coastal wetland sites (Galloway 2013), and another phase of peat formation is seen forming around the margins of the advancing sea, with a subsequent period of marine silt and silty clay deposition. This episode of marine transgression appears to have advanced further inland in places, but perhaps not so far in others, and may have reached a level of approximately 3–3.5 m AOD.

Evidence for the late Roman Phase 4 marine transgression has been seen in some of the archaeological assemblages. TAM04 located directly to the northeast of SMR01 was a primarily Romano-British site near Anderby Creek (Fig. 2.2). Midden 8 (deposit 4.34) was dated to the late Roman period, and it was noted that unlike in earlier fills, shells of brackish water snails were present, possibly suggesting that the site was prone to intermittent periods of inundation. The presence of wetland plants seeds, such as sedge, club rush, and rush in the later midden deposits also attests to the wetland conditions on site (Fryer and Bailey 2024). Wood charcoal recovered from archaeological samples included fragments of alder (*Alnus glutinosa*) and willow (*Salix* sp.), which may represent areas of higher ground in this area or perhaps freshwater wetlands; alder and willow are both tolerant of boggy or waterlogged soils characteristic of freshwater wetlands, where they are usually shrubby, sometimes forming dense thickets or carrs (Gale 2001, 155).

In the coastal Profile 08/05 (west of Addlethorpe, near Hildyke Drain; Fig. 2.2) there is the intriguing possibility of two distinct phases of land use present; one related to late Iron Age–early Roman saltmaking, and a probable later land use shown by burials that are almost certainly later Roman, with their stratigraphic location being above the nearby saltern deposits and below what are presumably post-Roman sediments (Rackham 2019). The presence of later Roman land usage here further indicating that the Phase 4 transgression may not have reached all inland coastal areas, or that the effects of the transgression were rather short-lived in some areas.

Medieval and post-medieval land reclamation

The medieval period saw a growth of ecclesiastical power, and various monasteries made attempts to drain parts of the fens and reduce flood risks from both rivers and the sea (Gardiner 2021). There were initially no overarching schemes to maintain or create these drainage solutions though, with the landowners largely responsible for maintenance of their own frontages, and degradation of the drains was a frequent political issue (Chisholm 2012). Plague deaths, and the associated losses of peasant labour to maintain drains, are also thought to have been contributing factors to increased flooding events that were recorded in the 14th century (Galloway 2013). It was not until 1531, when Henry VIII passed the *Act of Sewers*, creating Commissions and Courts of Sewers to investigate flood defences in coastal areas, that more formalised systems were created to establish which landowners were liable to pay for their repairs, with rates enacted for the upkeep of drains (Morgan 2017). Unfortunately, the Dissolution of the Monasteries in the 1530–40s only exacerbated issues of drain neglect by creating a vacuum in the ownership of the medieval fenland flood control measures (Galloway 2013). In 1568 work began on the Maud Foster Drain to the north of Boston to start draining the West Fen, before being enlarged by gentleman adventurers in 1631 (Kane 2011).

Seaports such as Boston (founded in the 11th century on a River Witham roddon), Ingoldmells, and Skegness were important to the medieval Lincolnshire economy, but all depended on safe and deep havens for boats. Weather during the medieval period was thought to have been particularly stormy, and there are some suggestions that storms in the 12th century may have destroyed a string of offshore barrier islands that had previously sheltered the Wash and other sea-facing areas of Lincolnshire (Pawley 1984; Galloway 2013; Green 2023a; Fig. 2.4). It appears that Skegness, despite being recommended as 'a good port' in 12th century sailing directions, was destroyed by a storm at some time in the 16th century (Green 2023a), possibly an event made more likely by the earlier destruction of offshore barrier islands. Whereas Ingoldmells was a shallow estuary, which appears to have partially silted by the end of the medieval period. Silting was a major concern for fleets and was also recorded at other towns such as Wainfleet, Saltfleet Haven, and Friskney during this period; silted areas were often reclaimed as farmland (*ibid.*).

There is very little existing environmental archaeology evidence for the post-medieval period towards the south of the Lincolnshire fens (Carruthers and Hunter Dowse 2019, 145–153). It seems likely that the roddons associated with the later marine transgressions now became important features within the medieval and post-medieval landscape, both for farming and settlements (Galloway 2013). Sites established during this period were likely to have been utilised into modern times following drainage of the peatlands. Plant remains that were assessed across the route showed an increase in dryland habitats and expansion of farming areas (Fryer and Bailey 2024; Fryer and Turner 2024; Wallace and Fryer 2024). Therefore, despite mixed fortunes in terms of weather and flooding, the landscape became more habitable during this period, with increasing amounts of farm land, and the beginning of more unified approaches to land management (Kane 2011; Galloway 2013).

Medieval

It appears that roddons continued to influence the landscapes colonisation, as while the grouping of features is generally less dense than during the Roman period, there are still clusters of features (ridge-and-furrow systems, field boundaries, and trackways) that suggest localised habitation, again, mainly restricted to the location of former and likely earlier settlements (Allen Archaeology 2021b).

Post-medieval

As has already been highlighted, there is very little existing environmental archaeology evidence for the post-medieval period towards the south of the Lincolnshire fens (Carruthers and Hunter Dowse 2019, 145–153). This is likely in part due to the deflation and desiccation of near-surface deposits due to post-medieval drainage schemes. Assessment of environmental samples collected from excavations on the Triton Knoll Electrical System though has added slightly to our understanding of this period.

The archaeobotanical assemblage suggests a fluctuating environment across the region. SMR12 near Sibscy Northlands (Fig. 2.3) is today located at the confluence of two major drainage channels at a low point along the Stickney Moraine, and it is perhaps unsurprising that this area was found to be a wet place during the post-medieval era. The SMR12 wild taxa were found to have a distinct wetland signature, though taxa from drier areas also contributed to the sample. The economic plants of SMR12 were dominated by barley; perhaps an indication that the saline tolerance of this crop was of value here (Wallace and Fryer 2024).

This contrasts with SMR09 (near Burgh le Marsh; Fig. 2.2), which had a greater diversity of economic plants and dryland wild taxa. SMR09 is very different to the other rural sites, in that it is the focus of brick manufacture and may have had a high input of imported material for fuel and/or for food stuffs. In contrast, the other sites appear more in keeping with rural agrarian settlements. SMR09 appears to have had a dryland character despite the most common plant recorded in samples being sea club-rush or club-rush, a wetland taxon. Club-rush may have been deliberately collected for craftworking or fuel, which is supported by a corresponding abundance of rush stems. It is interesting that, while the presence of such plants indicates that wetter areas were accessible to local inhabitants, both the wild seed and the molluscan assemblages from this area are more suggestive of dry land habitats, consistent with a crop profile that emphasises the cultivation of wheat. It therefore appears SMR09, as well as SPE03 (Mere Booth Road, West Fen; Fig. 2.3), had access to drier land areas despite the fen edge setting (Wallace and Fryer 2024).

The diversity of food plants being grown in the region is greater than seen in earlier periods, as is the norm for the post-medieval period when trading networks were more developed than in preceding periods. The pulses common pea and broad bean, as well as oat, are recovered in small proportions, along with durum wheat, bread wheat, apple or pear, and barley at SMR09. Durum wheat, which today is used more for pasta and biscuits, is found somewhat further north than is typical in medieval Britain (Moffett 2006, 49). Crop dominance appears to differ by area. At SMR09 wheat, and probably bread wheat, appear to be predominant. In the SMR12 sample, however, most of the food plant remains are barley grains. Bread wheat was a typical primary crop in the post-medieval era, being the favoured cereal for human consumption (*ibid.*, 48).

Bread wheat, however, would require relatively light, free-draining soils. The use of barley, as represented in the SMR12 sample, is by no means unusual (Carruthers and Hunter Dowse 2019, 145), but the selection of this less favoured crop (Newman and Newman 2006) could indicate the cultivation of saline ground at this time (*e.g.* Murphy 2001a, 154; Wallace and Fryer 2024).

Modern period

The modern period has seen arguably the most significant changes to the fens landscape since the first post-glacial marine transgression. Throughout the modern period, drainage schemes have been created to reclaim thousands of hectares of land across Lincolnshire fen areas for agriculture. The network of dykes and drains created to remove water from the fens is a distinctive feature of the modern landscape, with deep ditches bordering the field systems created by the drainage. These flat lowland Lincolnshire farmlands are now amongst the most fertile in the UK due to the presence of peat within the soils (DEFRA 2023). However, the impact of the drainage schemes continues into the present day, and the ongoing dewatering and shrinkage of peat areas has led to large peat losses in the East Fen which were noted during the geoarchaeological fieldwork phase. The continued losses of peat are a potential problem for the future of the fen landscape as they reduce the fertility of soils as well as releasing large amounts of CO_2 (DEFRA 2023). Additionally, the peat shrinkage leads to down wasting of the surface profile which, in our current period of modern anthropogenically driven climate change with rising sea levels, once again puts this dynamic landscape at risk of marine transgression.

Draining the fen

Following on from the early canals created during the Roman period to improve navigation inland, and the works of various monasteries and commissions during the medieval and post-medieval period to control flooding, the process of draining the fens largely began in the modern period (Galloway 2013). Early attempts to substantially drain the fen had been largely unsuccessful, with several of the attempts made in the 16th and mid-17th centuries purposely thwarted by unhappy Fenland residents, gentlemen adventurers, and Corporations (Kane 2011). Some improvements were made however, and pumping engines initially driven by horses were installed to remove the water as the drainage schemes had caused peat shrinkage, increasing the relative sea level, and decreasing the efficacy of the drainage channels, which in some cases led to increased flooding (Kane 2011). By 1763, there were 50 windmills recorded at work in Deeping Fen (Miles 1965).

Further attempts were made in the early 19th century, and Mr John Rennie recommended a scheme that was put into effect with Acts of the Parliament in 1801 and 1803 (Barton 2011). The Hobhole Sluice drain was constructed diverting waters of the East Fen to meet the Witham near Boston and opened in 1806, and the New Maud Drain opened in 1807. The industrial revolution led to further improvements in pumping, and the windmills were largely replaced by steam engines in the 19th century which realised the economic benefits of the fen drainage (Kane 2011), and these in turn were replaced by diesel and electric engines in the 20th century (Miles 1965).

The impact of this drainage was to reduce the depth of surface peat in East Fen, evidence for which was seen in works conducted for this project. Prior to drainage the East Fen was a boggy 'queachy' environment with numerous small lakes 'deepes' in the fen, possibly formed from peat cutting (Dugdale 1662), with earlier medieval reclaimed 'firm' surrounding the basin (Simmons and Foster 2023). The BGS records show extensive surface peats across this area (Fig. 2.3), but in our study, despite the ploughsoil being peaty only traces of compacted humified peat were identified in small discrete hollows beneath the ploughsoil from Profiles 24/01 to 28/04. As Robson (1985) had also recorded that there were rare patches of thick peaty soils present 40 years ago, this suggests that most peats must have been lost through agriculture and drainage over the last few decades, demonstrating that landscape changes are ongoing in the modern period. Drainage and peat losses in the fens are a complex issue, but their ongoing effects are important to consider in the preservation of the archaeological record (French 2000).

Glossary of terms

Alluvium: Alluvial deposits are unconsolidated material (clay, silt, sand, and gravel) deposited by running water such as rivers or streams. Material may be sorted or semi-sorted in a stream bed or its floodplain, and gravels are generally rounded.

Anoxic: A condition or environment that is completely lacking in oxygen.

Bedrock geology: The main mass of rocks that form the Earth. The British Geological Survey (BGS) refers to everything older than 2.6 million years as bedrock.

Carr: A wetland wooded environment dominated by shrub vegetation.

Clast: A single constituent part of a sediment deposit produced by fragmentation of a larger part (*e.g.*, gravel).

Clastic sediments: Detrital sediments that are formed of broken rocks (clasts) or sometimes shell fragments, that have been eroded, transported, and then redeposited at a new location. They are common in littoral zones where significant redeposition occurs. Particle sizes can range from silt to boulder.

Colluvium: Colluvial material or hillwash is unconsolidated material (silt, sand, gravel, and rock) that has been deposited at the base of a hillslope by processes like rainwash and downslope soil creep (erosion and gravity). Material is generally poorly sorted, and gravels are generally angular. May cap paleosols and important palaeoenvironmental deposits.

Detrital sediments: Fragmented rocky material produced by weathering and then transported from its original site.

Embayment: An open bay forming a recess in a coastline. The Wash is the UK's largest embayment.

Estuary: The tidal part of a river mouth, where it broadens and enters the sea. The fluctuating influence of the rivers discharging freshwater and saltwater from tides can create brackish shoreline environments. These are usually zone of deposition and can have complicated channel systems.

Eustasy/eustatic change: Global changes in absolute sea level without regards to local isostatic changes. These changes have in the Pleistocene been almost entirely the result of glacial cycles which have sequentially stored water as ice causing sea level drops (regressions) and then melted and released water causing sea level rises (transgressions), a process also called glacio-eustasy.

Fen: A low, marshy, sometime wooded area of land with waterlogged soils, that are usually alkaline or neutral. The Fenlands in eastern England around The Wash have been largely drained for arable agriculture since the 17th century.

Holocene: The current geological period, beginning 11.7 ka BP. The Holocene has been subdivided into three geological ages. The Greenlandian is the earliest age of the Holocene epoch (11.7–8.2 ka BP); this is followed by the middle Holocene age called the Northgrippian (8.2–4.2 ka BP), and then the Meghalayan (4.2 ka BP to present) is the second Quaternary period epoch.

ka BP: Thousand years before present.

Intertidal zone: The part of the shoreline that is covered at high tide but uncovered at low tide.

Isostasy/isostatic change: Changes in the relative mass and buoyancy of a landmass, that causes its subsidence (*e.g.*, due to growth of mountains or icesheets) or uplift (*e.g.*, due to erosion of mountains or loss of icesheets). In the UK the melting of ice sheets at the end of the last glacial period is continuing to cause the crust to rebound in previously glaciated areas. This is known as an isostatic sea level change.

Landscape: All the visible features of an area of land, its landforms both natural and man-made.

Last Glacial Maximum (LGM): The coldest part of the last glacial period (Devensian) when ice sheets were at their greatest extent, in the UK this was between 27–18.5 ka BP.

Last Glacial Period/Devensian: This is also called the Devensian Glaciation (in the UK), and was the most recent phase of glaciation to have occurred in Britain, covering the period of 115–11.7 ka BP. It had fluctuating interstadial periods (less cold) and stadial periods (cold periods), with the most significant cool period and maximum ice sheet advance occurring in the Late Devensian. The glacial period followed the Ipswichian Interglacial.

Late Glacial Period/Late Devensian: This is defined as the period of rapid climate fluctuations in the lattermost part of Devensian glaciation that occurred between 25–11.7 ka BP that covers the LGM and then rapid warming and retreat of ice sheets up to the start of the Holocene epoch. Coastal lowland areas in eastern Lincolnshire were covered by an onshore incursion of the North Sea Lobe (NSL) of the British–Irish Ice Sheet between *c.* 29–14.7 ka BP.

Littoral zone: A shoreline area, either relating to the sea or a lake.

Ma BP: Million years before present.

Paleosol: An ancient soil formed on a past landscape, that has been buried by later sediments such as flood deposits, river terraces, landslides, or further soil profiles. They can also be exposed be later erosion of the overlying sediments.

Palaeochannel: An abandoned fluvial channel – either a river or a stream – that has been infilled with later sediments.

Peat: A brown to black deposit formed of fibrous, partially decomposed organic matter that has accumulated in a waterlogged, anoxic environment. It can rapidly form under cool, humid conditions that have been common in the post-glacial British climate.

Pleistocene: The Pleistocene epoch occurred between 2.58 Ma to 11.7 ka BP, it was dominated by cycles of glacial and interglacial periods. This was the first Quaternary period epoch.

Preboreal: An informal stage within the Holocene epoch, following the Tarantian and preceding the Boreal. It occurred between 10,300 and 9,000 years BP.

Quaternary period: The most recent geological period from 2.58 Ma to present, including both the Pleistocene epoch (2.58 Ma to 11.7 ka BP), and the Holocene epoch (11.7 ka BP to present).

Regression: A fall in relative sea level.

Relative sea level: The height of the sea relative to a particular location, it is affected by both isostasy and eustasy.

Roddon: Dry raised beds of former river channels in the Fenland of east England. They are characterised by the fine sands that are deposited within former creeks and estuarine channels. The roddon forms as surrounding peat dries out or is drained causing the surface elevation of the formerly saturated peat areas to drop and leaving the roddon sands as areas of higher ground. Roddons also create natural banks when flooding creating levees.

Soil: The unconsolidated mixture of organic matter, minerals, gas, water, and organisms in which plants grow.

Superficial geology: The looser surface material. The British Geological Survey (BGS) refers to all geologically recent (Quaternary: 2.6 Ma to present) deposits as superficial deposits.

Till: Unsorted, and generally very consolidated mix of material (clay, silt, sand, gravels, and boulders) deposited by and underneath a glacier. Glacial till has historically been also referred to as drift, glacial clay, boulder clay, and diamicton.

Transgression: A rise in relative sea level.

Water lain deposits: These are deposited directly in water *e.g.*, lakes, ponds, estuaries, the sea. They are distinct from alluvium and are described by the environment they were deposited in.

3

Prehistoric landscapes

Claire Christie
With contributions from Michael Bamforth, Rebecca Davaney, Rebecca Sillwood, Ian M. Rowlandson, and Hugh G. Fiske

The Triton Knoll Electrical System extends through a landscape which witnessed significant change across the prehistoric period. This impacts the distribution and density of activity with the scarcity of evidence a consistent theme throughout this chapter (Fig. 3.1). The Mesolithic and Neolithic evidence comprises pits and artefact scatters indicating an early prehistoric presence moving across the landscape to access the rich variety of resources (Fig. 3.2). This picture continues into the Bronze Age as evidenced by the preserved timber structure excavated at Northlands (HDD95). The timber structure provides an opportunity to consider local resources, construction techniques, and the purpose of such structures. From the middle–late Bronze Age there was an expansion of evidence for salt production. The features excavated at SPE01 in the Coastal Landscape Parcel represent the earliest salt production evidence uncovered across the Scheme with activity continuing into the Iron Age. The site sits within a landscape with abundant evidence of later Iron Age salt production. Despite evidence of salt production, further evidence of Iron Age activity across the Scheme was rare comprising a limited number of features and pottery sherds recovered from later features.

Mesolithic and Neolithic: Prehistoric patterns

The identification of early prehistoric activity in Lincolnshire is problematic due to the development of peat in later periods potentially masking the evidence in low-lying areas (Membery 2000). At the beginning of the Mesolithic the lowland plains of Doggerland would have been accessible with the Lincolnshire coastline forming part of a wider low-lying landscape (Green 2023b). Geoarchaeological work indicated that at around 4000 BC the Scheme was located within a terrestrial landscape but 90% of this area became inundated by rising sea levels over the next 4000 years (Rackham *et al.* 2021, see Chapter 2). Extensive survey work conducted as part of The Fenland Project has identified Mesolithic activity primarily located at or near the present-day sea level at the edges of the Fenland basin (Hall and Coles 1994, 28). Evidence of Mesolithic activity has largely been confined to lithics scatters as opposed to *in situ* features. The excavation of Pit 0037 at SPE01, located towards the northern end of the Scheme between the towns of Anderby (in the north) and Hogsthorpe (in the south), provides a rare example of an *in situ* assemblage (Gaunt and Roberts 2024; Fig. 3.3). Pit 0037 contained an assemblage of Mesolithic or early Neolithic lithics with the worked flint including evidence for planned blade production (see below). The site is located in a coastal area to the north of the fens with scarce surrounding evidence of prehistoric activity, with the exception of find spots along the coast or further inland (Fig. 3.2).

The evidence for Neolithic activity is equally scarce with a sweep of find spots, largely flint assemblages, found from Willoughby to Welton le Marsh (Fig. 3.2). The find spots are located within a topographically transitional landscape with scattered areas of high ground extending from the Lincolnshire Wolds to the west. The extent of sea level rise, as indicated by the geoarchaeological work, places the coastline further inland during this period with only specific locations such as the hillocks at the edge of the Wolds potentially suitable for settlement (Rackham *et al.* 2021; see Chapter 2, Figs 2.4 and 2.6). The Neolithic–Bronze Age

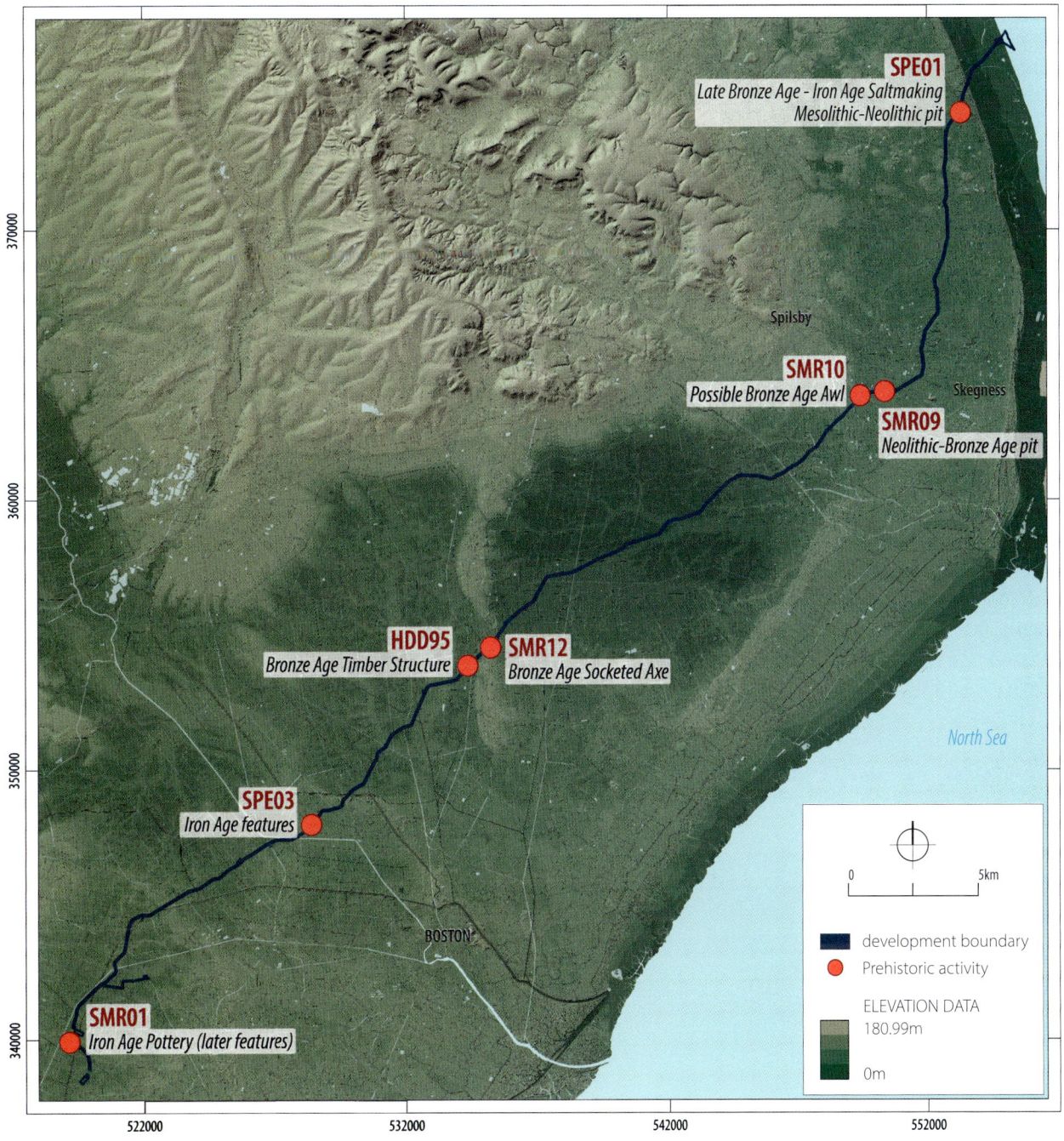

Figure 3.1 Prehistoric activity identified along the route of the Scheme

activity identified at SMR09 is located at the southern extent of this transitional landscape. A single pit, Pit 0014, from which lithics and pottery dated to the late Neolithic–early Bronze Age were recovered, represented the only surviving evidence of prehistoric activity within a site dominated by medieval and post-medieval rural industry (Stockdale *et al.* 2024). The lithic assemblage recovered from the pit was reminiscent of the later Neolithic or early Bronze Age and did not include any evidence of planned blade production (see below). The prehistoric pottery represented seven or eight vessels which, except for two vessels, could all be assigned to the 2nd millennium BC (Chowne 2024). The pit appears to represent the curation and deliberate deposition of material, a practice not uncommon in prehistory (Stockdale *et al.* 2024).

The site at SMR09 is located to the south of Burgh le Marsh with several find spots highlighting a prehistoric presence (Fig. 3.2). The excavated evidence is scarce with Neolithic–Bronze Age flints recovered during a watching brief near Hall Lane, Burgh le Marsh (MLI98787) and a sherd of middle Neolithic Impressed ware recovered during an evaluation at 2 High Street (Archaeological Project Services 2006; MLI89560). To the south, a flint scatter was recovered during works for The Hollies Solar Park, Croft (MLI99383). To the west, prehistoric activity was identified surrounding Spilsby during the Viking Link cable route mitigation works, which runs roughly parallel to the Scheme to the west (Wessex Archaeology 2023). Area 39 (TF 37289 63805) was notable for the relatively high number of struck flints including early Neolithic and Mesolithic material with a Neolithic pit uncovered at Area 37 (TF 39265 68928) (*ibid.*).

Lithics

Rebecca Devaney

A small assemblage comprising 78 pieces of worked flint (weighing 513 g) and 41 fragments of burnt unworked flint (weighing 247 g) were recovered from the excavations along the entirety of the Scheme (Table 3.1). The larger groups of flint were recovered from pits, with the flint from SPE01 dating from the Mesolithic or earlier Neolithic, and that from SMR09 potentially dating from the later Neolithic or early Bronze Age. However, chronologically diagnostic tools were not recovered and dating is based on the presence or absence of technological features relating to planned blade production.

Overall nature and significance of assemblage

The worked flint from the Scheme comprises two distinct assemblages dating from the Mesolithic or earlier Neolithic (SPE01) and the later Neolithic or early Bronze Age (SMR09). Chronologically diagnostic tools are not present in the assemblage, however, differing technological characteristics are present which determines the dating. The worked flint from Pit 0037 at SPE01 includes evidence for planned blade production indicating a Mesolithic or earlier Neolithic date for this assemblage. In contrast, the flint from Pit 0014 at SMR09 is more reminiscent of assemblages from the later Neolithic or early Bronze Age and did not include any evidence for planned blade production. The pottery also recovered from Pit 0014 suggests a broader date range, partially consistent with the later Neolithic to early Bronze Age date indicated by the flint and may therefore indicate the presence of a curated assemblage. Structured deposition in Neolithic pits is common, as documented by Bradley (2007) and Garrow (2007), and the pits may be viewed as part of this tradition. Similar pits have been found in the region, for example at Tattershall Thorpe (Chowne *et al.* 1993).

Overall, the volume of flint recovered from the excavations is small, merely comprising the two pit deposits and sporadic residual finds, suggesting limited activity in the area during the Neolithic and early Bronze Age. Evidence for settlement during this period in the region is rare (Clay 2022) however recent work at Lincolnshire Eastern Bypass, although predominantly comprising Mesolithic scatters, also included large numbers of flint tools spot-dated to the earlier Neolithic through to the early Bronze Age (Devaney 2021), perhaps suggesting a focus of activity elsewhere in the region. However, the presence

Table 3.1 Summary of lithics by Landscape Parcel, site, and lithic type

	Coastal		Fen Edge			Lincolnshire Marsh			Total
	SMR04	SPE01	SMR09	SMR10	SMR16	SMR06	SMR07	SPE02	
Flake	1	12	20	–	1	–	–	–	34
Blade	–	4	–	–	–	–	–	–	4
Bladelet	–	2	–	–	–	–	–	–	2
Blade-like flake	–	6	2	–	–	–	–	–	8
Irregular waste	–	2	8	–	–	–	–	–	10
Sieved chips	–	2	12	–	–	–	–	–	14
Multiplatform flake core	–	2	–	–	–	–	–	–	2
End scraper	–	–	1	–	–	–	–	–	1
End & side scraper	–	–	2	–	–	–	–	–	2
Disc scraper	–	–	1	–	–	–	–	–	1
Total	1	30	46	–	1	–	–	–	78
Total weight (g)	*0*	*211*	*286*	–	*16*	–	–	–	*513*
Burnt unworked	1	8	7	1	–	11	12	1	41
Burnt unworked weight (g)	*0*	*225*	*8*	*0*	–	*14*	*0*	*0*	*247*

3 Prehistoric landscapes

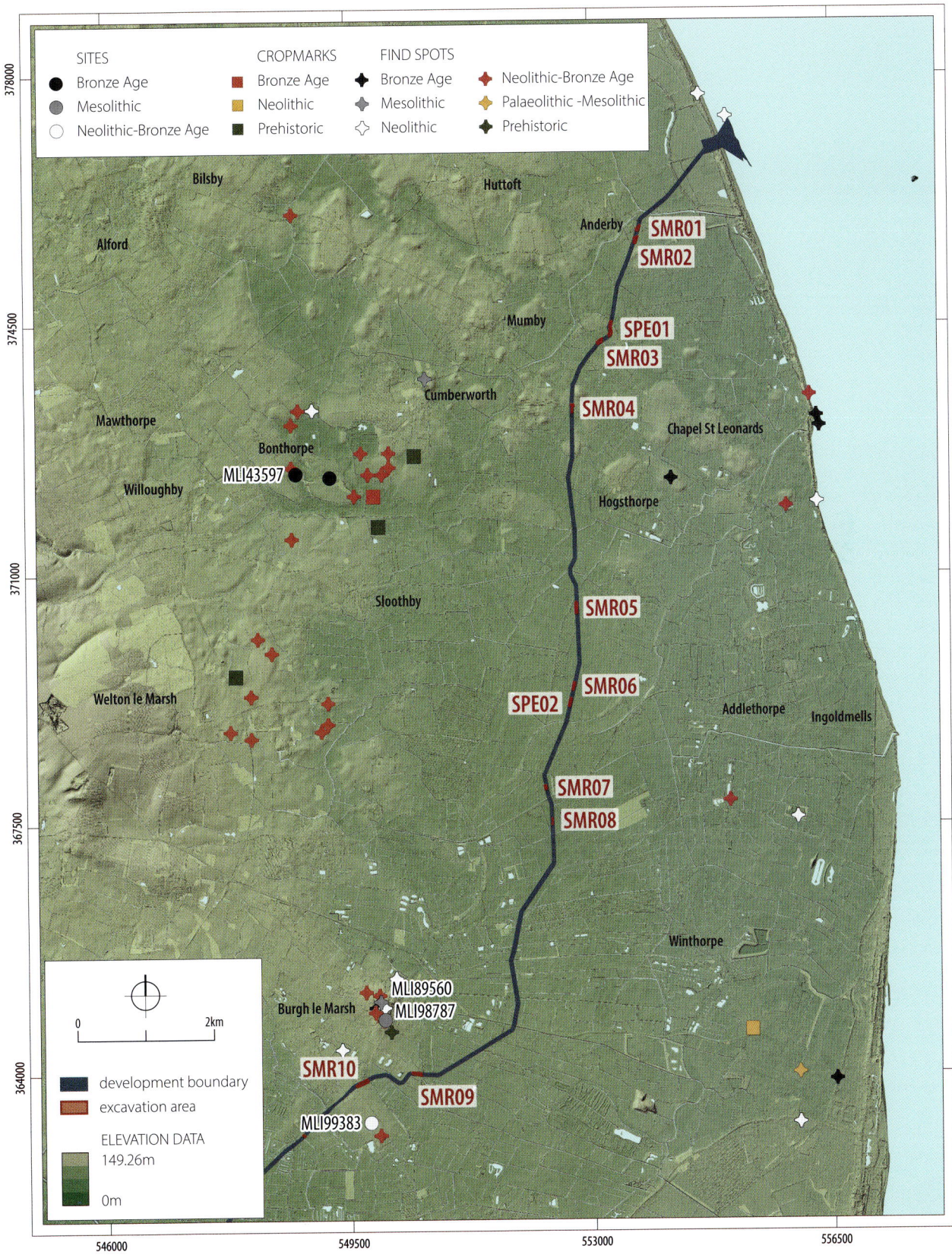

Figure 3.2 Prehistoric activity identified in the Historic Environment Record (HER) 1 km from the route of the Scheme from SMR01 to SMR10

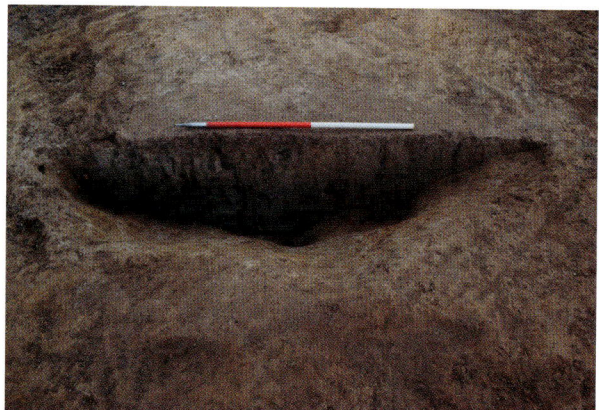

Figure 3.3 East-facing section of Pit 0037, SPE01

of the Mesolithic–earlier Neolithic flint from SPE01 and the later Neolithic–early Bronze Age flint from SMR09 is significant in terms of its demonstration of activity, albeit potentially minimal, along the Scheme.

Coastal communities

This limited evidence of earlier prehistoric activity is unsurprising given changing environmental conditions. As detailed in Chapter 2, marine transgression during the later Mesolithic–early Neolithic pushed the coastland westward with much of the Scheme route invaded by the sea. Coastal wetlands developed into the middle Bronze Age with the limited islands of high ground at the edge of the Wolds potentially providing limited areas above Mean High Water Spring Tide level. The progression of these changes, over 4000 years, would not have been uniform creating a dynamic landscape likely offering access to a variety of coastal and freshwater wetland resources potentially exploited seasonally with groups moving between the coastal lowlands and the chalk uplands of the Lincolnshire Wolds. The distribution of find spots combined with the excavated evidence points to sporadic activity with the flint scatters and isolated pits representing mobile communities. Landscape change during this period undoubtedly influenced the distribution of prehistoric activities but also their archaeological visibility. An impression of movement is reinforced by the distribution patterns of Mesolithic and Neolithic activity across the Wolds with flint scatters primarily identified along watercourses (Last and Willis 2023, 13). Neolithic long barrows and Bronze Age round barrows have been identified across the Wolds potentially providing a focus for activity (Field 2006; Drury and Allen 2020). The understanding of monuments as focal or anchor points for more mobile communities has been proposed in neighbouring regions such as Cambridgeshire (Brück 2019; 2000; Christie 2024). The pits uncovered at SPE01 and SMR09 provide only glimpses into the activities taking place in the Mesolithic and Neolithic. Their discovery on sites otherwise dominated by later activity points to the potential longevity of key locations, and the selective and specific use of areas of high ground across this landscape throughout the Holocene.

Bronze Age: Timber and tides

The Fenland witnessed continued environmental change with work conducted as part of the Fenland Surveys indicating that marine and freshwater deposits were laid down over wide areas with the sea beginning to withdraw post-1700 BC followed by renewed marine flooding c. 1400 BC (Hall and Coles 1994, 65; see Chapter 2; Fig. 2.7). Geoarchaeological work conducted along the Scheme suggested peat development beginning in the early Bronze Age along with the short-lived expansion of alder and willow (Rackham *et al.* 2021, 58; see Chapter 2). This was followed by the development of saltmarsh environments with a brackish landscape surrounding the Stickney Moraine (Rackham *et al.* 2021, 60). In the Bronze Age, cereal pollen and pastoral indicators were identified with peat again forming in the middle Bronze Age in an open landscape but with alder and willow present (*ibid.*). This landscape context provided rare evidence of Bronze Age activity with a preserved timber structure excavated to the north of the village of Northlands at HDD95 (Fig. 3.4).

The structure, located approximately 0.70–1.00 m below ground level, was composed of two sets of parallel timbers spaced 5 m apart supported by a series of vertical piles (Stockdale *et al.* 2024, Figs 3.5 and 3.6). On the exterior face of each line of timbers was a 0.35 m thick deposit, into which the posts were cut. This deposit was either natural or could represent the remains of a bank which was formed prior to construction. On the interior face were two deposits which appeared to have accumulated after the structure was no longer in use. Above this and the timbers was a 0.70 m thick layer of alluvial silt (*ibid.*).

The oak timbers can be described as good quality, being derived from straight grained, slow grown trunks with a diameter varying from *c.* 300–700 mm (Bamforth 2024a, 124; see below). The woodworking was restricted to simple splitting and trimming with an axe or adze with the relatively large and concave tool facets consistent with the use of a bronze axe (*ibid.*). Dendrochronological analysis of the timbers revealed that they date to the middle part of the 2nd millennium BC (Tyers 2024; Table 3.2).

The structure was located to the west of the Stickney Moraine, a spur of glacial till extending into the fen, which would have existed as a dry island even during higher levels of marine transgression (Lane 1993; Lane and Morris 2001; Fig. 3.4). Given these drier conditions, this part of the landscape appears to have formed a focus for agricultural activities from the middle Neolithic to middle Bronze Age as indicated by the palynological sequence

3 *Prehistoric landscapes*

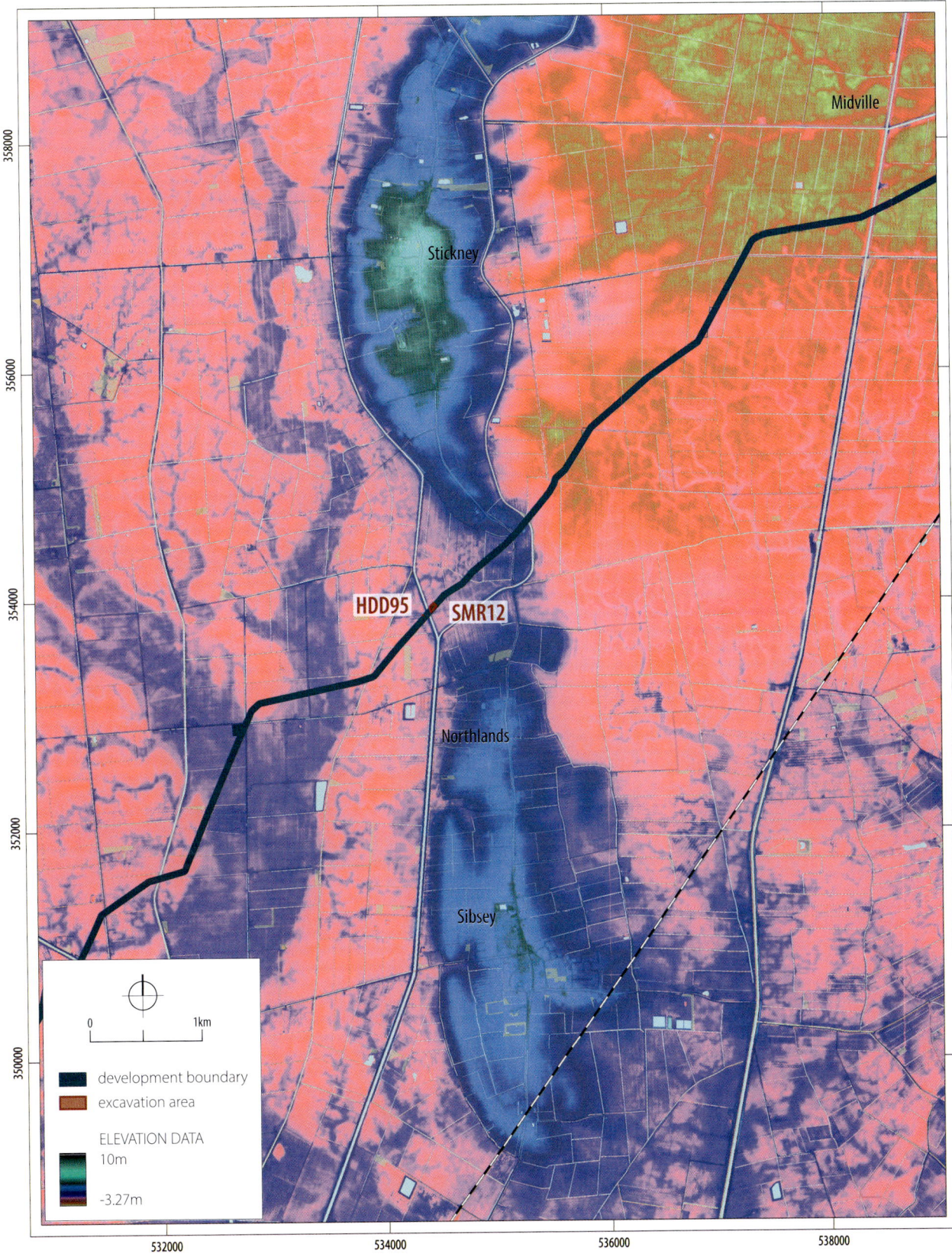

Figure 3.4 The topographic setting of HDD95 and TAM14 (LiDAR: Environment Agency reproduced under Open Government Licence v3.0; Environment Agency 2024)

Figure 3.5 Southwest facing photograph of the wooden structure in HDD95

Figure 3.6 The wooden structure in HDD95 during excavation

Table 3.2 Details of the seven dendrochronological samples taken from the timber structure at HDD95 All oak (Quercus spp).

Sample number	Cross-section (mm)	Rings	Sap	AGR	Result	Interpretation
2	180 × 120	199	–	0.86	1654–1456 BC	after 1446 BC 2
3	275 × 75	185	–	0.98	−30–154	not dated 5
5	135 × 90	157	–	0.87	9–165	not dated 5
6	130 × 90	59	–	1.23	105–163	not dated 5
7	135 × 55	149	–	0.88	1–149	not dated 5
8	135 × 85	102	–	1.15	−28–73	not dated 5
9	110 × 80	97	–	1.01	1658–1562 BC	after 1552 BC 2

KEY AGR growth rate mm/year, dimensions to nearest 5mm; sap column; –: no sapwood. 2: part of tree 2, 5: = part of tree 5 (after Tyers 2024)

(see Chapter 2). The placement of the structure along the western edge of this island potentially extends across the dryland/wetland divide linking or facilitating movement between the two. However, the form of the structure does not match the comparative examples of timber walkways or trackways. Bronze Age walkways or trackways, such as those identified in the Middle and Lower Thames Valley, are typically formed of pairs of vertical piles set *c.* 2 m apart (Brunning 2007; Stafford 2012, 136). The causeway uncovered at Must Farm, Cambridgeshire, was also formed of two parallel rows of piles set 1.2–1.6 m apart to support a raised wooden trackway (Knight *et al.* 2024, 58). No cross beams or horizontal timbers spanning the 5 m wide gap were uncovered at Northlands to indicate the presence of a raised platform or walkway. While not contemporary, the Iron Age timber causeway at Fiskerton, north of the River Witham, potentially provides an example of a low trackway. The timber causeway at Fiskerton, was formed of two rows of posts 2.4 m apart with no evidence of cross beams tying the opposing side together (Field and Pearson 2003, 8–9). This led to the favoured interpretation of the structure as a low trackway with layers of peat, brushwood, and silt excavated between the post rows overlain by a limestone rubble layer later in its development (*ibid.*, 10). At HDD95, no such deposits were identified. A layer of mid-grey silt was overlain by a 0.30 m thick mid-orange-brown silty clay that reached the height of the preserved stakes but did not extend beyond them. It is unclear if the interior deposits developed as mounded material or after the structure fell out of use.

The construction technique observed at HDD95 is closely comparable to Bronze Age timber revetments. A comparable revetment was excavated at Anslow's Cottages, Burghfield, Berkshire where two parallel rows of stakes with pieces of wood lying horizontally between, which were not worked or attached to the stakes, were set at the edge of a river channel (Butterworth and Lobb 1992, 89). Bronze Age revetments have also been recorded at Runnymede Bridge, Surrey (Needham 1991), Friar's Oak, West Sussex (Butler 2000), and Whitecross Farm, Cholsey, Oxfordshire (Cromarty *et al.* 2006, 23). At Whitecross Farm, Cholsey, excavations revealed a later Bronze Age waterfront site with timber structures including a possible revetment formed of a single row of vertical piles (*ibid.*). Timber revetments are typically formed of one structural feature making the parallel revetments uncovered at Northlands unusual. No finds were recovered at HDD95, but two fragments from a late Bronze Age socketed axe were recovered from TAM14, *c.* 1 km to the NNE, also on the Stickney Moraine (Fig. 3.1). The important relationship between metalwork deposition, ritual, and watery places is a theme of the Bronze Age. An alternative interpretation of the structure is that it may have facilitated this practice or marked an important space (see discussion below).

The wooden structure
Michael Bamforth

The analysis of the structure uncovered in HDD95 applied the system of categorisation and interrogation developed by Taylor (1998; 2001) and the condition scale developed by the Humber Wetlands Project (Van de Noort *et al.* 1999) has been adopted (Table 3.2). All the wood was identified as oak (*Quercus* sp.) based on characteristics visible with a ×10 hand lens. The identifications follow anatomical guides (Wheeler *et al.* 1989; Schoch *et al.* 2004) and modern reference material. The condition varied from poor to good. The boundary for meaningful technological analysis is set at 3/moderate with 78% of the wood records fulfilling or exceeding these criteria (Table 3.3).

The wood

The lifted material consists of cleft horizontal timbers, retained by seven vertical, driven piles – five on the 'inside' of the inner horizontal timber and two on the 'outside' of the outer horizontal timber. The piles were variously radially and tangentially cleft. Where the lower

Table 3.3 Condition scale used in this report (after Van de Noort et al. 1995, table 15.1)

Condition score		Museum conservation	Technology analysis	Woodland management	Dendrochronology	Identification to taxa
5	excellent	yes	yes	yes	yes	yes
4	good	no	yes	yes	yes	yes
3	moderate	no	yes/no	yes	yes	yes
2	poor	no	yes/no	yes/no	yes/no	yes
1	very poor	no	no	no	no	yes/no
0	non-viable	no	no	no	no	no

ends survived, they have been trimmed to a tapered point while the upper ends have degraded away where they pass through the preservation horizon for waterlogged wood (Fig. 3.7). Sub-samples of the piles were all submitted for dendrochronological analysis, which showed they probably derived from two trees: Tree 2 (SF2 and SF9) and Tree 5 (SF3, SF5, SF6, SF7, and SF8) (Tyers 2024).

The two timbers of Tree 2 (SF2 and SF9) are both approximately radial eighth splits, with SF2 describing a parent timber with an original diameter of at least 440 mm (Fig. 3.8). Whilst it is important to note that the Tree 5 timbers may be derived from different lengths of the same parent trunk, it is interesting to note that they can all fit into the cross section of a single parent timber, with plenty of timber left to spare (Fig. 3.7). SF6 describes a parent timber with a diameter of at least 700 mm – quite a substantial size. Three of the timbers are radially aligned (SF5, SF6, and SF7) whilst two are tangentially cleft (SF3 and SF8). The Tree 5 piles vary in length from 535–1230 mm. SF6 shows slight traces of possible water wear to one of the split faces.

The horizontal timbers (SF1 and SF4) are both relatively large (measuring 975 × 220 × 160 mm and 1960 × 290 × 145 mm respectively). They are both in poor condition and the ends have either degraded or been sawn during excavation. SF1 is a radial quarter split whilst SF4 is tangentially cleft. Both show traces of wet rot on the upper/outer face (Eaton and Hale 1993) and have either side branches or burrs present.

Discussion

The Tree 2 sequence provided a dendrochronological cross match with a terminal growth ring dating to 1456 BC (Tyers 2024; Table 3.2). Given the lack of sapwood and the narrow terminal growth rings, it is likely that the timber was felled around 1400 BC, placing the structure firmly in the middle Bronze Age (*ibid.*). The timbers have been identified as oak and are derived from large diameter tree trunks (varying from *c.* 300–700 mm in diameter) which are straight grained, almost entirely devoid of side branches and knots, and slow grown (average growth ring

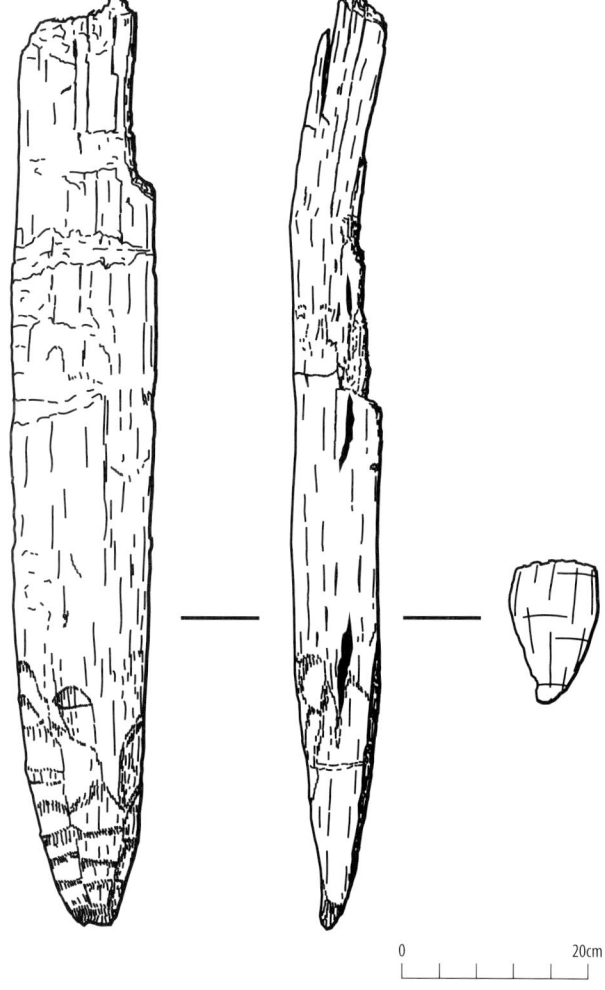

Figure 3.7 HDD95: driven oak pile SF5, Tree 5

estimates vary from 1–2 mm), describing good quality timber. These traits are indicative of 'wildwood' grown trees, a resource that becomes scarcer over the course of later prehistory. The best quality material, perhaps derived from the larger diameter butts of trees, was used for the piles, which required the most working in terms of splitting to size and trimming to points in preparation timbers and uprights of a similar size but they do tend to be much busier with no void between the two sides (Pryor 2001; Pryor and Bamforth 2010; Gearey *et al.* 2011; *et al.* 2016). As highlighted, the plan form of the timbers led to the suggestion by the excavation team that the two sides of the structure were perhaps used to revet a channel or to support a bund or bank. Further examples have been recorded at Friar's Oak, West Sussex (Butler 2000) and two phases of a more substantial late Bronze Age piled revetment or palisade were recorded at Runnymede Bridge, a settlement on the banks of the Thames, with around 150 driven piles and associated horizontal wood encountered (Needham 1991). The late Bronze Age occupation site at Whitecross Farm, had a possible revetment or palisade running along at least part of the edge of the gravel eyot it occupied in the Thames floodplain, formed of a series of posts 140–300 mm in diameter (Cromarty *et al.* 2006).

Taylor (2010) suggests a link between Big Trees and monumental structures in the Neolithic and Bronze Age, pointing out the relative difficulty of felling large trees and cleaving them down into useable sized timbers against the practice of felling trees, the trunks of which are already of suitable size. Bronze Age monumental wooden structures from the region that utilise large, oak timbers split down from Big Trees include the middle Bronze Age post alignment/causeway and platform at Flag Fen (Pryor 2001), and the early Bronze Age funerary monument excavated in the intertidal zone at Holme Next the Sea (Brennand and Taylor 2003). The Big Trees/monumental, smaller trees/domestic theory has recently been lent further weight by the complete lack of Big Trees used in the construction of the later Bronze Age stilted settlement at Must Farm, Cambridgeshire (Robinson *et al.* 2024).

In conclusion, the timbers are most certainly of a suitable size and form to have acted as a revetment for a channel, bund, or bank and there are archaeological parallels for similar structures from the Bronze Age. However, given the short stretch of structure excavated and the lack of clarity around the context of the structure, alongside the use of timbers split down from relatively large trees, it cannot be ruled out that the timbers formed part of an unknown structure, perhaps with a ritual function or significance.

Bronze Age finds
Rebecca Sillwood

A late Bronze Age socketed axe and a possible late Bronze Age awl are the only two small finds from the Scheme to have come from the early prehistoric period. The copper alloy finds were both recovered from sites within the Fen Edge Landscape Parcel, from TAM14 and SMR10 respectively. The socketed axe recovered from TAM14 located *c.* 1 km to the NNE of the timber structure

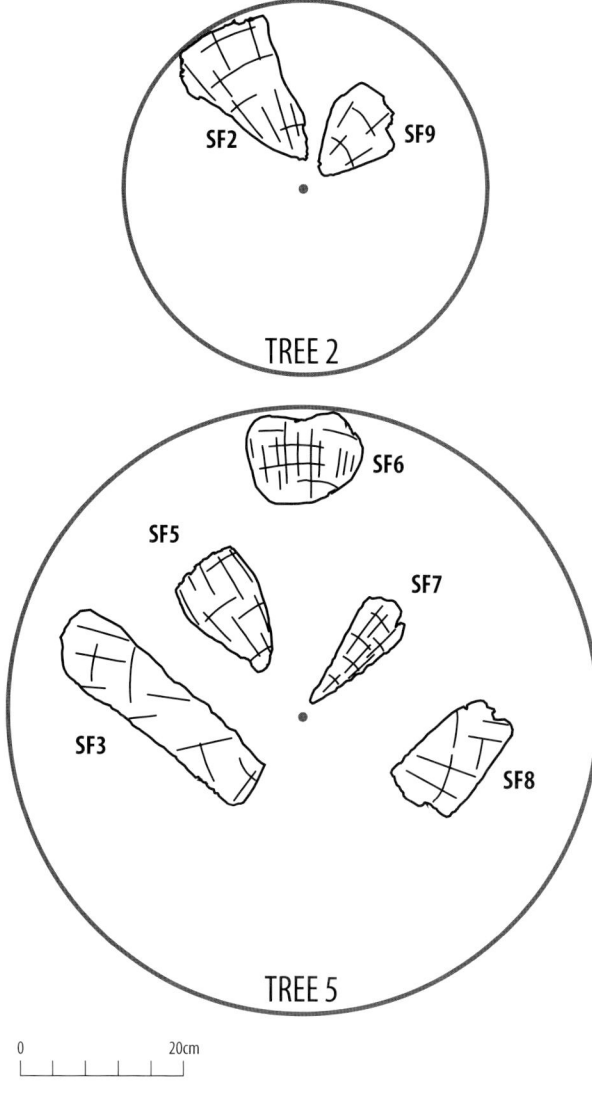

Figure 3.8 HDD95: cross sections of driven piles arranged by position in parent timber and dendrochronological grouping

for driving. Slightly poorer quality material was used for the horizontal timbers, each of which had a side branch or burr present, suggesting they were derived from slightly poorer quality material, perhaps taken from slightly higher up the trunks. Oak grows on a variety of soil types and conditions in stands and mixed deciduous woodland and is likely to have been growing in the vicinity of the site (Gale and Cutler 2000). Oak is an easily worked and hard-wearing timber that is frequently used in prehistoric structures and is relatively durable in wet environments (Wilson and White 1986; Gale and Cutler 2000).

Given that the two sides of the structure are some 5 m apart, as discussed it seems unlikely that they form part of a trackway, causeway, post alignment, or bridge. Further comparable examples at Yarnton, Oxfordshire (Hey *et al.* 2016) and Vauxhall, London have been interpreted as causeways, jetties, or platforms (Sidell *et al.* 2002). Substantial ground-level trackways can incorporate

Figure 3.9 The late Bronze Age socketed axe from TAM14

(Fig. 3.9). It is in two pieces, incomplete, and unfortunately unstratified. This axe was identified as being part of the Wilburton/Ewart Park phase of Bronze Age metalwork and dates to between *c.* 1100 BC and 700 BC. Bronze Age metalwork, such as the axe, is frequently found as stray finds or as part of hoards in Lincolnshire, more rarely they are found in burials (Davey 1973, 53).

The possible Bronze Age awl was found within an early medieval phased feature but can be compared to a late Bronze Age awl found at Billingborough (Bacon and Fitzpatrick 2001, 22, fig. 13, no. 2). If this is an awl, it is an unusual object to find in copper alloy, though not unheard of; awls are more usually found in iron and sometimes, bone. Copper alloy is a metal normally reserved for attractive and personal finds, such as brooches and buckles, but here it may have been utilised as a craft tool. Copper alloy awls of Bronze Age date make up 76% of those recorded on the Portable Antiquities Scheme (PAS) database (https://finds.org.uk/database/search/) with undated and other time periods only forming low percentages. These percentages are mainly a reflection of the unstratified nature of the finds recorded on the PAS database, but it does also raise the possibility that the Triton Knoll awl may be of earlier date than Anglo-Saxon, though possibly being re-used or curated during this period. If an awl, this object points to late Bronze Age craftworking evidence, specifically leatherworking but with the possibility of other crafts and it appears to be residual in a later context.

Late Bronze Age–Iron Age beginnings

Features indicating late Bronze Age–Iron Age activity were uncovered at the northern extent of the Scheme within SPE01 (Gaunt and Roberts 2024; Fig. 3.10). The early Iron Age structures were defined by ring-ditches each enclosing a space *c.* 5 m in diameter (E1.02 and E1.03). Three intercutting post-holes were recorded along the inner edge at the northeastern terminus of ring-ditch E1.03 and could relate to a possible entrance (*ibid.*). It is possible that both ring-ditches represent the remains of ephemeral structures akin to windbreaks. The two ring-ditches were separated by a narrow gully (E1.04) with a large Pit 0088 immediately to the west (Fig. 3.10). Fragments of briquetage, typically associated with salt-working, were recovered from the structures (Lane and Morris 2001; see Chapter 5). Among the briquetage was a pedestal fragment with moderate bleaching. Further evidence of salt production was found within Pit 0088 with hearth and container briquetage recovered from the fill (Lane 2024a). The pit contained evidence of a clay and sand lining suggesting this may have been used as a salt settling or storage pit similar to those found elsewhere on the Scheme.

The form of the pit is analogous to other examples of Iron Age sites, including at Hinkley Point, Somerset (Mudd *et al.* 2024, 332). The ceramic assemblage from the features was broadly dated to the late Bronze Age–early Iron Age with parallels also found in early–middle Iron Age assemblages (see pottery discussion below). Activity continued into the middle Iron Age with a further ring-ditch E1.05, pits, and ditches uncovered from which briquetage and sherds of middle to late Iron Age pottery were recovered. The briquetage from SPE01 fits within the latter stages of Morris' Briquetage Phase 1, with the key identifier being the presence of the pedestal form PD4 (*e.g.* Morris 2007, fig. 3, no. 16). Such pedestals rise from a wide rectangular base narrowing towards the top and are thought to be used within an open hearth. Fragments of 'gutter-shaped troughs' were also recovered with only a limited number displaying the characteristic shelly fabric common at other fenland sites (Lane 2024a). The difference may reflect the local clay supply with the overall assemblage dated from the middle–late Bronze Age to the middle Iron Age.

The features at SPE01 represent a comparatively rare, excavated example of a late Bronze Age–middle Iron Age salt production site on the Lindsey Marshes. The majority of excavated examples of early salt production are situated to the south at sites with Langtoft, Welland Bank, Pode Hole, Fengate, and Northy on the inner edge of the fenland (Lane 2017, 158). On the fen edge, comparable evidence of middle–late Bronze Age salt production was uncovered at Billingborough where pottery and briquetage were recovered from an enclosure, a pit and several post-holes. Activity at SPE01 continued into the Iron Age with further enclosures, hearths and possible structures identified (Chowne *et al.* 2001, 7–13, 15). In contrast, few early salt production sites have been excavated on the Lindsey Marshes despite the abundance of evidence

3 Prehistoric landscapes

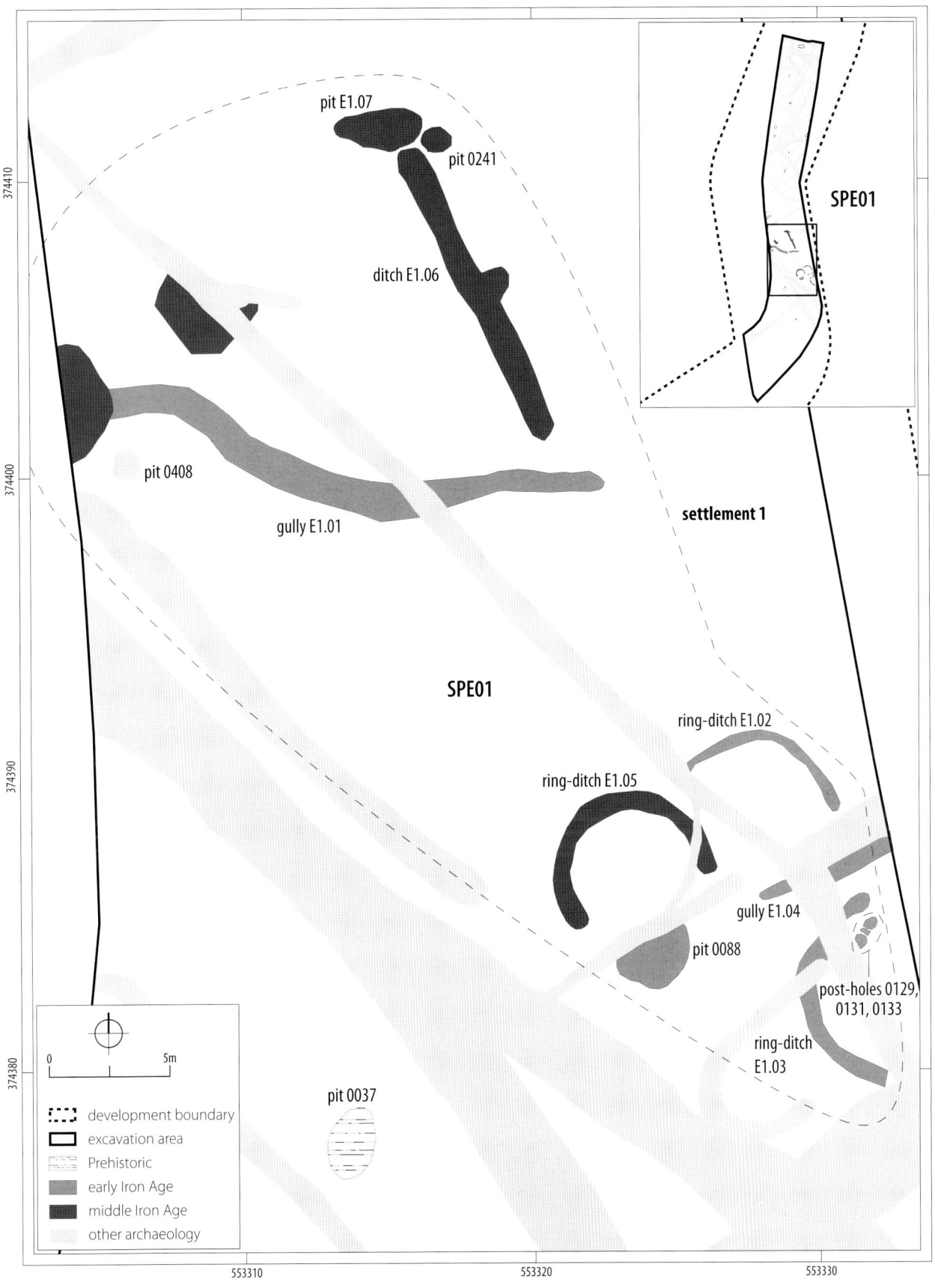

Figure 3.10 Iron Age features at SPE01

for later Iron Age–Roman salt production (see Chapter 5). To the north of SPE01, excavations at Newton Marsh near Tetney revealed deposits of fired clay and briquetage adjacent to a large pool within which further briquetage deposits were identified (Palmer-Brown 1994, 2). The features encountered include a small fire pit or hearth which was radiocarbon dated to the late Bronze Age–early Iron Age (2460±70 BP; *ibid.*, 4). The landscape of the Lindsey Marshes witnessed significant environmental change with sites potentially buried under later land surfaces (Lane 2017, 16; see Chapter 2).

The excavations at SPE01 provide the earliest evidence of salt production identified across the Scheme, likely representing small-scale local industry. The extent to which the activity was taking place seasonally is unclear but salt production was likely occurring alongside a suite of activities including agricultural activities, such as grazing, in the wider region. The incorporation of this activity into wider settlement patterns may contribute to the difficulties in identifying earlier sites. At SPE01 the difficulties are heightened by the extent of later activity with the development of a Roman field system, medieval ditches, and post-medieval boundaries. To the south of SPE01, Iron Age sites have been identified at Addlethorpe (Cope-Faulkner 2006) and during the Fenland Survey (Hayes and Lane 1993) representing the beginnings of more widespread salt production activities typically identified through large spreads of briquetage and associated features (see Chapter 5).

Limited further evidence of Iron Age activity was encountered across the Scheme with the traces primarily comprising Iron Age sherds recovered from later features. A small number of middle Iron Age features were identified at SPE03 in the Fen Edge Landscape Parcel, comprising a curvilinear ditch and ditches. The curvilinear ditch enclosed an area of *c.* 250 m² with a single hazelnut shell recovered from the ditch radiocarbon dated to 380–170 cal BC (95% probability; 2210±30 BP, Beta–667275). Iron Age pottery was found scattered across the site, largely recovered from later features (see below). A similar pattern was observed at SMR01 in the Inland Fen Edge Landscape Parcel, where Iron Age pottery was recovered from later features.

Iron Age pottery
Ian M. Rowlandson and Hugh G. Fiske

A limited range of Iron Age pottery was recorded during the project. The most significant group was recorded from the SPE01 in the Coastal Landscape Parcel where pottery stylistically dated to the middle Iron Age was recorded. A few assemblages contained vessels with a late La Tène III influence (see Knight 2002) but many of these vessels were of transitional types known to be made in the peri- to post-Roman conquest period and continuing in circulation into the early years of the 2nd century AD.

The saltmakers assemblage

The majority of the pottery from SPE01, Coastal Landscape Parcel, was from handmade vessels gritted with quartz and rocks probably derived from the local Boulder Clay deposits (ETW* fabrics; Fig. 3.11). A small quantity of shell-gritted pottery was also present probably produced to the west of the Lincolnshire Wolds, including a single sherd of the fine, shell-gritted IASH2 fabric from Pit 0246 that was probably of mid–late Iron Age date.

This assemblage had form parallels with a group considered to be of late Bronze Age date at Tetney (Knight 1994) but also to the early phases of pottery from the Iron Age settlement at Weelsby Avenue, Grimsby (Elsdon 1996). The pottery of this sort, mostly consisting of

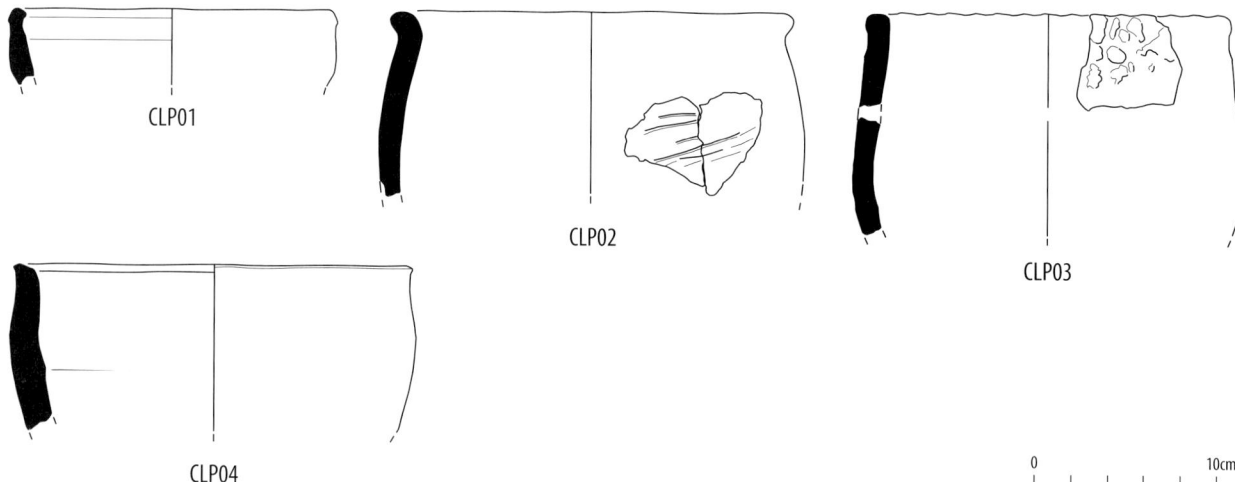

Figure 3.11 Examples of Iron Age pottery from SPE01: CLP01. handmade jar with in-turned rim; CLP02. handmade jar with Scored Ware surface treatment; CLP03. handmade jar; CLP04. handmade jar

'Barrel Jars' with in-turned rims (Challis and Harding 1975), is difficult to date closely as this is a long-lived form which continued to be produced into the later Iron Age and beyond into the Roman period in some places. What is notable is that the fabric of and firing of all the rock-gritted wares appear fairly similar and a few sherds show signs of Scored Ware surface treatment. Scored Ware has been considered to date to the mid- to late Iron Age (see Knight 2002; 2010 for discussion) if this is the case then it is possible that, in the absence of quantities of late La Tène II/III wares, much of the pottery from this site should be placed in the Middle Iron Age.

The carbonised residues and Organic Residue Analysis (ORA) evidence suggests that the inhabitants of the site were not exclusively engaged in saltmaking and the Iron Age vessels in use were probably used for a range of cooking and rendering functions in a similar way to some of those recorded from other sites, such as at Immingham (Rowlandson and Fiske 2016, 2019c; Dunne and Evershed 2018a). It is difficult to assert that the activity that the pottery was used for on this site, located in the vicinity of saltmaking, was substantially different from domestic sites located further inland.

In addition to the assemblage from SPE01, two handmade, shell-gritted IASH1 sherds were recovered from SMR05 (Lincolnshire Marsh Landscape Parcel). The sherds broadly date from the late Iron Age–early 2nd century AD. Little more can be said about this small assemblage but it may hint at earlier activity at SMR05.

The later Iron Age assemblages
The assemblage from the Fen Edge and Inland Fen Edge Landscape Parcels included transitional wares. Although a range of transitional wares with late La Tène III traits (Knight 2002) were recorded from some of the Fen Edge Landscape Parcel sites, including a storage jar with combed decoration, none of the more distinctively Iron Age handmade, shell-gritted types were noted. All the Iron Age tradition material was associated with groups of early Roman wheelmade wares. The sites encountered along the route of this part of the Scheme appear to represent activity that began after the Roman conquest. A few handmade, Iron Age type shell-gritted sherds (IASH1 and IASH2) were recorded from the Inland Landscape Parcel sites SMR01 (Structure Complex 16) and TAM04 (Deposit 4.33) including a necked storage jar. All this material appears to be in a late La Tène III style and may represent material brought to the sites in the peri- or post-conquest periods rather than suggesting definite pre-conquest activity on these sites.

Conclusions
The Scheme encountered only limited activity for Iron Age activity. At the northeastern end, the inhabitants of the SPE01 site utilised the local Boulder Clay deposits to produce the majority of their pottery, similar to sites known from Tetney and the Immingham area in northeastern Lincolnshire, augmented with a few fossil shell gritted vessels that were probably produced to the west of the Lincolnshire Wolds (Rowlandson and Fiske 2023b). The small number of sherds with Scored Ware surface treatment including an example in a local rock-gritted fabric (ETW2, CLP2) suggests that the local potters and consumers at the Anderby site used pot styles more commonly seen in southern Lincolnshire and other parts of the eastern Midlands. The rest of the Scheme did not encounter significant groups of Iron Age pottery and this may be in part due to the route of the Scheme largely passing through areas of modern day Lincolnshire that would have been extremely low-lying during much of the Iron Age (May 1996, fig. 24.6).

Traces and transitions
The Iron Age across the Scheme is marked by the continued scarcity of evidence, excluding salt production, mirroring the situation for much of the region. Evidence of Iron Age settlement is largely located inland from the Scheme with a concentration of activity identified surrounding Sleaford *c*. 13 km west of the Triton Knoll route. A possible substantial enclosure was excavated at Mount Lane (MLI82561), a further enclosure was identified at East Road (MLI60812), an Iron Age settlement was excavated at Bone's Farm, Kirkby la Thorpe (MLI89706), and late Iron Age activity was identified at Half Mile Lane (MLI82557). Excavations for the Hatton to Silk Willoughby Gas Pipeline revealed ring-ditch defined structures, enclosures, and boundaries at Kirkby la Thorpe and Ewerby with activity occurring from the early–late Iron Age (Network Archaeology 1999). Further to the northeast the Viking Link Interconnector mitigation excavations between Haugh and Bicker Fen identified limited Iron Age activity at ten sites (Wessex Archaeology 2023, table 3). Curvilinear ditches, representing a possible roundhouse, and ditches were uncovered at Area 41, Stickford *c*. 6 km north of Triton Knoll. An assemblage of Iron Age and prehistoric pottery was recovered from the features (*ibid.*, 78). Iron Age settlement has been identified and excavated to the north and west of the Scheme with limited evidence, particularly at SPE03, potentially marking the fen edge limit of Iron Age activity. This likely reflects the landscape location of the Scheme with areas only becoming suitable for settlement in later periods. All Landscape Parcels witnessed a significant expansion of activity in the Roman period (settlement and saltmaking) with no evidence of continuity. At SPE03 and SPE01 no relationship was observed between the Iron Age and Roman features with the Roman activity marking a new phase of use.

4

Living near the edge:
Settlement and agriculture in the Roman period

Maria Stockdale and Owain Scholma-Mason

*With contributions from Laura Bailey, Marina Chorro-Giner,
Hugh G. Fiske, Val Fryer, Kevin Hayward, Gwladys Monteil,
Ian M. Rowlandson, Hannah Russ, Kate Turner, Rebecca Sillwood,
Ruth Shaffrey, Zoe Tomlinson, and Michael Wallace*

Towards the end of the Iron Age, the landscape along the route of the Scheme underwent significant change, with a third episode of marine regression (Fig. 2.8). In the wake of this, a broad swathe of land was available for settlement and agricultural exploitation. As evidenced through wide-ranging surveys across the region, this area formed a focus for salt production, potentially reflecting a point of continuity with the preceding Iron Age (see Chapter 5). Alongside this, there is evidence for widespread agriculture in the form of enclosures and field systems, often aligned along the course of roddons (Taylor 2007, 65). Evidence for settlement, in contrast, is more constrained, with a limited number of farmsteads or settlements known, although this may in part reflect low levels of excavation within the low-lying Lincolnshire Coast and Marshes, rather than a genuine absence (Hall and Coles 1994; Tuck 2023, 333). The most recent review of settlement patterns within this area, undertaken as part of the *Roman Rural Settlement Project* (RRSP), showed that the majority of settlement evidence was seemingly restricted to the Lincolnshire Wolds just to the west, with further major settlements including Lincoln located beyond this (Allen 2016; see Chapter 6).

Consequently, given the lacuna in our understanding of settlement to the east of the Wolds, the data from the Scheme provide a unique opportunity to explore the nature of land use within this dynamic region. A total of 11 Roman sites were recorded, whilse further evidence for Roman activity was noted in several horizontal directional drilling (HDD) pits and Joint Bay sites, for the most part comprising possible agricultural remains and saltern deposits (Fig. 4.1; Table 4.2). Possible Roman activity was also noted at SMR09 and SMR10, comprising a single pit and possible deposit but, due to the ephemeral and uncertain nature of these, they have not been included alongside the principal sites. The overall distribution of these sites is in part reflective of environmental conditions during the period, with the sites clustering into two groups, the first located to the north of Burgh le Marsh and Skegness, occupying the area of the Lindsey Marshes. The second, extending from Boston to Bicker, occupies the area of the Fens and, unlike the northernmost group, contains a series of large complex farmsteads which are further outlined in this chapter. In between these groups there was limited evidence for Roman activity with few such sites being noted in the HER. This apparent dearth of settlement may in part be attributed to environmental conditions prevalent across this area in the Roman period, with the Fenland Surveys indicating that this area was peaty and seasonally inundated (Lane 1993; see also Green 2023a; 2023b for a wider discussion of the region).

The 11 recorded sites have been grouped into four broad categories: farmsteads, salt production, funerary, and agriculture (Table 4.1). Agriculture sites encompass those with evidence of agricultural activity in the form of ditches or enclosures relating to arable and/or pastoral farming but lacking strong evidence for a domestic component. These sites in turn form part of wider agricultural landscapes associated with farmsteads or larger settlement sites (Taylor 2007; Allen and Smith 2016). Salt production sites can be interpreted in a similar vein, reflecting areas associated with saltworking located within the larger agricultural landscape, potentially being utilised on a seasonal basis. A more detailed review of the characteristics and nature of salt production at these sites is set out in Chapter 5. A single funerary site was also noted, comprising a group of three burials at the southern end of SPE02, preceding the later use of the site for saltworking (Scholma-Mason 2024; see Chapter 5). The final category, farmsteads, incorporates a range of sites, often with evidence for enclosures and ditches, but with stronger indications of domestic occupation.

The overall morphology and function of the farmsteads and agricultural sites is further examined in the opening section of this chapter. Following this, a summary of the environmental and artefactual evidence is outlined. A detailed discussion of the key themes emerging from this chapter is reserved for Chapter 6, which follows the review of the evidence for Roman salt production in Chapter 5.

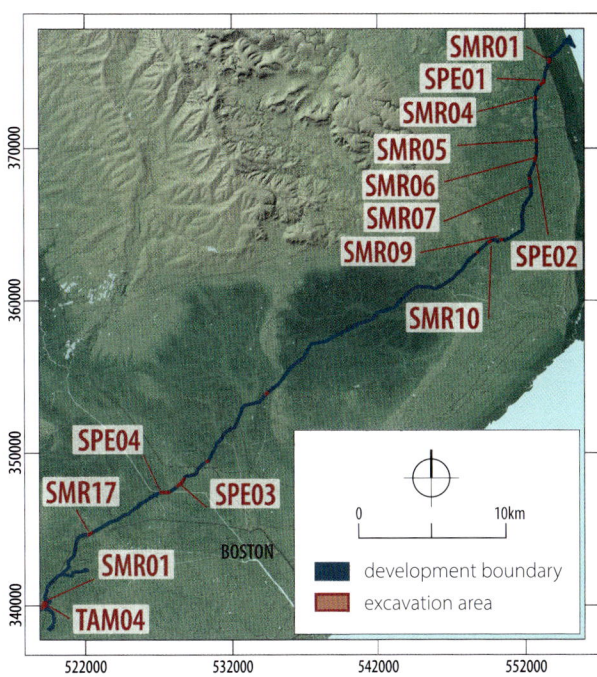

Figure 4.1 Roman sites excavated along the route of the Scheme

A Roman agricultural landscape

The sites located within the Fen Edge and Inland Fen Edge Landscape Parcels in the southern portion of the Scheme represent the remains of complex and well-defined Roman farmsteads. In the case of the Inland Fen Edge, the excavated sites at SMR01 and TAM04 reflect elements of a single farmstead and are treated as one site in the following review. Chronologically,

Table 4.1 Principal Roman sites recorded across the Scheme

| | | Early to mid-Roman | | Later Roman | Roman (not closely datable) |
| | | Early Roman | Mid-Roman | | |
		c. AD 43–100	c. AD 100–250	c. AD 250–410	c. AD 43–410
Coastal	SPE01		Agriculture		
	SMR01			Agriculture	
	SMR04		Agriculture		
Lincolnshire Marsh	SMR07		Salt production		
	SPE02		Funerary activity	Salt production	
	SMR06		Salt production		
	SMR05				Salt production
Fen Edge	SMR09				
	SMR10				
	SPE03		Farmstead		
	SPE04	Agriculture	Farmstead		
	SMR17		Agriculture		
Inland Fen Edge	SMR01		Farmstead		
	TAM04		Farmstead		

Table 4.2 Iron Age and Roman evidence excavated at other locations along the Scheme

Site	Location	Iron Age	Roman	Undated	Archaeology	Site type
TAM07	TF52697221				Finds of Roman pottery	Find spot
TAM19	TF21034306				Roman pit & ditch	Agricultural
HDD10	TF5313974222				Undated saltern deposits	Salt production
HHD14	TF5276973352				Roman ditch	Agricultural
HDD24	TF5280769862				Iron Age–Roman saltern deposit	Salt production
HDD26	TF52623868964				?Middle Iron Age saltern?	Salt production
HDD27	TF5232468234				Undated saltern deposits	Salt production
HDD35	TF5181765601				Iron Age–Roman saltern deposit	Salt production
HDD55	TF4762861897				Iron Age–Roman pit	Agricultural
JB05	TF5275469455				Saltern deposit	Salt production
JB06	TF5235867906				Material from alluvial deposit	Find spot

the sites spanned the early to late Roman period with many displaying multiple phases of development (Table 4.1). Evidence of early Roman (AD 43–100) activity was also found at SPE01, SPE04, SPE03, and SMR01/TAM04 (Table 4.1). The evidence from SPE01 comprised a probable Roman field system with a preceding phase of late Bronze Age–middle Iron Age saltworking (Gaunt and Roberts 2024; see Chapter 3). Similarly, at the southern end of the Scheme at SPE04, a series of scattered ditches, probably relating to early Roman agricultural activity, were identified. At SPE03, within the same landscape parcel, further evidence for early Roman activity was identified, comprising a series of enclosures, ditches, and a possible structure defining a farmstead (Stockdale *et al.* 2024). During the latter half of the early Roman period a post-built structure encircled by a ditch was constructed at TAM04 but appears to have been levelled in the middle Roman period, when a larger farmstead was established.

There is a notable expansion in the number of sites in the middle Roman period (AD 100–250). These include three salt production sites within the Lincolnshire Marsh Landscape Parcel as well as the development of the farmsteads at SPE03 and SPE04 in the Fen Edge Landscape Parcel. The earlier ditches at SPE04 were replaced during this period by a series of enclosures relating to a larger farmstead (Stockdale *et al.* 2024). A farmstead was established at SMR01/TAM04 in the middle Roman period, formed of a series of adjoining enclosures, superseding the early Roman post-built structure identified at TAM04. Six of the recorded sites persisted into the later Roman period (AD 250–410), including the settlement at SPE04.

Farming from Anderby Creek to Hogsthorpe

The landscape extending from Anderby Creek to Hogsthorpe on Lincolnshire's east coast is characterised by a scatter of irregular, higher plateaus surrounded by lower-lying silt lands. The excavated sites are located on these high plateaus with potential evidence for the use of locations formally utilised in the Iron Age for salt production, including SPE01 (see Chapter 3). At the northern extent of the Scheme, evidence of Roman activity was scarce, except for a small late Roman enclosure identified at SMR01 (TF 53726 75826) located in Anderby flanking the southwest side of the Sea Road (Figs 4.1 and 4.2). The relatively low quantities of finds from the fills of the enclosure ditch suggest that it was associated with agricultural activities rather than domestic occupation. The limited features uncovered at SMR01 contrast with the stratigraphically complex site excavated at SPE01, 1.32 km to the south.

4 Living near the edge: Settlement and agriculture in the Roman period

Table 4.3 Radiocarbon dates from Roman sites

Landscape Parcel	Site	Group/feature	Context	Sample	Material dated	Lab. code	δ13C	Radiocarbon age BP	Radiocarbon date (95.4% probability)
Lincolnshire Marsh	SPE02	Oven 2.19	0161	33	Charred culm nodes	Beta-667274	-26.8	1760±30	cal AD 230–390
Lincolnshire Marsh	SPE02	Oven 2.18	0303	40	Charred culm nodes	Beta-667276	-24.3	1740±30	cal AD 240–410
Lincolnshire Marsh	SPE02	Oven 2.18	0306	44	Charred culm nodes	Beta-667277	-24.1	1780±30	cal AD 210–370
Lincolnshire Marsh	SPE02	Inhumation burial 2.29	0009	3	Tibia: human	SUERC-87856	-19.9	1814±30	cal AD 130–340
Lincolnshire Marsh	SPE02	Inhumation burial 2.30	0056	–	Rib: human	SUERC-87855	-20.7	1910±30	cal AD 20–220
Fen Edge	SPE03	Curvilinear ditch 3.01	30016	39	Hazelnut shell	Beta - 667275		2210±30	380–170 cal BC
Fen Edge	SPE04	Structure 4.4	45057	–	Animal bone	Beta - 667278		1920±30	cal AD 20–210
Fen Edge	SPE04	–	42047	–	Animal bone	Beta - 667279		130±30	cal AD 1770–1950
Lincolnshire Marsh	SPE02	Inhumation burial 2.28	0006	2	Tooth/skull human	GU 51893	–	Failed due to insufficient carbon	

Between Anderby, Hogsthorpe, and Mumby, the cable route crossed the Roman site at SPE01, situated *c.* 130 m southeast of Manor Farm (TF 53315 74417; Fig. 4.1). The site is positioned on a crescent-shaped plateau (*c.* 2.6–2.9 m AOD) within a landscape scattered with amorphous islands and meandering former creeks (see Chapter 2; Fig. 4.3). The site had previously been host to a late Bronze Age–middle Iron Age salt production site,

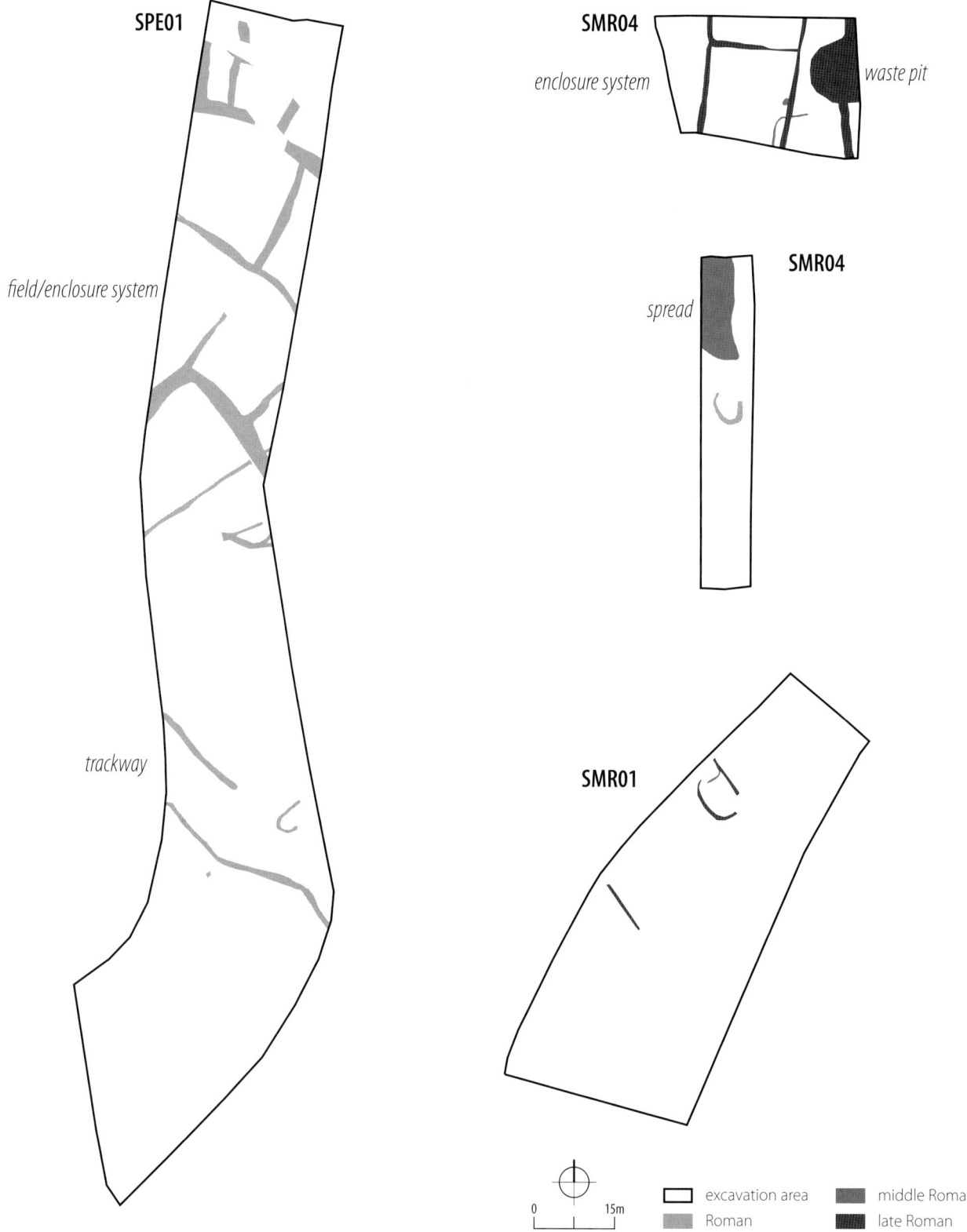

Figure 4.2 Comparative site plans of Roman features at SMR01, SPE01, and SMR04

elements of which were truncated by the various Roman ditches (see Chapter 3).

The ditches at SPE01 defined multiple phases of a field or enclosure system with the limited ceramic assemblage supporting only a broad Roman date (Rowlandson and Fiske 2024a). The fields extended across the northern half of the site, continuing off the raised plateau. The environmental and limited artefactual assemblages suggest a primarily agricultural function with small quantities of cereal grains and animal bone recovered. Among the animal bone were multiple fragments of cattle and sheep/goat, although these comprised high value meat bearing elements and could have been brought to the site. In contrast, there was evidence for the butchery of pigs on site (Chorro-Giner 2024a; see discussion on the role of animals). It is possible that the enclosures at SPE01 were associated with the seasonal movement of livestock, which may have been moved across this landscape to access wetland meadows, marshes, and fields post-harvest. Movement across this landscape is suggested by the presence of two parallel northwest to southeast oriented ditches along the southern extent of the site likely representing a track- or droveway (Fig. 4.2). The trackway appears to follow the southern edge of the crescent-shaped plateau and may have continued further northwest along the plateau terminating at the lower-lying land (Fig. 4.3). Following the plateau towards the southeast the trackway may have linked neighbouring agricultural land and settlements.

Further agricultural activity dating to the late Roman period was identified at SMR04, 0.5 km northwest of Hogthorpe and south of Langham Road (TF 52684 69195; Fig. 4.1). The presence of a spread of dumped material containing middle Roman pottery attests to some activity prior to the late Roman period, although the precise character of this is uncertain (Gaunt and Roberts 2024). To the south of this spread was a curvilinear ditch; to the north was a shallow ditch and pit, both of which were truncated by the late Roman, rectilinear enclosure system (Fig. 4.2). From the fills of the enclosure ditches sherds of 3rd–4th century AD pottery, fragments of vessel glass, ceramic building material (CBM), animal bone, and marine shells were recovered. A large waste pit, measuring *c.* 12 m across and 0.60 m deep, was cut through one of the enclosure ditches and contained backfill material of pottery, Roman brick/tile, and animal bone (Fig. 4.2). The greater range of finds recovered from SMR04, when compared to SMR01 and SPE01, suggests that the enclosures at SMR04 may have lain in proximity to a settlement. The activity at SMR04 is located on a high point in the surrounding landscape, a pattern mirrored in the scarce distribution of surrounding sites such as Mumby and Hogsthorpe. A recent geophysical survey conducted at Sea Lane, Hogsthorpe (Allen Archaeology 2022b), *c.* 2.2 km southeast from SMR04, revealed an amorphous network of possible enclosure ditches, preliminary interpreted as prehistoric in date but plausibly later (Fig. 4.4). To the east of

SPE01 possible settlement remains were identified at land off Hogsthorpe Road (MLI82496), whilst to the south-west further settlement remains are indicated by a panoply of cropmarks (MLI90836). Elsewhere in the landscape, the Roman presence is meagrely represented by find spots and artefact scatters (Simmons 2022; Lane 2024b).

The sites located from Hogsthorpe to the north of Burgh le Marsh are primarily focused on salt production with some evidence of earlier activity (see Chapter 5). This includes the only funerary remains uncovered across the Scheme at SPE02, on land adjacent to South Ings Lane. A sequence of three inhumation burials was uncovered with further funerary activity in the form of a cremation burial noted just to the east within Tr 254 (Allen Archaeology 2018d). The three inhumation burials included the poorly preserved remains of an individual estimated to be around 6 years old (burial 2.28; Boyle 2024; Fig. 4.5). To the north was a pair of burials orientated northeast to southwest including that of a young adult female who had been buried with hobnail boots and placed within an oak coffin (burial 2.30; Boyle 2024; Bamforth 2024). The second burial comprised a shallow cut containing the remains of an adult of unknown sex with elevated proportions of carbon and nitrogen isotopes suggesting that marine resources formed a significant component of their diet (burial 2.29; Boyle 2024). Radiocarbon dating places all the burials within the middle Roman period (Table 4.3).

Farming from Sibsey to Bicker Parish

The landscape from Burgh le Marsh to Bicker Parish (incorporating sites within the Fen Edge and Inland Fen Edge Landscape Parcels) follows the fen with the excavated Roman sites being located on islands of glacial till and outwash. At the northern extent of this landscape was the peninsula of Burgh le Marsh, which was connected to an inland trade route to Lincoln via Ulceby Cross to the northwest and over the Wolds (Whitwell 1993; see Chapter 6, Fig. 4.6). Multiple Roman finds, including pottery and coins, have been recovered from the vicinity of the modern town. Limited excavations within Burgh le Marsh have recorded the presence of possible stone buildings, alongside evidence for crop processing (Malone 2001; Bradley-Lovekin and Kitch 2006). Despite this, the Scheme revealed scant evidence of Roman activity at SMR09 and SMR10 located only *c.* 0.5 km from Burgh le Marsh. SMR09, west of 'Jock Hedge' and directly south of Beechwood House (TF 50453 64004), provided some indications of saltworking with a small dump of material containing ceramic building material and briquetage. The site was heavily truncated by later industrial activities of medieval and post-medieval brickmaking (described in Chapter 7) limiting the identification of earlier features. Further scant evidence of a Roman presence was identified at SMR10 located between Low Lane and High Lane on the southwest outskirts of Burgh le Marsh (TF5241 67494 and TF 5241 67755). Two pits were situated within

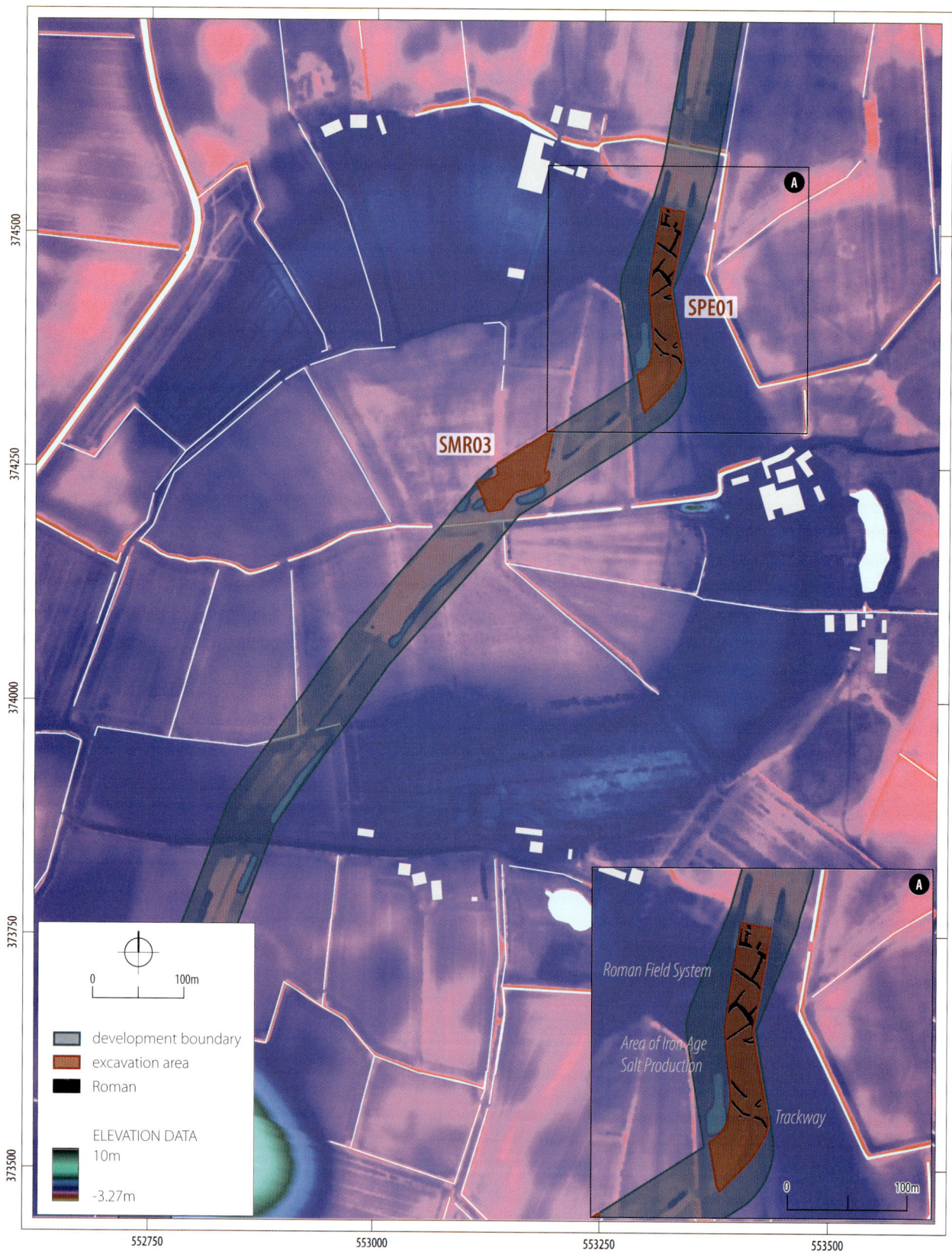

Figure 4.3 Roman features at SPE01 aligned to the crescent-shaped plateau

4 Living near the edge: Settlement and agriculture in the Roman period

Figure 4.4 The coastal landscape showing the location of the excavated sites and Roman sites identified in the Historic Environment Record (HER) 1 km from the route of the Scheme

Table 4.4 Summary of Roman artefacts from the Coastal Landscape Parcel

Site	Pottery (no. of sherds)	Pottery (MNV)	Samian	Small finds	Glass	Ceramic Building Material/fired clay
SPE01	1 (+ frag.)	–	–	–	–	1 small frag. abraded *tegula* flange
SMR01	69	27	–	–	–	10 small frags fired clay
SMR04	69	62	2	2 iron nails	1 blue-green sherd	24 small frags brick or tile

an early medieval field system from which late Roman pottery was recovered.

The evidence recovered from the northern portion of the landscape contrasts with the farmsteads identified to the southwest, from Sibsey to Bicker Parish (Fig. 4.7). The excavations conducted at SPE03, SPE04, SMR17, and SMR01/TAM04 offer valuable insights into the development, expansion, and activities occurring at Roman farmsteads within this region. A high number of Roman sites have been identified in the surrounding area including enclosures (MLI12705), earthworks (MLI40719), field systems (MLI40720, MLI40721) and

Figure 4.5 Roman burials at SPE02: left. burial 2.30; right: burial 2.29

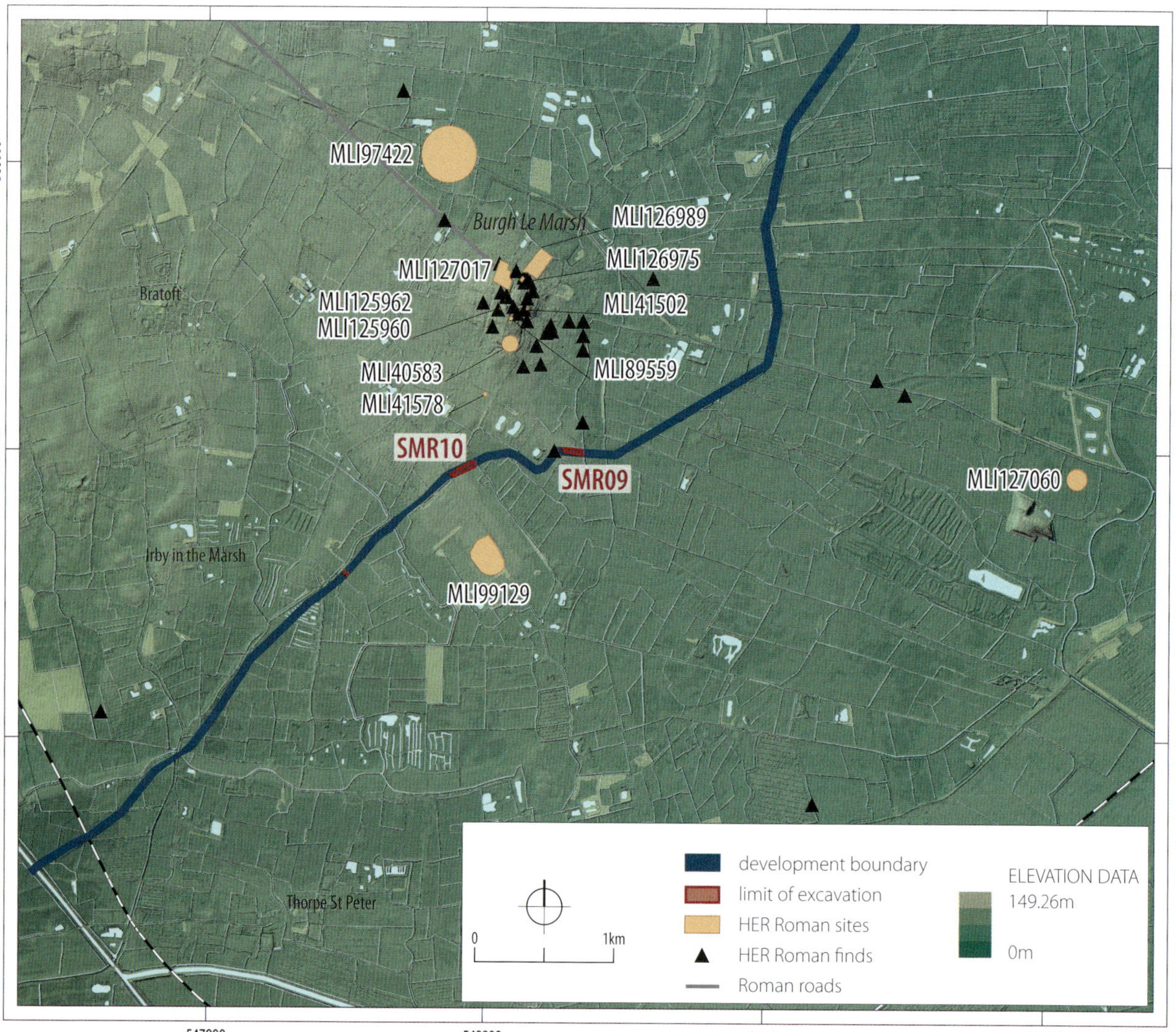

Figure 4.6 Landscape around Burgh le Marsh showing the location of the excavated sites and Roman sites identified in the Historic Environment Record (HER) 1 km from the route of the Scheme

farmsteads (MLI12605) (Fig. 4.7). More recent work in the near locale such as the Heckington Fen Energy Park (Dabill 2023) flanking the east side of the Viking Link excavations (Daniel and Halldórsdóttir 2023), has increased the number of excavated sites in the area.

At SPE03 an early–middle Roman farmstead was uncovered to the southeast of Rectory Farm flanking the south side of Mere Booth Road in the parish of Langriville (Fig. 4.8). The features are concentrated within the northeastern portion of the site with previous investigations indicating intense activity directly east and northwest with less intense activities on the north side of Mere Booth Road, showing an estimated spread of archaeology across *c.* 2.9 ha (Allen Archaeology 2018b; 2018d). During the early Roman period (AD 43–100) activity was concentrated towards the western limit of SPE03, comprising a series of enclosures and ditches to the southwest of Structure 12 (Figs 4.8 and 4.9). The earliest iteration of the farmstead comprised Enclosures 10 and 11, with the latter located within the footprint of Enclosure 10. Sherds of later Iron Age and 1st–2nd century AD pottery were recovered along with several fired clay balls from the eastern ditch of Enclosure 10 (Fig. 4.9). The precise function of these enigmatic objects is unclear, but they may have encompassed a range of uses, including as net weights, sling shot, stoppers, and kiln related activities, although there was no evidence for a kiln on site.

The enclosures underwent modification at some point in the early Roman period with an expansion of activity to the east of Enclosure 10 (Fig. 4.8). These changes included the construction of Structure 12, defined by a pair of beam slots, with a line of post-holes extending from its western edge (Figs 4.9 and 4.10). This row of posts may

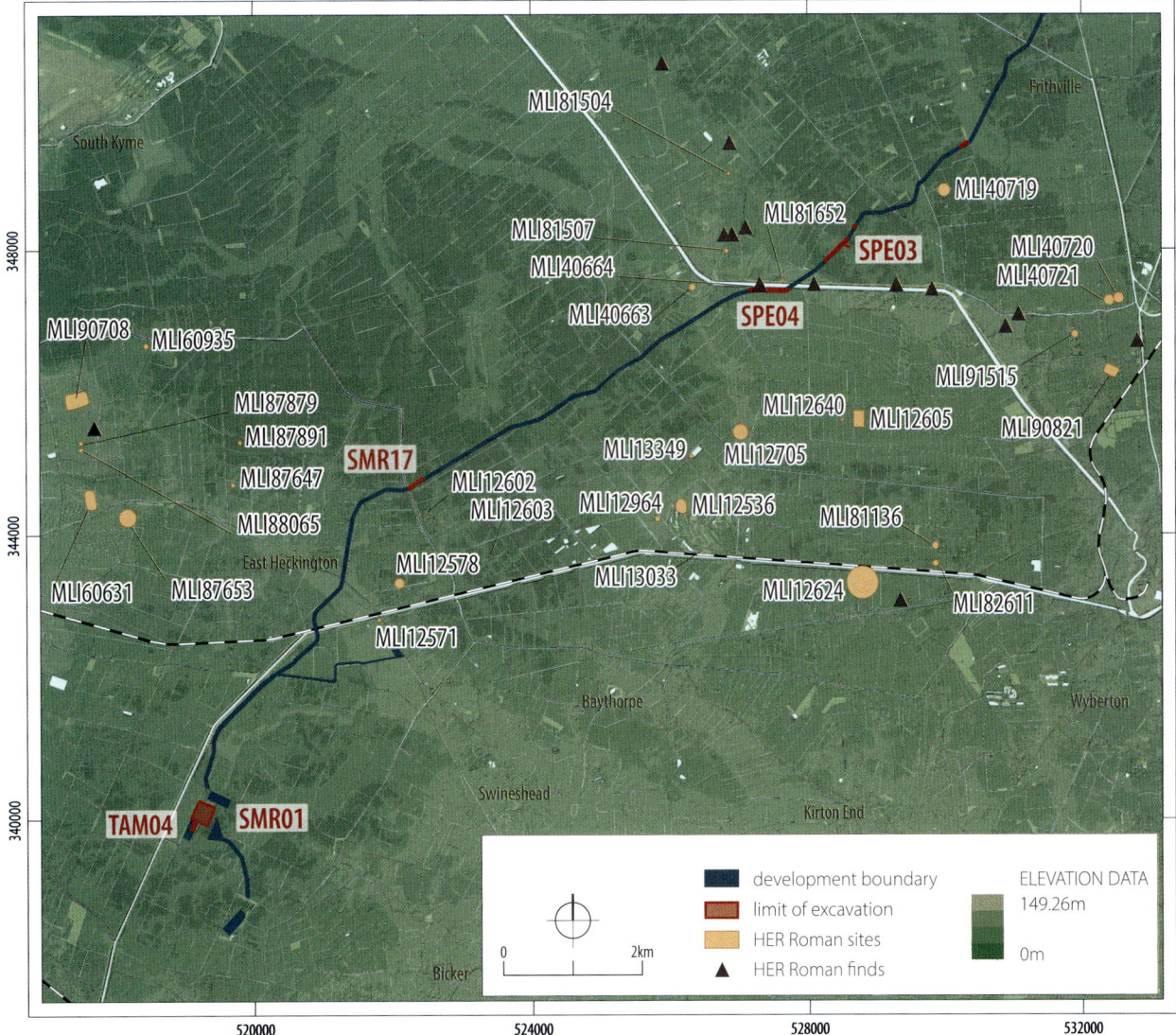

Figure 4.7 The landscape between Sibsey and Bicker Parish showing the location of the excavated sites and Roman sites identified in the Historic Environment Record (HER) 1 km from the route of the Scheme

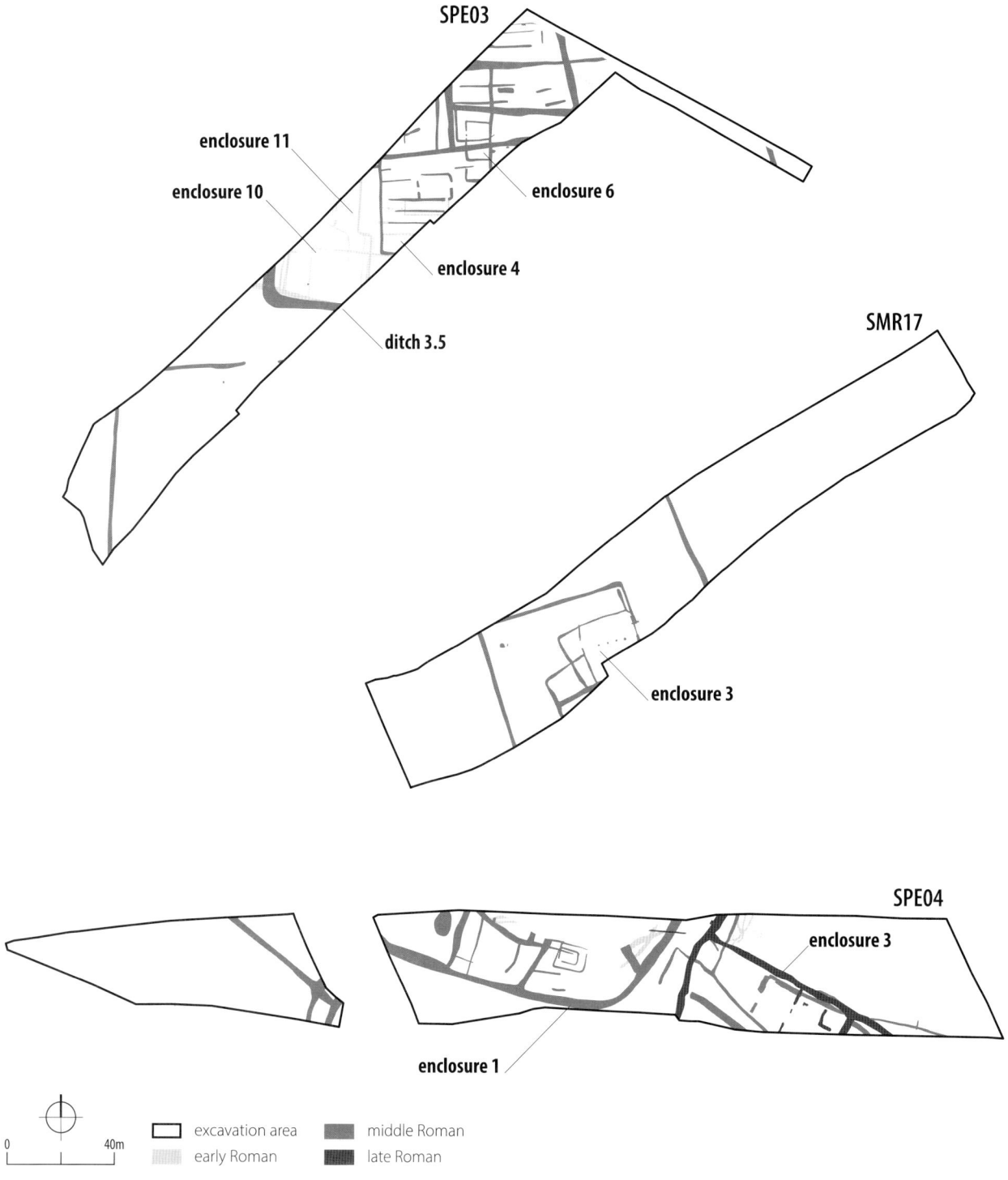

Figure 4.8 Comparative site plans of SPE03, SPE04, and SMR17

have defined a small fence associated with the building, which measured *c.* 16 m in length with an internal area of *c.* 80 m². The only features located within the footprint of the building were two post-holes, which could relate to elements of the superstructure, supporting parts of the roof (Fig. 4.10). The general absence of other internal features such as hearths may suggest an agricultural function. Thirty-two sherds from four late 1st to mid-2nd century AD vessels were recovered from the fill of beam slot 3.18, while the fill of post-hole [30356] contained 30 sherds of 2nd–3rd century pottery (Fig. 4.9). During the middle Roman period Structure 12 was replaced by a larger structure, Structure 5, as the farmstead expanded (Fig. 4.10).

The middle Roman period (AD 100–250) witnessed further expansion of the rectilinear enclosures at SPE03,

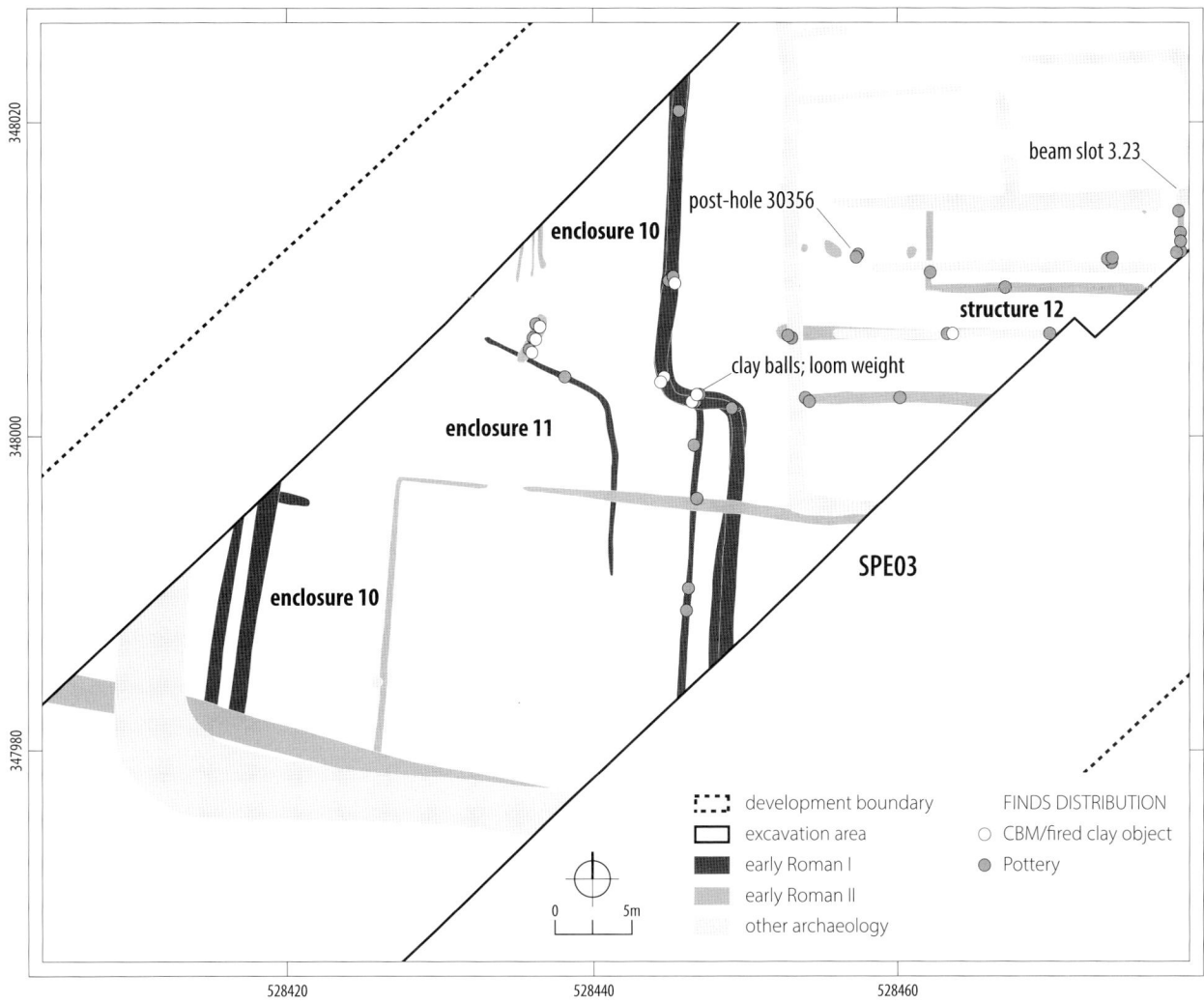

Figure 4.9 Early Roman phases of SPE03 showing the distribution of key artefacts

developing into a more complex farmstead potentially enclosed by Ditch 3.5 (Fig. 4.8). The enclosures to the north extended beyond the excavated area as indicated by the earlier geophysical survey and evaluation (Allen Archaeology 2018b; 2018d). The enclosures appear to have been recut multiple times to form a series of larger enclosures with sub-divisions. However, activity continued to be focused to the south, within Enclosure 4, with Structure 5 replacing the earlier Structure 12 (Fig. 4.11). Enclosure 4 measured c. 35 m north to south and a maximum of 55 m was encountered east to west before it extended beyond the limit of excavation, leaving an overall area of c. 960 m² enclosed. A high concentration of artefacts was recovered from Enclosure 4 and included sherds of later 2nd and 3rd century AD pottery (Fig. 4.11), including two sherds with evidence of lipids. Quantities of animal bone were also recovered with a slightly higher concentration being noted at the northeast, which could derive from activities associated with Structure 5.

Some of these objects probably derive from activities associated with Structure 5: a large rectangular two-celled structure defined by beam slots which truncated the northern edge of Structure 12. It measured c. 25 m east–west, with an internal space almost twice as large as Structure 12 (Fig. 4.10). A possible entrance was noted at the eastern end of the building, aligned to the internal partition. The structure contained no internal post-holes, floor surfaces, or hearths. Although the artefactual assemblage from the beam slots included fragments of tile, brick, and fired clay (Tomlinson 2024), these likely originated elsewhere and were not part of the overall superstructure. The artefacts provided clues to the function of the building with finds relating to personal adornment as well as craftworking activities. These included bone hairpins, an awl, fragmented loom weights, and a significant number of clay balls, similar to those from Enclosure 10, from the surrounding ditches. The ceramic assemblage from the structure included a nearly complete stamped mortaria produced in Lincoln in AD 90–115, alongside several greyware vessels with indications for both dairy and plant processing (Dunne *et al.* 2023; Rowlandson and Fiske 2024b).

The complex farmstead at SPE03 developed throughout the middle Roman period with activity focused to the south and enclosures expanding to the northeast and northwest. The enclosures likely relate to livestock management with smaller paddocks, such as Enclosure 6 (Fig. 4.8), located closer to the focal point of activity. The enclosures may also relate to cereal production within a mixed agricultural regime with the analysed palaeobotanical assemblage containing rare cereal grains but abundant cereal chaff, predominantly from spelt (Wallace and Fryer 2024). Two quern stones were also recovered from ditches immediately to the north of Enclosure 4 and Structure 5 suggesting limited cereal processing on site. The farmstead at SPE03 was not exposed in its entirety which poses some limitations to the interpretation of form. The successive realignment of enclosures and the more substantial boundary ditch to the south would nonetheless suggest that the arrangement of enclosures is comparable to an enclosed farmstead where the expansion takes place within a limited (enclosed) space rather than extending along a linear form. It has been estimated that nearly 10%

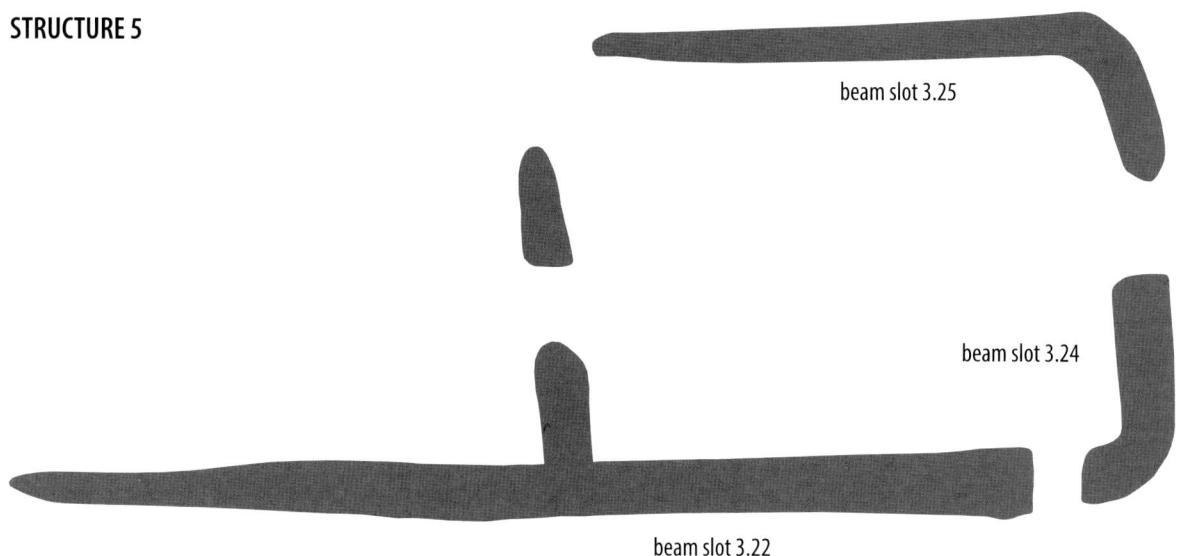

Figure 4.10 Plans of Structure 12 and 5 at SPE03

of the farmsteads in the Fens are enclosed while a larger percentage have been identified as complex farmsteads with a transition from the former to the latter throughout the Roman period in the Central Belt region (Smith *et al.* 2016). The excavation at SPE03 suggests something in between an enclosed farmstead and a complex form as apart from the main enclosing boundary, the site also features a putative rectangular structure. This mix of forms has been excavated elsewhere such as at Langtoft (Hutton 2007) which displayed both enclosures with rectangular post-built structures and an outlying field system, the Fen Edge site at Parnwell, Peterborough (Webley 2006), and Love's Farm, St Neots, Cambridgeshire (Hinman and Zant 2018).

The occurrence of two beam slot buildings within SPE03 is also particularly notable, finding parallel with other examples of Roman farmsteads across Britain (Fig. 4.10). The rectangular architectural form of both Structures 12 and 5 fits well into the Smith *et al.* (2016) model of rural buildings encountered within complex farmsteads from the central region of Britain, where the rectangular form surpassed the circular roundhouse by the 2nd century AD. Rectangular structures, both post-built and trench-built, have been identified within neighbouring regions such as at Love's Farm in St Neots (Hinman and Zant 2018). Rectangular structures with uncertain function have been encountered in the enclosed Roman farmsteads at Marsh Leys, Bedfordshire (Luke and Preece 2011) and at the Roman farmstead in Scalford Brook, Leicestershire (Beamish 1990). The precise function of the two structures at SPE03 is unclear but it is possible that Structure 12 had an agricultural function, while Structure 5 was used for a range of craft activities. The latter structure is associated with the peak of activity at the farmstead in

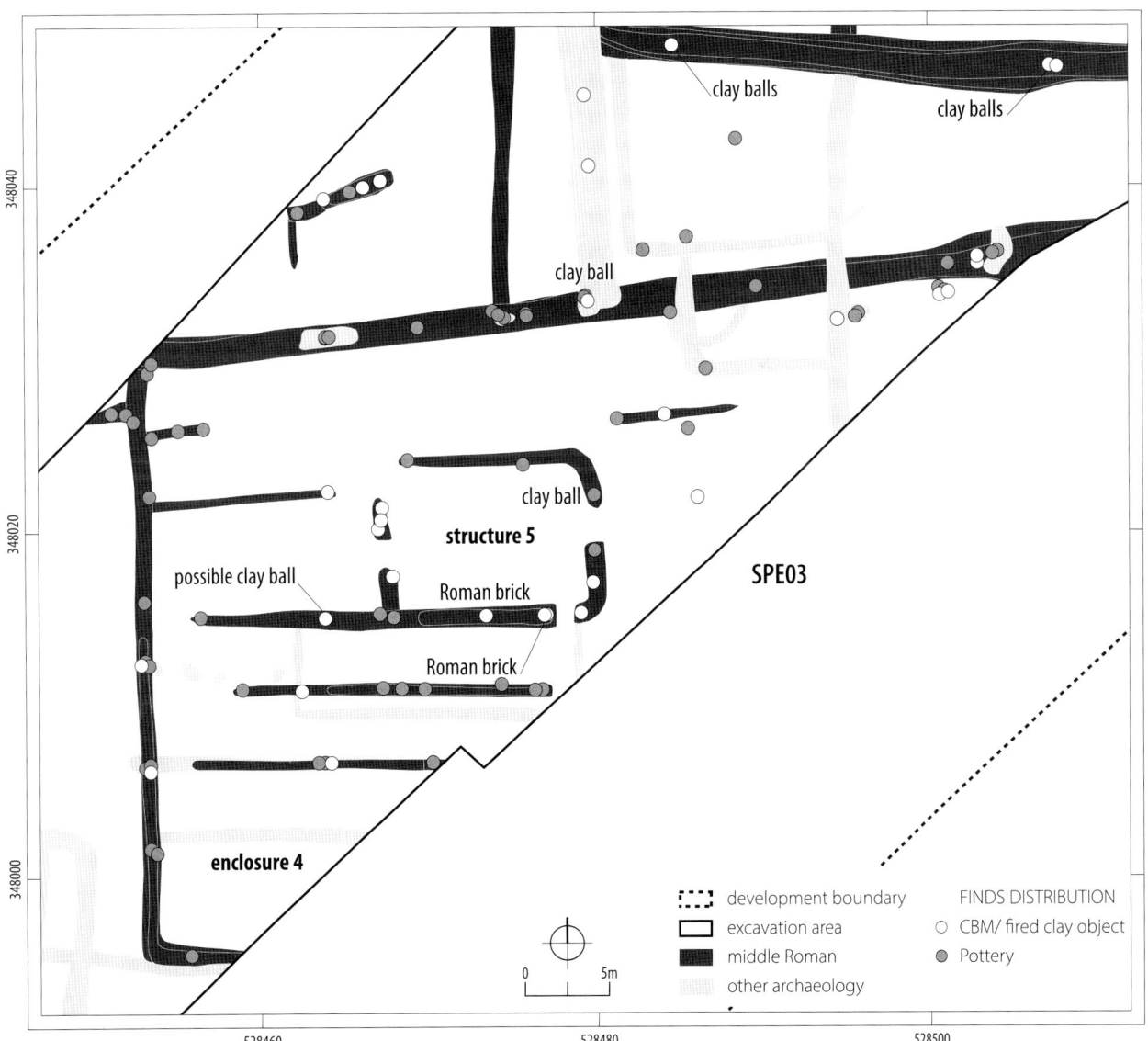

Figure 4.11 Middle Roman phases of SPE03 (Enclosure 4) showing the distribution of key artefacts

the middle Roman period when the farmstead was at its largest and most complex form. Pinpointing the decline of the settlement is problematic but this appears to begin in the mid-3rd century AD with no artefactual evidence, with little definitive evidence of late Roman pottery types (see Rowlandson and Fiske, below).

A similar pattern of development was identified at SPE04 at Langrick Bridge, *c.* 750 m east of the village core and 2 km to the west of Anton's Gowt (Fig. 4.1). The excavated area ran parallel to the southern bank of the current canalised course of the River Witham (see Chapter 2). There was no prehistoric presence on site which at its closest point lay only *c.* 130 m away from the non-canalised stretch of the river to the north. The earliest Roman phase was defined by fragmented ditches likely impacted by water incursions from the river (Fig. 4.8).

It was not until the 2nd and 3rd centuries AD that the farmstead at SPE04 became well established (Fig. 4.8). The 2nd–mid-3rd century AD farming activities would have been contemporary with the farmstead at SPE03. The middle Roman period saw the establishment of a grid-lined network of ditches that stretched across an area of at least 40 m north to south and 260 m east and was bound at its western edge by Enclosure 1. The Enclosure 1 ditch measured 1.90 m in depth and contained waterlogged deposits with insect analysis revealing the presence of dung beetles suggesting it enclosed a small number of livestock paddocks (Allison 2024). The presence of a central, spiral-shaped corral, devoid of finds, may indicate the seasonal or periodic corralling of animals within the enclosures (Fig. 4.12). The main boundary of Enclosure 1 was maintained but the internal paddocks, including the corral, were superseded by recut and newly established drainage ditches. The enclosures extended to the west, adjacent to a ring-ditch structure, from which no artefacts were recovered, seemingly located away from the main activity and animal enclosures. Circular ditches with a similar lack of artefacts suggested to be of agricultural function have been encountered in corners of Roman fields at Christchurch, Upwell, Norfolk and near Bourne-Morton canal, Lincolnshire (Coles and Hall 1994). Two similar-sized ring-ditches to SPE03 were excavated at Love's Farm and interpreted as potential drainage ditches for hayricks (Hinman and Zant 2018). Hay would have ensured fodder for the livestock in the winter when grazing may have been limited. The management of water across the site is a distinctive feature with water incursion potentially leading to the abandonment

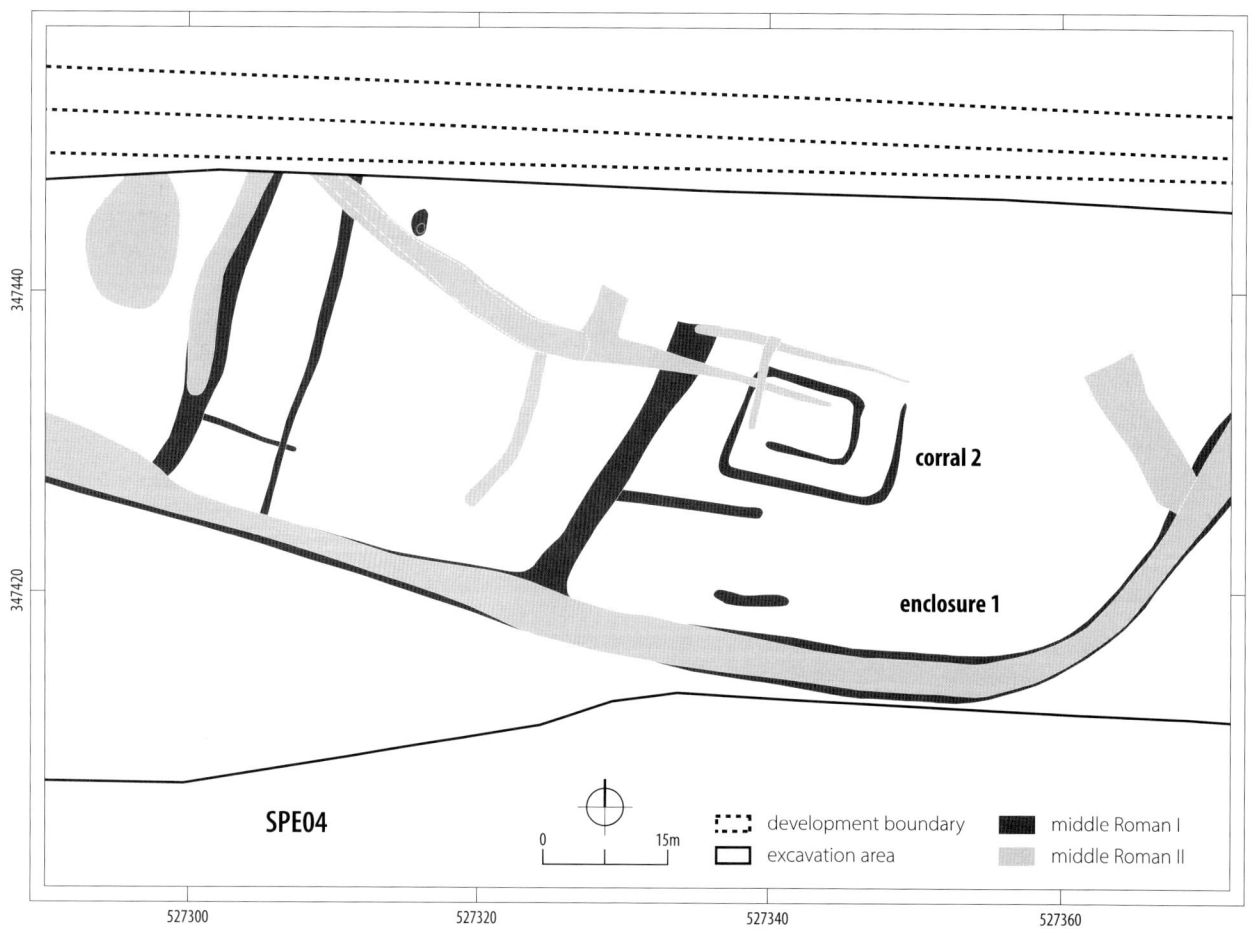

Figure 4.12 Middle Roman phases of SPE04

of Enclosure 1. Insect remains indicatie the ditch was permanently waterlogged with surrounding land of rich lowland fen vegetation (Allison 2024).

Activities continued within the farmstead at SPE04 into the 3rd century AD when activity shifted to the east (Fig. 4.8). A limited area of the later Roman farmstead was uncovered comprising a T-shaped ditch defining Enclosure 3 (Figs 4.8 and 4.13). The density of finds and dumped deposits encountered within the internal features of Enclosure 3 in the 3rd and 4th centuries AD suggests they are close to domestic activities, perhaps beyond the area of excavation to the south as indicated by preceding geophysical survey results (Allen Archaeology 2018b). The large group of pottery from a southwest branch of Enclosure 3 included imported wares such as a Dressel 20 amphora, a Mancetter-Hartshill mortarium, Dales ware, a Nene Valley greyware strainer, and a Bourne type shell-gritted bowl with dairy residues (Rowlandson and Fiske 2024b). The imported pottery wares were found in smaller quantities than at SPE03 but suggest connections to trade and that the farmstead was not functioning in isolation (see Chapter 6). From the same area came a beehive quern reused as a rubstone, perhaps related to the sharpening of tools for crafting or general farm use (Hayward and Shaffrey 2024a). Four quern stones in the same vicinity, all recovered within a 110 m^2 area of ditches and pits associated with Enclosure 3, indicate grain processing on site despite the relatively low quantity of cereal remains recovered from across SPE04 (Fig. 4.13). The largest assemblage was recovered from L-shaped Ditch 4.21 within the enclosure and included a very small amount of possibly roughly milled grain fragments. There appears to be a distinct shift at SPE04 from a focus on animal husbandry to a more mixed agricultural regime with evidence of cereal processing and the on site processing of dairy produce. With such a short distance between the two settlements of SPE03 and SPE04 it is not inconceivable that they may have been economically tied particularly during the 3rd century AD when a degree of specialisation may have developed (see Chapter 6).

A farmstead, also dated to the 2nd–3rd centuries AD, was excavated at SMR17, at Amber Hill (TF 2228 4472), *c.* 1.75 km north–northeast of Swineshead Bridge (Fig. 4.1). This farmstead is located at the northern extent of a spread of Roman sites extending from Bicker to Swineshead and Boston (Phillips 1970; Figs 4.7 and 4.14). The site also neighbours a series of cropmarks covering 19 ha *c.* 1.1 km to the south (TF 2253 4324). Therefore, while the excavated site is smaller in scale than SPE03 and SPE04 it may have formed part of a wider group of sites. The farmstead at SMR17 comprised two phases of enclosure, all extending beyond the limit of excavation to the north and south where the remainder of the Roman activity is thought to lie (Fig. 4.8). A series of intercutting enclosures defined this period of activity, with areas of the site reconfigured over time. The main area of activity was defined by a gated enclosure, Enclosure 5, with an internal partition indicated by a row of posts presumably representing a more substantial fence line with smaller ditched paddocks extending beyond the limit of excavation (Fig. 4.14).

A potential gated enclosure, identified as two intercutting post-holes at the end of the enclosure ditch, was excavated at the Roman farmstead in Marsh Leys, Bedfordshire (Luke and Preece 2011). The enclosure was interpreted to be domestic with an associated structure. Similarly, a gated enclosure surrounding a domestic aisled building with six furnaces/ovens, dated to the late 2nd century AD, was excavated at Lynch Farm, Peterborough (Upex 2018). Further domestic examples of gated enclosures of 2nd and 3rd century AD date have been found at Love's Farm (Hinman and Zant 2018). While a rectangular structure was encountered within the enclosure at SMR17, it was deemed to be associated with the medieval farmstead, as such there were no domestic or industrial structures associated with the enclosure. The lack of domestic activity is supported by the limited artefactual assemblage. Despite the recovery of three Millstone Grit querns and millstones (the largest of which was found in a medieval beam slot), the overall impression of the enclosure suggests a focus on livestock with cattle being the most dominant species within the animal bone assemblage.

The farmsteads at SPE03, SPE04, and SMR17 form part of a network of enclosed and complex farming settlements in the Lincolnshire Fen Edge. Recent Viking Link excavations of the *Mown Rakes*, 1 km to the east of SMR17, have revealed two main Roman foci in the area (Daniel and Halldórsdóttir 2023). To the north (Area 52), pits and ditches dated from the 1st–2nd centuries AD confirm the presence of early Roman occupation in the area. Artefacts from salt production were also present amongst several features with a potential production site to the south (Area 53) dating between the Iron Age and the 2nd century AD. Second and 3rd century AD settlement was exposed within a 'ladder enclosure' with internal sub-divisions which also included a cremation deposit (*ibid.*). This would have been a neighbouring focus of activity, potentially contemporary with the farmstead at SMR17. The full extent of the settlement form could not be defined within the limit of excavation although some complexity is indicated by its extent, internal features, and recuts. Further south, a second settlement was identified (Area 55) dating from the late 1st century AD to the 3rd century AD. The site was dominated by numerous enclosures with internal features including a pond indicating a former extraction site or waterhole for livestock. The artefactual assemblage linked the site to pottery and salt production as well as the malting of spelt. Roman settlement has also been recorded at Heckington Fen to the east of the Viking Link excavations (Dabill 2022). The site comprised an enclosure system with the artefactual

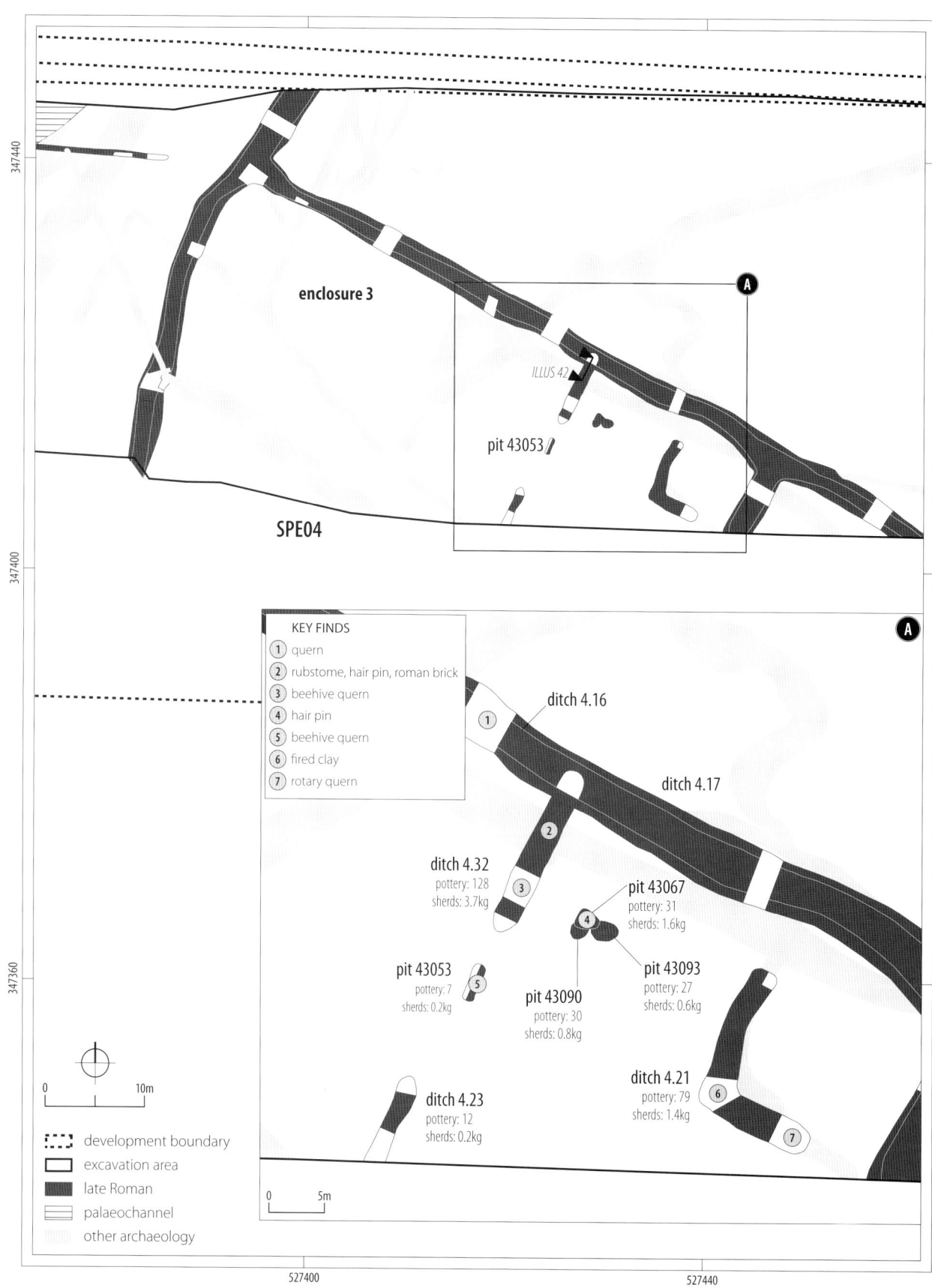

Figure 4.13 Late Roman phases of SPE04

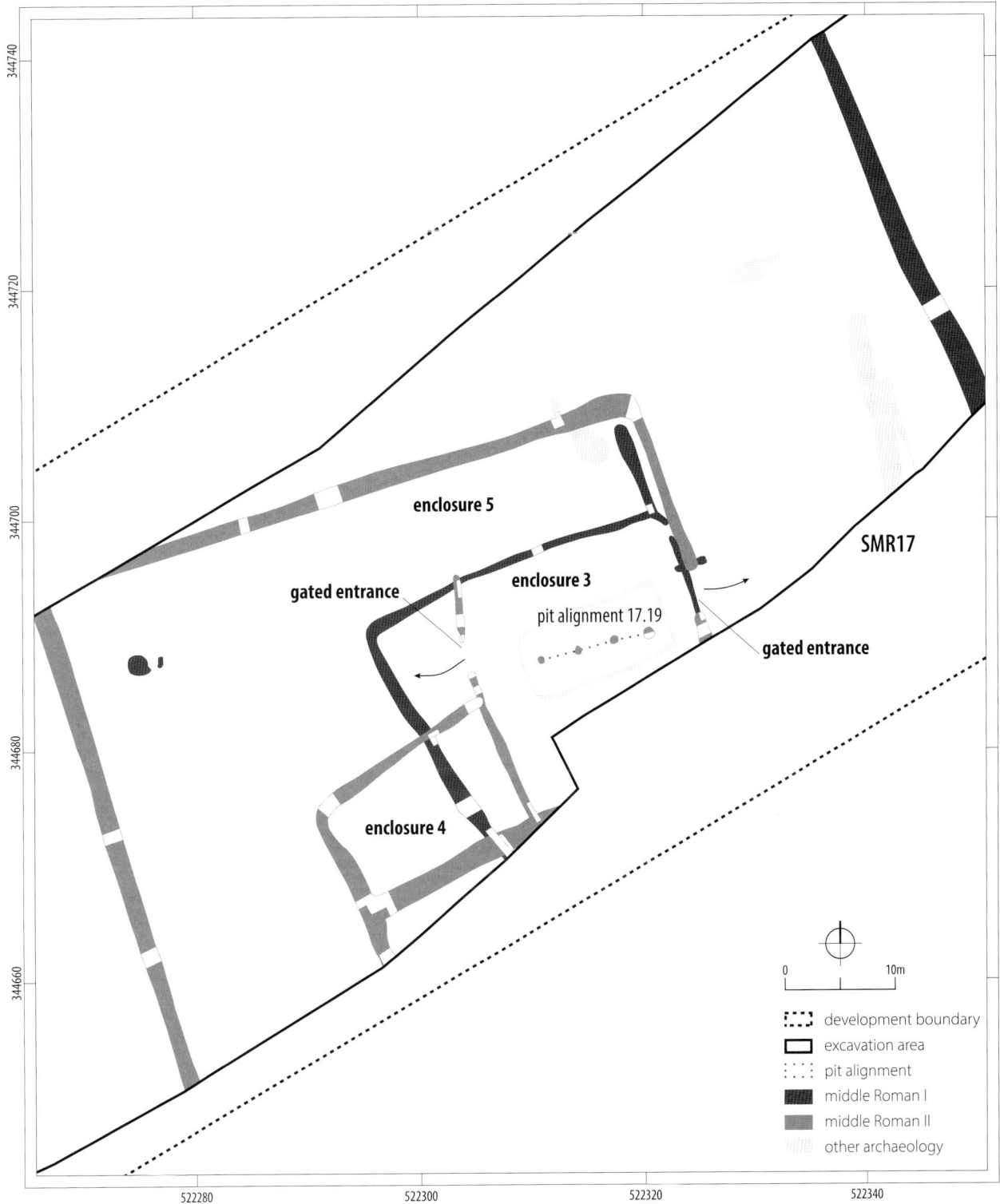

Figure 4.14 Roman phases of SMR17

assemblage indicating links to saltmaking and wider trade links with both imported and fine wares recovered.

The seeming expansion of activity from the middle Roman period onwards is exemplified by the farmstead excavated at SMR01/TAM04 located on a pronounced roddon within the Bicker Fen landscape. The excavations revealed evidence for early Roman (AD 43–100) activity centred on a moated post-built structure tentatively related to an unenclosed farmstead west of the excavation area. The middle Roman period (AD 100–250) saw an expansion of an enclosure system defining a complex farmstead with conjoined enclosures best relatable to SPE04 with a

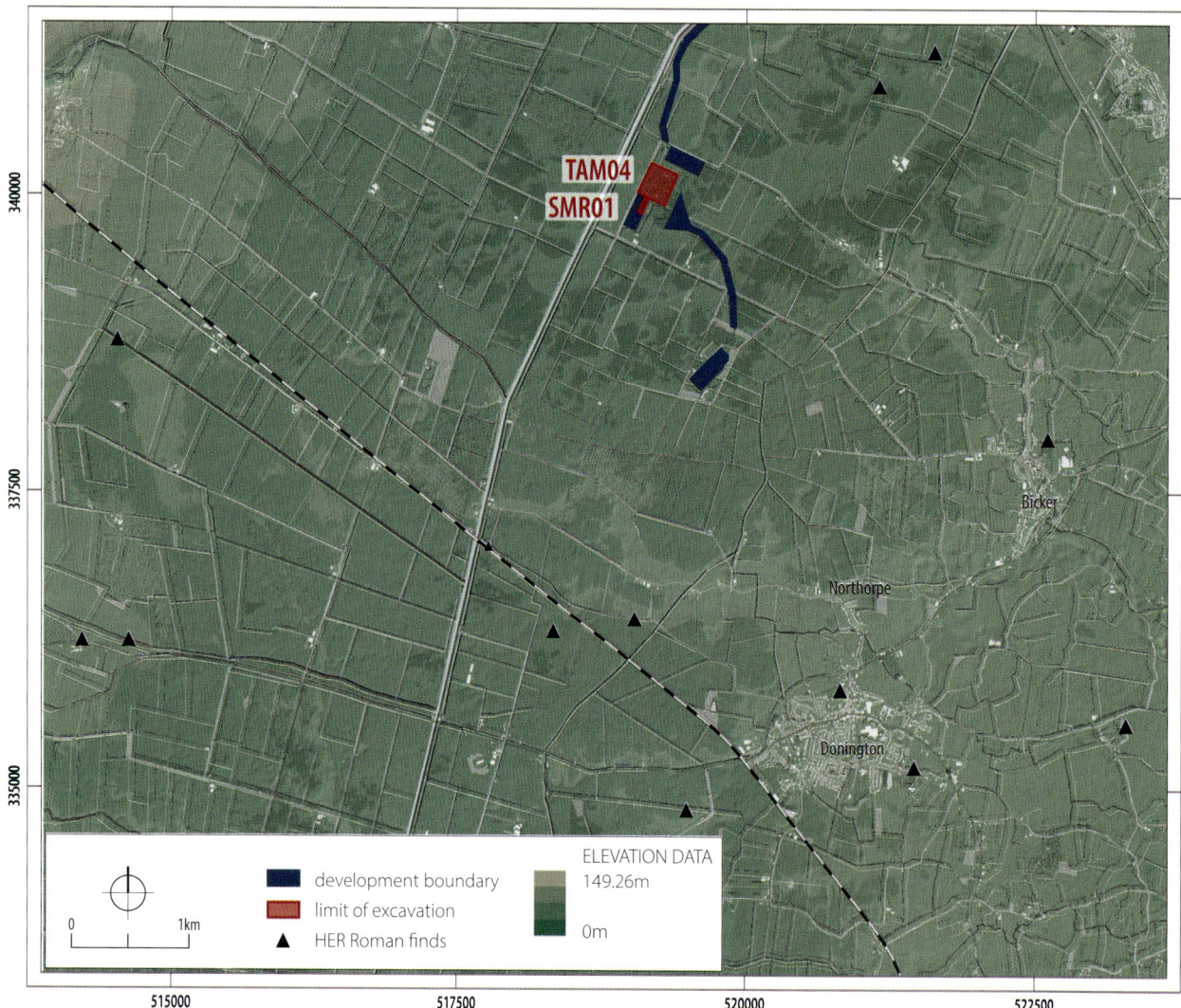

Figure 4.15 The landscape around SMR01/TAM04 showing the location of the excavated sites and Roman sites listed in the Lincolnshire HER (1 km)

livestock focused economy. In the late Roman period (AD 250–410), the site was reshaped and previous enclosures were superseded by a curvilinear 'ladder enclosure' to the north with potential domestic focus situated further south (Fig. 4.16).

In the latter part of the early Roman period, activity is represented by Structure Complex 2 at the western edge of TAM04 (Figs 4.16 and 4.17). The post-built, sub-rectangular structure with rounded corners was constructed on a prepared platform of packed clay and surrounded by a circular ditch or moat encroaching upon an earlier boundary to the south (Fig. 4.18). A bridge may have braced the ditch as indicated near the east entrance to the building. The 0.60 m deep ditch may have protected against the high water-table and episodes of flooding, and fire, much like medieval moated manors (Steane 1984). The structure displayed evidence for three construction phases comprising sturdy timbers initially set in two even rows of seven posts with additional stakes (Figs 4.17 and 4.18). These become less frequent over time with successive rebuilding of the platform. A hearth was located in the centre and the entrance faced east. The artefactual assemblage was largely lacking in structural elements apart from some fired clay. However, it seems most likely that the walls primarily consisted of wattle and daub and, with its position on the fen edge, thatching (perhaps of reeds) seems the most likely contender for roofing. The form of the structure appears to be unique to its setting and may reflect a particular response to local ground conditions. The adaptation of structures in response to flooding or high water-tables can be seen in other fen regions, such as the raised platform-like structures at Colne Fen, Cambridgeshire (Evans 2013). A possible comparison to the arrangement of features seen at TAM04 was uncovered at Cambridge Biomedical Campus where post-built structure (Structure 3), dated to the mid-2nd to early 3rd century AD, was surrounded by an enclosure (Compound B; Tabor and Phillips 2024). There is some

4 Living near the edge: Settlement and agriculture in the Roman period

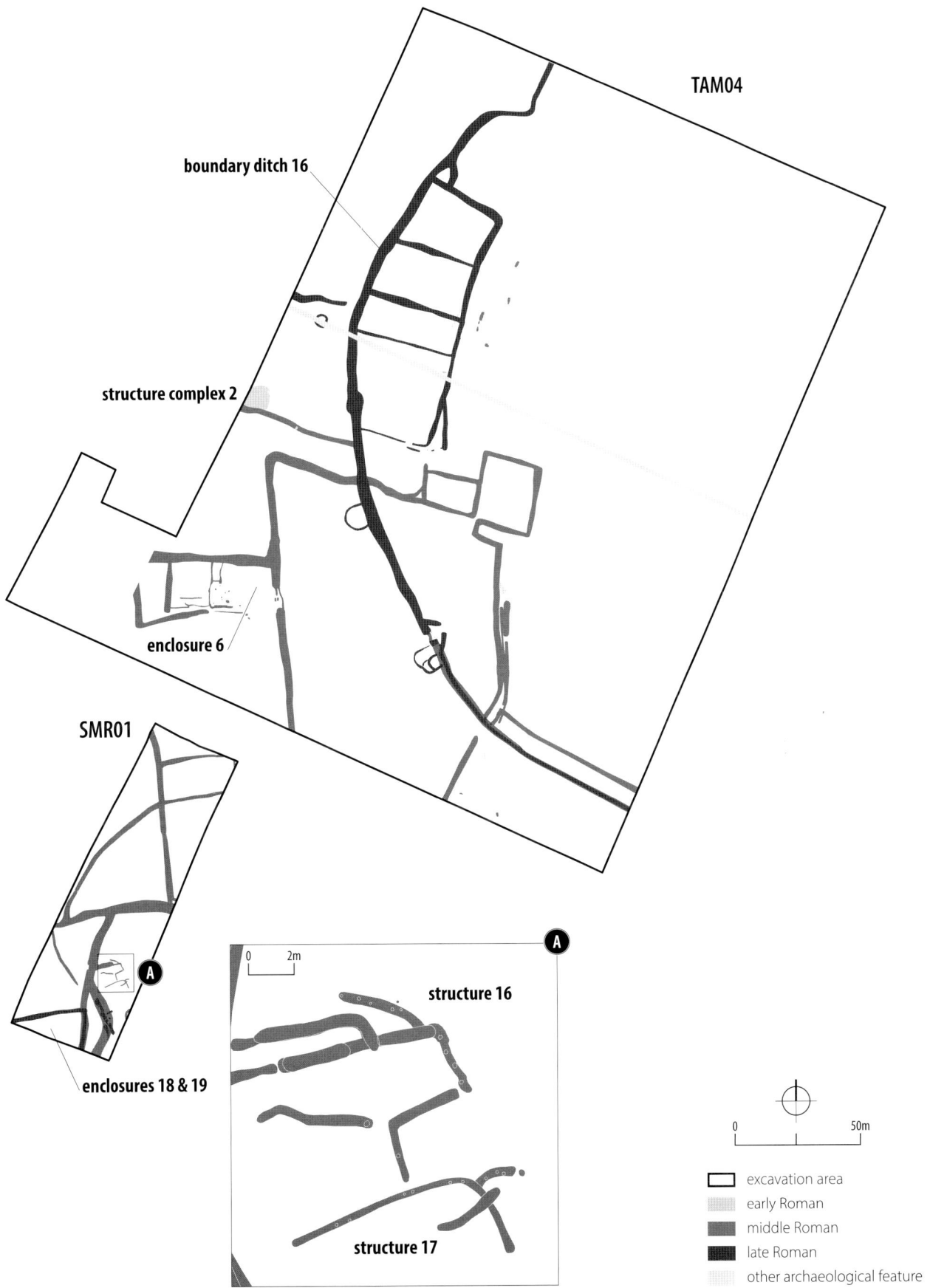

Figure 4.16 Roman activity at SMR01 and TAM04

debate as to whether the enclosure is contemporary but the shallow enclosure, which measured 0.7–1.1 m wide and 0.3–0.4 m deep, may have served a similar function to that proposed at TAM04 (*ibid.*). Ditches and enclosures surrounding structures may have developed as a means to control fluctuating water levels while simultaneously influencing access to resources or activities.

The function of the structure at TAM04 was not immediately apparent, however, the large dump of material positioned to the north is likely to have derived from periods of clearing out and rebuilding. The material included domestic items, potentially linked to the phase of the structure when a central hearth was present, including limited tableware, a storage jar with cooking residues, bowls with evidence of dairy processing, and a loom weight. The structure may have also been associated with saltmaking or the storage of salt as indicated by environmental samples of midden deposits despite being devoid of briquetage. Salt may have been procured from production sites to the south such as at Bicker (MLI12523) and Hurn Fen Farm (MLI33320). Evidence for the use of the structure for storage towards the end of its lifespan was recovered from the latest ditch fills on the north side of the structure which contained sherds from large storage jars. The successive episodes of rebuilding and repair may suggest that the building was in seasonal use serving a variety of functions. The structure fell out of use in the 2nd century AD. The area was levelled and may have been marked by a timber screen to the south evident as a linear cluster of post- and stake-holes.

During the 2nd and 3rd centuries AD several phases of a complex farmstead of adjoining enclosures was constructed south of the 'moated' structure (Fig. 4.16). These enclosures appeared to follow the natural curvature of the underlying roddon. The eastern half of the site comprised a large polygonal enclosure, with two smaller enclosures located on its northern edge. Entrances into and out of the enclosure were located on the eastern and western sides. Along the western side was a further series of enclosures, which extended southwards into SMR01. The smaller ancillary enclosures may have been utilised as livestock pens with animal husbandry primarily focused on cattle within a mixed agricultural regime that also included low-level crop production. The larger enclosure may have been used for the corralling of livestock, potentially including for the overwintering of animals.

The principal area of domestic activity was located to the west, within Enclosure 6. A series of fragmentary beam slots and post-holes defining possible structures were located to the west of a gated entranceway from the central enclosure (Fig. 4.16). The precise form of this structure though, unlike those at SPE03, is unclear. A limited artefactual assemblage, including pottery and a quern stone, was recovered from the structural features. However, a richer assemblage was recovered from the surrounding enclosure ditches and the entranceway from the main enclosure. This included domestic refuse and debris such as cooking pots, pot boilers, vessels for processing dairy and carcass products, as well as discarded animal bones. There were also personal effects and crafting objects such as a knife blade and a pin beater for weaving. Further evidence for domestic activity was noted in the southern extension of the enclosures in SMR01.

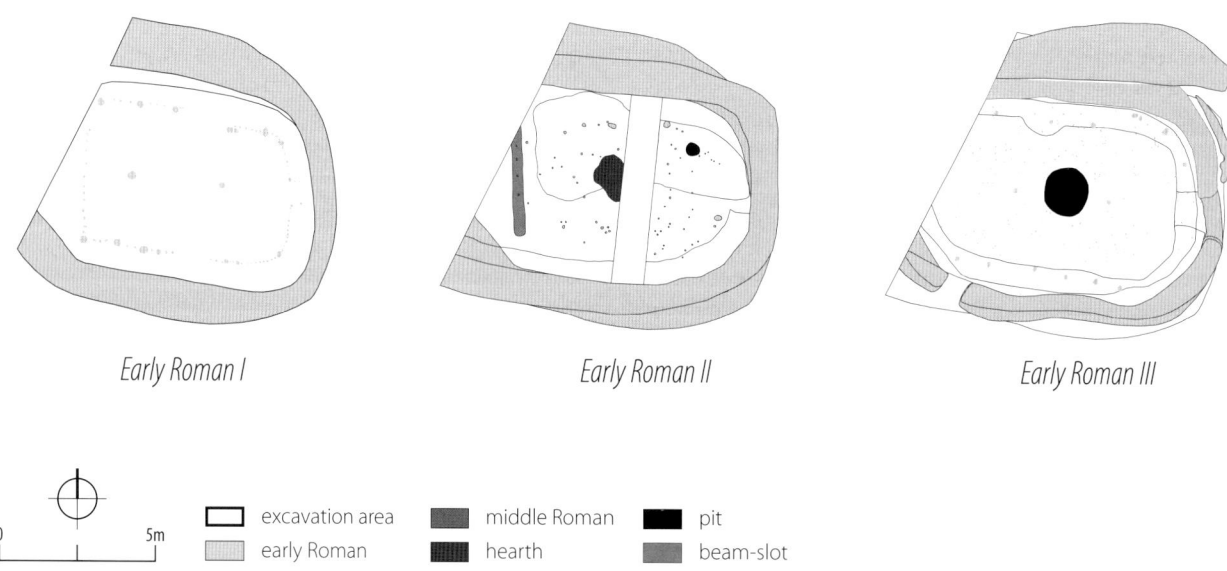

Figure 4.17 Development of Structure Complex 2 at TAM04

Figure 4.18 GoPro Photograph of Structure Complex 2 at TAM04

Here, further enclosed structures defined by a series of shallow gullies, beam slots, pits, and post-holes were identified. The beam slots and post-holes defining Structures 16 and 17 in SMR01 appeared to be focused around the entrance into the enclosure and could represent features associated with livestock management (Figs 4.16 and 4.18). The artefactual and environmental assemblage in and around the structures included a copper alloy bracelet. Activity may have continued into the later Roman phases with an enclosure (Enclosure 18 and 19) in the southwestern corner of the site with a fragmented beam slot structure and a series of pits located just east of the enclosure. From one of these pits a possible weaving tablet or a small musical instrument was recovered, located in the same area (Fig 6.6, IFE-1.3-249). The neighbouring ditches contained domestic debris including a high concentration of samian ware. That this site practised some regional trade is evident from pottery imports as well as a Whitby originating jet bead and by the plain column shaft from SMR01 probably made of Ancaster stone from approximately 40 km away (Hayward and Shaffrey 2024b). The shaft potentially formed part of a dwarf column in a portico or veranda in a high-status farmstead or possibly a villa, neither of which was evident in SMR01 or TAM04. This modest interaction with other communities and trade routes follows the trend seen both in the Triton Knoll and Viking Link material encountered at the other middle Roman farmsteads along the Lincolnshire Fen Edge.

TAM04 was reshaped in the 3rd–4th century AD by a substantial curvilinear Boundary Ditch, 16, which extended through the site aligning with the palaeochannel and roddon system. A funnelled entranceway was identified in the southern portion of the boundary ditch used to manage the movement of livestock and people across the site (Fig. 4.16). A group of penannular ditches on the western side of the ditch at the entrance may have functioned as corrals or paddocks to facilitate this movement. These types of entrances have been recorded in livestock enclosures from various periods, for instance within Bronze Age livestock enclosures at Cambridge Biomedical Campus (Tabor and Phillips 2024) and stock enclosures excavated at the Iron Age/Roman settlement in Horndean, Hampshire (Hopkinson 2014). A series

Figure 4.19 GoPro photograph of excavated Structures 16 and 17 at TAM04

of rectangular enclosures lay to the north adjoining the eastern side of the boundary. The site, particularly in this area, is reminiscent of a 'ladder enclosure', a system common for the late Roman period where enclosures were formed along a trackway. These are more common within the northeast region (Smith *et al.* 2016) such as at Newbridge Quarry, Pickering, North Yorkshire (Williams 2010), but present themselves elsewhere, such as those uncovered during the Viking Link excavations on Langton Hill in the Lincolnshire Wolds and at The Rakes in the parish of Swineshead near SMR17 (Daniel and Halldórsdóttir 2023). Potential Roman ladder settlement observed on satellite images has also been encountered in South Hykeham, Lincolnshire (MLI125635).

Environmental evidence

A range of environmental data was recovered, including assemblages of cereal remains and collections of faunal material, providing insights into agricultural regimes across the Scheme. In the following section, the principal aspects of this material are outlined, opening with a review of the botanical data, followed by the faunal data. This section concludes with a summary of the stable isotope evidence and the implications for this on our overall understanding of agricultural regimes across the Scheme, informing the wider discussion of agriculture in Chapter 6.

Cereal production and plants

Kate Turner with contributions from Laura Bailey, Val Fryer, and Michael Wallace

The early Roman period was characterised by an increase in arable agriculture across the Fenland area, with the bulk of the evidence for such activity being recorded on sites in the Fenland Edge Landscape Parcel. Charred plant assemblages recovered from samples of early Roman date suggest the continued cultivation of cereals, predominantly hulled wheats, such as spelt, and free-threshing wheats, with evidence for barley also present, particularly on areas of higher salinity land in proximity to saltmarshes. The crop profile represents a continuation of the trend seen in the early Iron Age assemblage from across the route. Spelt is a cereal better suited to heavy, clay soils prone to waterlogging. Barley, on the other hand, is a particularly hardy crop that is often used on drier or less fertile land where a wheat yield would be unreliable. Barley, furthermore, also has a degree of salinity tolerance and so may have been important on higher salinity land. Saline tolerance may have contributed to the predominance of barley at other sites in the area, such as Oakham (Beamish 1997) and the Roman saltern site of Morton (Murphy 2001a, 152).

Evidence from the botanical assemblage suggests the presence of open and dry environments in the area of the Fen Edge Landscape Parcel during the early Roman period, which may have been suitable for use as arable land. Grass seeds were common in deposits from this landscape block, with many being larger-seeded soft-brome/rye-brome (*Bromus mollis/secalinus*) though there were also larger numbers of small-seeded grasses. The other taxa present in greater numbers were oraches (*Atriplex* sp.), buttercups (*Ranunculus acris/repens/bulbosus*), knotgrass (*Polygonum aviculare*), and docks (*Rumex* sp.). Other notable taxa present in low quantities were fairy flax (cf. *Linum catharticum*), lesser chickweed (*Stellaria media*), thistles (*Cirsium* sp.), and scentless mayweed (*Tripleurospermum inodorum*). Wetland plant seeds lacked diversity, comprising only sedges (*Carex* spp.) and very few seeds of spike-rushes (*Eleocharis* sp.). Given that the SPE03 area was located in proximity to fen and marshlands, the clear emphasis on dryland wild species taxa is notable. The wild assemblage is quite different to that for nearby sites such as Cowbit (Murphy 2001b), Morton (Murphy 2001a), and Market Deeping (Branch and Lowe 1996, 15). The assemblage for SPE03 is more similar to inland sites such as Stamford Road (Monkton 1997) and Wing-to-Whatborough (Beamish 1997), both near Oakham. The wetland taxa that do occur are indicative of freshwater environments (*e.g.* sedges) and are not characteristic of saltmarsh taxa seen elsewhere in Roman Lincolnshire (Murphy 2001a; 2001b).

Cultivation of wheats and barley appears to continue into the middle Roman period, albeit the reliance on barley is seen to reduce in favour of a mix of spelt and bread wheat, with spelt being dominant. This is more typical of Roman assemblages in Britain. Indeed, it is notable that anything other than spelt dominance at Roman Lincolnshire sites is unusual (Carruthers and Hunter Dowse 2019, 63–65; Murphy 2001b, 154). Bread wheat performs poorly on waterlogged soils and so would not be suited to the wetter or marshy land of the Lincolnshire Marsh area.

The botanical assemblage from the Fen Edge Landscape Parcel supports the presence of dryland, open habitats including arable land, during this period. Wetland taxa were significantly more abundant at SPE04, and this may reflect the distribution of wetlands during the Roman period. In the case of SPE03, it appears that the focus was on accessing and farming drier lands that were free of waterlogging or high salinity. While the early Roman wild taxa are consistent with the weed assemblage of open, dryland crop fields, the materials could also represent the harvesting of hay meadow. This may have been collected as livestock fodder or as fuel. In either scenario, the wild plant remains could have been mixed with excess or spoilt crop material to bulk out the fodder or fuel. There were, however, a lack of charred mollusc shells, which has been proposed as an indicator of turf burning (Murphy 2003). Charred stems, on the other hand, were found in multiple Roman samples from SPE03, SPE04, and SMR17. Overall, the data point towards spatial and temporal variation in agricultural activities and local environs during the early and mid-Roman period. In the early Roman period at SPE03 (Fen Edge) there is some indication that crops were being produced locally and hay meadows harvested, with both activities occurring on dry lands.

There is also evidence of agriculture taking place in the marshy landscape surrounding the sites in the northern half of the Scheme, with evidence for the cultivation of spelt supplemented by barley and oat. Spelt would have had multiple uses, being principally used in the production of flour and for brewing beer, with the presence of detached coleoptiles and embryos indicating that crops may have been stored on site, perhaps in damp conditions that lead to spoilage. There is no evidence to suggest that crops were being grown on soils with a significant saline influence, which would be likely to have resulted in a preference for barley and a greater presence of salt-tolerant plants in the weed assemblage. Cereal agriculture is likely to have been supported by the cultivation of horticultural plants, including legumes, and the utilisation of wild plants and exotic imports, with seeds of coriander (*Coriandrum sativum*) and possible dill/fennel (*Anethum/Foeniculum*) recovered, in addition to wild carrot (*Daucus carota*), bramble (*Rubus* sp.), and fragments of hazelnut shell.

There is evidence to indicate that attempts were being made to improve the fertility of the soil from the mid-Roman period onwards, perhaps in order to expand arable agriculture more widely. Seeds of nitrophilous plants, such as common nettle and henbane, were recovered from deposits of middle and late Roman date in fenland and marsh areas and are likely to be indicators for nutrient-rich soils. Whether these are the result of arable management or due to the presence of grazing livestock is unclear. During the Roman period, the practice of manuring was widespread as a means of restoring soils depleted by intensive farming, as well as improving the working properties and boosting drainage. Leguminous plants were also found in the charred assemblage and may be linked to improved soil quality.

These assessed assemblages were comparable to those from other Romano-British sites in the Lincolnshire Fenland (*e.g.* Giorgi 1998; 2000; Lane and Morris 2001; Rayner *et al.* 2003). The saltmarshes of the Lincolnshire coast are dynamic and ecologically sensitive environments, characterised by varying water levels and a rich diversity of plant life, and influenced by historical marine regressions and flooding during the middle–late Holocene period (Green 2023b). This distinct habitat likely served as a valuable resource for Roman inhabitants, supporting local salt production and providing fertile soils for the cultivation of crops and the raising of livestock. Adapting to the challenges of living and working in such a diverse and ever-changing environment was likely a fundamental aspect of daily life for Fenland communities during this period (Fryer and Turner 2024).

The role of animals at Roman settlements
Marina Chorro-Giner and Hannah Russ

A total of 8303 fragments of animal bone were recovered from Roman features and deposits within the excavated sites, with most of them dating to the middle Roman (57.7% by count, n=4788) and late Roman (34.4% by count, n=2859) periods. A small portion of the Roman assemblage (n=355 fragments) could only be attributed to the Roman period more broadly (AD 43–410) (Fig. 4.20). This material is not included in further discussions. A comparison of the assemblages and the wider regional context provides an opportunity to better understand animal roles and human-animal relationships at Roman period settlement sites, looking at trends in human diet as well as agricultural practices at the sites during this time.

In the last major review of archaeological sites in the East Midlands (Cooper 2006), it was recognised that evidence for this area was relatively sparse compared with southern regions of England. While many sites have been excavated since that review took place, the general pattern that fewer sites in the East Midlands have been excavated remains. In 2019, a review of animal bone from archaeological sites in the Midlands recorded 31-40 archaeological sites of any period in Lincolnshire, <0.005 sites per km² (Albarella 2019, 14–15), nine of these were dated to the Roman period (Albarella 2019, 100). Moreover, the animal bone assemblages from Roman period sites in the East Midlands tended to be smaller than those in the rest of the Midlands and in southern England. This means that the large assemblage recovered as part of the Scheme is highly significant in contributing to further understanding the role of animals in human diet, economy and lives of people living in Lincolnshire during the Roman period but that comparative sites were few; drawn from Lincolnshire, Leicestershire, and Northamptonshire.

Early Roman (AD 43–100)

Animal bone from features and deposits dating to the early Roman period (AD 43–100) were only recovered from the sites between Sibsey and Bicker Fen (Fen Edge and Inland Fen Edge Landscape Parcels). The assemblages were broadly similar with cattle as the dominant domestic taxon followed by sheep/goat. In the early Roman period, there was a notable switch from sheep to cattle-dominated husbandry in the region, for example at Nettleton and Rothwell (Rackham 2013) and Cowbit (Albarella and Mulville 2001) in Lincolnshire. This change is also seen in the wider East Midlands region, like, for example, at Redlands Farm (Davis 1997). While there was insufficient data for pigs and sheep/goat, differences in the age at death for cattle were identified between the sites. At SMR01/TAM04; age at death for cattle, calculated based on epiphyseal fusion, indicates that most animals were killed in the first and second year of their lives which is consistent with slaughter ages expected where meat is the primary resource being exploited. However, a small number of cattle were kept beyond the age expected for meat production and these could represent animals kept for traction, milk, or breeding purposes. Age at death for cattle remains from SPE03, SPE04, and SMR17 was estimated based on tooth eruption and wear and suggested that cattle were being kept to an age of over 5 years, which is well beyond the optimum for meat production. Skeletal element representation for cattle indicated a prevalence of forelimb elements over those of the hindlimb, perhaps suggesting that hindlimb joints of meat were taken away for trade or sale; the recovered cattle teeth and foot elements indicate that whole carcasses were present and overall waste from both primary and secondary butchery were represented. However, the assemblage is small, and interpretation should be considered tentative.

Middle Roman (AD 100–250)

The largest proportion of animal bones from Roman period activity was recovered from features and deposits dated to the middle Roman period (AD 100–250). Overall, cattle were the most common domesticate identified in the Fen Edge and Inland Fen Edge Landscape Parcels

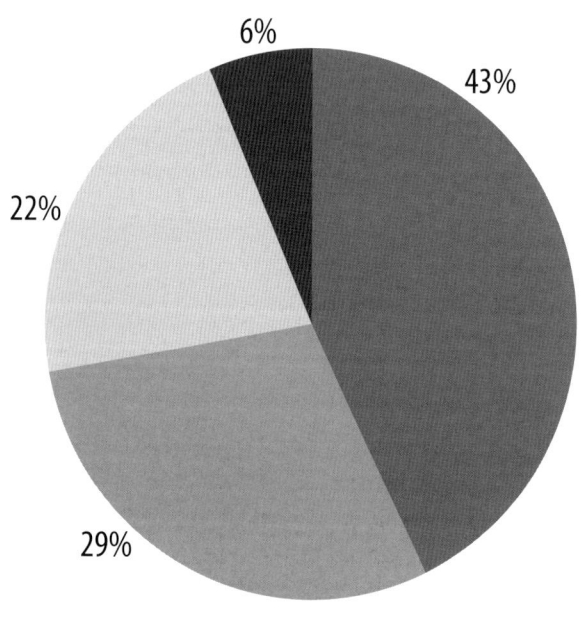

Figure 4.20 Comparative chart of the animal bone assemblages (by fragment count) of the Coastal, Lincolnshire Marsh, Fen Edge, and Inland Fen Edge Landscape Parcels

followed by sheep/goat, many, if not all of which, were sheep (Table 4.5). As previously seen in the early Roman period, cattle-dominated husbandry is expected for the Roman period and can be seen in different sites around the area. The analysis of age at death and skeletal parts present revealed notable patterns at both Fen Edge and Inland Fen Edge sites including the slaughter of neonate and infant cattle at these locations, which could be linked to dairying and/or veal consumption. The consumption of young animals was also noted in the pig remains from Fen Edge where evidence of neonatal mortality could be related to the consumption of suckling pigs (this may also represent naturally occurring deaths at or shortly after birth). The other cattle remains from the Fen Edge indicate that animals were slaughtered at an age consistent with meat exploitation. At both, most skeletal elements were recorded, indicating that whole carcasses were present at the sites, and so primary and secondary butchery occurred as well as kitchen and table waste. Some animals survived into old age (10–14 years), which might represent traction animals. The mixed role of cattle during the Roman period was also suggested at Dragonby (Harman 1996), Lincolnshire, and Stretton Road, Leicestershire (Browning 2015), where they were kept for meat and traction. The ageing data for equids also indicates they were kept for traction and travel.

The age of death for sheep indicates that at Fen Edge most were slaughtered before their second year, with only a small number surviving into late adulthood (around 10 years of age). This pattern is consistent with that expected when dairying is the primary role for sheep, with meat (lamb and mutton) and wool being secondary resources, *i.e.* a mixed husbandry regime. However, at the Inland Fen Edge sites, the pattern suggests a mixed economy focused on meat production as there is some infant mortality, with animals being slaughtered between 6 and 12 months of age, but with most slaughtered consistently at two or three years, and some surviving into late adulthood (5–10 years). The assemblage contained selected elements, with mandibles being the most common, suggesting animals may have been butchered for consumption elsewhere.

The assemblages also included wild animals such as deer, birds, fish, and marine molluscs. The presence of roe deer (*Capreolus capreolus*) and possible red deer (*Cervus elaphus*) recovered from the farmsteads of the Fen Edge and Inland Fen Edge Landscape Parcels is notable. Roe and red deer are expected from Roman sites in Britain with the small numbers representing hunting or scavenging activity for resources. No antler was recovered at any of the Triton Knoll sites, with deer instead being represented by skeletal elements which may suggest very occasional hunting of deer for their meat, adding venison as a rare part of the human diet. Red and roe deer were also recovered at Overstone (Harman 1976), Clay Lane (Jones *et al.* 1985), Dragonby (Harman 1996), and Redlands Farm (Davis 1997).

The inclusion of wildfowl in the diet was also noted with duck comprising part of the assemblage, although it is unknown whether they represented domestic animals or birds hunted in the surrounding landscape. The bird remains also included chicken and pheasant, with the overall species range being typical for Roman sites in Britain. However, it is more common for chicken to be the most common species, which is not the case at Triton Knoll. Chicken has been known to be the only identified bird species at some Roman period sites, such as Clay Lane (Jones *et al.* 1985), but it is more usual to find bird bone assemblages that also include ducks and/or geese alongside chickens, which was the case at Wakerley (Jones 1978), Nettleton and Rothwell (Rackham 2013), and Stretton Road (Browning 2015). Pheasant has been a difficult bird to understand in terms of establishing a precise date for its introduction in Britain and its subsequent spread and population size across Britain. It is thought that it was introduced during the Roman period; pinpointing a specific introduction date has been impeded by the osteological similarity between domestic fowl/chicken and pheasants, the two species being closely related within the Galliformes order (Cooper *et al.* 2022).

The fish remains suggest that fishing took place in freshwater and/or estuarine environments rather than marine; while the European eel (*Anguilla anguilla*) can be found in marine environments during some stages of its life cycle it is usually caught in its freshwater phase or during its migration to the sea for breeding. The flounder can tolerate low levels of salinity and is found in estuaries and rivers some distance inland. Marine mollusc shells were only present at SMR01/TAM04 with these species expected at Roman period sites in Britain, where oyster is typically the most frequently recovered taxa, followed by mussel (*e.g.* Cool 2006), with other species such as cockle also known to have been consumed. However, it is interesting that they were only present at SMR01/TAM04, rather than any site closer to the sea. This potentially supports evidence for established trade connections with coastal areas for the transportation and trade of these dietary resources.

The remains of dogs (some of which have the potential to represent red fox (*Vulpes vulpes*) rather than domestic dog) were rare across the sites. Dog remains are common at Roman period sites across Britain including those located close to the Triton Knoll sites, including Wakerley, Northamptonshire (Jones 1978), Billingborough (Chowne *et al.* 2001) and Cowbit (Albarella and Mulville 2001) in Lincolnshire, and Stretton Road, Leicestershire (Browning 2015). During the Roman period dogs served as herding animals, pest control, guard animals, hunting aids, companion animals, as status symbols, and played roles in ritual activities (*e.g.* Bellis 2020). 'Dwarf' and miniature dogs also appear in Britain for the first time during the late Iron Age–Roman period (Baxter 2006; 2010; Bennett and Timm 2016, Bennett *et al.* 2016).

Table 4.5 Presence/absence of identified taxa for the middle Roman period

Identified taxa	Domesticates							Deer		Bird			Fish					Mol.	Micro-fauna		
	Cattle	Sheep/Goat	Equid	Pig	Canid (dog/fox)	Canis familiaris	Domestic cat (Felis catus)	roe deer (Capreolus capreolus)	possible red deer (Cervus elaphus)	mallard/duck (Anas platyrhynchos)	domestic fowl/chicken (Gallus gallus domesticus)	pheasant (Phasianus colchicus)	Flatfish (European plaice (Pleuronectes platessa)	European flounder (Platichthys flesus)	common dab (Limanda limanda)	northern pike (Esox lucius)	European eel	Marine Mollusc	Mouse/small vole (Mus sp./Apodemus sp./Myodes sp./Microtus sp.)	Frog/toad (Anura)	Snake (Serpentes)
Coastal	■	■	■	■														■			
Lincolnshire Marsh	■	■		■	■					■	■		■	■	■				■	■	■
Fen Edge	■	■		■	■						■					■	■	■			
Inland Fen Edge	■	■		■																	

Late Roman (AD 250–410)

In total, 2859 fragments of animal bone were recovered from late Roman features and deposits (AD 250–410) across the four Landscape Parcels. The main domesticates (equid, cattle, pig, and sheep/goat) are present in all Landscape Parcels (Table 4.6). When considering minimum number of individuals (MNI) values, which are less affected by taphonomic and recovery biases, the proportions of cattle and sheep present at the sites shift in favour of caprines (sheep/goat). This shift back to a more sheep dominated husbandry seems to begin in the late Roman period throughout Britain (King 1999). The Landscape Parcels show very similar patterns for the exploitation and husbandry of sheep, with some infant mortality present but, overall, most animals slaughtered between their second and fourth years and a few surviving until they are 8–10 years. This is consistent with a mixed husbandry exploitation in which meat, wool, and milk were exploited. The husbandry regimes evidenced at the sites during the Roman period compare well with those seen at other contemporary sites in the region; both cattle and sheep from Nettleton and Rothwell (Rackham 2013) in Lincolnshire appear to have been kept following the same mixed regime with exploitation of both primary and secondary resources, while at Redlands Farm, Northamptonshire (Davis 1997) it seems that sheep were kept primarily for wool and milk.

There are differences observed in the cattle assemblages from the Coastal, Fen Edge, and Inland Fen Edge Landscape Parcels. On average, the cattle remains from the Coastal Landscape Parcel represented animals that died at a younger age, including some that died during their first 7 months, with almost 20% having died by 1 year of age; most of the animals appear to have been slaughtered between their first and third year with few surviving into their fourth year. This infant mortality pattern might suggest that a portion of the herd was kept primarily for dairying, where young male cattle are culled as they are surplus to requirement in dairying herds. However, cattle were almost certainly also used for meat, either after their primary dairying function had been surpassed, or as a mixed economy herd where dairy and meat production herds were simultaneously kept. It should be noted, however, that only epiphyseal fusion data were available for cattle from the Coastal Landscape Parcel, which may have biased the data. In opposition, in the Inland Fen Edge Landscape Parcel, cattle were surviving to much older ages, with epiphyseal fusion data showing that all animals survived into their third year, with some surviving until their fourth, but most being slaughtered in their second or third years. The dental wear data from the Inland Fen Edge, however, give a different age at death profile, with half of the specimens recorded being 8–18 months at death and the remainder 10–14 years of age. This may be due to low sample size but, combining both datasets, most cattle died between their second and fourth year with few surviving until late adulthood (>10 years). In this case, we could be seeing the exploitation of these animals for dairy and traction as well as meat. Almost all elements are present including skulls, carpals, tarsals, and first phalanges. The high proportions of low meat-bearing elements often removed during the primary stages of butchery observed at the Inland Fen Edge indicate the presence of whole carcasses at the site, with disposal of these low meat-bearing elements at the location. Despite this, it is clear that some high meat-bearing elements remained at the site, suggesting that at least some of the beef butchered at the Inland Fen Edge was also consumed there but that some fore- and hindlimb joints were taken elsewhere for trade, sale, and/or consumption. Evidence from Roman sites within Lincolnshire shows that it was usual for different butchery activities to be taking place at different locations, for example, at Dragonby (Harman 1996) and Billinborough (Chowne *et al.* 2001), all elements were present, interpreted as primary butchery, while at Clay Lane (Jones *et al.* 1985) and Stretton Road (Browning 2015) secondary butchery is interpreted for both cattle and sheep.

The assemblages of pig and equid remains were considerably smaller than those for cattle and sheep. For pigs at the Inland Fen Edge the humerus was the most common element, likely resulting from kitchen/food waste since humeri are one of the high meat-bearing elements of a pig. Metapodials and phalanges could be linked to consumption of 'pig feet', though it is not possible to distinguish this activity from the discard of these elements which would generally be regarded as low meat-bearing. It was interesting that pig skulls were absent; pig skulls produce the highest quantity of edible muscle when compared with cattle and sheep/goat and, as a result, might not be discarded at as an early stage of butchery (Jones 1978). Their absence from these locations remains unexplained. For equids, epiphyseal fusion data suggests that breeding may have been occurring at the Inland Fen Edge sites. Neonatal and infant remains were recovered, with most of the animals dying within their first year, and only some surviving until they were older than 3 years. While the use of epiphyseal fusion data for estimating age at death for equids is limited due to the completion of fusion at around 3.5 years, after which no further age estimation can be attempted, it is expected that animals surviving until 3.5 years of age likely continued to live into late adulthood, serving as transportation and/or traction animals, and this is supported by tooth wear data from the Inland Fen Edge, which indicate that some individuals were surviving to 20–40 years of age.

There are distinctions identifiable in the presence or absence of wild game and other animals such as birds, fish, and marine molluscs. This suggests that while the

Table 4.6 Presence/absence of identified taxa for the late Roman period

Identified taxa	Domesticates				Deer	Bird		Fish					Mol.	Micro Fauna		
	Cattle	Sheep/Goat	Equid	Pig	Red deer (*Cervus elaphus*)	Mallard/duck (*Anas platyrhynchos*)	Domestic fowl/chicken (*Gallus gallus domesticus*)	Haddock (*Melanogrammus*) *aeglefinus*)	European eel	Atlantic herring (*Clupea harengus*)	salmon/trout (*Salmo sp.*)	flatfish (*Pleuronectidae*)	Marine Mollusc	Mouse/small vole (*Mus sp./Apodemus sp./Myodes sp./Microtus sp.*)	Frog/toad (*Anura*)	Snake (*Serpentes*)
Coastal																
Lincolnshire Marsh																
Fen Edge																
Inland Fen Edge																

main meat aspect of the human diet was comparable between the sites, the resources supplementing meat from domestic livestock animals varied. Red deer were only identified on the Inland Fen Edge, which could point to the continuity of wild game exploitation since deer were also exploited on a small scale during the middle Roman period. There also seems to be continuity in the species of birds exploited during the late Roman period. Ducks were identified in both the Fen Edge and Inland Fen Edge, while chickens were only found at the Inland Fen Edge. However, it seems that birds were a less important resource in the late Roman period.

Fish remains were only recovered from the Inland Fen Edge and Lincolnshire Marsh Landscape Parcels, with the larger assemblage recovered from the latter. It is interesting that only one marine species is found in the Inland Fen Edge, but this is also consistent with the fact that this is the only landscape parcel in which marine molluscs are found both in the middle and late Roman periods, further demonstrating the established trade and communication networks between this site and the coast. The haddock remains from the Inland Fen Edge represent two cleithra (skull fragments), one of which had a cutmark. The cleithrum is a common bone on which to find cutmarks since its position in the head of the fish means it is usually damaged during head removal. Interestingly, the only fish bone recovered from Billingborough was a haddock cleithrum (Chowne *et al.* 2001, 80), two of which were recovered as the only fish remains from the Inland Fen Edge (from late Roman deposits). This bone is particularly dense, as it naturally exhibits hyperostosis, and perhaps as a result survives preferentially over other fish remains. The use of this bone as a raw material in artefact production is known for later periods (*e.g.* Batey 2005), as such it is possible that the presence of this bone specifically is evidence for the retention or differential treatment of this element due to its value as a raw material. Marine mollusc shell was also only recovered from the Inland Fen Edge, representing edible oyster and common cockle (*Cerastoderma edule*) species consistent with those expected during the late Roman period. What is interesting is the fact that they must have been brought to the sites intentionally, probably along with the haddock remains (see above).

Grazing and grain: Isotopic analysis

Michael Wallace, with contributions and data analysis from Derek Hamilton, Kerry Sayle, Steven Brookes, and Christine Stockton

Stable isotope analysis was undertaken on crop grain remains and livestock faunal remains from the Triton Knoll project (Tables 4.7 and 4.8). Stable isotope ratios are influenced by the life history of organisms and, as such, provides novel insights into both the environmental conditions, and husbandry practices experienced by past crops and livestock (Fiorentino *et al.* 2015; Szpak 2022). Full details on the analytical methodology are provided in the Lincolnshire Marsh Landscape Parcel Collection available as part of the ADS archive. Stable carbon isotope ratios are measured as $\delta^{13}C$ values (per mil), and in the case of plant-samples the results may be converted to $\Delta^{13}C$ values to account for changes in atmospheric CO_2 (Ferrio *et al.* 2005a), whilst stable nitrogen isotope ratios are always measured as $\delta^{15}N$ values.

Crops and animals reared in the Inland Fen Edge Landscape Parcel are expected to be typical of other stable isotope evidence for Roman Britain. The stable isotope record for Roman Britain is still modest in scale, and it largely comprises inland, terrestrial sites. For the Fen Edge and Lincolnshire Marsh Landscape Parcels, the influence of waterlogged soils may be detectable. In the marshes and coastal areas soil salinity may be an important factor, including an increased prevalence of C_4 plants. It is noted at the outset, however, that crop products or livestock may have been moved from the place of their growth to their place of deposition.

Results

CROPS

Evaluation of data quality for the stable isotopes values (Reed and Wallace 2024; Styring *et al.* 2024) by examining the C:N molar ratio and the stable isotope values of untreated and pre-treated pairs, indicates some evidence of diagenesis. The narrower, and more normal, distribution of C:N ratio values for pre-treated samples may indicate that untreated samples were subjected to varying degrees of contamination (Fig. 4.21), which is unsurprising given the diversity of environments sampled. Accordingly, only data from pre-treated samples are used here and, while these samples may not be ideal candidates for stable isotope analysis, interpretations based off their stable isotope data are likely to be sound.

The $\Delta^{13}C$ values for the wheat grains fall between 16.1‰ and 18.8‰ (Table 4.9). These span the moderately-watered through to beyond the well-watered bands based on experimental crop growing (Araus *et al.* 1997;

Table 4.7 Archaeobotanical samples subjected to stable isotope analysis

Landscape	Area	Sample	Context	Period	Taxon	Material
Fen Edge	SPE03	016	30287/8	Early Roman	Spelt/bread	7 grains
Lincolnshire Marsh	SMR06	005	0026	Late Roman	Emmer/spelt	8 grains
		009	0032		Spelt/bread	9 grains
		012	0089		Emmer/spelt	6 grains
Coastal	SMR01	004	0032	Late Roman	Spelt/bread	4 grains
	SPE01	011	0423	Roman	Bread type	4 grains
		011	0423	Roman	Spelt type	7 grains

Table 4.8 Archaeozoological samples subjected to stable isotope analysis

Landscape Parcel	Area	Context	Period	Taxon	Mandibular bone samples	Age stage	M3 tooth increments
Inland Fen Edge	SMR01	0564	Middle Roman	*Bos*	1	Adult	4
		0580	Middle Roman	*Bos*	1	Old adult	4
Fen Edge	SPE03	30204	Early Roman	*Bos*	1	Senile	4
		30404	Middle Roman	*Bos*	1	Old adult	4
	SPE04	44265	Middle Roman	*Bos*	2	Senile	4
Lincolnshire Marsh	SMR06	0025	Late Roman	*Bos*	1	Indet.	4

NB: aging data was supplied by Hannah Russ

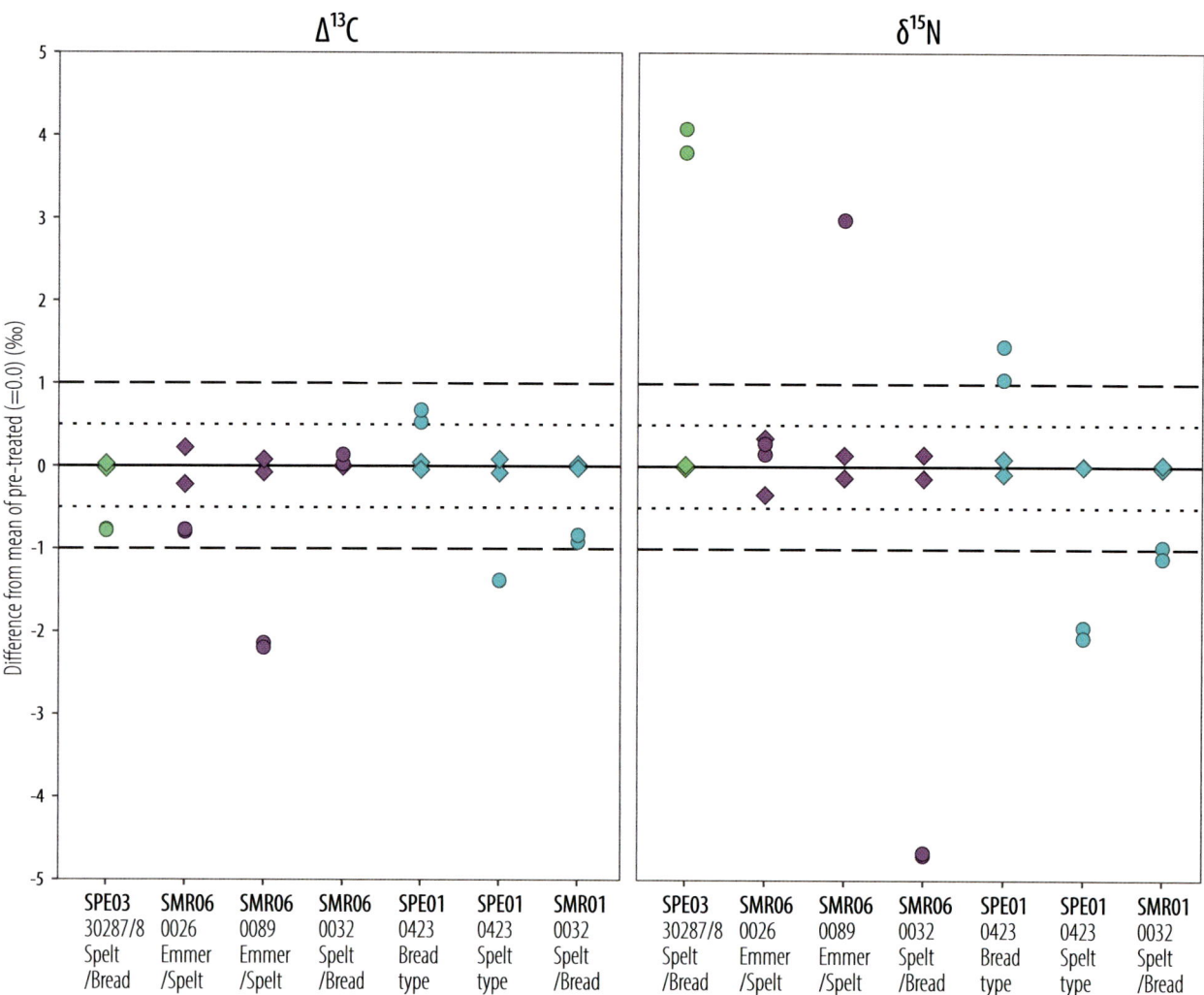

Figure 4.21 Comparison of untreated and pre-treated analysed charred grain samples. Results have been normalised to mean of each sample's pre-treated samples, such that deviation from zero indicates the difference between an individual analysis and the value used in the analysis. Left panel: $\Delta^{13}C$ values. Right panel: $\delta^{15}N$ values. Colour denotes Landscape Parcel: green = Fen Edge, purple = Lincolnshire Marsh, blue = Coastal. Shape denotes whether an individual analysis was of pre-treated grain or not: circles = untreated, diamonds = ABA pre-treated. Samples within ±0.5‰ (within the dotted lines) represent a small deviation from the pre-treatment mean; samples within ±1‰ (within the dashed lines) represent a moderate deviation from the mean; samples >1‰ different from the mean represent a major difference from the mean used in interpretation

Wallace *et al.* 2013). One Coastal sample (SPE01 0423 bread-type) has a value close to 19‰, which is unusually high for charred wheat grains. The four samples from the Fen Edge and Lincolnshire Marsh Landscape Parcels span 16.7–18.0‰, which is a high degree of variability but all exhibit high $\Delta^{13}C$ values consistent with wetter conditions. The three samples from the Coastal Landscape Parcel exhibit even greater variation, spanning a range of 2.7‰. Such a high range from just three samples indicates that these crops grew in varied conditions.

The stable nitrogen isotope values for the wheat grains typically fall between 8.8‰ and 11.8‰. One sample, from the Lincolnshire Marsh, has a lower value, at 6.6‰ and another has a higher value of 17.0‰, also from the Lincolnshire Marsh. Taking the main group of five of the seven samples, their range is much narrower at 3%. The lower value (SMR06 0089 emmer/spelt) is conceivable at the lower end of the same growing conditions that produced the majority of results. If reliable, the sample with an exceptionally high $\delta^{15}N$ value (SMR06 0032 spelt/bread) is unlikely to be grown in comparable conditions (the untreated grains have more comparable $\delta^{15}N$ values, but these are excluded as discussed above). There is no apparent taxonomic dimension to the distribution of results, nor is there in terms of chronology (Fig. 4.22).

LIVESTOCK

Bulk isotope analysis: For animal collagen samples, the likeliness of diagenetic contamination is lower and all the samples fell within an acceptable C:N range.

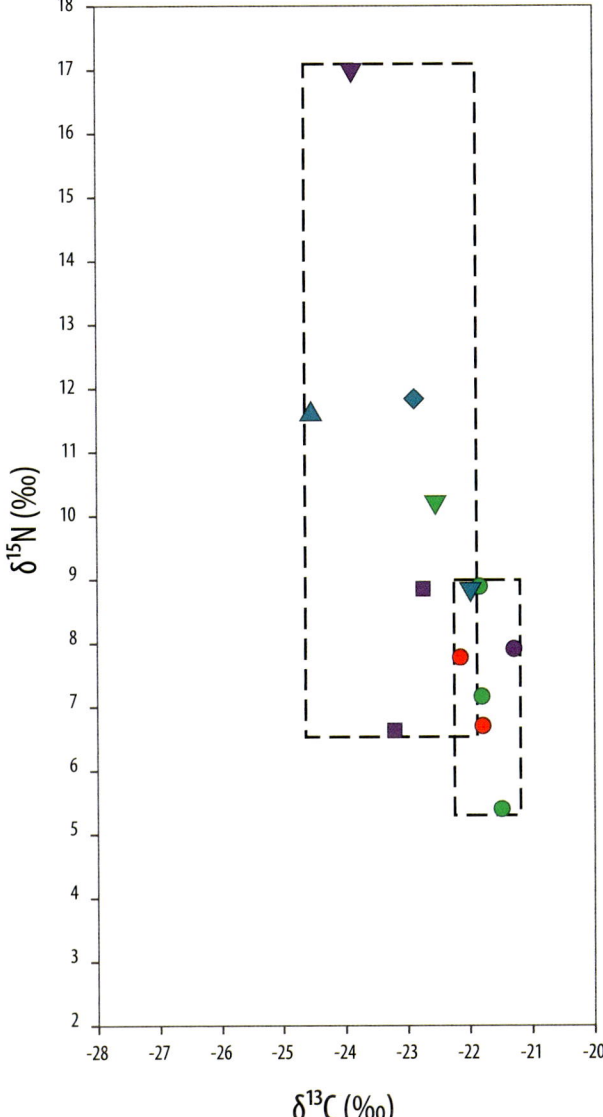

Figure 4.22 Results of Δ¹³C and δ¹⁵N analysis of charred wheat grain and cattle mandibular bone. Colour denotes Landscape Parcel: red = Inland Fen Edge, green = Fen Edge, purple = Lincolnshire Marsh, blue = Coastal. Shape denotes taxon: circle = cattle, square = emmer/spelt, diamond = spelt, downward triangle = spelt/bread, upward triangle = bread-type. Dashed line rectangles are bounding boxes for the range of δ¹³C and δ¹⁵N values for crops and cattle

The analysis of cattle mandibular bone produced $\delta^{13}C$ results in a narrow band between –21.7‰ and –22.2‰ (Table 4.10). This lack of variation is consistent with cattle reared in comparable conditions. The absolute value (mean –21.9‰) indicates consumption of a terrestrial diet in Britain. The three samples from Fen Edge have the higher values (mean –21.8‰) than those from the Inland Fen Edge and Lincolnshire Marsh Landscape Parcels (mean –22.1‰); this difference is statistically significant (t-test, t = –5, df = 3.2, p = 0.01), but the sample size is very small (n = 6).

Cattle mandibular bone $\delta^{15}N$ values ranges from 5.4‰ to 7.8‰. This range is also consistent with single herd reared in unvaried conditions. Only one sample has a $\delta^{15}N$ value below 7‰, and this is from the Fen Edge (SPE04, 44265). The Fen Edge actually spans the $\delta^{15}N$ range, producing bone with the lowest and highest $\delta^{15}N$ values.

Incremental stable isotope analysis (Figs 4.23 and 4.24): The teeth of cattle generally form from the tip to the base though this formation is not linear. The implication for stable isotope analysis is that increments from nearer the top of the tooth form earlier than nearer the base, and therefore isotope composition nearer the tooth tip represents an early stage during the tooth formation period. For cattle, the M3 forms over an animal's second year of life and so the isotope data from across the length of the M3 reflects that year. Teeth are, however, subject to wear which may have resulted in some loss of tooth matter and as this wear occurs at the tip it may shorten the earlier part of the time span recorded by the tooth. All the aged mandibles were over 3 years old and so the M3 should be fully formed. As two of the samples were from senile aged cattle, for these at least some loss of tooth due to wear is likely (Table 4.10).

The two cattle from the Inland Fen Edge exhibit minimal variation in $\delta^{13}C$ values across their four increments. The dentine $\delta^{13}C$ values are also comparable to those of their mandibular bone. In combination, these results indicate that the animals did not experience any marked change in their diet during their second year of life. The animal from the Lincolnshire Marsh has comparable dentine $\delta^{13}C$ values to those of the inland cattle. In the cases of the Lincolnshire Marsh animal, however, there is a c. 0.8‰ difference between the dentine and the mandibular bone. This animal, therefore, may have experienced a dietary change between its second year of life (represented by the dentine) and the last couple of years before death (represented by the bone).

The $\delta^{13}C$ incremental data for the Fen Edge Landscape Parcel is somewhat different to the inland and marshes areas. In all three cattle specimens from the Fen Edge the mandibular bone is within the bounds of fairly varied dentine increments. This indicates that the at-death diet of the animal was comparable to the second year of life. It also means that these animals experienced greater dietary variation than the other three. In all the Fen Edge cases, at least one increment elevated, to around –21‰, above the typical values for these animals (c. –22‰).

The $\delta^{15}N$ incremental data shows that four of the animals (those from Inland Fen Edge and Lincolnshire Marsh, plus SPE03 30204 from the Fen Edge) have fairly flat variation in dentine $\delta^{15}N$ values, which align closely to the $\delta^{15}N$ value from their mandibular bone. The remaining two animals tell different stories. SPE03 44265 initially has $\delta^{15}N$ values comparable (*i.e.* c. 7‰ to 8‰) to the other animals, but

Table 4.9 Summary results for stable isotope analysis of crops samples. In all cases the value shown is a mean

Sample details			Untreated				Pre-treated			
Landscape Parcel	Sample	Taxon	$\delta^{13}C$ (‰)	$\Delta^{13}C$ (‰)	$\delta^{15}N$ (‰)	C:N	$\delta^{13}C$ (‰)	$\Delta^{13}C$ (‰)	$\delta^{15}N$ (‰)	C:N
Fen Edge	016	Spelt/Bread	−23.3	17.5	14.1	10.9	−22.5	16.7	10.2	17.1
Lincolnshire Marshes	005	Emmer/Spelt	−23.5	17.7	9.1	18.5	−22.7	16.9	8.9	15.9
	009	Spelt/Bread	−23.8	18.0	12.3	19.4	−23.9	18.0	17.0	18.9
	012	Emmer/Spelt	−25.4	19.6	9.6	16.9	−23.2	17.4	6.6	15.6
Coastal	011	Bread type	−23.9	18.1	12.9	13.4	−24.5	18.8	11.6	15.4
	011	Spelt type	−24.3	18.5	9.8	20.2	−22.9	17.0	11.8	15.9
	004	Spelt/Bread	−22.9	17.0	7.8	21.2	−22.0	16.1	8.8	18.7

Table 4.10 Summary results of stable isotope analysis of faunal remains. Values shown are mean unless stated to be a minimum (Min.) or maximum (Max.)

Sample details			Mandibular bone		Dentine increments			
Landscape Parcel	Area	Context	$\delta^{13}C$ (‰)	$\delta^{15}N$ (‰)	Min. $\delta^{13}C$ (‰)	Max. $\delta^{13}C$ (‰)	Min. $\delta^{15}N$ (‰)	Max $\delta^{15}N$ (‰)
Inland Fen Edge	SMR01	0564	−21.8	6.7	−22.2	−22.0	6.6	7.6
		0580	−22.1	7.8	−22.4	−22.1	7.1	8.1
Fen Edge	SPE04	44265	−21.5	5.4	−22.2	−21.2	5.2	7.4
	SPE03	30204	−21.8	7.2	−22.2	−21.1	7.7	8.4
		30404	−21.8	8.9	−22.4	−21.2	4.8	9.4
Lincolnshire Marshes	SMR06	0025	−21.3	7.9	−22.4	−22.0	7.3	8.3

one increment is considerably lower at around 5‰, which is similar to its mandibular bone. This indicates a substantial drop in dietary $\delta^{15}N$ in the animal's final years, which encompasses the last part of the animal's second year. For SPE03 30404, the $\delta^{15}N$ values are initially below the norm, but then rise steeply to slightly above the norm. In this case, as was the case for the previous, the final increment $\delta^{15}N$ value is comparable to the mandibular bone.

Discussion

CROP HUSBANDRY REGIMES

The most striking aspect of the crop stable isotope data is the high degree of variability between the samples. There are substantial differences in the $\delta^{15}N$ and, to a lesser degree, the $\delta^{13}C$ values of the different cereal grains. Variation in $\delta^{13}C$ may be greater in the Coastal Land Parcel, and $\delta^{15}N$ values seem most varied in the Lincolnshire Marsh Landscape Parcel, but the small sample size means it is difficult to compare areas with confidence. The samples were also variable in terms of their level of contamination based on the pre-treatment results, again with no apparent pattern to which samples exhibited the greater or lesser contamination. Nevertheless, restricting data analysis to only samples that were pre-treated means that the variation in isotope values may be assumed to be a genuine reflection of variation in growing conditions. In such a case, it must be inferred that these crops do not derive from a consistent, singular crop husbandry regime applied in the same kinds of environmental conditions.

The $\delta^{13}C$ (or $\Delta^{13}C$ to account for changes in atmospheric CO_2) are affected by environmental factors that influence stomatal conductance and this can provide a link to inferring water availability (Farquhar and Richards 1984; Araus et al. 1997; Ferrio et al. 2007; Wallace et al. 2013; 2015). In Britain, however, water management is unlikely to be a major component of crop husbandry regimes and it is likely that a myriad of other environmental factors could also influence stable carbon isotope ratios in plant remains. Natural variation in grain $\delta^{13}C$ within an ear can also be in the region of 0.5‰ (Heaton et al. 2009), and individual plants grown under similar conditions may vary by 1–2‰ (Heaton 1999). The range of $\delta^{13}C$ of the

4 Living near the edge: Settlement and agriculture in the Roman period

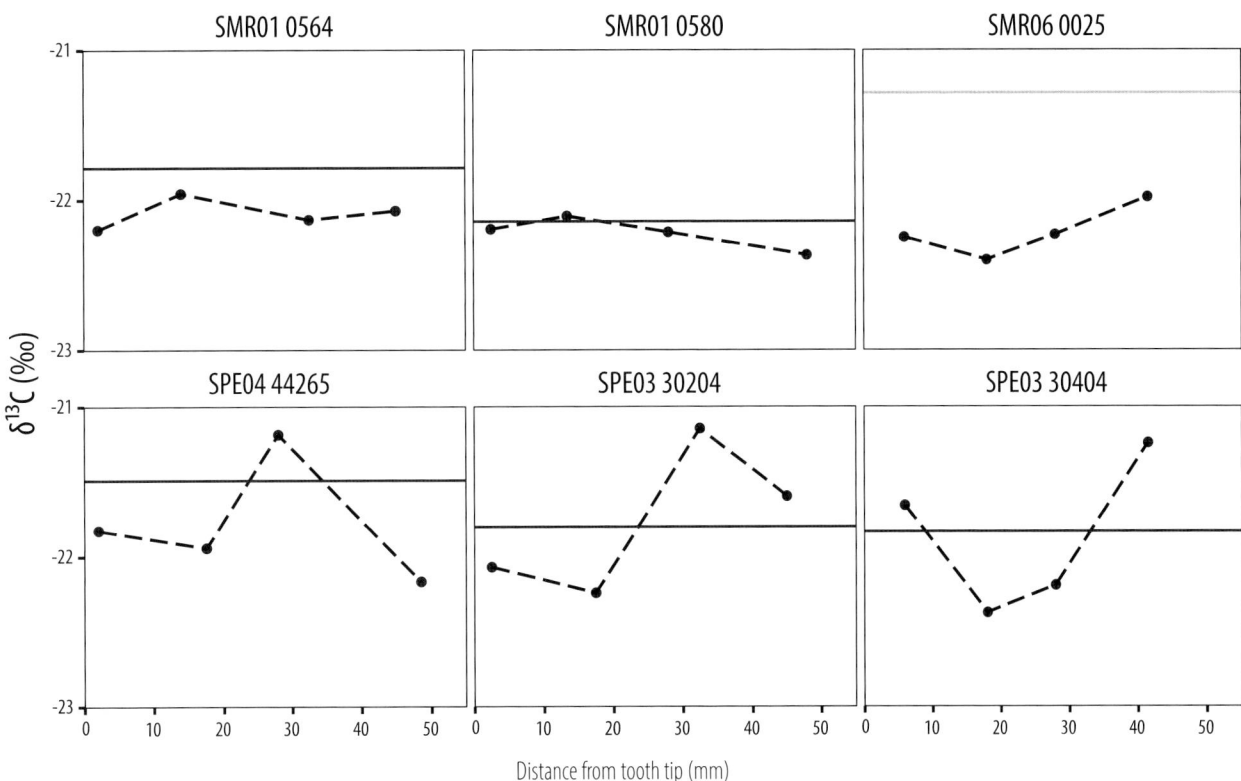

Figure 4.23 Results of $\delta^{13}C$ analysis of tooth increments. Each panel represents a single M_3 tooth. The $\delta^{13}C$ value for dentine at each increment is shown as dots joined by dashed lines. The x-axis represents the distance from the tip to the base of the tooth (i.e. from older to younger). The solid line denotes the $\delta^{13}C$ value of bone from the same mandible

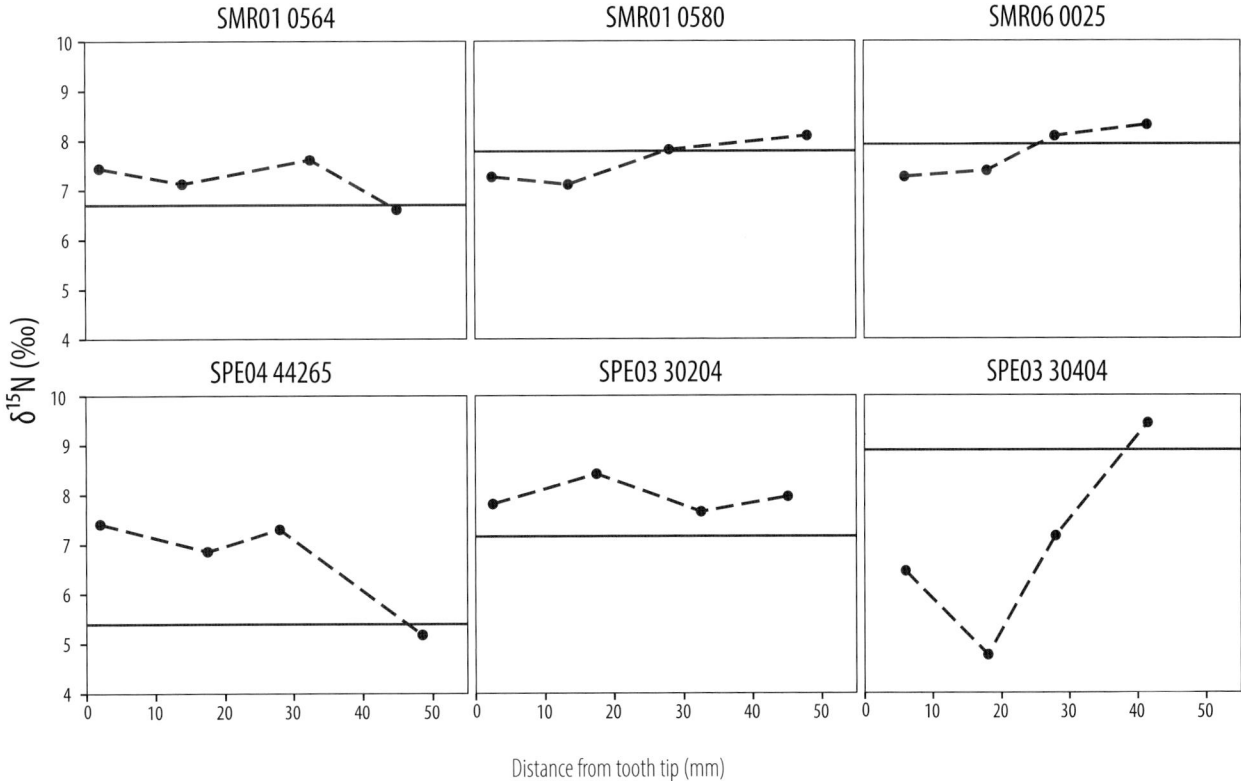

Figure 4.24 Results of $\delta^{15}N$ analysis of tooth increments. Each panel represents a single M_3 tooth. The $\delta^{15}N$ value for dentine at each increment is shown as dots joined by dashed lines. The x-axis represents the distance from the tip to the base of the tooth (i.e. from older to younger). The solid line denotes the $\delta^{15}N$ value of bone from the same mandible

Triton Knoll grains, despite the small sample size, exceeds this at 2.4‰. Stable carbon isotope evidence from other Romano-British sites is limited, but the δ¹³C range tends to be in the region of 0.5–1.0‰ (Lodwick et al. 2021; Lodwick 2023). The Triton Knoll results are, therefore, consistent with crops having been grown in a variety of distinct conditions, albeit these environs do not appear to map to the land parcels in which the grains were deposited or to taxa. The highest Δ¹³C values are from the Coastal and Lincolnshire Marsh Landscape Parcels, which indicates crops deposited in these areas were not exposed to high salinity soils (which would manifest as water stress).

The robustness of the link between water status and Δ¹³C (e.g. Araus et al. 1997; Wallace et al. 2013), which is based on experimental crop growing in semi-arid regions, in temperate Britain is uncertain but crops from other Romano-British sites – such as Stanwick, North Yorkshire (Lodwick et al. 2021) and the Dunkirt Barn, Hampshire and Grateley, Gloucester, villas (Lodwick 2023) – tend to have somewhat lower Δ¹³C values, of 16–17‰. One of the larger stable isotope studies for Britain was that of the A14, Cambridgeshire (Moore et al. 2023), which included crop samples from Roman rural settlements. On the A14 Δ¹³C values tended to span 16.5–17.5‰, which is more akin to the upper range of the Lincolnshire Marsh and Coastal Landscape Parcels. It can be inferred that past agricultural fields of the Triton Knoll inland land parcel were drier than those in the marshland and coastal land parcels as well as the fields exploited on the A14 scheme, which were likely located in fen-edge or river-edge places. Roman agriculturists were apparently prepared to utilise local, wet soils rather than import crop from farmers on drier lands. Albeit, they avoided constantly wet or saline affected soils. This corresponds to the well-attested favouring of spelt by the Romans, a wheat species that performs better on heavy and damp soils (Van der Veen 2014; Allen and Lodwick 2017). The high variation in the coastal area could be attributed to either the isotopically more varied conditions in coastal zones or the mixing of grain from coastal and non-coastal areas.

The variation in the δ¹⁵N values of wheat grains is even more pronounced than that for δ¹³C. The results span several trophic levels (= 3–5‰) and it is likely that these crops were grown in notably different conditions in terms of soil nitrogen content. It cannot, however, be assumed all crops were grown in soils with the same δ¹⁵N starting point. Soil δ¹⁵N can reasonably be assumed to range between 0‰ and 4‰ (Bakels 2019), but higher values are conceivable, and so this could account for some of the variability. Generally, elevated δ¹⁵N values in an arable context may indicate manuring (Fraser et al. 2011; Bogaard et al. 2013). Though other factors could cause increased δ¹⁵N values, those relevant to Triton Knoll include the bacterial action associated with waterlogged soils (Handley et al. 1999; Stroud 2022) and the role of salinity in saltmarshes (Cloern et al. 2002) and coastal lands (Heaton 1987). High δ¹⁵N values, however, do not relate directly to the Landscape Parcels with the greater availability of wet soils. The implication of this is that either conditions were variable – i.e. some waterlogged soils were present in all or most Landscape Parcels, but crops were not systematically grown on wet or dry soils – or crops were moved between the Landscape Parcels after harvest – and so their place of deposition and place of growth are not necessarily the same. The region around Triton Knoll was both diverse and highly dynamic and this dynamism may explain the high isotopic variability as arable fields may have been subjected to periodic flooding and salt influx.

The Triton Knoll crop δ¹⁵N values are ostensibly high, with values consistently above 6‰ and frequently much higher. For comparison, crops from Stanwick (Lodwick et al. 2021) and Grateley (Lodwick 2023) reached only as high as 6‰ and, at Dunkirt the δ¹⁵N values were yet lower at 1–3‰ (ibid.). On the A14, δ¹⁵N values for wheat were a little higher, roughly 6.5–8.5‰, and included some markedly higher specimens (Moore et al. 2023; Wallace et al. 2024) but, overall, the A14 results are lower than those from Triton Knoll. The high δ¹⁵N could plausibly be explained by manuring because similar values have been achieved experimentally (Fraser et al. 2011) but given that the values are higher than those seen from other Romano-British sites this indicates that either the Triton Knoll crops were manured to a far higher extent than elsewhere in Roman Britain or that waterlogged soils were contributing to increased δ¹⁵N values.

LIVESTOCK HUSBANDRY AND MOBILITY

The δ¹³C and δ¹⁵N values for the mandibular bone exhibit considerably less variation than seen for the crops. This may be in part due to the averaging effect of bone. The stable isotope values of crop grains largely reflect growing conditions during c. 6 weeks of grain filling, whilst bone isotope values reflect conditions throughout the bone turnover period of c. 2 years. Nevertheless, whilst the data indicate evidence for varied environments and practices influencing the small crop sample, in the case of the livestock there is no indication that any of the five animals were reared in manifestly different environments.

There is a substantial amount of stable carbon and stable nitrogen isotope data for cattle from Roman Britain (e.g. Britton et al. 2008; Chenery et al. 2010; Redfern et al. 2010; Müldner 2013). A consistent trend has emerged for inland sites, with cattle bone producing δ¹³C of < –21‰ to c. –22‰, and δ¹⁵N values between 5‰ and 7‰. In the case of Triton Knoll, the cattle data fall within the lower part of the δ¹³C range and the δ¹⁵N values are very slightly elevated from what is recorded elsewhere. Saltmarsh grazing has been previously detected in archaeological faunal remains by elevated $\delta^{13}C$ values (c. >–21‰) and $\delta^{15}N$ values (c. >7‰) (Britton et al. 2008; Müldner et al. 2014). While the Triton Knoll $\delta^{15}N$ values are slightly heightened, the $\delta^{13}C$ and $\delta^{15}N$ values in combination do not align as evidence for saltmarsh grazing. Indeed, the stable isotope data for Triton Knoll appear to align closely with that for Vale of the White Horse, Oxfordshire, where lower $\delta^{13}C$ values combine with increased $\delta^{15}N$ values, that are in turn attributed primarily to natural nitrogen cycle processes (Iorga et al. 2021). It is most likely that the Triton Knoll cattle grazed primarily inland areas in a manner consistent with most cattle reared in Roman Britain.

The above interpretation of the cattle isotope data can be enhanced by higher resolution analysis using the incremental tooth data. The third molar of cattle begins to form at 9–10 months after birth and ceases formation at 23–24 months (Brown 1960). Increments across the tooth therefore span approximately an animal's second year of life. The four increments taken per tooth are fewer than is typical in similar studies but is able to give a resolution broadly equating to one season per increment. The cattle from the Inland Fen Edge Landscape Parcel were the most homogeneous. The one marshes cattle also showed little variation, with the exception of a higher mandibular bone $\delta^{15}N$ than the dentine $\delta^{15}N$ values. The Fen Edge SPE03 30204 individual showed greater fluctuation in $\delta^{13}C$ through the increments. The two remaining cattle from the Fen Edge Landscape Parcel exhibit variation in increment $\delta^{13}C$ and $\delta^{15}N$ values.

All three Fen Edge Landscape Parcel cattle have a single dentine increment with a $\delta^{15}N$ value that is around 1‰ higher than is typical for their other increments and other Triton Knoll cattle. These animals' spike in $\delta^{13}C$ value reaches c.–21‰. This value is not of itself unusual and $\delta^{13}C$ values of up to –21‰ are widely reported for Roman Britain (e.g. Britton et al. 2008; Chenery et al. 2010; Redfern et al. 2010; Müldner 2013). What the results do show, however, is that these animals experience a brief but substantial period in which their diet became relatively ^{13}C enriched. Furthermore, the mandibular bone for the one marshes cattle is also closer to –21‰ than the dentine increments; in this case it implies that the $\delta^{13}C$ dietary increase occurred after the animals second year when dentine had matured. The implication is that four animals (all from the Fen Edge and Lincolnshire Marsh sites) experienced a change in diet during their life. As stated above, higher $\delta^{13}C$ values are associated with saltmarsh environments (Britton et al. 2008; Müldner et al. 2014). Only one of these individuals is associated with a $\delta^{15}N$ spike too – SPE03 30404. Nevertheless, these fleeting changes in diet could correspond with temporary grazing access of saltmarsh environments, potentially on a seasonal basis.

THE BROADER IMPLICATIONS OF THE TRITON KNOLL STABLE ISOTOPE DATA

Comparing the Triton Knoll crop and livestock stable isotope data, it is clear that these cattle were not consuming these crops. Bone collagen $\delta^{15}N$ values increase by around 3–5‰ (a trophic level), and $\delta^{13}C$ by around 1‰, for each step in the food chain (Bocherens and Drucker 2003). This means that the $\delta^{15}N$ value of the plants consumed by these cattle would have had stable isotope ratios that are a trophic level lower than that of the cattle which, in this case, would indicate consumed plants had $\delta^{15}N$ values around 2–5‰. This is below the crops (with $\delta^{15}N$ values mostly between 6‰ and 12‰) and so crops cannot have contributed substantively to the diet of the cattle. Indeed, the cattle were clearly grazing plants under quite different conditions than those found on the arable land.

A further implication is that any palaeodietary study of humans from the Scheme would need to account for the reversal in the $\delta^{15}N$ values for crops and livestock from expectations. The relative proportion of plant and animal based foods in human diets can be estimated by determining whether the $\delta^{13}C$ and $\delta^{15}N$ human remains are closer to one trophic level above crops (indicating a plant-rich diet) or livestock (indicating a meat-rich diet) (Richards and Hedges 1999; Hedges and Reynard 2007). It is often assumed, however, that the crop stable isotope ratios will be one trophic level below those of the local herbivores (e.g. Cummings 2009). The dangers of this assumption have been previously highlighted (Fraser et al. 2013) and has been demonstrated on the A14 where crop and animal $\delta^{13}C$ and $\delta^{15}N$ values overlapped to the extent that palaeodietary reconstruction was largely impossible (Wallace et al. 2024). Similar overlaps have also been recorded elsewhere in Roman Britain (Lodwick 2023). In the case of Triton Knoll, there is overlap here too making palaeodietary reconstruction problematic, but the technique would be potentially viable if expectations were reversed – with higher human $\delta^{15}N$ values being used as an indicator for a plant based, rather than animal based, diet.

The Roman economy and the Scheme's environments were both sufficiently complex to result in important isotopic changes in crops and livestock, which provides clues on past husbandry practices. The small sample size of this study limits the extent to which husbandry patterns can be explored, but the fact that some patterns were discernible indicates that this region is ripe for further stable isotope work. Developer-led archaeology has an important role to play in advancing stable isotope research. The nature of such archaeological research may mean it is not uncommon for contributions to be incremental – in which modest project-specific insights can be gleaned as well as contributing to the creation of regional and period-specific stable isotope records. This study represents the first isotopic evidence for saltmarsh grazing in Roman Britain, to the author's knowledge, and advances understanding of Roman agriculture, in turn setting priorities for future research in the region.

Conclusion

The Scheme spans a vast area stretching through inland, fen edge, marshland, and coastal regions, with evidence for saltmaking in the Roman period (see Chapter 5). The stable isotope study was undertaken to explore livestock mobility, crop husbandry practices, and evidence for saltmarsh or coastal land utilisation in the agricultural system. Variable preservation of plant and animal remains meant that the material suitable for stable isotope analysis was modest. Nevertheless, the results provided important insights into the Roman agricultural system around the Triton Knoll sites. An important consideration for future work is that the unusually high crop $\delta^{15}N$ values would need to be taken into account for any future palaeodietary research, and serve as a general warning against inferring crop $\delta^{15}N$ values from herbivore $\delta^{15}N$.

The Triton Knoll crops were exceptionally varied in the $\delta^{13}C$ and $\delta^{15}N$ values. Greater $\delta^{13}C$ variation in the coastal region may indicate that locally grown crops were mixed with those from inland areas. While also varied, $\delta^{15}N$ values were very high for most crops samples, indicating that not only manuring was probably practised but also some arable land may have been located on waterlogged or higher salinity soils. Livestock for the most part produced stable isotope ratios consistent with terrestrial farming in Roman Britain. This was unexpected given the diversity of environments within the Triton Knoll Scheme and implies that Roman cattle farmers favoured consistency. There was, however, potential evidence for fleeting periods of saltmarsh grazing for some of the cattle. Finally, it is important to highlight that the Triton Knoll project extends the geographic range of stable isotope studies of Roman agriculture in Britain and takes in types of sites not previously studied; as the corpus of stable isotope data grows for Roman Britain, the Triton Knoll assemblage will be an important comparator.

Artefactual evidence

Roman pottery

Ian M. Rowlandson and Hugh G. Fiske with a contribution from Gwladys Monteil

It is possible to outline a changing pattern of pottery usage, with the range of pottery used by the inhabitants of the sites on the east coast of Lincolnshire (Coastal and Lincolnshire Marsh) differing from that available to those living at the southern end of the Scheme near Bicker (Inland Fen Edge). The Roman pottery assemblages from the north of the Scheme suggest supply from the known industries in the Market Rasen and Tattershall Thorpe areas augmented by a limited range of regional and continental traded wares that were probably acquired from merchants in exchange for valuable commodities produced on site, such as salt. Towards the south of the Scheme a broad range of pottery from the modern counties of Lincolnshire and Cambridgeshire were utilised by the inhabitants of the sites who were connected with Lincoln, northern Lincolnshire, Cambridgeshire, and beyond by the River Witham and its tributaries.

The study of the pottery from the Scheme has served to demonstrate the intra-regionality of pottery supply across a large county such as Lincolnshire where there was a range of different industries providing pottery that were no doubt influenced by the ability to access goods by being close to waterways and having valuable commodities such as salt that could be exchanged for table wares and other goods. The use of Organic Residue Analysis (ORA) has also helped to further inform us about the diet and 'foodways' of the inhabitants of the sites and have shown different strategies of vessel use on sites in the south of the county in contrast to contemporaneous sites from northern Lincolnshire. This section is supported by full pottery reports provided as part of the ADS archive.

The assemblage shows that the inhabitants of the sites had access to a range of table wares and highlighted the difference in pottery supply, from the areas at the south of the route in the lower Witham valley to the area at the north near Burgh le Marsh. The parishes to the north of the study area evidently received their pottery from local industries in the historic region of Lindsey, augmented by samian, amphorae, and mortaria from further afield. Areas closer to Boston had local grey wares with shell-gritted wares from the Bourne area, a greater range of material from the Nene Valley, and imported Black Burnished ware 1 and 2. The assemblages from further south, within the Inland Fen Edge Landscape Parcel, also included a greater number of sherds of imported fine wares including a single possible example of a Colchester colour-coated beaker from Trench 125 close to the River Witham in the Langriville and Holland Fen with Brothertoft parishes (Rowlandson and Fiske 2018).

The Eastern coast to Burgh le Marsh

Pottery from the Landscape Parcels to the north of the Scheme in the parishes towards Ingoldmells can be paralleled with a range of sites located in the vicinity of Skegness and Burgh le Marsh (Precious and Rowlandson 2008; Leary 2013; Rowlandson 2013; 2014a; 2014b) which show a greater dependence on grey wares more typical of the Bain Valley, Market Rasen area and perhaps rare vessels from the Lincoln industries. Colour-coated wares were scarcer among these assemblages due to their location some distance away from the Nene Valley production sites to the south and a bias among these small assemblages to the 2nd century AD. The presence of stamped decoration in a 'Parisian ware' style and forms such as grey ware collared jars (JCR) and developed wide-mouthed bowls

(BWM3) suggest vessels produced in the northern Lincolnshire style seen from kilns such as Rookery Lane and Swanpool in Lincoln and kilns in the vicinity of Market Rasen (Samuels 1983). Other Swanpool type material has been recognised from assemblages at Burgh le Marsh (Rowlandson 2014b). This area appears to lie outside the main area of distribution of Nene Valley products, such as Nene Valley grey ware in the 2nd and 3rd centuries AD, and the suite of 4th century AD colour-coated jars, large bowls, bowls, and dishes that are common on sites in the Nene Valley and more southerly reaches of the historic county of Lincolnshire (Perrin 1999, Darling *et al.* 2020), exploiting local sources instead (see discussion in Rowlandson *et al.* 2014; 2015; Rowlandson and Fiske 2022; Fiske *et al.* 2023).

A number of sites in this area have shown evidence for small quantities of imported Black Burnished ware 1 and 2 along with Dressel 20 amphora. A noteworthy vessel is a fragment from a Dressel 20 amphora that has a circular pattern of carbonised deposits suggesting that it had been used as a makeshift lid during cooking or processing activities over an open fire. The presence of these traded wares is noteworthy as imported Black Burnished ware 1 and 2 is seldom seen on inland rural sites in northern Lincolnshire. The proximity to the coast and significant sites at Burgh le Marsh and perhaps Skegness may explain the presence of some coastal traded wares along the eastern coast of Lincolnshire (Darling and Precious 2001).

The pottery recovered from sites within the Coastal Landscape Parcel is fairly typical of 'basic rural' Roman pottery assemblages from this part of Lincolnshire. A total of 69 sherds were recorded from SMR01 located at the northern extent of the Scheme. The range of materials is typical of late Roman groups recorded from the east of the Lincolnshire Wolds, such as Nettleton Top and Stallingborough Hobson Way (Rowlandson 2011a; Rowlandson and Fiske 2019a). It is likely that all the pottery was produced in northern Lincolnshire with some of the Dales ware sherds possibly produced in northwestern Lincolnshire (*e.g.* Loughlin 1977; Darling 2009). The material from SMR04 is also a fairly limited range of mid–late Roman pottery with most of the activity dating to the later 2nd–3rd centuries AD. The inhabitants from this site had a mortarium from the Mancetter-Hartshill industries and sherds from two samian vessels. A typical range of grey ware was also recorded, which included a wide mouthed bowl, lipped bowl, a plain rimmed dish, and a carinated B334 type bowl.

Burgh le Marsh to Boston

There are no groups among the pottery studied from this part of the Scheme that could be considered as distinctively 'high status'. The groups are either typical 'basic rural' or similar assemblages associated with salt production. There were no sites that were akin to what might be expected from a fort, large civilian settlement, or roadside settlement (*e.g.* Rowlandson 2011b; Darling and Precious 2014) or more sophisticated rural sites (Spence 2009; Rowlandson and Fiske 2021). The route that this part of the Scheme passed through was an area of land which would have predominantly consisted of dry islands and low-lying marshes which would have been connected to Lincoln by the River Witham (see Simmons 1993; 2010). The location of these sites on the riverine link between Lincoln, London, and the near continent probably explains the greater diversity and proportion of regional and international imported pottery present in contrast to groups in the Ancholme Valley. Groups of material from the Viking Link Scheme have also recently been recorded where a similar pattern of small but diverse quantities of imported pottery was recorded (Rowlandson and Fiske 2023a; 2023b).

The main groups from this area have a broadly similar composition reflecting the waterborne transport links. The small assemblage retrieved from SMR17 mostly dates to the mid–late 2nd century AD with small quantities of early Roman and 3rd century AD wares present. Grey wares, Bourne type shell-gritted jars, and shell-gritted Dales ware jars are all well represented, with only small quantities of Nene Valley grey ware vessels present, a reflection of the location of the site close to the River Witham where pottery from Lincoln and the Nene Valley were both readily available

The main sites investigated, SPE03 and SPE04, were both located close to the modern course of the River Witham. As part of the archaeological evaluation, two trenches from the earlier phases of work on the Triton Knoll Scheme were excavated by Allen Archaeology in 2017 and produced evidence of what might be considered a 'structured deposit' of Roman pottery with a range of fresh fine ware (Rowlandson and Fiske 2018; Fig. 4.25). Trench 125 from Langriville Parish, Plot 37/11, contained a significant range of pottery with 177 sherds (3.618 kg, 3.09 Rim Equivalent (RE)) retrieved. The mean sherd weight at 20.44 g is high with a significant proportion of samian. Fresh fragments from rough-cast beakers, one with a cornice rim and a Colchester type colour-coated beaker (Rowlandson and Fiske 2018, figs 2.3 and 2.2 respectively) are also present. The fresh vessels from this feature suggest a primary and probably structured deposit. The other pottery present includes a white ware mortarium with a hooked rim, a possible sherd of Black Burnished ware 2, a fine grey ware sherd, a range of grey ware including a necked jar, a lipped bowl, and a wide-mouthed bowl. Nene Valley grey ware is well represented including a wide-mouthed jar and a necked jar or beaker. Early Roman grey ware (NVGY) and native tradition wares are also well represented suggesting activity on the site in the first half of the 2nd century AD or earlier. Shell-gritted wares including Bourne type shell-gritted jars along with a small quantity of Dales ware suggest activity continued into the 3rd century AD.

The other assemblage is from Trench 136 in the Holland Fen with Brothertoft Parish, Plot 37/23 (Rowlandson and Fiske 2018). A total of 198 sherds (4.485 kg, 7.36 RE) were retrieved. The mean sherd weight of 22.65 g is high, suggesting proximity to an area of Roman settlement. The majority of the pottery dates to the later 2nd–early 3rd century AD with two very fresh groups retrieved from ditch termini (13612 and 13616). The terminus ends of linear features have often been found to contain some form of structured deposition and the groups from both features in this trench appear to have unusual deposits with very fresh fragments of vessels. It is also notable that there were cross-vessel joins between the features which suggested that the two features may have been backfilled at a similar time. The features contained fresh fragments from a samian cup, colour-coated beakers including a scale decorated vessel (Rowlandson and Fiske 2018, fig. 3.10), a Black Burnished ware 1 dish (*ibid.*, fig. 3.11), fresh fragments of bowls mimicking Black Burnished ware types (*ibid.*, figs 3.12–3.14), and a grey ware jar (*ibid.*, fig. 3.16). Other pottery present includes smaller fragments of Nene Valley grey ware and a sherd from a Mancetter/Hartshill mortarium. A further fresh assemblage was retrieved from possible Ditch 13628, which includes sherds from at least four carinated drinking vessels (B334, *e.g. ibid.*, fig. 3.15). The feature also included fragments from grey ware lipped bowls and jars in the Bourne type SLSHB fabric (*e.g. ibid.*, fig. 3.17). These unusual deposits suggested some element of selective deposition in some of the features on the site with a higher proportion of table wares present. A more mundane range of pottery dating to the 3rd century AD was retrieved from Ditch 13621, with a lower mean sherd weight and higher proportion of grey ware more akin to what might be expected from a rural site in this region. Although smaller sherds of samian, Dressel 20 amphorae, and a Mancetter/Hartshill hammer head type mortarium are present there are far fewer fresh fragments and little table ware.

One note of caution with this interpretation is the way taphonomic process will have affected levels of preservation across the study area. Observations on the basis of assemblages from recent investigations in the south of Lincolnshire from this Scheme and others are beginning to show a pattern – where sites investigated within particularly low-lying areas the ditches appear to have been dug a deeper depth than those in the higher areas of land, presumably to service a pressing need for drainage, with pottery assemblages tending to have a higher mean sherd weight and be in fresher fragments. Excavations inland, particularly on sites with acidic soils, appear to have lower sherd sizes and the pottery may have only found itself deposited in shallow ditches after having first spent time in a midden (see Rowlandson and Fiske 2023a; 2023b).

The material from these excavations and trenches suggests the possibility that some groups may have been deposited in a 'structured' fashion (Hill 1995). Much of the material is similar to assemblages recorded from Boston (Rowlandson 2014a; Rowlandson and Fiske 2019b) but with a greater, more diverse range of imported material. In composition, it appears similar to the unquantified material from Gold Dyke Bank, Wrangle (Darling and Precious 2001). The more diverse range of imports recorded on sites from this project and from Wrangle may be in part due to a higher proportion of the pottery dating to the 2nd–3rd century, when imported pottery was more common. The assemblages from Boston have a higher proportion of late Roman pottery and this chronological bias may be responsible for the greater proportion of local pottery present in that assemblage. As such, the assemblages from the trial trenches, particularly those from Langriville and Holland Fen, are small but offer interesting groups to help categorise the range of pottery in use in this riverine landscape (Simmons 1993), and potentially an insight into the lives and perhaps beliefs of the inhabitants of these liminal islands (Brown 2013).

The main excavation areas from the Fen Edge area, SPE03 and SPE04, were also located in the Langriville and Holland Fen with Brothertoft parishes. The majority of the pottery from SPE03 dates to the 2nd century with activity continuing on site until the middle of the 3rd. There is limited evidence of activity on the site in the later 1st century AD. Among the material from SPE03 was a fragment of a Lincolnshire White Ware mortarium with two stamps of Vitalis i, dating to AD 90–115. Unusually there was a counter-stamp at right angles to both main impressions, which appears to consist of the letters CO[, a third unclear letter is also evident (Fig. 4.26). The excavations at the SPE04 site, located in the Holland Fen with Brothertoft parish, has a similar range of activity to the SPE03 site. The majority of the pottery appears to date to the mid–late 2nd–earlier 3rd century. The pattern of pottery from this site is more typical of other assemblages from this area with the majority of the pottery comprising local grey wares augmented by shell-gritted Dales ware, Bourne type jars, and a small quantity of Nene Valley grey ware. A small number of colour-coated and other fine wares are also present as would be expected for a rural site from this part of Lincolnshire. A mortarium from the Lincoln potter Senico was retrieved from this site along with mortaria sherds from the Mancetter-Hartshill industry. The presence of Dales ware from these sites is of interest as it is usually a rare find from sites located in the south of Lincolnshire, but the riverine link north towards Lincoln perhaps explains its presence amongst this assemblage. Black Burnished ware 1 and 2 are also present in higher proportions that are typically seen from rural sites to the west of the Wolds, however this is also most likely due to the riverine trade.

Simmons (2010 and see Chapter 2) has suggested that, in the late Roman period, the climate deteriorated and that there was a marine transgression in this part of the fens. As such the limited evidence for late Roman pottery from the SPE03, SPE04, and SMR17 sites might be in part due to the sites becoming unviable during the late Roman period. Although Nene Valley grey ware continued to be produced until the end of the 3rd century AD, and shell-gritted Dales ware was produced into the 4th century AD, there is little definitive evidence for pottery types that developed in the late Roman period. No straight-sided bead and flanged bowls typically dated to the later 3rd–4th century AD was recorded and there are no developed grey ware wide-mouthed bowl types (BWM3). Distinctive late Roman beaker types such as slit-folded or pentice moulded types are absent and all the beakers could date to the mid-2nd–mid-3rd century AD and, with the exception of one flagon or jar that might date to the 3rd century AD or later, there are no other potentially late Roman forms. Types such as plain rimmed dishes are only present in small quantities suggesting that little if any new ceramics reached the sites in the late Roman period.

Organic residue analysis on vessels from this area showed that the Dales ware jars sampled had been used for processing ruminant carcass fats in a similar fashion to Dales ware vessel samples from northern Lincolnshire (see Rowlandson and Fiske 2023c). Bourne shell-gritted jars appear to have been utilised for processing ruminant carcass and dairy products. The samples from this site appear to suggest that Bourne type shell-gritted jars may have also fulfilled similar cooking functions to the shell-gritted Dales ware jars. Sampled Black Burnished ware 1 jars were also used for both dairy and carcass products. It was noticeable that a higher proportion of the vessels sampled from this area produced evidence for dairy processing than some of the sites from northern Lincolnshire, perhaps suggesting a more mixed approach to farming on the SPE03 and SPE04 sites.

North of Bicker Southern section, south of Boston

The excavations along the Scheme in parishes near the River Witham have some similarities with groups from Boston and areas further south towards Spalding (Rowlandson 2014a; Rowlandson and Fiske 2019b; Rowlandson *et al.* 2020). While the Fenland Survey undertook a vast fieldwalking survey, little synthesis and publication was undertaken on the Roman pottery, even from areas that were extensively excavated (Hayes 1988; Crowson *et al.* 2000; Lane and Morris 2001; Lane and Trimble 2010). Other key groups which might be suitable for comparison also remain unpublished, such as the Wygate Park excavations at Spalding (Darling 2007). The pattern becoming evident from this area is of a range of pottery similar to that seen in Lincoln comprising Bourne type shell-gritted wares and a range of Nene Valley and kindred grey wares in a similar tradition (*e.g.* NVGWC). Further south, for example, in the recently published assemblage from Baston (Darling *et al.* 2020), the forms and fabrics more typical of Lincoln and the northern Lindsey districts of Lincolnshire are almost absent and the suite of pottery suggests that the inhabitants were within the main distribution of the Nene Valley and kindred industries in the Gwash and Welland valleys (*e.g.* Corder 1961; Perrin 1999; Hunt 2011; McConnell *et al.* 2012). The pottery from the TAM04 area appears to represent the southern edge of the area where Dales ware might be expected, possibly due to the link to the River Witham and tributaries. Parishes further south towards Spalding were probably more easily linked to industries upstream along the course of the Welland and Glen.

The relatively small assemblage from SMR01 has a high mean sherd weight of 26.33 g and, as noted above, this may be due to taphonomic processes with fresh pottery deposited into ditches; mineralised deposits were noted on a number of vessels suggesting that they may have been discarded into standing water. The Bourne type shell-gritted jars show signs of carbonised deposits suggesting that they were utilised for cooking processes and a worn Mancetter-Hartshill mortarium was also recorded. Small quantities of white ware flagons and samian suggest that the inhabitants had access to specialist table wares. Activity on the site appears to have been from the later 1st to sometime in the 3rd century AD with no evidence that activity needed to have continued into the second half of the 3rd century AD. It is noticeable that there are no examples of shell-gritted Dales ware jars from this site which may be in part due to lying towards the edge of the main distribution of this ware and also due to the site perhaps ceasing to receive much new pottery during the 3rd century AD.

The TAM04 site produced an unusual assemblage with activity beginning sometime in the second half of the 1st century AD with unusually fresh groups of pottery being recovered but also continuing into the later 3rd–4th century when some of the ditches were finally backfilled. The samian assemblage, analysed by Gwladys Monteil, includes a new die with the name stamp for the potter *Perpetus* ii who worked in both Rheinzabern and Trier in eastern Gaul in the middle of the 3rd century AD (Fig. 4.26). Examples of colour-coated necked jars, Dales ware, a grey ware plain rimmed dish, a jar with a collared rim (JCR), Dales type grey ware jars, and Nene Valley mortaria with reeded rims all suggest that activity on the site may have continued into the second half of the 3rd century AD. The absence of straight-sided bead and flange rimmed bowls from this site and some of the other key indicators typically seen amongst assemblages dating to the 4th century suggest that this site may have prevailed longer than the other groups recorded from the

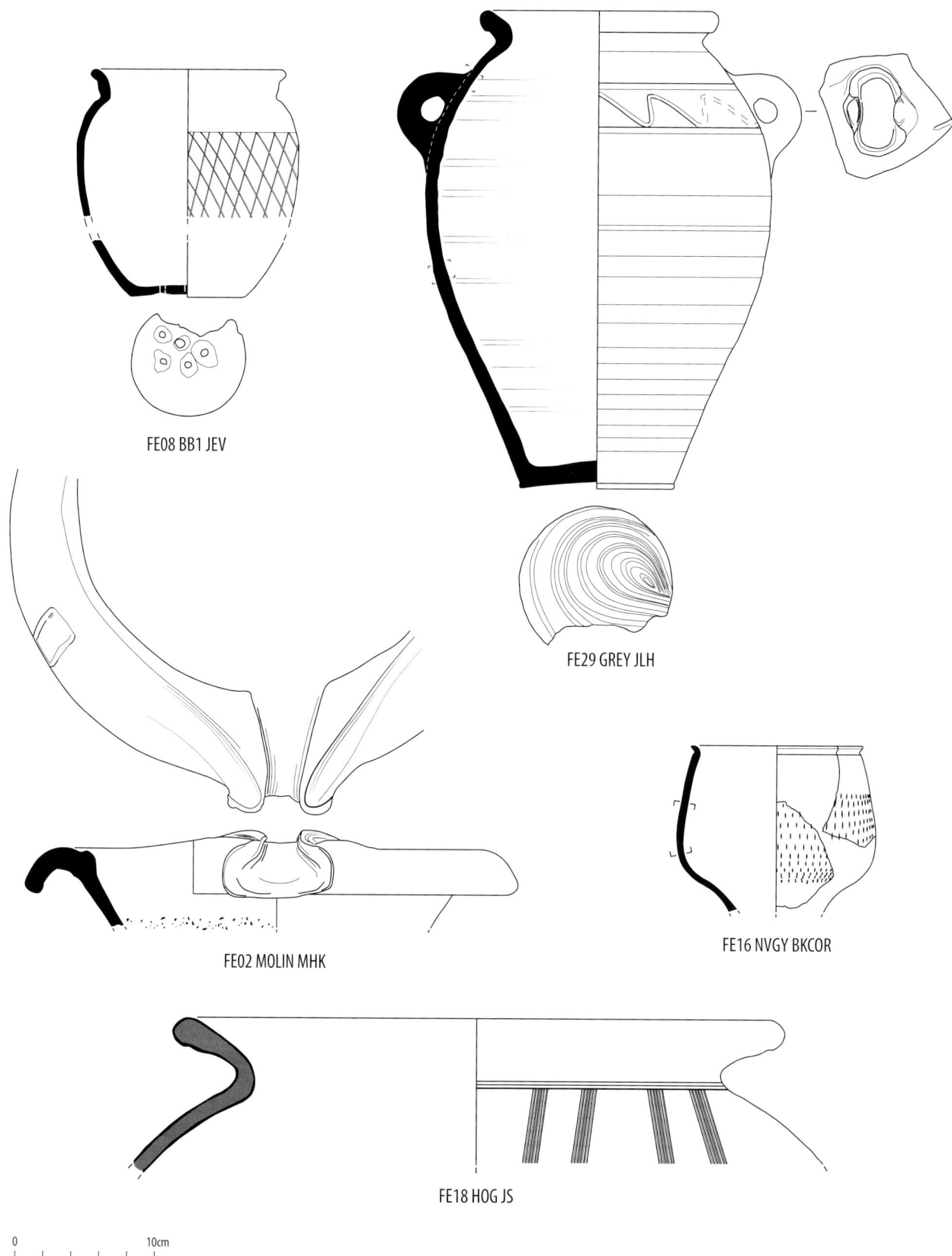

Figure 4.25 Examples of Roman pottery from SPE03 and SPE04: FE08. Black Burnished Ware 1 jar; FE29. grey ware lug-handled jar; FE02. Lincoln white ware mortarium with heavily excoriated potter's stamp; FE16. Nene Valley grey ware bag-shaped beaker; FE18. grey ware storage jar

Inland Fen Edge and Fen Edge Landscape Parcels but did not thrive during the late Roman period. The absence of a significant proportion of diagnostically late Roman pottery also suggests that the site had probably ceased to receive new pottery by the earlier 4th century AD.

Although the author has recorded a number of sites in southern Lincolnshire with cross-joining vessels, the TAM04 area appears to have a large number of such vessels perhaps as a result of levelling a midden to build up the ground for construction and backfilling of negative features. The mean sherd weight of 24.27 g is also relatively high with less than a third of the vessels showing signs of abrasion. Sherds from two Nene Valley mortaria (contexts 1779 and 1875) show signs of internal use-wear from grinding. A large storage jar represented by sheds in several contexts (IFE06) shows signs of internal excoriation, presumably from cleaning or chemical surface damage caused by brewing or other processes. The same vessel also shows signs of an internal white residue that may have been caused by a process such as boiling liquids. The salt surface reaction often seen on briquetage used in the brine boiling process was not recorded amongst the pottery assemblage. A further seven vessels also show signs of similar internal white mineralised deposits. Three further vessels show signs of internal excoriation (all from context 1960). Three vessels have post-firing basal piercings suggesting that they had been repurposed for straining liquids or as planters (contexts 1370, 1813, and 2274). The occurrence of these pierced vessels is similar to the groups studied from the Port of Immingham Scheme (Rowlandson and Fiske 2019c). There are few fine wares and no coarse ware vessels showing signs of repair. It appears from this assemblage that the pottery was primarily used for cooking and processing tasks.

The multiple samples submitted for ORA from TAM04 are of interest as there is a greater bias towards dairy processing activities in contrast to many of the groups that have been studied from northern Lincolnshire. While a number of the shell-gritted Dales ware jars and a grey ware jar with a Dales type lid-seated rim produced the ruminant carcass fats that have been seen from sites in the north of the county and some of the Bourne type shell-gritted jars and coarse gritted lid-seated jars also produced evidence of carcass fats, the main point of interest is the high proportion of samples producing evidence for dairying. A shell-gritted Bourne type bowl (TKN01) produced evidence for lipid and dairy residues which have been seen on a number of smaller bowls from elsewhere in the county. What is noticeable is that a number of the Dales ware jars had been used for dairy processing and a further Dales ware jar (TKN35) has a basal piercing and registered evidence of dairy processing, perhaps suggesting it had a role in straining for activities such as cheese or butter production. Evidence for dairy processing was also recorded on a number of the large jars, notably the large, necked storage jar (TKN13, TKN21-4), bowl (TKN27-30), wide-mouthed jar (TKN25), and large jars (TKN33 and TKN34). The samples from jars in the coarse Nene Valley grey ware NVGWC fabric group TKN26 and TKN32 also showed evidence of dairy processing. This group has been one of the few assemblages sampled from Lincolnshire so far where dairy processing appears to have been a significant element of vessel use for a number of the jars. The presence of porcine fats from sample TKN28 is also of interest as examples of this from groups studied from northern Lincolnshire have thus far been rare (J. Dunne pers. comm.). This study suggests that dairy processing may have been one of the key activities on the site in contrast to the evidence from coastal sites in north Lincolnshire, such as the Goxhill Feeder 9 project where, by the late Roman period, the site appears to have focused on cooking and processing ruminant carcass fats (Dunne and Evershed 2018b; Rowlandson and Fiske 2020).

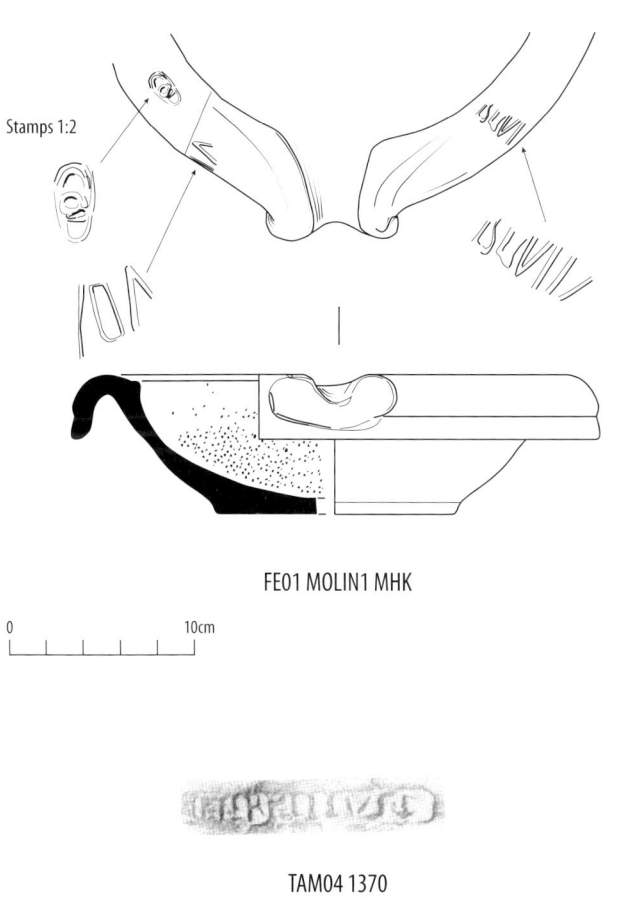

Figure 4.26 Pottery stamps from the Fen Edge and Inland Fen Edge: FE01. Lincoln white ware mortarium from SPE03 a new counter stamp of three letters CO[with the third letter unclear; TAM04 1370. New die for Perpetus ii (PIIRPIITVSF)

Other finds
Rebecca Sillwood

Roman small finds were recovered from all Landscape Parcels with 128 from Roman phased features (this figure does not include any unstratified Roman finds) across the Scheme, with the vast majority (81%) coming from middle Roman features and the remainder from late Roman features (Table 4.11). The object types encountered are diverse, with 38% of the assemblage taken up by iron nails and 17% by iron hobnails, beyond which finds types become more varied. Only 12 unidentified objects remain, whilst six pins and three pin roughouts were recovered, along with six iron coffin fittings. Many of the nails are likely to be coffin nails, though have not been specifically named as such within the data as they have no differences to any other kind of nail and fit within the same typology (Manning 1985, 133, fig. 32). A single brooch was recovered comprising five fragments. Although not unusual, coins are an obvious important Roman find type which is almost absent from the assemblages. The single coin recovered is a silver denarius which would have been a fairly valuable loss. Other Roman finds from the sites include low numbers of tools and personal possessions, plus an important and enigmatic bone find which may have been a stringed instrument tailpiece or possibly a weaving tablet.

Roman burial: Lincolnshire Marsh

A collection of small finds was recovered from a small cemetery at SPE02 (see Fig. 5.6) with other finds from the site indicating probable bone pinmaking activity in the later Roman period. Two of the graves contained coffin nails and fittings indicative of coffined burial which is an uncommon practice in Roman Britain. The *Roman Rural Settlement Project* (RRSP) dataset contained only *c*. 20% coffined inhumation burials (Smith 2018, 254). It has been suggested that the use of coffins in Roman burials in Britain was reserved for individuals of high status (Philpott 1991, 53). The RRSP dataset recorded over 20 rural cemeteries that have particularly high proportions of burials within coffins (*c*. 60% or more), and Smith (2018, 254) believes that their use was in part due to the choices of individual communities rather than any consistent, province-wide, association with higher status, which appears to be the case here at SPE02. One sample of coffin wood was identified as oak, which is the commonest material used for Roman coffins (*ibid.*). The second sample was uncertainly identified as field maple, which would seem odd as it came from the same coffin as the oak sample, but the condition of the sample precluded any certainty (Bamforth 2024). One of the graves contained all the hobnails found along the entire length of the cable route, pointing to the presence of hobnailed shoes most likely worn on the feet of the deceased. The presence of hobnails within an inhumation burial is not unusual, though it becomes more common from the mid-2nd century AD onwards, and the question could be asked why only one of the three burials contained hobnails – this could be a preservation or truncation issue but could also be a deliberate choice and may imply that either no shoes were placed in the other graves, or that they were not hobnailed and only organic, which is not always likely to survive the burial environment.

Table 4.11 Quantification of Roman small finds by object type and phase

Object type	Middle Roman	Late Roman	Total
Nail	43	6	49
Hobnail	22	–	22
Unidentified	12	–	12
Pin	4	2	6
Coffin fitting?	6	–	6
Brooch	–	5	5
Pin roughout	1	2	3
Nail?	2	–	2
fragment	2	–	2
Point	2	–	2
Toilet spoon?	–	2	2
Hobnail?	2	–	2
Awl	2	–	2
Knife	1	–	1
Tack	–	1	1
Spoon	–	1	1
Handle	1	–	1
Bead	–	1	1
Peg/pin roughout	–	1	1
Bracelet	1	–	1
Strip	1	–	1
Pin beater	1	–	1
Musical instrument?/ Weaving tablet?	–	1	1
Coin	1	–	1
Pin/needle	–	1	1
Adze-hammer?	–	1	1
Total	104	24	128

Farmsteads: Craft, personal, and agriculture objects

The small finds recovered from the Fen Edge Landscape Parcel also indicate craft activities with bone pins and roughouts recovered from SPE03 and SPE04. Bone hair-pin working evidence was present at SPE03, once again with an apparent roughout plus three pins, all middle Roman in date. A bone awl was also recovered, created from a sheep metatarsal with remaining butchery marks. An iron knife fragment plus the bone handle for a possible knife (which could equally be a different type of tanged tool) were also recovered which could have been used in craftworking, though might also be domestic in nature. Further evidence of craft activities was provided by the recovery of a possible loom weight (see discussion of CBM below). SPE04 produced another small assemblage of small finds which included bone pins and a bone point from middle and late Roman features.

One of the most important finds from the whole Scheme came from the Inland Fen Edge Landscape Parcel (SMR01): a bone object which was flat in profile and T-shaped in plan with four drilled holes in the wide end and one in the narrow end (Fig. 6.6). It is possible that this object derives from a lyre, although comparable examples are often of a different form and made of wood (cf Wardle 1981). Alternatively it is possible that the object was part of a weaving tablet, although again there are no direct parallels with other recorded examples typically being of triangular or rectangular form (Crummy 1983). That said, other textile working equipment was found at SMR01, which may reinforce the idea that this enigmatic object was used for weaving. Other possible weaving equipment from the site includes a bone awl and a bone point, both of which could also have been used for other activities. An awl is more usually associated with leatherworking but the tool itself is very versatile and would have worked in many scenarios. Other Roman material from this area is more mixed, including nails but also a delicate, incomplete bracelet of 1st–2nd century AD date and an incomplete bone spoon. A silver denarius, dated to the reign of Hadrian (AD 117–138), was also recovered (Enclosure 12). Many of the metal finds from SMR01 are in poor condition and though some point to domestic and settlement activity of a low level, they may also be midden material, with only the bone objects being in fair, unworn, condition.

The neighbouring TAM04, which likely formed part of the same site, contained a small quantity of probable weaving related finds, such as an unfinished bone pin beater of cigar-shape, more usually associated with the Anglo-Saxon era, but occasionally associated with Roman features. Also found here was a pin/needle and an iron adze-hammer. This iron tool was for use in carpentry and may point to the construction/maintenance of wooden structures on the site. Also recovered from TAM04 was a complete spherical jet bead and an extremely fragmented brooch, plus the usual small collection of nails. Birley (2012, 1–2) has discussed Roman jet beads and that much of the jet in Roman Britain was sourced from Whitby, North Yorkshire with an upsurge in production in the 3rd century AD presumably reflecting fashion trends for its use in jewellery. Allason-Jones (2011, 2) discusses the Roman use of jet as being generally believed to be a 4th century AD phenomenon, but that jet carving was already fully established in York as early as the late 2nd century AD. The use of jet and other black materials (such as shale, *etc.*) as beads for use in both necklaces and armlets is well-attested, with the black sometimes being used as a contrast colour with beads of other material, such as amber or glass for example. Allason-Jones (*ibid.*, 6) also discussed the apparent 'magical' significance of jet for the Romans and also the suggestion that it may have had an association with both Christianity and the worship of Bacchus.

Worked stone
Kevin Hayward and Ruth Shaffrey

The moderate quantities (62 examples) of worked stone recovered from all four Landscape Parcels, stretching from Anderby to north of Bicker, were all found to be middle–late Roman in date. The worked stone artefacts comprise rotary querns, millstones, whetstones, and other processing tools used for rubbing or pounding tasks.

QUERNS, MILLSTONES, AND WHETSTONES

An understanding of the petrology of the entire worked stone assemblage has had to take into account the poor quality of the underlying bedrock geology (Whitaker and Jukes-Brown 1899), consisting of Upper Cretaceous Burnham Chalk Formation (Coastal), Upper Cretaceous Welton Chalk Formation (Lincolnshire Marsh), older sandy oolitic mudstones of the Early Cretaceous Roach Formation (Fen Edge), and finally Upper Jurassic (Oxfordian) clays and siltstones of the West Walton Formation (Inland Fen Edge). All these material types are too soft and friable to be worked into portable utilitarian stone objects suitable for grinding and milling (quern and millstone) or sharpening tools (whetstone). A majority of the worked stone (with the notable exception of the much harder Lower Greensand Spilsby sandstone used in quern which outcrops 5–10 km due west of Burgh le Marsh in the Lincolnshire Wolds) has therefore come from older, harder sediments, all of which lie well to the west of the Inland Fen Edge Landscape Parcel.

The worked stone assemblage at all four Landscape Parcels is dominated by quern and millstone fragments. Millstone fragments, unlike querns, are typically over 500 mm in diameter and associated with more intensive processing through mechanical mills powered by animals, people, or water (Shaffrey 2015). At the Fen Edge, quern and millstone fragments account for 27 kg (91%) of all stone while, at the Inland Fen Edge, five of the seven fragments of worked stone (71%) are either quern or millstone. Two material types have been identified. Spilsby sandstone, a grey, loosely compact, glassy quartz gritstone with small glassy black chert and rod shaped foraminifera, was identified in quern at the two Landscape Parcels: Lincolnshire Marsh and Fen Edge closest to the outcrop on the West Lincolnshire Wolds. This use of this durable local stone as an important Roman quern material in this part of Lincolnshire has been demonstrated at other local sites in the Lincolnshire Wolds such as at Hatcliffe Top (Willis 2019, 247–248) although at sites much further west, such as at North of Bicker Inland Fen Edge, it is completely absent and the reliance is on other material choices from much further afield. Its use in two large beehive hand querns and a third in a small, standard, round upper or nether stone from the Fen Edge (SPE04) shows how important to the local rural economy this stone was for flour production. Spilsby sandstone, has, however, also been identified in querns and millstones at farmsteads and villas far outside the immediate rural setting of provincial Lincolnshire, at Stanwick Villa, Northamptonshire (Coombe *et al.* 2021), Thorpebury, Leicestershire (Hayward 2023a), and sites along the A428 in Bedfordshire (Hayward 2023b), showing that a much wider provincial trade in this stone was also in operation.

Millstone Grit, a coarse grained, open textured, cream-grey, angular quartz sandstone (arenite) was the principal quern and millstone material type to be identified in these Roman settlements. Present in all four Landscape Parcels, the stone came from Upper Carboniferous (Namurian) exposures of the Peak District, 75–100 km due west. It would have probably come into this part of the province via Lincoln by road or via the Car Dyke and even the River Witham in the case of the Inland Fen Edge north of Bicker (Hayward and Shaffrey 2024b), which would have flowed into the estuary (Bicker Haven) of the Roman coastline. As well as its use in fragments of hand quern (35 mm thick) and smaller millstone (50 mm thick) in the Inland Fen Edge sites, especially the middle Roman and late Roman fills of Enclosures 6 and 9, there were much larger millstones with a defined profile from the Fen Edge Landscape Parcels. Even allowing for some recycling of the fragments away from their initial places of use, the recovery of millstones from separate sites suggests that centralised milling of either water-powered or animal-powered type was a regular occurrence in the landscape of the area. This is a significant discovery that changes our understanding of agricultural practices in the region during the Roman period, an understanding which is variable and typically focused on land use patterns and archaeobotanical remains (Taylor 2006, 150). The addition of this key strand of evidence is critical. The *Rural Settlement of Roman Britain* project found possible millstones only at one site approximately 20 km to the west of Skegness; no dimensions are available so the classification is uncertain (Critchley 2005, 34). More recently a probable millstone was found during work on Viking Link Connector Station by Headland Archaeology *c.* 15 km to the south of the southern end of SPE04 (Shaffrey 2024).

The millstones from Triton Knoll indicate that even in these rural settings cereal processing included both household level activity and centralised grinding. The existence of mills means there was an important shift away from individual households or familial groups feeding themselves to some people bringing their cereal to a central point to be ground. This might have allowed them to specialise in other activities (saltmaking for example) or created a surplus of flour that could be traded for other resources. All of the millstones were recovered from late Roman or residual contexts, but evidence from elsewhere in the country suggests a typical pattern of centralisation from the 2nd century AD with some use from the 1st century AD (Shaffrey 2015). The recovery of further closely dated millstones, along with an analysis of unpublished museum archives, would help us understand when the organisation of the processing of agricultural produce began to change.

Whetstones, fine, hard, even-grained sandstones used for sharpening tools are represented at the Fen Edge Landscape Parcel (Hayward and Shaffrey 2024a) by secondary whetstones, that is fashioned from stone imported to a site for some other purpose (Allen 2014, 6). Here it is the reuse of durable angular Millstone Grit quern and Spilsby sandstone beehive quern. The reuse of quern as secondary whetstone merely reinforces the value of the stone in this region where the local underlying geology is in the main too soft to be worked into portable utilitarian objects as well as reflecting its geographical isolation away from established provincial networks of whetstone trade (Allen 2014).

Column shaft

The objects of greatest petrological and functional interest are a column shaft section from the Inland Fen Edge Landscape Parcel and a paving slab from the Fen Edge Landscape Parcel.

The small (130 mm diameter) plain column shaft section was made from Ancaster stone, a fine, sparry (Bajocian) oolitic limestone from central Lincolnshire. The stone may have formed part of a dwarf column in a portico or veranda to the entrance of a high-status farmstead, or possibly even in a villa from an as yet to be discovered high-status building in the immediate vicinity and is certainly atypical of the Roman settlement and activity north of Bicker. Ancaster stone has been identified in Roman London in the Dioscuri sculpture from the Temple of Mithras (Coombe *et al.* 2015, no. 55) and the grave of a child from Crosswall (*ibid.*, no. 84) both later 3rd–4th century AD in date, but rarely locally to the outcrop. Other than its identification in a late Roman mother goddess sculpture in Lincoln and sarcophagi from Ancaster, nothing else has been discovered locally including villas in the Lincolnshire area (Scott 1993). The same is true for a small paving slab fragment in Barnack stone from an unphased post-hole [30502] in the Fenland Edge Landscape Parcel. This hard, shelly, oolitic limestone sourced even further away to the Middle Jurassic (Bajocian) of north-west Cambridgeshire is found in great quantity in late Roman London (Coombe *et al.* 2015, nos 71, 119, 133–141, 143, 144, 146–148, 151–155, 159–165, 186, 187) and at villas in East Anglia (Hayward and Meckseper 2022), but as yet not in this region.

Ceramic building material (CBM)
Zoe Tomlinson

A small amount of Roman brick and tile was recovered from interventions in the Roman settlement areas of the Fen Edge and Inland Fen Edge Landscape Parcels. Fired clay was the most common material recovered from both Landscape Parcels. This fired clay is more domestic than industrial in nature. Of particular note are a number of fragments of loom weights, fragments of kiln or oven, and a significant number of complete and incomplete fired clay balls. Only a small number of fragments of abraded daub with either wattle or withy impressions were recovered. The daub may have derived from parts of structures or objects but the fragments are too small and abraded to be certain. In the Fen Edge Landscape Parcel just over half of the material recorded was found to be fired clay, most likely Roman in date. A small amount of Roman brick and tile was also recovered. Most of this material was from SMR09 and SPE03. Several of the Roman brick fragments join and have evidence for burning and reuse as does the single fragment of Roman tile.

LOOM WEIGHTS

Fired clay recovered from SPE03 included fragments of a possible loom weight recovered from Ditch 3.43. Two joining fragments of fired clay with rounded corners and a groove in the top appear to be parts of a loom weight, from fill (30503). The groove in the top, often referred to as a saddle, is typical of triangular shaped loom weights. Although traditionally considered to be of Iron Age date there is increasing evidence that triangular loom weights continued in use into the Roman period (Tyrrell 2015) suggesting some continuity in production activity.

Several fragments of what appears to be loom weights were also recovered from sites within the Inland Fen Edge Landscape Parcel including three fragments from TAM04 and one from TAM19. A single fragment of abraded loom weight recovered from Pit 2103 (2211) at TAM04 had smoothed edges and an angled oval-shaped aperture. The suspension hole had evidence for wear, probably caused by a cord having been tied through the hole to suspend the weight from the warp. Although the shape of this object is unclear it most likely would have been used with a warp-weighted loom. It was recovered from a late Roman midden layer.

A further five fragments from TAM19 joined to form what appears to be the corner of another triangular shaped loom weight (19017). There were no suspension holes visible in the remaining fragments of this piece. These fragments were recovered from a pit fill also containing Roman ceramics possibly dating to the 2nd century AD.

FIRED CLAY BALLS

The group of fired clay balls from SPE03 is of particular interest with eight complete fired clay balls recovered from enclosure ditches (Fig. 4.11). A further 38 incomplete rounded objects likely to have originally been parts of similar clay balls were also recovered. Most were retrieved from middle Roman phases with a small number from an early Roman phase. The fired clay balls are all roughly spherical in shape and have a diameter or width of between 50 mm and 63 mm, with most being around 60 mm (Fig. 4.27). The surfaces have been smoothed either during manufacture or use. Two examples have what appears to be a deliberately cut side, possibly to prevent rolling. Most of the clay balls have patches of burning to the surface and some have an iron rich concretion which is probably post-depositional. Although clay balls similar to these are known from several sites in Lincolnshire (generally towards the East coast in fenland areas) a group of this many is notable.

The clay balls may be associated with kilns but as there is no evidence for kilns on the site their presence may suggest kilns were relatively close by. However, most of the clay balls were found associated with other finds of a more domestic nature. Similar clay balls have been recorded from other sites within the region. Six examples of spherical clay or fired clay balls are known from the site at Dragonby (Barford *et al.* 1996). These were of an Iron Age to Romano-British date, and some were interpreted as sling shots. Although clay balls are often interpreted as sling shots, smaller biconical shaped fired clay objects are more commonly thought to represent sling shots or projectiles. The clay balls are however similar in shape and size to stone ballista balls and it has therefore been suggested that fired clay projectiles may have been used as 'practice' pieces (Vujovic 2009). If such objects were used as projectiles, they may possibly have been used in hunting small game or waterfowl.

Eleven rounded fragments derived from incomplete clay balls were recovered during archaeological investigations on land near Tytton Lane East in Boston

Figure 4.27 Fired clay balls from SPE03

(Tomlinson 2019). They were all the same fabric and probably dated to the 3rd century AD. Other fired clay material recovered from that site included a fragment with a partial large, rounded aperture and fragments of loom weights. A number of incomplete fired clay balls were recorded from St Nicholas C of E Primary School in Boston (Young 2010) also with a Roman date. The Fenland Project (Hayes and Lane 1992) noted three incomplete clay balls of roughly 50 mm diameter; one from Bourne and two from Gosberton. It was also mentioned that others had been found on sites in the area. In this case they were interpreted as possible net weights.

A confident determination for the function of these fired clay balls remains elusive and they may of course have had more than one use. Suggested functions include their use as weights, projectiles, stoppers, or in kiln related activity. Given the area they were recovered from it may have been that stone was not readily available and fired clay was used in situations where stone was exploited more commonly. It is possible that there was a relationship between the clay balls and the piece of fired clay recovered from SPE03 with the rounded aperture (Ditch 3.43). A clay ball could have been used as a type of 'plug' for the aperture, possibly to control heat or temperature in, for example, an oven.

Kiln fragments and structural pieces

Most of the fired clay recovered from the Fen Edge Landscape Parcel comprises small, abraded, formless fragments, although a number of pieces have smoothed or flattened surfaces and some have rounded edges. These featured pieces may have been parts of structures or objects but are too fragmentary to allow further identification. However, the assemblage also includes a number of pieces of possible oven or kiln fragments, some larger featured fragments, including pieces with smoothed surfaces, rounded edges, and also several thin, flat pieces. Some fragments are grass marked and have finger impressions. A piece of fired clay with a relatively large partial aperture or perforation, with a diameter of at least 55 mm, was also recorded from SPE03, Ditch 3.43. Fragments such as these are often found associated with kilns and formed parts of floors or vents (Swan 1984). It is possible however that this fragment may have been part of a vent for an oven.

Seven fragments of Roman tile were recovered from the Inland Fen Edge Landscape Parcel mostly from TAM04, along with single fragments of *tegula*, box-flue tile, and Roman brick. Most of these fragments are abraded and, having evidence for burning, most likely reused. This small group was unlikely to have originated from buildings on the site. The fabrics are however similar suggesting a relatively local source.

5

An esteemed resource: Roman saltworking at Triton Knoll

Owain Scholma-Mason and Tom Lane
With contributions from Hugh G. Fiske, Gwladys Monteil,
Ian M. Rowlandson, and Kate Turner

Pliny in his *Natural History* expounds on the virtues and properties of salt, highlighting the esteemed value of the resource and its importance in the ancient world (*Nat. Hist. 31.88–89*). This significance is, in part, due to the necessity of salt to enable a variety of essential bodily functions in humans and animals. As humans cannot naturally produce salt, we need an intake from our food (*e.g.* Williams 1977, 8; Lane 2018, 2). Much of this can be derived from plants and other foods without the need for supplements, although some animals, such as working oxen and horses, may have required supplementary salt (Kinory 2012, 105–106). In addition, salt plays a key role as a food preservative, its application to flesh facilitates moisture absorption and inhibits the growth of bacteria and mould. This enabled, for instance, salted fish, meat, and vegetables to be kept for considerable lengths of time, making long-term survival through winters and droughts easier. Salt also plays a key role in breadmaking, the production of butter and cheese, as well as leathermaking. Consequently, the acquisition and production of salt has been an important industry from antiquity through to the modern period (see Kurlansky 2002).

In this chapter the characteristics of the salt production sites at Triton Knoll are further explored, opening with a review of the components of the individual saltworking sites, focusing in particular on the data from the excavated sites (SMR05, SMR07, SPE02, and SMR06). This includes a summary of the briquetage from each of the sites, alongside a review of the structural evidence of salt production such as water channels and ovens. This is supplemented by a review of the environmental data, exploring the evidence for the diverse array of fuels utilised in salt production. Following this the pottery data is examined, exploring the role of pottery in salt production and the evidence for wider connections at these sites. The final section explores the wider context of the sites and their implications for our understanding of salt production, and in particular the importance of the evidence for late Roman saltworking.

Saltworking is widely known from across Roman Britain, with multiple sites attested within parts of the south and east coast, particularly the low-lying areas of Norfolk, Essex, Hampshire, Dorset, and Lincolnshire. The Lincolnshire coastal area is believed to have been one of Britain's longest running and most significant areas of salt production (Fig. 5.1). The earliest known Lincolnshire saltworking site at Deeping St James in the southern Fenland dates to the middle and later parts of the Bronze Age and into the early Iron Age (Lane 2007). Nearer to the Triton Knoll sites, at Tetney on the Lindsey Marshland, evidence for late Bronze Age saltworking has also been recorded (Palmer-Brown 1993). From this period on, evidence of saltmaking in Lincolnshire is attested across all the major archaeological periods (except early Saxon) until the demise of the industry in the earliest decades of the 17th century (Lane and Morris 2001; Lane 2018). The relative longevity of this industry in Lincolnshire compared to other parts of Britain is unusual and is probably closely related to the geography of these coastal regions, which can be divided into a Northern and a Southern section.

The Southern section of Lincolnshire's east facing coast extends south of Gibraltar Point down to the embayment of the Wash and the county boundary with Norfolk. Known as the Lincolnshire Fens or Fenland, this area is much wider, more extensive and better known archaeologically, with many investigations of its landscape and archaeology. In particular, an extensive fieldwalking programme with some subsequent excavations and environmental investigations, was funded by the then English Heritage (now Historic England) in the 1980s–1990s (Hall and Coles 1994). The fieldwalking, which covered some 32% of the Fenland area (Hayes and Lane 1992; Lane 1993), was supplemented by environmental investigations undertaken by Martyn Waller (1994). A second English Heritage funded programme, The Humber Wetlands Project, included the Lindsey Marshland and saltmaking sites in that area (Van de Noort and Davies 1993; Ellis *et al.* 2001; Van de Noort 2004). The Northern section of Lincolnshire's coast extends from Grimsby south to Gibraltar Point, just south of Skegness. This area is generally known as the Lindsey Marshland and is currently an approximate maximum 10–15 km wide expanse of former marshes extending from the present-day coast west to the beginnings of the Lincolnshire Wolds.

In the Fenland, the mid- to late Bronze Age up to the middle Iron Age saltern sites tend to occupy the western Fen edge, from Helpringham down to Market Deeping, presumably the inner edge of wide and extensive saltmarshes (Fig. 5.1). Due to the changing landscapes, the late Iron Age and Roman sites extend further east alongside

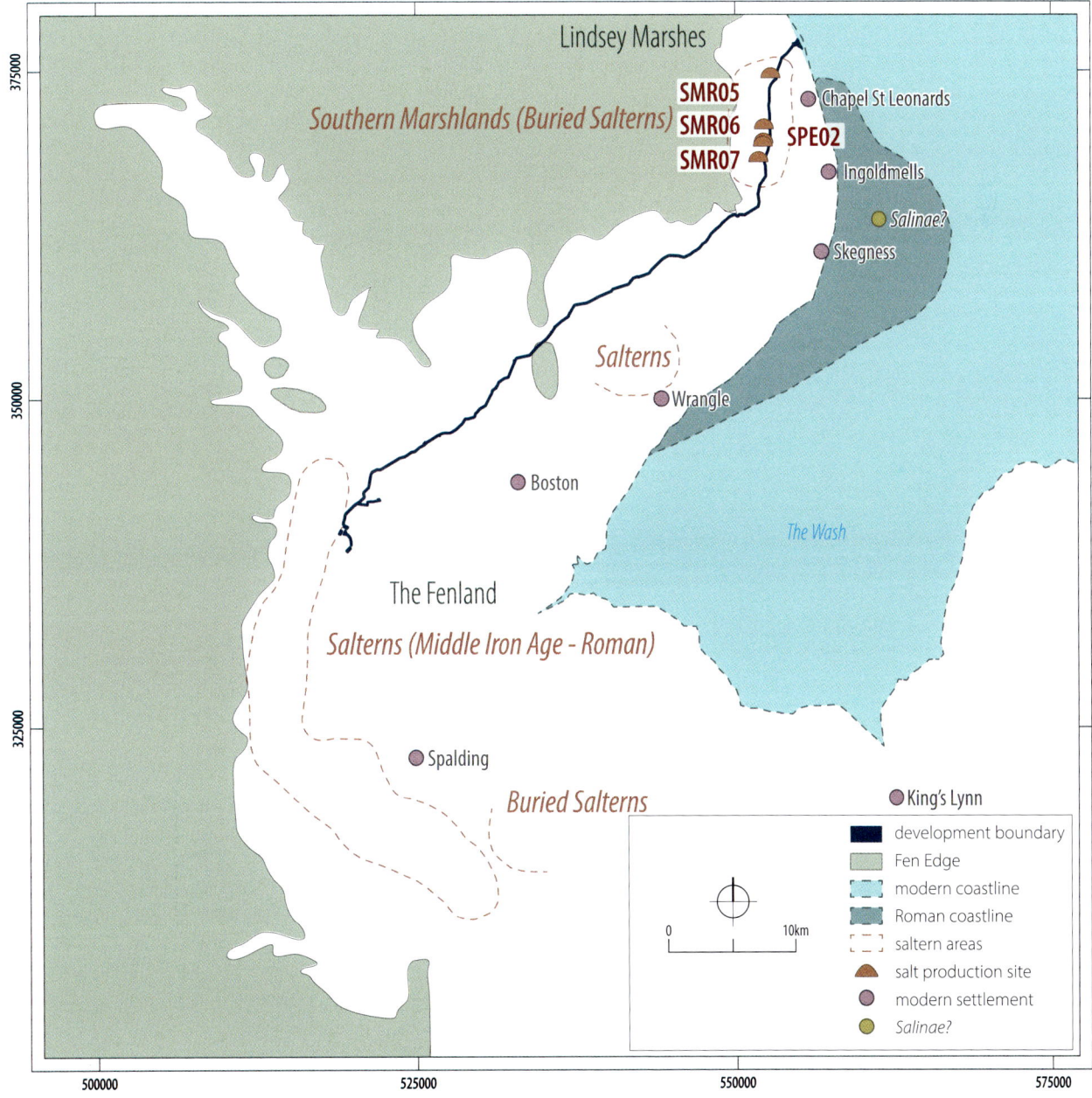

Figure 5.1 The geography and context of the principal saltern sites identified across the Scheme (after Lane and Morris 2001, fig. 2 and Lane 2017, fig. 1)

the broadly east–west aligned creeks (see Chapter 2). Traces of these creeks in the Fenland disappear under later, post-Roman silting seaward from the Spalding area. There, the salterns are sealed beneath an expanse of marine silts believed to be of late Roman and/or early Saxon date. Some of the earlier salterns in the Fenland, such as that at Welland Bank Quarry, Deeping St James, are up to 40 km inland from the present coastline. In contrast, the Lindsey Marshland sites in the Chapel St Leonards/Ingoldmells area extend only c. 5 km inland towards the Roman sites on high ground at Burgh le Marsh, but almost certainly extended eastward, where they are now beneath the sea. The fact that saltern sites have been found on the present-day beaches at places like Ingoldmells and Chapel St Leonards strongly suggests that a much larger area of the densely distributed sites now lies further east, beneath the sea (Figs 5.1 and 5.2). This includes the putative Roman settlement of *Salinae*, noted by Ptolemy, which may have been located near to or east of Skegness (Lane 2024b; see Chapter 6).

The majority of the Triton Knoll salt production sites were located within the Lindsey Marshland, in particular within the southern part, termed here the Southern Lindsey Marshland (Figs 5.1 and 5.2). These include the later prehistoric salt production site at SPE01 in the Coastal Landscape Parcel, discussed in Chapter 3, and four Roman salt production sites in the Lincolnshire Marsh Landscape Parcel (Fig. 5.2). Possible salt production was also noted at SMR09 in the Fen Edge Landscape Parcel, with fragments of briquetage recovered from a thin deposit at the western edge of the site, although this could relate to the movement of salt rather than on-site production (Stockdale *et al.* 2024, 8; see Chapter 4). In addition to these excavated sites, further saltern mounds were noted in six direct drilling sites situated within the Lincolnshire Marsh Landscape Parcel: HDD24, HDD26, HDD27, HDD28, JB5, and JB6 (Table 5.1; Fig. 5.2). The dating of these is reliant on the forms of briquetage recovered, with date ranges spanning the Iron Age to Roman periods. At HDD24 a sherd of middle Iron Age pottery was recovered from the mound, whilst from the top of the mound recorded in JB5, sherds of 3rd century AD pottery were recovered, but these may post-date the salt production (Allen Archaeology 2021b, 85, 95). During the trial trenching a further 14 saltern sites were identified within the vicinity of the excavated sites, including three with possible hearths and or ovens (Allen Archaeology 2018d). In two cases the evidence for hearths or ovens comprised multiple hearth fragments, whilst in Tr 231 a gully like feature and a potential flue were recorded (*ibid.*, 26).

The remains of salterns were recorded within SMR05 and SMR07, at the northern and southern ends of the Landscape Parcel (Fig. 5.3). SMR05 is broadly dated to the Roman period (AD 45–410), while SMR07 is dated to the middle Roman period (AD 120–250), although dating evidence was on the whole limited. For the most part the dating of these sites is contingent on the forms of briquetage recovered, although two sherds of 3rd century AD pottery were recovered from Saltern 1 at SMR07. This saltern comprised two distinct deposits of briquetage, separated by a 0.20 m thick alluvial layer, indicative of a flooding event (Fig. 5.4). In light of the limited dating evidence recovered from the saltern the precise date of the flooding event is uncertain, although sherds of 3rd century AD pottery were recovered from the upper deposit. The features identified at SMR05, at the northern end of the Landscape Parcel, comprised two saltern mounds, one of which was noted in section at the southern end of the site. These were recorded alongside a series of natural water channels and boundary ditches (Fig. 5.3). A small assemblage of pottery, broadly dated to the late Iron Age–early 2nd century AD, was recovered from a ditch sealed by the saltern. Unlike SMR07, the salterns at SMR05 comprised only a single deposit of waste, potentially suggesting a more limited phase of activity (Scholma-Mason 2024). It is also probable that both SMR05 and SMR07 were not the primary locations

Table 5.1 Overview of salt production sites recorded across the Scheme

Site	Date	Evidence
SMR05	Roman	2 saltern deposits & series of water channels
SMR07	Middle Roman	Single saltern deposit, with 2 phases of deposition
SPE02	Late Roman	Ovens, settling tanks & water management features associated with late Roman salt production
SMR06	Middle–late Roman	6 saltern deposits associated with middle Roman salt production. Succeeded by phase of late Roman salt production associated with oven & pair of wells
HDD24	Late Iron Age–early Roman	Saltern deposit
HDD26	Late Iron Age–early Roman	Saltern deposit
HDD27	Undated	Saltern deposit
HDD28	Undated	Saltern deposit
JB5	Roman	Saltern deposit
JB6	Late Iron Age–early Roman	Possible saltern deposits, finds of briquetage

5 An esteemed resource: Roman saltworking at Triton Knoll

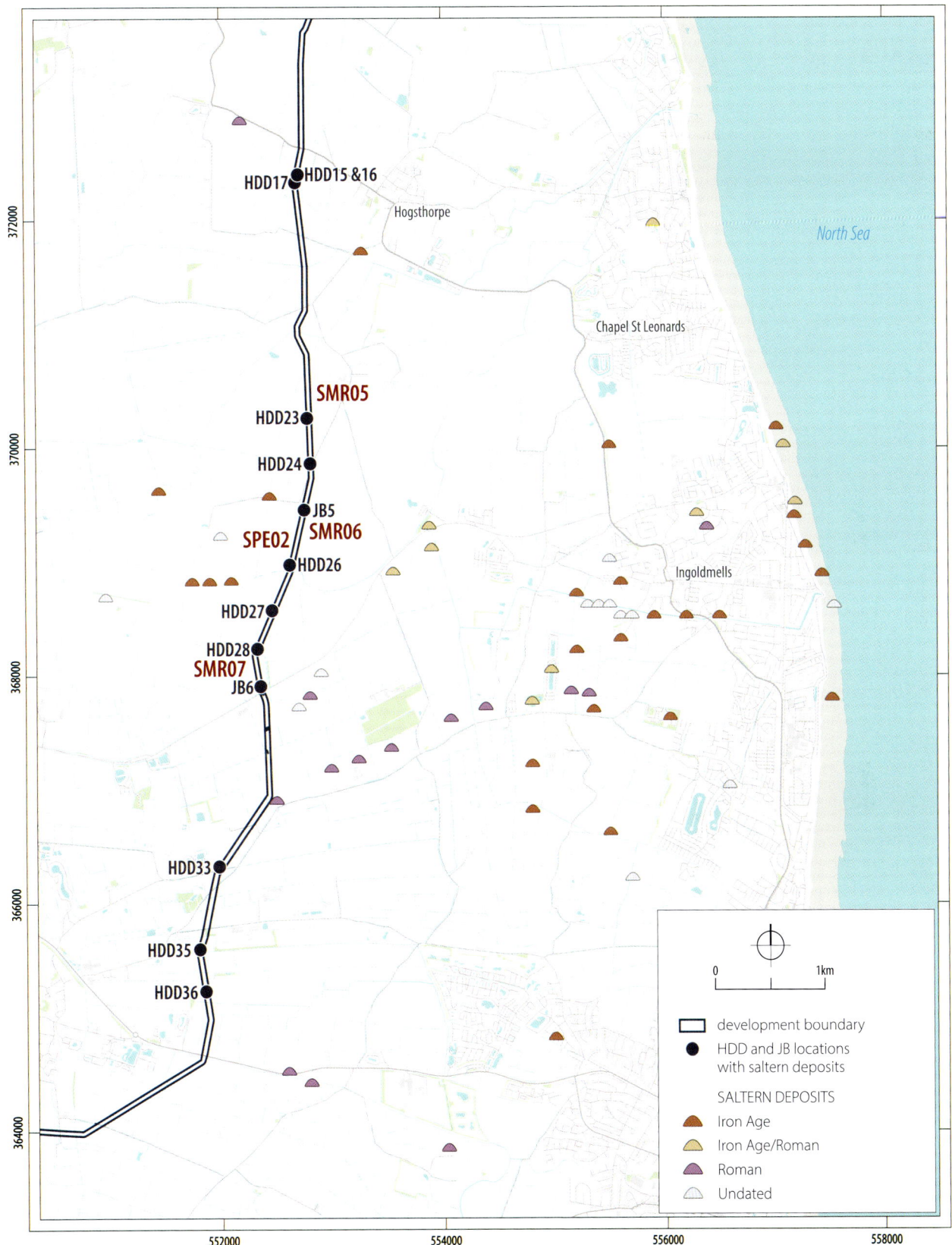

Figure 5.2 Triton Knoll saltern sites in relation to other known saltern sites recorded in the Historic Environment Record (HER) (1 km)

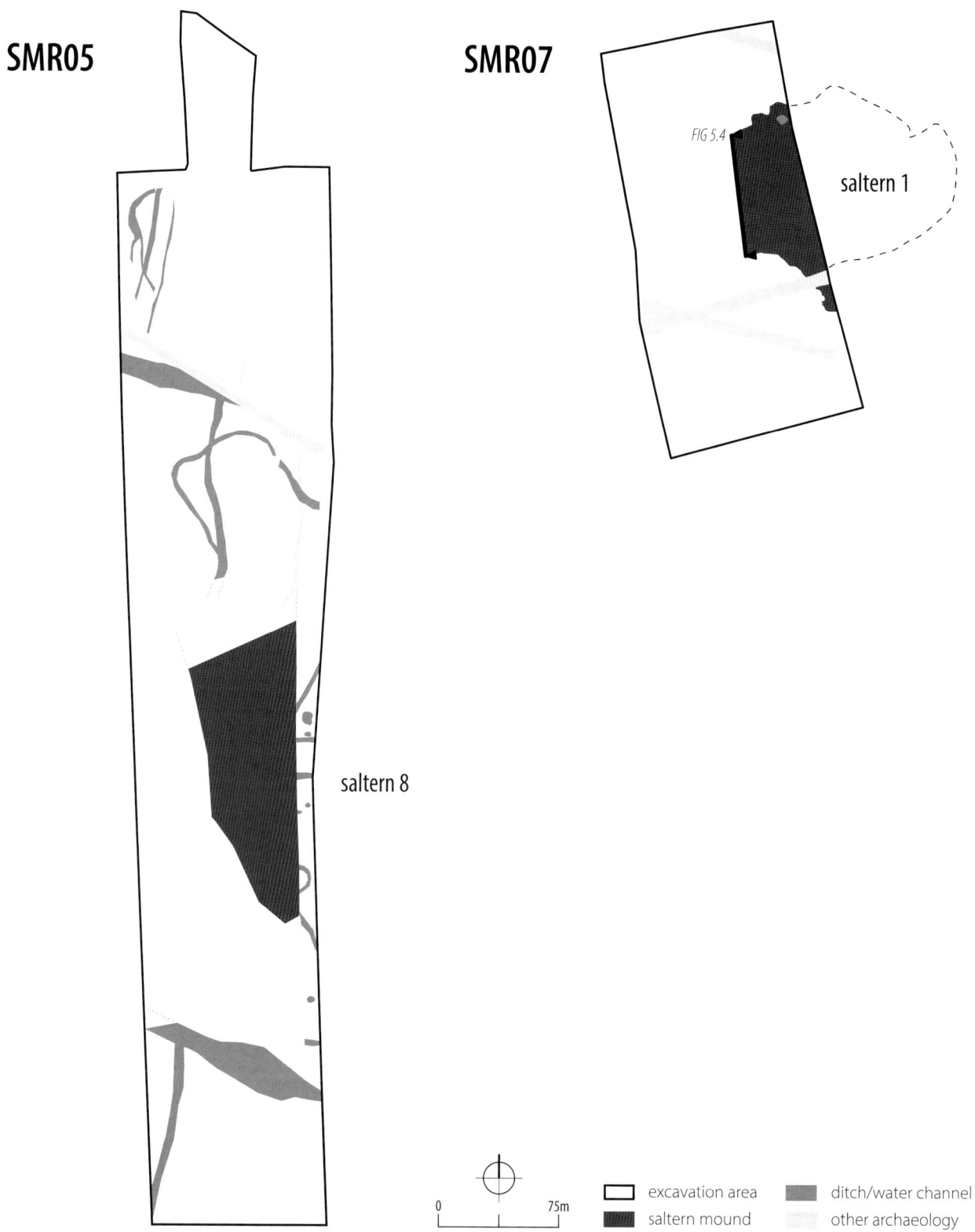

Figure 5.3 Plan of Roman features at SMR05 and SMR07

for saltworking but rather places where saltern waste was being disposed of.

Located between these two sites were the more extensive saltworking sites at SMR06 and SPE02 (Fig. 5.2).

A sequence of five middle Roman saltern deposits were recorded at SMR06 from which 12 kg of briquetage was recovered (Fig. 5.5). Some of these were partially identified in test pits, with a further saltern deposit recorded

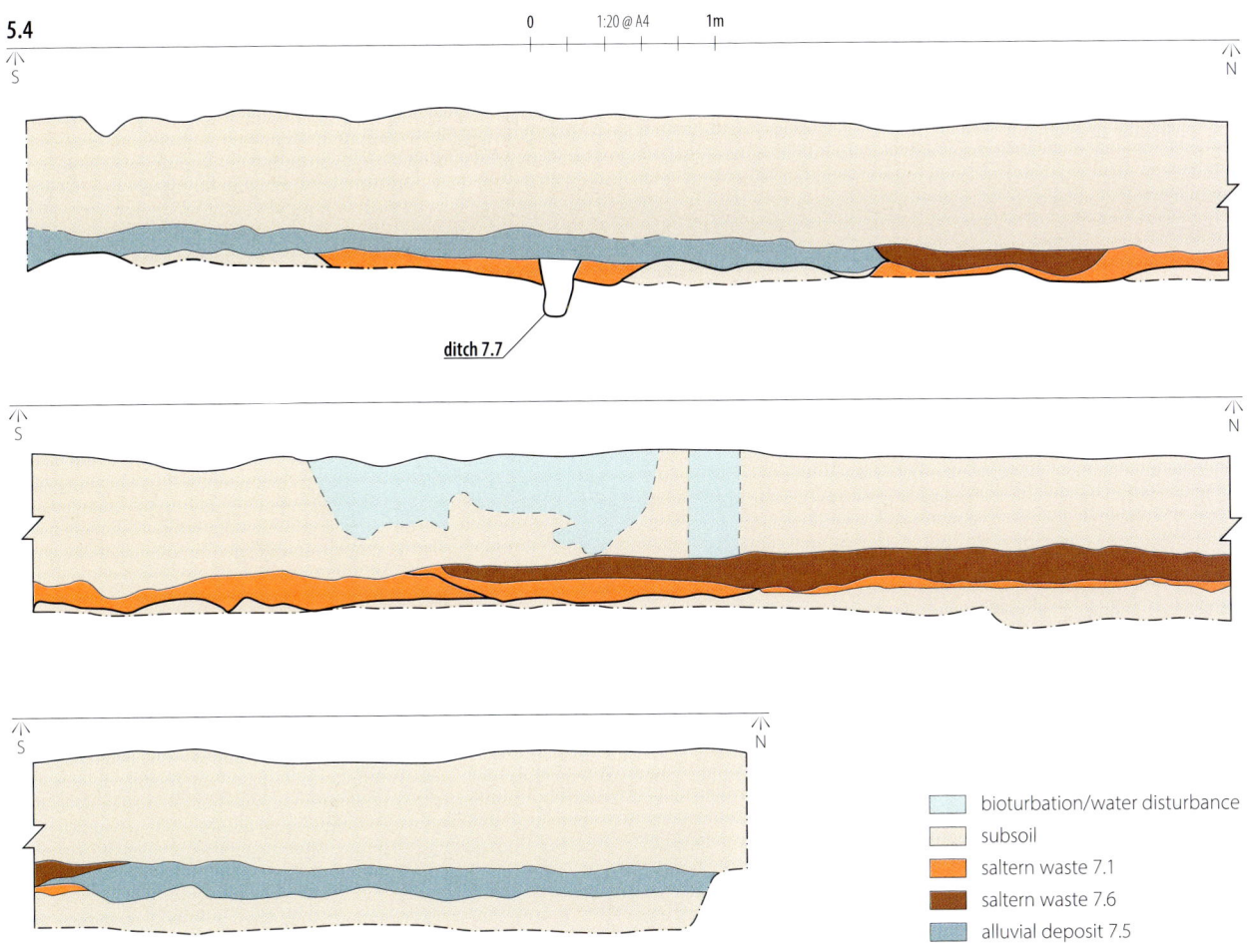

Figure 5.4 Section through Saltern 1 at SMR07 showing deposits of saltern waste and flooding events

in section (see Scholma-Mason 2024). Other finds from these deposits included sherds of 2nd century AD pottery, with a medium sized group of mid-2nd century AD pottery recovered from Saltern 4. Sherds of late Roman pottery were also recovered, but these could be intrusive material from the late Roman phases of the site. Between the middle and late Roman phases there is evidence for possible flooding, with alluvial deposits noted overlying Saltern 6, akin to those noted at SMR07. These could relate to episodes of seasonal flooding, with comparable flooding events being recorded in a cross section of the coastal zone from Burgh le Marsh to Ingoldmells, which shows layers of briquetage above peat deposits sealed by a significant late or post-Roman flooding event (Lane 2018, fig. 33). Whether this deposit, and indeed that from SMR06 and SMR07, is related to the episodes of marine transgression outlined in Chapter 2 is uncertain. During the late Roman period (AD 250–410) a series of features relating to salt production were dug into the flooding deposit at SMR06 (Fig. 5.5). This included a series of ditches, two wells, and a possible oven towards the western edge of the centre of the site, with sherds of late Roman pottery being recovered from the features (see Scholma-Mason 2024). This included a complete grey ware, lug-handled jar with burnished way line decoration dating to the 3rd–4th century AD (LM22; Fig. 5.17). These features were in turn overlain by a series of occupational deposits, into which several further ditches were cut. From the deposit and ditches came further sherds of later Roman pottery, including some residual early to middle Roman material and briquetage.

During the late Roman period at SPE02, *c.* 120 m to the south of SMR06, the site witnessed a period of reorganisation with the middle Roman features being replaced by a range of features associated with salt production (Fig. 5.6). The middle Roman phases of the site comprised a group of three inhumation burials at the southern end of the site, just to the north of the palaeochannel, with a further cremation burial to the east in Tr 254 (Allen Archaeology 2018d; see Chapter 4). Radiocarbon dating of the burials returned dates spanning the early to middle Roman period (Table 5.2). During the later 3rd century AD there is evidence for increased activity on the site, with a range of features

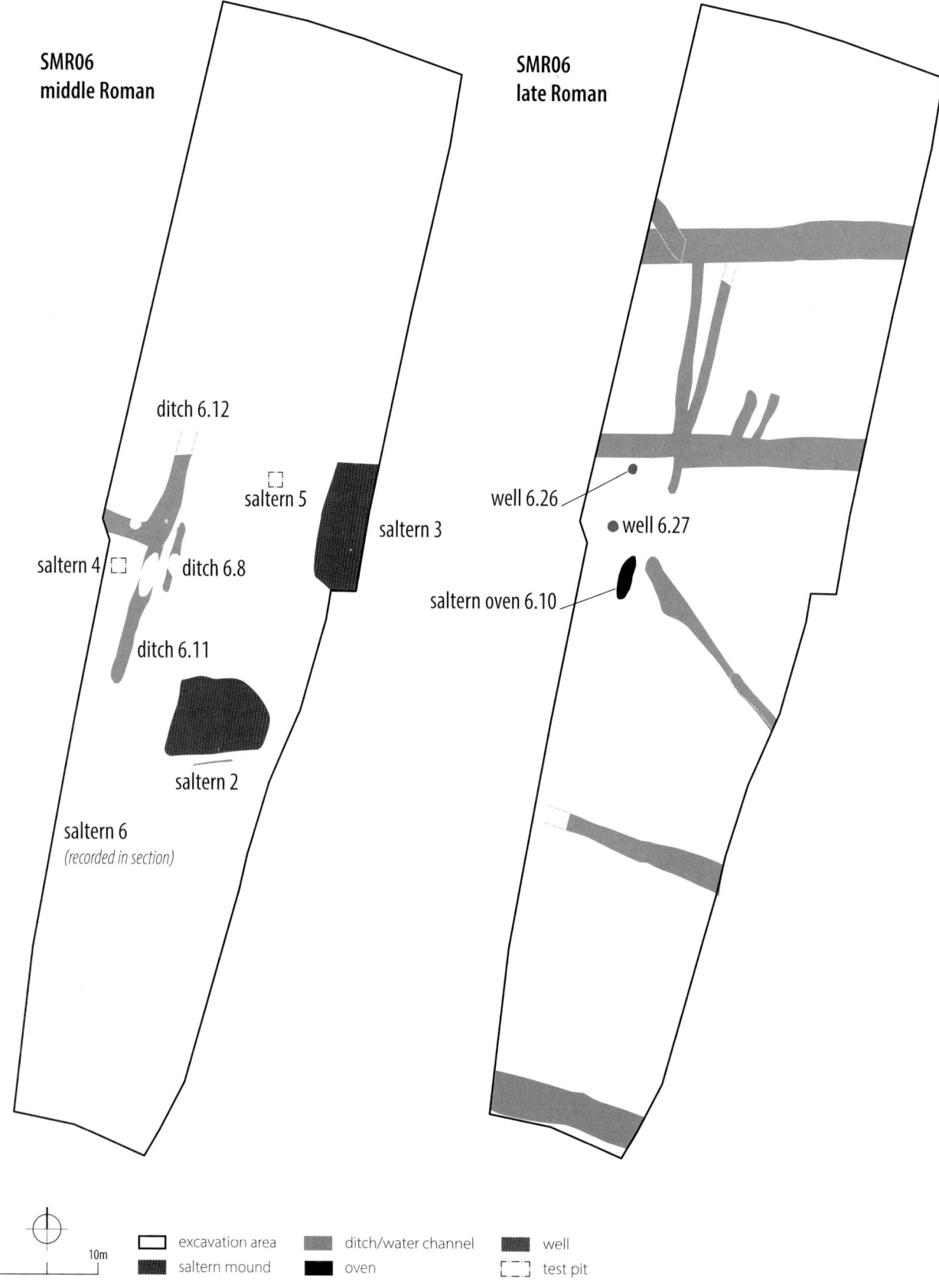

Figure 5.5 Plan of middle and late Roman features at SMR06

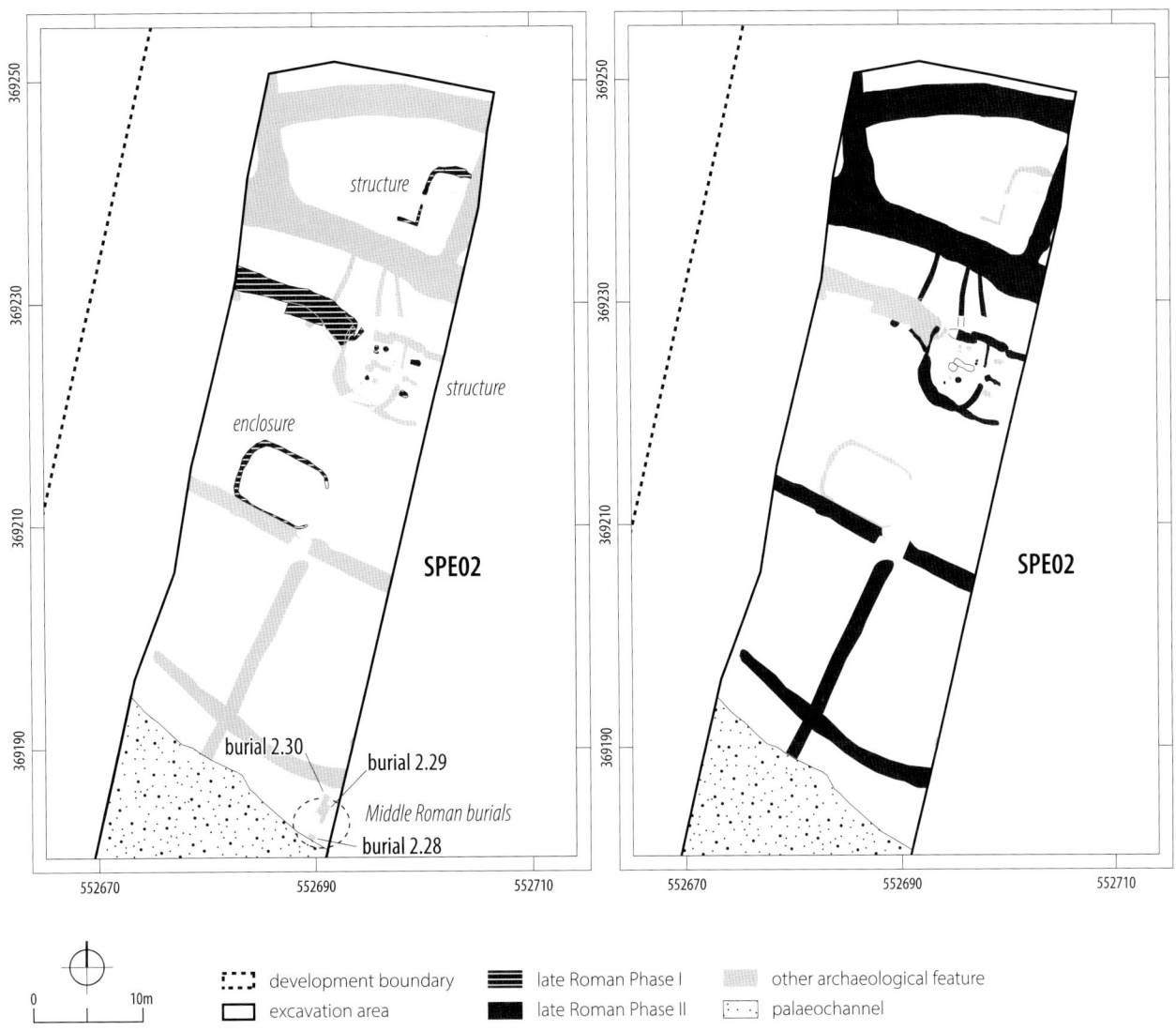

Figure 5.6 Plan of middle and late Roman features at SPE02

Table 5.2 Radiocarbon dates from SPE02, Lincolnshire Marsh

Group/feature	Context	Sample	Material dated	Lab. code	$\delta^{13}C$	Radiocarbon age BP	Radiocarbon date (95.4% probability)
Oven 2.19	0161	33	Charred culm nodes	Beta-667274	−26.8	1760±30	cal AD 230–390
Oven 2.19	0303	40	Charred culm nodes	Beta-667276	−24.3	1740±30	cal AD 240–410
Oven 2.19	0306	44	Charred culm nodes	Beta-667277	−24.1	1780±30	cal AD 210–370
Inhumation Burial 2.29	0009	3	Tibia: human	SUERC-87856	−19.9	1814±30	cal AD 130–340
Inhumation Burial 2.30	0056	–	Rib: human	SUERC-87855	−20.7	1910±30	cal AD 20–220

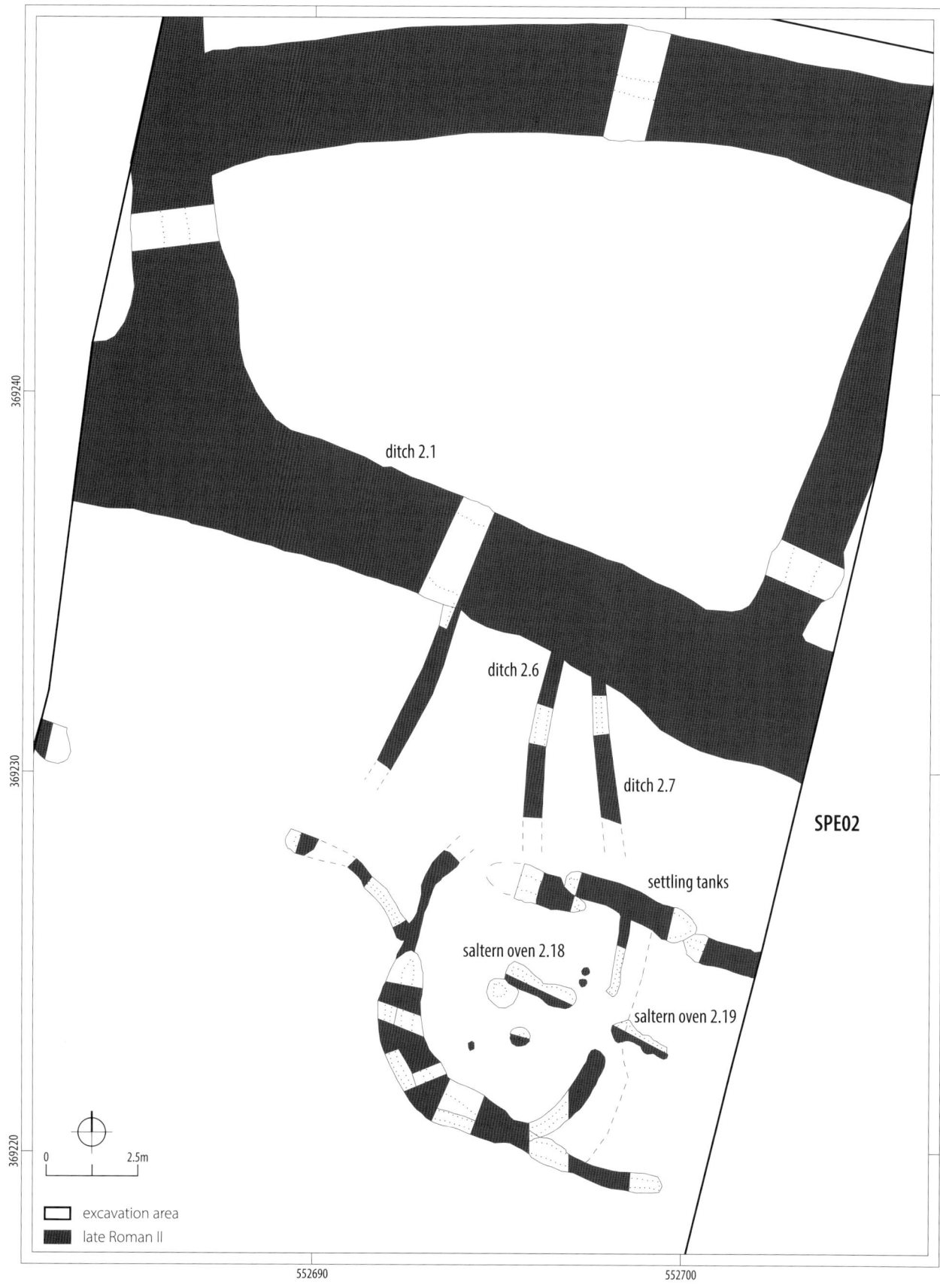

Figure 5.7 Plan of late Roman saltworking features at SPE02

established to the north of the palaeochannel. These include a C-shaped enclosure, a possible structure, and a series of ditches (Fig. 5.6). Sherds of late Roman pottery were recovered from these features, along with a very small assemblage of briquetage. The presence of the latter does not appear to relate to saltworking on site and could be material used to transport salt. It is possible that this material could have derived from salterns in the vicinity, such as that identified to the south of SPE02, in Tr 255, which has been provisionally dated to the late Iron Age–early Roman period (Allen Archaeology 2018d, 21). During the final phase of late Roman activity at SPE02 a series of saltworking features was established in the northern half of the site (Figs 5.6 and 5.7). These features were cut into a spread of occupation material, potentially representing midden material used to level the ground (Scholma-Mason 2024).

Among the features in the northern half were two saltern ovens, which were enclosed by a circular ring-ditch, which effectively defined the area of saltworking (Fig. 5.7). Radiocarbon dating of charcoal from both ovens returned dates spanning the late Roman period (Table 5.2). The incidence of late Roman saltworking at SPE02 and SMR06 is of particular note as to date, no late Roman salt production sites have been identified within Lincolnshire, although examples have been noted from across the southeast of England, including at Middleton, Norfolk and London Gateway, Essex (Crowson 2001; Biddulph and Stansbie 2012; Biddulph 2017). Consequently, the data from SPE02 and SMR06 offer a unique opportunity to explore the notion of later Roman salt production within Lincolnshire.

The anatomy of saltmaking

Before discussing the specifics of the saltworking sites from Triton Knoll, it is worth pausing to consider the salient points of salt production. Seawater contains in the region of 3.5% salts by weight, of which 77.8% is sodium chloride, the desired final product. To extract the sodium chloride, a variety of techniques could be employed, including solar evaporation, sandwashing, or the open-pan method. The latter is generally assumed to have been the principal method used to extract salt from seawater throughout the prehistoric and Roman periods in Britain (Lane and Morris 2001). This process involves the boiling of seawater, extracting the desired product, and leaving behind the leftover impurities, the bittern. Prior to boiling, seawater is initially collected in salt pans or settling tanks, being left to evaporate naturally, although this may have relied on the wind more than solar evaporation (Lane and Morris 2001, 96). Consequently, salt production was probably a summer activity, relying on the warmer summer months with the optimum time being suggested as May to September (Bradley 1975, 22).

Once the brine reached a certain concentration it was then transferred to briquetage or lead vessels, the latter being more common during the later Roman period (Biddulph and Stansbie 2012, 164). These containers were then placed over a hearth or oven to further crystallise the salt. This process was not necessarily particularly time consuming. It is estimated that brine poured to a 10 cm depth in a pan or trough with a base area of 1000 cm^2 could be converted into 300 g of salt in under an hour (Lane and Morris 2001, 132). Recovered fragments of briquetage often show yellow/white deposits, indicating prolonged contact with saltwater, which creates a bleaching effect (Lane 2018, 65). The levels of this bleaching can reflect on the intensity of use, with heavy bleaching often being indicative of a late Iron Age and early Roman date (Lane 2024c). Owing to the accumulation of bittern deposits within the briquetage vessels, these were frequently disposed of, possibly being used for a handful of evaporations (Lane and Morris 2001; Biddulph and Stansbie 2012, 167).

The waste from this process, including fragments of containers, troughs, and material associated with the hearths or ovens, provides the most visible evidence of salt production, forming the distinct 'red hills', which attracted antiquarian interest (see Lane 2018). As seen at Triton Knoll, these mounds could encompass multiple episodes of production, although whether these dumps cover the area used to make the salt or are deposits of industrial waste removed from salt manufacturing nearby, remains uncertain (Fig. 5.4). Either way, the finds strongly indicate that saltmaking was taking place either on site or very close by. Multiple saltern mounds were recorded across the Scheme, but of note is their absence at SPE02. Also, when compared with other sites from the Scheme, SPE02 had a relatively low volume of briquetage. This could suggest that waste was being dumped elsewhere within the landscape or, alternatively, it reflects changes in technology during the late Roman period when lead pans may have been employed (Biddulph and Stansbie 2012, 164).

Alongside the need for briquetage, which may have been produced on-site, saltmaking required a range of further resources including fuel for the ovens and hearths. Consequently, the production of salt was a multi-faceted and skilled process requiring a range of resources as well as specialised features such as ovens, water channels, and settling tanks (see Lane and Morris 2001). Evidence for all of these was noted across the Scheme, in particular at SMR06 and SPE02, where all of these elements were recorded (Scholma-Mason 2024).

In the following section the evidence for salt production from Triton Knoll is reviewed, situating the data within its wider local setting. Opening with a review of the briquetage from the Scheme, the section then considers the evidence for water management, ovens, fuel sources, and finally the ceramic data from the sites.

Briquetage

First used to describe the ceramic industrial waste found on salterns in the Seille region of France, 'Briquetage' is now the term used universally to describe the ceramic waste from all saltmaking sites (salterns). Earliest recognised discoveries of briquetage on the Lincolnshire coast came from the mid-19th century when pedestals in particular were found 'in no small quantities' on the beach at Ingoldmells, close to the Triton Knoll sites, and described as 'washed up after gales of wind, by which they are dislodged from the beds of black mud off that coast' (Reynardson 1850, 75). Since then, saltern sites have been found on the old land surfaces when storms have washed the sands from beaches along that stretch of coast (*e.g.* Maudson 1904; Swinnerton 1932; Baker 1960; Lane 2018, 13).

Over the years, numerous briquetage sites have been discovered. Because of the irregular and often amorphous nature of the finds, the items have been described in many contrasting and not always helpful ways, rendering it difficult to make sound comparisons with earlier or later superficially similar finds. In addition, the broad similarity of the individual briquetage pieces between sites and over a long time-scale has not made the creation of type-series easy. Moreover, the frequent lack of datable pottery associated with the salterns, along with, more recently, the relative paucity of the application of scientific dating to salterns, has hampered the formation of accurate chronologies for the saltern sites. Elaine Morris, in her review of briquetage from the Fenland Project, divided the material into three principal categories with a fourth encompassing miscellaneous material (Morris 2001, 374; see also Morris 2007; Table 5.3). In addition, Morris divided the material into a series of chronological phases providing a broad framework for dating (Morris 2007, 435; Table 5.4).

The bulk of the Lincolnshire Marsh briquetage can be dated to Morris's Phase 2 and 3, with the majority of the material deriving from SMR06 and SMR07 (Lane 2024c). Both SMR06 and SMR07 have pedestals that are cylindrical and overfired, along with heavily salt-bleached container fragments (Fig. 5.8). Little structural material came from SMR06, with slightly more from SMR07, where it tended to be overfired and with substantial amounts of green glaze adhering, indicating high firing temperatures, again suggesting Briquetage Phases 2 or 3. There was comparatively little briquetage at SPE02. Only ten fragments of containers were recorded and these had little or no evidence of salt bleaching, suggesting that they were little- or un-used. The relative absence of container sherds has in the past been cited as evidence for a later Roman date (Morris's Phase 4; Morris and Percival 2001, 339). Supports at SPE02 comprise 12 pedestals (four complete) and eight clips (three complete). While the pedestals resemble in shape those from SMR06 and SMR07, they were, in contrast, relatively small and not as heavily fired/subjected to intense heat as the examples from SMR06 and SMR07. They are mainly broken and certainly very abraded, as if they have been around a while. Two have salt bleaching on the bases, the remainder have little or no bleaching. No obvious structural material was present, although it is almost certain the many miscellaneous pieces contain small pieces of the oven structures. Alongside the briquetage containers several pottery vessels from SMR06 and SPE02 showed signs of use in salt processing, including the base of a large grey ware jar (SF002) from the middle Roman phases of SMR06 with a thick white internal deposit, although this could represent either the residue from brineworking or urine (Rowlandson and Fiske 2024c; Fig. 5.9).

At SMR05 a small assemblage of briquetage was recovered from a dumped deposit (Saltern 8), measuring some 40 m long by 13 m wide (Fig. 5.3). A sample from this site yielded two container sherds and 144 miscellaneous pieces. Excluding the unidentifiable miscellaneous pieces, a total of 47 pieces of briquetage was collected. These comprise eight pedestals, two spacer/clips, 32 container sherds, four bar fragments, and one structural piece (Lane 2024c). None of the pedestals contained any amount of salt bleaching and none was heavily fired/vitrified. Container sherds from SMR05 are small and unusual in that there are no rims or base/wall pieces. Moreover, as with the pedestals, the level of salt bleaching is remarkably low, with only one piece heavily bleached, nine (28%) with very light bleaching, and the remaining 22 (68%) exhibiting no bleaching.

Table 5.3 Principal forms of briquetage (after Morris 2007)

Containers	Hand-made & either 'gutter-shaped' ceramic troughs or 'wide, shallow, slightly curved but mainly flat pans' (Morris 2007, 430). Containers for heating brine were placed above or within heating sources (hearths or ovens) & held in position by a variety of 'supports'
Supports	These include pedestals, ranging from substantial pyramidal types in the Iron Age, developing into hand-squeezed cylindrical varieties on which containers were situated. In addition, & serving a similar broad purpose, were bars, rods, clips, bricks, & wedges (Morris 2007, 431)
Structural material	Classed as frags of broken-up heating structures, either walls or flooring
Miscellaneous	Refers to numerous unidentifiable ceramic frags present on all salterns

Table 5.4 Morris's briquetage phases (2007)

Phase	Period	Description
1	Middle/late Bronze Age– middle Iron Age	Typically found on sites adjacent to the Western Fen Edge from Billingborough south to Deeping St James. Typically, these tended to be made in a shelly fabric. Pedestals were 'horned', rising up from a wide rectangular base to a narrower top, the latter being described as similar to a pair of horns (*e.g.* Lane 2018, fig. 25). No clips or spacers tended to be found with these Phase 1 sites. By the middle Iron Age, the pyramidal pedestals, while retaining their broad pyramidal outline, had changed to a sloping top on which rested the containers. (Morris's PD4-type; Lane 2018, fig. 26)
2	2nd century BC & later	Unlike the shelly clays of the briquetage in Phase 1 sites, Phase 2 containers & supports were made from organic-tempered fabrics. Salt production took place out in the Fenland itself, as opposed to on the inner periphery of the Fenland. By then, clips & spacers were needed to make the set-up of containers-on-pedestals suitably rigid, particularly as the Pedestals had changed from the well-made & substantial pyramidal types to slighter, cylindrical, hand-squeezed varieties. Many of these in this Phase 2 & Phase 3 were heavily overfired & green salt glazed
3	Late 1st–2nd century AD	As with the previous phase the container fragments have salt 'bleach', a white 'skin' on one side or all through, indicating a greater intensity of use. No bleaching had been present at all on the Phase 1 container frags. Large quantities of structural material in Phase 3, much of it with green salt glaze adhering, were suggestive of the use of more substantial kiln-like Ovens, as opposed to the 'direct' heating systems of the hearths
4	Later Roman	Morris (2007, 436) stated that 'late Roman salt production sites have yet to be firmly identified in Lincolnshire' (but see text). Morris noted, however, that at Middleton, in Norfolk, a major complex had been excavated consisting of three phases of typically large ovens, settling tanks & brine channels, dating to the late 3rd and 4th centuries (Crowson 2001). Briquetage was confined to 'massive' pedestals & structural debris. Only 2 ceramic container sherds were present, with the containers at that time identified as being of lead

This is likely to indicate an earlier date than that for the nearby SMR06 and SMR07.

Channels and tanks: Procuring saltwater

The saltwater placed within the briquetage containers was obtained through a number of means, including the exploitation of natural channels. Sites were typically positioned close to creeks to take advantage of these natural streams, with the changing distribution of saltern sites from the middle Bronze Age through to the Roman period being partly reflective of wider environmental changes (see Lane 2018). Located between Plots 08/05 and 09/05 was a major palaeo-estuarine creek, identified within LiDAR and in the excavation of SPE02. In the vicinity of this creek were a number of saltern sites, including the late Iron Age–early Roman saltern deposits recorded within HDD26 (see Chapter 2, Fig. 5.2). At SMR05, at the northernmost end of the Landscape Parcel, a series of natural channels were identified which could have been exploited to capture saltwater (Fig. 5.3).

In a number of cases these natural channels were enhanced through the creation of man-made channels, which were often associated with settling tanks used for the collection of saltwater (Lane and Morris 2001, 349). At SMR07, at the southern end of the Landscape Parcel, the mid-Roman saltern mound was truncated by Ditch 7.7, which was only visible in section; while the precise function of this ditch is uncertain, it is possible that it was associated with water management (Fig. 5.3). More substantive evidence for water management was noted at SMR06 and SPE02, where a series of artificial channels was identified. Running parallel to Ditch 6.11 and 6.12 was Ditch 6.8, which could have functioned as a water trap, similar to the penannular ditches at SPE02 (Fig. 5.7). During the later Roman period, two Wells, 6.26 and 6.27, were recorded in the northwestern corner of the site, one of which was capped by wooden planks (Fig. 5.10; see Bamforth 2024). As in the middle Roman period, a series of ditches was recorded, relating to wider water management systems, although unlike SPE02 no evidence for settling tanks was noted (Fig. 5.5). The settling tanks located towards the centre of SPE02 formed part of a small complex of features defining an area of salt production (Fig. 5.7). As outlined previously, this space was partly enclosed within a ring-ditch and included the remains of two saltern ovens. The arrangement of the features at SPE02 is characteristic of the period, although enclosing ditches of this type have not been previously recognised in the Lindsey Marshland, being more typically associated with Fenland sites (*e.g.* Lane 2018, figs 44 and 45). The overall layout of the features at SPE02 closely resembles the arrangement of features at Middleton, Norfolk. Located 4 km to the southeast of Kings Lynn, the site comprised a sub-rectangular enclosure with a saltmaking

Figure 5.8 Examples of key briquetage forms from Lincolnshire Marsh Landscape Parcel sites

oven and settling tank located within the southern half. The enclosing ditches probably served to trap water, although in its second phase these ditches fell out of use, with a series of settling tanks and ovens established just to the north (Crowson 2001).

The ring-ditches at SPE02 may have served a similar function to those at Middleton, supplementing the water collection taking place within the three settling tanks (Fig. 5.7). These tanks were linked to Ditch 2.1 by two 'feeder channels', Ditches 2.6 and 2.7, drawing saltwater into the settling tanks. The three tanks intercut each other, hinting at multiple episodes of activity, or alternatively the existence of a three-celled tank, similar to examples at Middleton which was sub-divided by a series of clay walls (Crowson 2001, 178). Such a system would have allowed for the first tank to be filled with saltwater, undergoing initial evaporation, before being moved into the second, and then after a further period of time into the third. Through this process, the saltwater becomes progressively more concentrated, with impurities and silt being removed (Hoover and Hoover 1950, 546–547). The concentrated brine would then have been scooped out and heated over the ovens just to the south, where the next stage of the process would have occurred.

Figure 5.9 Base of large grey ware jar (SF002) in situ at SMR06

Figure 5.10 Timber planks in upper fill of Well 6.26 at SMR06

From brine to salt, hearths, and ovens

Two principal forms of heating were employed in salt production, the simplest of which comprised saltern hearths, a fireplace where saltwater was heated. Pedestals were placed directly into the feature with the containers positioned atop these. More complex saltern ovens are typically below-ground features and include a stoke pit and flue (Lane and Morris 2001, 373). The features at SPE02 fall into the latter category and are outwardly similar in form to examples of pottery kilns. In plan, both ovens had an elongated figure of 8 shape, with Oven 2.19 measuring 1.7 m long and Oven 2.18 around 1.6 m (Fig. 5.7). The easternmost oven, 2.19, was partially truncated during machining, and it is unclear if the tapering at the eastern edge of the feature relates to a flue (Fig. 5.11). In the case of the westernmost oven, 2.18, a possible flue was located on the western edge, sloping into the oven chamber (Figs 5.12 and 5.13). Both ovens were lined with clay and filled with charcoal rich fills. The western oven, 2.18, contained evidence for two firing events, separated by a layer of clay perhaps representing a raised floor surface (Fig. 5.14). Radiocarbon dating of the lowermost fill returned a similar date range to the eastern oven, cal AD 240–410 (95% probability; 1740±30 BP, Beta-667276), and the uppermost fill, cal AD 210–370 (95% probability; 1780±30 BP, Beta-667277; Table 4.3). Radiocarbon dating of material from the easternmost oven, 2.19, returned a date of cal AD 230–390 (95% probability; 1760±30 BP, Beta-667274; Table 5.2). The lowermost fill of Oven 2.18 also contained a complete grey ware beaker or jar and may reflect a structured deposit (Fig. 5.15). Set into the ground close to the oven were two further grey ware vessels, which could have been associated with the storage of brine.

At SMR06 north of SPE02, Oven 6.10 comprised a 4.2 m long, 1.32 m wide and 0.30 m deep feature (Fig. 5.5). The basal fill contained high quantities of charcoal, similar to the deposits noted within the ovens at SPE02, although in contrast no evidence for a clay lining was noted (Scholma-Mason 2024, 39). Within three of the trial trenches the presence of probable oven lining fragments is suggestive of further ovens or hearths but no actual structures, except for a possible flue in Trench 231, were identified (Allen Archaeology 2018d, 26).

Cultivating fuel and food: The environmental assemblage

Kate Turner with contributions from Val Fryer, Marina Chorro-Giner, and Hannah Russ

The landscape of the Lincolnshire Marsh Landscape Parcel during the Roman period is likely to have been characterised by areas of wet managed and semi-derelict grassland, with species of trampled ground suggesting human or animal movement. There appears to be little variation across the Lincolnshire Marsh area, although the lack of well-preserved waterlogged remains from SMR06 could indicate that conditions were generally drier than at SPE02 and SMR07. Late Roman plant assemblages are dominated by grassland taxa and wetland plants. Species present are largely indicative of damp, open grassland, with numerous seeds of rush, docks, and silverweed in several deposits perhaps representing rush pasture. Rushes were by far the most numerous taxa in all of the analysed samples, perhaps signifying the existence of extensive rush beds in the locality that might have been utilised for fuel or other purposes such as flooring or thatching. Wet hay meadows are suggested by the presence of potential indicator species including greater burnet-saxifrage (*Pimpinella major*), hogweed (*Heracleum sphondylium*), and buttercup (Greig 1984; Hodgson *et al.* 1999). Unburnt straw and stem-type material could be the remains of grassland or marsh hay. Seeds of silverweed and red goosefoot provide evidence for trampling by human or animals, perhaps supporting the presence of managed pastures along some parts of the route during this period.

Figure 5.11 Oven 2.19 at SPE02

Figure 5.12 Mid-excavation photo of Oven 2.18 at SPE02 with elements of charcoal in fill in situ

Figure 5.13 Post-excavation photo of Oven 2.18 at SPE02

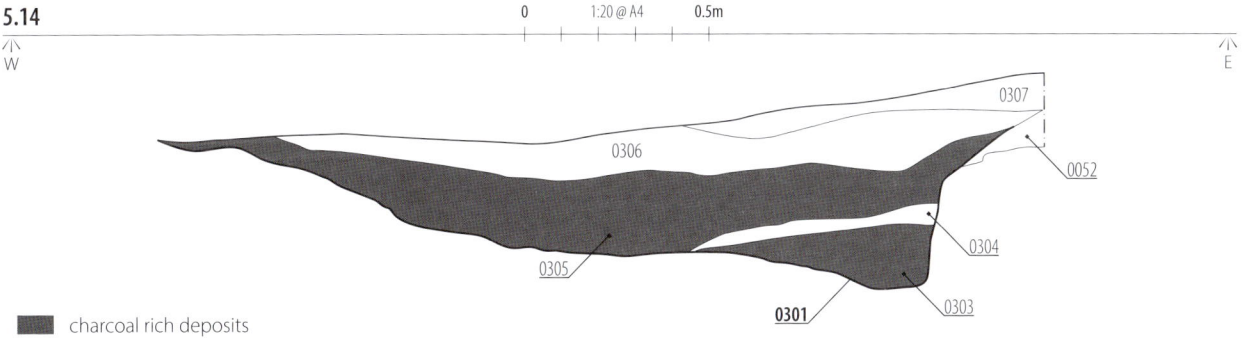

Figure 5.14 Section through Oven 2.18 at SPE02

Analysis of charred and waterlogged plant remains from this area also emphasised the probable links between salt production and the surrounding environment during the middle and later Roman periods. The composition of the charred assemblage indicates that vegetation growing locally may have provided an important source of fuel for industry in the area. This could have included the use of peat, with some evidence for the use of this fuel type being noted at Saltern 7.1 at SMR07 (Fryer and Turner 2024), and plants gathered from hay meadows, reed beds, and managed grassland, the latter in the form of cut turves.

The utilisation of cut turves is suggested by the presence of charred root material and the remains of compressed stem 'mats' in the ovens which could represent the burnt remains of spent flooring. The practice of collecting local vegetation as fuel for the saltmaking industry is not uncommon, with raw materials likely chosen based on seasonal and spatial availability, as seen at other Fenland sites (Gale 2001). This material is likely to have been used in conjunction with other readily available fuels, notably crop processing waste. Variations in the composition of primary deposits of fuel waste, such as those

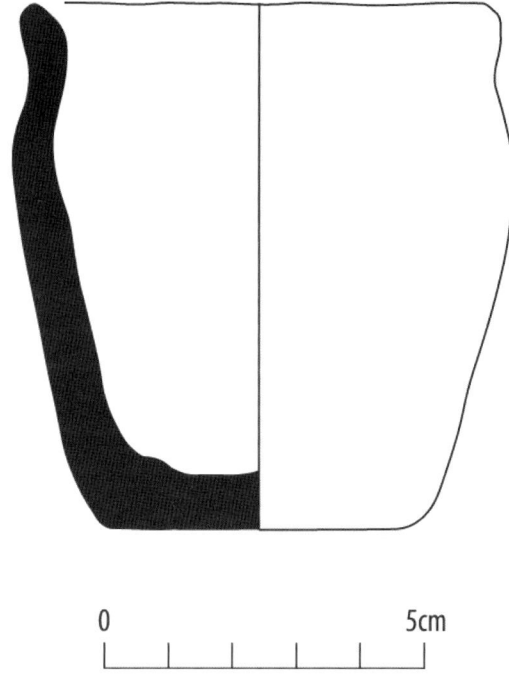

Figure 5.15 Grey ware beaker from Oven 2.18, SPE02

associated with Ovens 2.18 and 2.19 (SPE02) and deposit 6.13 (SMR06), are of particular interest, and support the hypothesis that fuel use may have fluctuated periodically.

The presence of mixed plant assemblages comprised of cereal processing waste in conjunction with evidence for hay, as well as possible turves and peat, in the samples from SMR07, SPE02, and SMR06, indicates that a variety of raw materials were being exploited to fuel domestic and industrial activities, including salt production. Use of a range of plant based fuels is not unusual in fenland areas, with assemblages often containing a combination of wood charcoal, crop processing waste, peat or turves, and cut vegetation (Gale 2001, 456). Charred plant assemblages with evidence for mixed fuels have been recorded at other fenland locations, including the saltern site at Morton Fen (Murphy 2001a), the Iron Age/Roman settlement site at Bourne Road, Spalding (Giorgi 1998), and also on sites in the Cambridgeshire Fenland (Andrews 2006). In addition to being utilised as fuel, it has been suggested that crop waste and gathered plants may also have been used as a tempering for briquetage in some areas (Murphy 2001b).

Wood charcoal was comparatively rare from within not only the Lincolnshire Marsh Landscape Parcel, but across the route as a whole. Fragments of oak charcoal were recorded in several deposits across the Scheme, along with charred acorn shell and cupules, which indicates that there may have been oak woodland in the local area, although the lack of such material in the Lincolnshire Marsh assemblages suggests that oak wood may not have been widely used as fuel at these sites.

Gale (2001) proposed that other industries in the region could have strained limited local woodland resources, leading to the utilisation of alternative fuels. It is also plausible that raw materials possessing a high calorific value, such as oak charcoal, were more suited to and reserved for high intensity industries like smelting, while lower value fuels, such as peat or cut vegetation, were reserved for low intensity tasks such as brine evaporation. As highlighted in Chapter 2 there are abundant peat deposits within the local vicinity and these could have formed the primary fuel source for saltworking. Peat is known to have been used as the principal fuel source during the medieval period, with grants for salterns also included rights to cut peat (Lane 2018, 47). Given that peat burns so comprehensively it can be difficult to identify within assemblages (Lane and Morris 2001, 351), but as at Saltern 7.1 there are some indications for peat use within the Scheme. Beyond the Scheme evidence for the use of peat was noted at Nordelph, Norfolk, whilst evidence for Roman peat cuttings were noted in the vicinity of Morton Fen (Lane 2018, 44–45).

The absence of halophytes in the Lincolnshire Marsh plant assemblage is notable, with a single record of sea arrowgrass perhaps the only evidence for the use of saltmarsh vegetation during salt extraction. It is probable that such vegetation may have been used more widely outside of the saltmaking industry, but there would be little evidence for this in the archaeological record unless these materials were being burnt after use.

Alongside the botanical remains, a panoply of faunal remains were also recovered, suggesting some pastoral activity taking place alongside the salt production. In the middle Roman period cattle were the main domesticate identified, with the pattern of mortality suggesting meat exploitation with no evidence for older animals that might be linked with traction. In the late Roman period epiphyseal fusion data show that around 20% of cattle were being slaughtered during their first year but most of them were slaughtered by their third year, with few surviving past 4 years of age. The assemblage includes an over-representation of the upper forelimb (scapulae and humerii) compared with other skeletal elements. This may suggest that choice cuts were being brought onto site, echoing patterns from elsewhere across the Scheme (see Chapter 4). In the case of the Lincolnshire Marsh sites this material may have been brought onto site for salt curing, a notion that is further explored in Chapter 6. Sheep, in contrast, appear to have been processed on-site, with most carcass elements present. Epiphyseal data show that most of the sheep seem to have been killed after their first month and up to their second year, with some surviving up to their third year and a half. This pattern is consistent with animal husbandry focused on meat production (Chorro-Giner 2024b). Pig may have also been brought to site with teeth being the most common element present, with skulls, radii, femora, and tibiae also present. An absence of scapulae and humerii might suggest that shoulders of pork prepared at the site were transported elsewhere for consumption, sale, and/or trade.

No equid remains were recovered from middle Roman features or deposits at the Lincolnshire Marsh Landscape Parcel, which may suggest that the settlement there was of low status given the resources required to keep a horse. Equids were present at the location during the late Roman period, during which activity at this location seems to intensify compared with the middle Roman period and potentially reflects economic growth and an increase in status and wealth of those living at the Lincolnshire Marsh, a change that can also be seen in aspects of the pottery from each of the sites.

Collection, storage and trade: The pottery assemblage

Ian M. Rowlandson and Hugh G. Fiske with a contribution from Gwladys Monteil

The assemblages from SPE02 and SMR06, largely dated to the late Roman period provide insights into the storage practices and trade connections at each of the sites. Pottery dating to the middle Roman period was present at SMR06 suggesting a long period of occupation with multiple phases of activity. At SMR06 the pottery was fresh with a number of fragments from large storage jars or bowls that were probably used as part of the industrial process. It is also possible that some of the recovered amphorae sherds had been reused for this function. It was notable that the inhabitants of this site appeared to be far more integrated with Roman trading networks and dining practices than their contemporaries living on inland rural sites to the west of the Lincolnshire Wolds. These coastal dwellers had sherds of late Roman table ware from Argonne, Northern Gaul and a stamp decorated bowl from Hertfordshire or Essex of a type that is seldom seen on sites in Lincolnshire. Other table ware present included colour-coated sherds probably produced in the Nene Valley and local fine grey wares. The production and exchange of salt with coastal traders may have resulted in the offloading of such trinkets to the Lincolnshire coast rather than to consumers in the north at York or Hadrian's Wall. Although these vessels may suggest the inhabitants had some urge to consume distinctive 'Roman' table ware, it may be that such unusual ceramic vessels were merely easier to acquire in exchange for trading salt at a coastal site than for the average rural labourer seeking table ware at a regional market swamped with the products of the local kilns at Market Rasen.

At SPE02 the assemblage was more functional including mostly grey ware and Dales ware with only small quantities of table ware reinforcing the impression that the area was primarily for salt production. The range of pottery present was mostly utilitarian grey ware and burnished grey wares similar to those recorded at the more ambiguous industrial site further north at Stallingborough (Rowlandson 2011a). Much of the pottery was well preserved, high-fired occasionally with burnished surfaces. Whilst there were a few sherds that showed signs of warping it does not appear that there was large scale pottery production on the site (Scholma-Mason 2024). The most notable vessel was a complete miniature beaker or jar that had been crudely handmade that was found in Oven 2.18 (LM21). Darling (unpublished data from Market Rasen) and others have postulated a ritual function for such vessels and the find spot within the oven might support some form of 'structured deposition' or 'closure' interpretation (Hill 1995).

A small quantity of samian, fine grey ware beakers, colour-coated bowls, and beakers was recorded along with a few sherds of Swanpool type oxidised ware that would have functioned as table ware suggesting some domestic activity (Fig. 5.16). Shell-gritted Dales ware jars were also present as would be expected from a site of this date. The samian ware assemblage includes a limited number of earlier vessels from La Graufesenque dated to the late Flavian–early Trajanic period (AD 80–120). These few vessels either represent earlier occupation or perhaps a slightly higher status revealed by access to samian. A new die was also identified among the name-stamps for the potter *Fuscus* ii who worked in the late Flavian and Trajanic period in La Graufesenque in South Gaul (see Monteil in Rowlandson and Fiske 2024c, 26).

It was notable that, although there was evidence for activity in the 4th century AD, there were none of the key indicators present that represented activity in the later 4th–early 5th century AD (see Darling 1977; Rowlandson *et al.* 2017) suggesting that the site may have fallen out of use by that stage. However, many of the grey ware forms that were present continued to be produced until the end of the Roman period and it may be we merely lack the key type fossils from this sample.

Triton Knoll and salt production in Lincolnshire

Taken as a whole, the data for salt production across the Scheme is typical of the region, encompassing mounds of briquetage and evidence for salt production in the form of hearths and ovens. The sites themselves form part of a wider landscape of salt production located within the Lindsey Marshland. Many of these are known through surface scatters of briquetage often revealed through fieldwalking. The present day location of these is in part reflective of changing environmental conditions, with many salterns sites being located along the lines of former creeks (see Lane 2018). In addition a number of coastal saltern sites have likely been lost owing to coastal erosion.

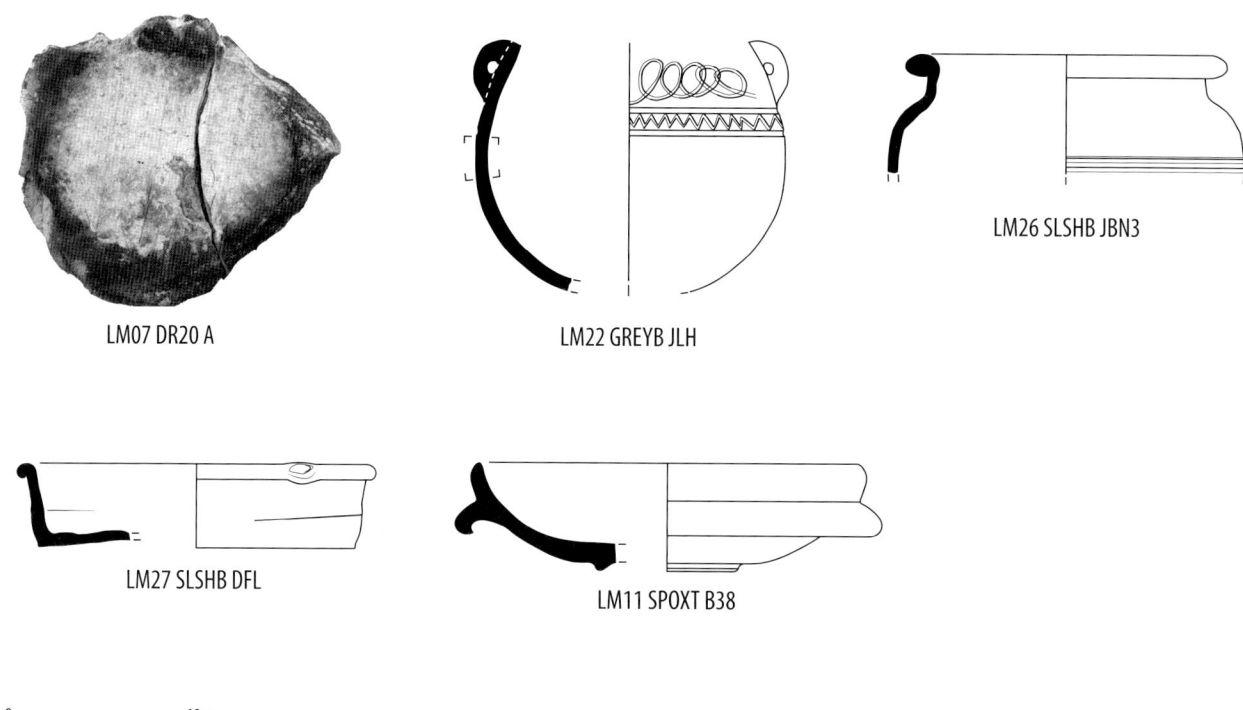

Figure 5.16 Examples of Roman pottery from SMR06 and SPE02: LM07. fragment of Dressel 20 amphora; LM22. grey ware lug-handled jar with burnished wavy line and scroll decoration; LM26. Bourne-type shell-gritted jar; LM27. Bourne-type lipped dish; LM11. Swanpool flanged bowl

At present, dating evidence from these sites suggests that salt production was a long-lived process, with several examples spanning the middle and later parts of the Bronze Age and into the early Iron Age (Lane 2007). The saltern at SPE01 in the Coastal Landscape Parcel, can be fitted within this early phase of production and it is also possible that the saltern in HDD24 is of a similar date, although the dating evidence for the feature comprises one sherd of pottery. Salt production continued into the middle–late Iron Age with salt production potentially playing a key role in Iron Age economies of the region (Elsdon 1996, 5). None of the recorded salterns from the Scheme can be assigned to this period although, given the limited dating evidence for the saltern sites recorded in the direct drilling sites and the trial trenches, it is possible that some of these pre-date the later Iron Age.

A high percentage of the salterns recorded within the wider area have been dated to the late Iron Age–early Roman period, predominantly on the basis of briquetage. The salterns at SMR05 and SMR07 probably form part of this group, sitting at the western extent of a group of salterns extending from Ingoldmells (Figs 5.1 and 5.2). The data from SMR05 and SMR07 relate to the waste deriving from salt production and it is unclear if these sites were also the centres of salt production. At SMR06 the multiple saltern deposits are indicative of more sustained salt production. As at SMR07 there was evidence for episodes of flooding although the dating and nature of these events is unclear. While episodes of marine ingress are known to have occurred in the later Roman period, it is difficult to ascertain if these events recorded in section relate to a larger episode of flooding or more localised seasonal flooding events.

Traditionally saltworking is seen as having reached a peak in the 1st century AD, with the industry declining by the mid-2nd century AD (Hallam 1970, 70; see Lane 2018, 128–129). The salterns from SMR06 and SMR07 could relate to this 'final' phase, with the pottery suggesting a 2nd century AD date for their use. Various explanations have been put forth to explain this apparent decline, including changes in sea levels and impeded drainage (Gurney 1978, 8), as well as a wider shift in the location of salt production to inland sites in the midlands (Rodwell 1976). The relative absence of dating material could also be cited as a further factor, prohibiting nuanced dating of saltern sites (see Hayes and Lane 1992, 218). Additionally, if late Roman saltmaking was less reliant on briquetage, this would remove one of the key indicators of saltmaking, the 'red hills', inhibiting the recognition of such sites (Bradley 1975, 25). As noted, previous discoveries from other regions indicate a continuation of the industry into the 3rd century. Archaeomagnetic dating at Morton Fen returned dates of cal AD 294–375 (68% confidence) and cal AD 125–188 (68% confidence level), although the veracity of these dates is uncertain (Lane and Morris 2001, 157). Instances of 3rd and 4th century AD pottery have also been noted at several saltern sites in Lincolnshire, but this material often appears to post-date the industrial use of the site and reflects later occupation (Crowson 2001, 245). Briquetage from four sites in the Wrangle parish could also fall within Morris's Phase 4 as container sherds were uncommon (Morris and Percival 2001, 327). Container sherds were also limited at SPE02, reinforcing the idea of the site belonging to a late Roman phase of production.

The site at SPE02 shows a high degree of organisation with a series of water management and processing facilities. This layout finds parallel at both London Gateway in the Thames Estuary and Middleton in Lincolnshire. At London Gateway, Saltern 5808 had a comparable layout to both SPE02 and Middleton but appeared to be situated atop a middle Iron Age saltern (Biddulph and Stansbie 2012, 115). The dating evidence for Saltern 5808 is equivocal, comprising three sherds of pottery, and a middle Roman date is possible. At Middleton, the dating evidence comprises a more substantive collection of late Roman pottery (Crowson 2001, 216). The arrangement of the features at Middleton was suggested to reflect the existence of a more formalised salt industry, moving away from *ad hoc* models of production in the early Roman period towards possibly a more centralised and controlled mode of production (Crowson 2001, 248).

The formal planning of the SPE02 production area could also be attributed to a similar model, with the apparent levelling of the space prior to construction and the creation of an ordered central working space. It is also possible that the establishment of the late Roman saltworking features at SMR06 is part of a similar process, although unlike SPE02 there was evidence for a preceding phase of middle Roman saltworking. The length of time for which SMR06 was 'abandoned' is uncertain, the overlying alluvial deposits could reflect seasonal flooding or the accumulation of deposits over multiple years. Nevertheless, the establishment of SMR06 and SPE02 in the late Roman period suggests a persistence of saltworking into the 3rd century AD, potentially stimulated by continued demand for salt, an aspect that will be further reviewed in the following chapter which draws together the key themes emerging from this review of the evidence of salt production and the data from Chapter 4.

6

Inhabiting the fens: Communities and connections during the Roman period

Owain Scholma-Mason, Maria Stockdale, and Tom Lane

In the preceding two chapters the Roman archaeology from the Scheme has been set out, highlighting aspects of settlement morphology and economy. This has included, in Chapter 4, a detailed review of the environmental and artefactual data while in Chapter 5 the evidence for salt production was further outlined. What is apparent from these reviews is the varied nature of settlement and associated activity across the Scheme, with subtle variations in morphology and economy evident between each of the sites. The data relating to the agricultural economy showed varying emphases within arable and pastoral regimes across each of the Landscape Parcels. This included differences in the levels of arable cultivation and processing, with SPE03 and SPE04 in particular showing high levels of cereal processing compared to other sites on the Scheme. Within the faunal data, variations in livestock regimes were identified with some sites partly relying on imported joints of meat to supplement their diet. The differences in agricultural regimes across the Landscape Parcels reflect a series of choices contingent on local environmental conditions alongside wider socio-economic factors.

These aspects are synthesised in this chapter, building on the data from Chapters 4 and 5 to develop a clearer picture of the agricultural strategies that underpinned the economies of the Triton Knoll sites. Inter-site variability is further explored to understand how these strategies reflect environmental conditions and socio-economic choices across the Scheme and how these changed between the earlier and later Roman periods. To this end, the evidence for arable production is first reviewed, exploring variations in crop choice and how these were in part informed by environmental factors. This is followed by a summary of the evidence for crop processing and the movement of chaff across the Scheme, highlighting the importance of this secondary product. There is then a review of the evidence for pastoral regimes, complemented by a synthesis of the evidence for salt production and particularly its relationship to other industries across the region, building on the data from Chapter 5. In the final section, the concepts of wider connections and interconnectivity across the region are explored, with an emphasis on the changing nature of the socio-economic landscape from the early to late Roman period.

Veni, vidi, colui: Roman agriculture at Triton Knoll

Before reviewing the data from Chapters 4 and 5 it is worth expanding on the context of agricultural production within the Scheme, highlighting the particular environmental and socio-economic circumstances in which it took place. This provides an important context in which to discuss aspects of not only organisation but also the generation of agricultural surplus, which was key to the operation of the Roman economy. Turning to the environmental factors first, as highlighted in Chapters 2 and 4 the route of the Scheme crosses a number of distinct environmental zones, including areas of marsh, regions prone to seasonal flooding, as well as expanses of heavier clay soils (Fig. 6.1). Importantly these environments were subject to change across the period, with evidence for marine ingress occurring in the later Roman period flooding areas of the recolonised landscape (Elsdon 1997, 5; see Chapter 2). These varied conditions will have impacted on the suitability of the land for arable cultivation, pastoral farming, and settlement. This is observed at SPE02 where the marginal land was probably seasonally exploited for sheep grazing as well as salt production. The identification of late Roman salt production is in itself, as highlighted in Chapter 5, of particular significance, countering previous perceptions of the decline of the industry in this region during the early Roman period. Towards the southern end of the Scheme at Langrick (SPE03, SPE04, and SMR17) and Bicker (TAM04/SMR01) there is a correlation between the increased use of cattle for traction and the evidence for the cultivation of clay soils. While in part driven by changes in technology, such as heavier ploughs, the decision to expand onto or utilise marginal land will also have been informed by socio-economic factors, the first and most important being the provision of enough food to support basic subsistence. What was left above this would have been employed for paying rents or taxes, leaving a potentially small 'disposable surplus' (Bang 2008, 77; Gerrard 2013, 97–99). This surplus could have been utilised to buy other products such as pottery, clothing, and agricultural implements, or be converted into gold and silver coinage. The overall disposable surplus would have in many cases been minimal and would have been impacted by a range of aspects including increases in rent alongside environmental factors such as flooding, crop failures, or disease among livestock impacting overall yields (*e.g.* Gerrard 2013, table 3.1).

Consequently, most farmsteads would have operated at a subsistence level, although some may have pursued strategies to optimise this, including placing an emphasis on particular products, and/or hiring seasonal labour

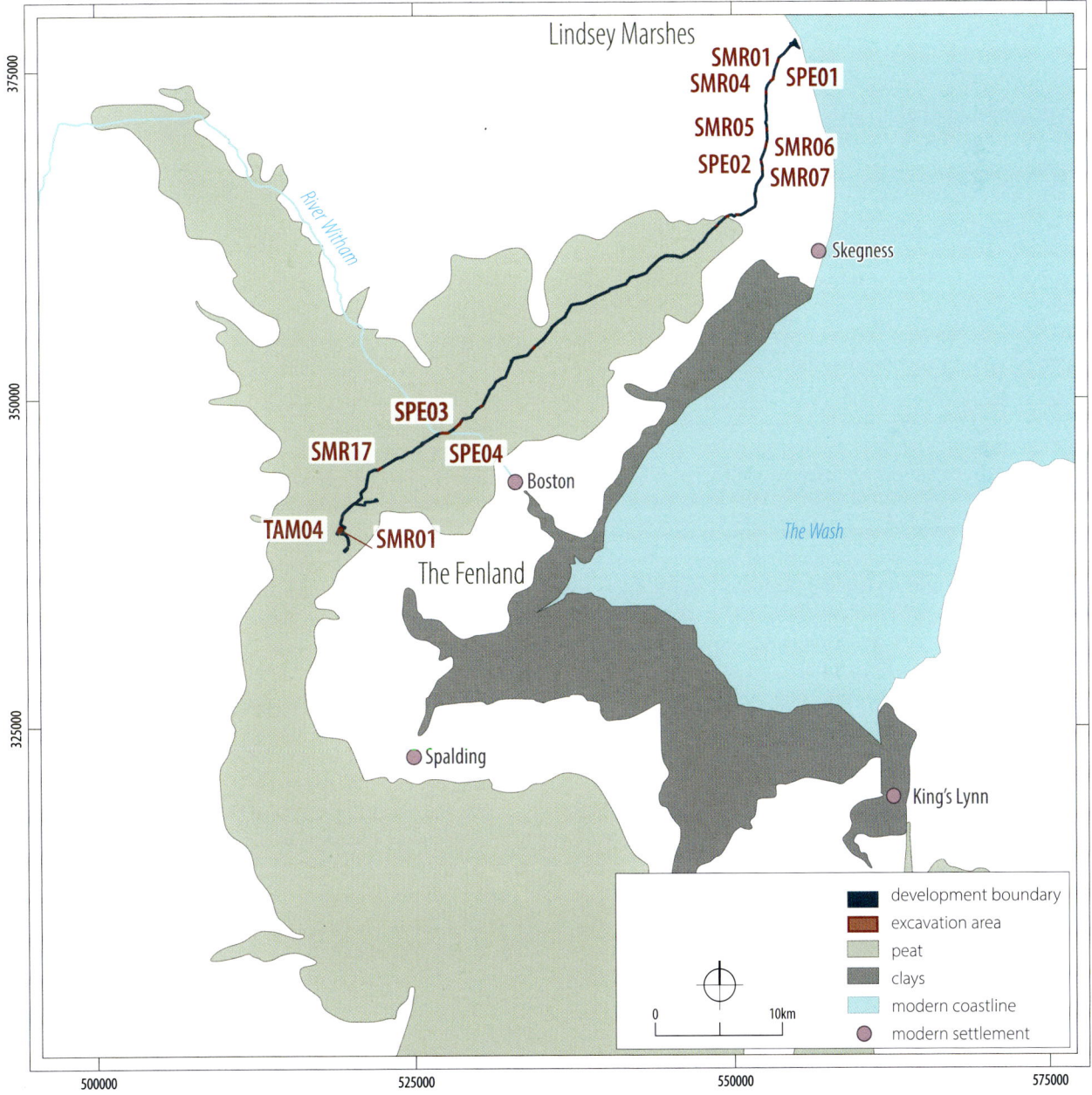

Figure 6.1 Sites in their Roman landscape context (the Fenland in c. AD 100, after Hall and Coles 1994, fig. 68)

as well as investing in land improvements (McCarthy 2013, 11; Erdkamp 2015, 27). The inter-connections between individual sites may have allowed for some of these impacts to be offset and could have enabled some farmsteads to focus on particular products or processes such as milling, dairying, or salt production. These products were still couched within a wider agricultural regime and reflect a diversification of production which may in part have been stimulated by the supra-regional networks within which the sites were located. In the case of Triton Knoll the supra-regional aspects encompass the relationship of its sites to other settlements within the region, including the *colonia* at Lincoln (*Colonia Domitiana Lindensium*), *c.* 54 km to the west of SPE02. Founded in the mid-1st century AD as a legionary fortress, Lincoln became a colony in the Flavian period and, in the 4th century AD, a provincial capital (Wacher 1974, 120–137; Jones 2002). Alongside the development of Lincoln, several other larger settlements are known from across the Wolds, including at Caistor, Horncastle and possibly Burgh le Marsh. These centres, as well as being key consumers of agricultural produce, will probably have acted as points for the collection of taxes, as well as being host to regional markets providing a forum for the exchange of surplus for other items such as imported pottery. At a higher level, demands by the state in the form of tax (either in kind or cash) will also have created an economic stimulus which may have partly driven an intensification in agricultural regimes and the development of centralised processes (Garnsey and Saller 2014, 82). This includes provisioning for the Roman army, which was reliant on external suppliers, although how this was organised is unclear; produce may have been directly requisitioned by the army or through military contracts (Thomas and Stallibrass 2008; Allen and Lodwick 2017, 174). Gauging the degree to which this took place and its impact on local communities is beset by a range of problems. Nevertheless, alongside the expansion of new settlements and wider markets it may have provided a key stimulus for the expansion and diversification of agricultural regimes.

To examine these further the following section weaves together multiple strands of data from Chapters 4 and 5 to explore the nature of arable and pastoral farming from across the Scheme and how this changed over time. The review aims to understand the scale and intensity of agricultural regimes, in particular whether we can identify surplus production. To this end the discussion is largely centred on data from the SPE03 and SPE04, which produced the bulk of the data for cereal processing. The second half of this section looks at livestock strategies, highlighting the subtle differences in husbandry regimes between sites and what this reveals about the role of livestock and their secondary products and how these changed during the period.

Feeding the fens: Crop choice and processing

During the Roman period arable regimes were generally focused on the cultivation of barley and spelt wheat across most of Britain (Lodwick 2017). These occurred in varying quantities across the Scheme, with variations in crop choice being partly driven by underlying soil conditions, with barley particularly suited to saline conditions. Spelt wheat in contrast was ideal for heavier soils and was the preferred crop throughout the Roman period, reflecting a shift towards more extensive cultivation (Van Der Veen and O'Connor 1998, 131; Lodwick 2017). This trend was observed at SPE03 where the change towards spelt and bread wheat, alongside the weed ecologies, in the middle Roman period suggests the exploitation of drier soils, possibly to the west of the farmstead. This pattern of exploitation appears to indicate an expansion of arable activity at this time and can be seen as part of a broader expansion of agriculture across the region during this period (see Allen 2016).

Both SPE03 and SPE04 contained evidence for crop processing in the form of quantities of cereal waste and querns or millstones (Fig. 6.2). Crop processing was a multi-stage process involving threshing, winnowing, and sieving to remove weed seeds, and hand cleaning (White 1970, 185; Stevens 2003; Van der Veen and Jones 2007). Glume wheats such as spelt were also pounded to remove glumes, though this occurred after parching to ensure the individual spikelets were sufficiently brittle (Lodwick 2017, 49). The first stage, threshing, involves the separation of the spikelets from straw, which is left as a by-product (*ibid.*). The following two stages see the winnowing of the light chaff, followed by coarse and fine sieving. The presence or absence, as well as the quantity of cereal waste, is often taken as an indicator of the scale of arable cultivation and has in the past been used to define consumer and producer sites (*e.g.* Jones 1985). Recent critiques have highlighted the multiple factors that can influence the presence, absence, as well as quantity of cereal waste on site (see Van Der Veen and Jones 2007).

In the context of SPE03, while the data indicate early and late stage crop processing, it is difficult, given the relatively small sample size to determine if this reflects domestic production or if cereals were being produced in quantities beyond those needed by the immediate community (Wallace and Fryer 2024). The relatively low number of querns on site alongside the dearth of grain suggests as well that the semi-processed grain from SPE03 was probably dispatched elsewhere for consumption, storage, or grinding into flour. At SPE04, 0.8 km to the southeast, five quern and two millstones were recovered indicating the grinding of grain into flour on site during the middle–late Roman period, an impression reinforced by the presence of possible milled grains (see Fig. 4.13). No indication of an actual mill structure was noted during the excavations, although evidence for such structures across the country is comparatively rare (Smith 2016,

Figure 6.2 Spilsby sandstone beehive quern from SPE04

60). Nevertheless, the proximity of the site to the River Witham could have facilitated the use of a watermill. The presence of milling at SPE04 could also reflect a shift towards increasing centralisation of grain processing during the later Roman period, echoing trends from across the country (Lodwick 2017, 72; see conclusions below). It is also worth reiterating that activity at SPE03 seemingly came to an end in the mid-3rd century AD, given the proximity of the two this could suggest a relocation of cereal processing from SPE03 to SPE04 (Fig. 6.3). This centralisation is closely allied to shifts in the scale of production and it is probable that the flour produced at SPE04 may not have all been intended for on site consumption but instead could have then been moved off site via the River Witham for onward distribution, either to the west towards Lincoln or along the east coast.

The pattern of crop processing at SPE03 and SPE04 contrasts with the early–to late Roman farmstead at SMR01/TAM04 within the Inland Fen Edge Landscape Parcel at Bicker Fen. Here, low quantities of cereal waste and few querns were recorded, suggesting that crop processing was occurring on a reduced scale, though given the narrowness of the excavated area the possibility that these activities were taking place within an unexcavated portion of the site cannot be ruled out. It is also possible that the processing waste that was recovered was brought in from elsewhere for a specific purpose such as fodder and/or fuel (Van der Veen 1999; Fryer and Bailey 2024, 60). At SPE02, within the Lincolnshire Marsh Landscape Parcel, there was evidence of cereal waste being used for fuel in the saltern ovens (see Chapter 5), which may explain the varied isotopic picture of this material, it being waste from cereals grown over a wide area with different soil conditions. The utilisation of alternative fuels is noted across the region, including at Morton Fen in southern Lincolnshire, where wetland plants and cereal waste were used (Trimble 2001). This may reflect a lack of fuelwood or the practice of reserving timber for construction and other industrial processes. Additionally, while millstone fragments were recorded at SPE02 and could have been employed for cereal processing, they could also reflect secondary material imported for a range of alternative uses, such as the crushing of salt, as documented in ethnographic studies (Peacock 2013, 21; Watts 2014, 38). On balance the data from the Lincolnshire Marsh and Inland Fen Edge sites do not suggest that these settlements were engaged in large-scale cereal cultivation, although this is difficult to prove based on the archaeobotanical assemblage.

Shepherds and cowherds: Pastoral regimes at Triton Knoll

Livestock formed the second key component of Roman agricultural regimes, providing a range of primary and

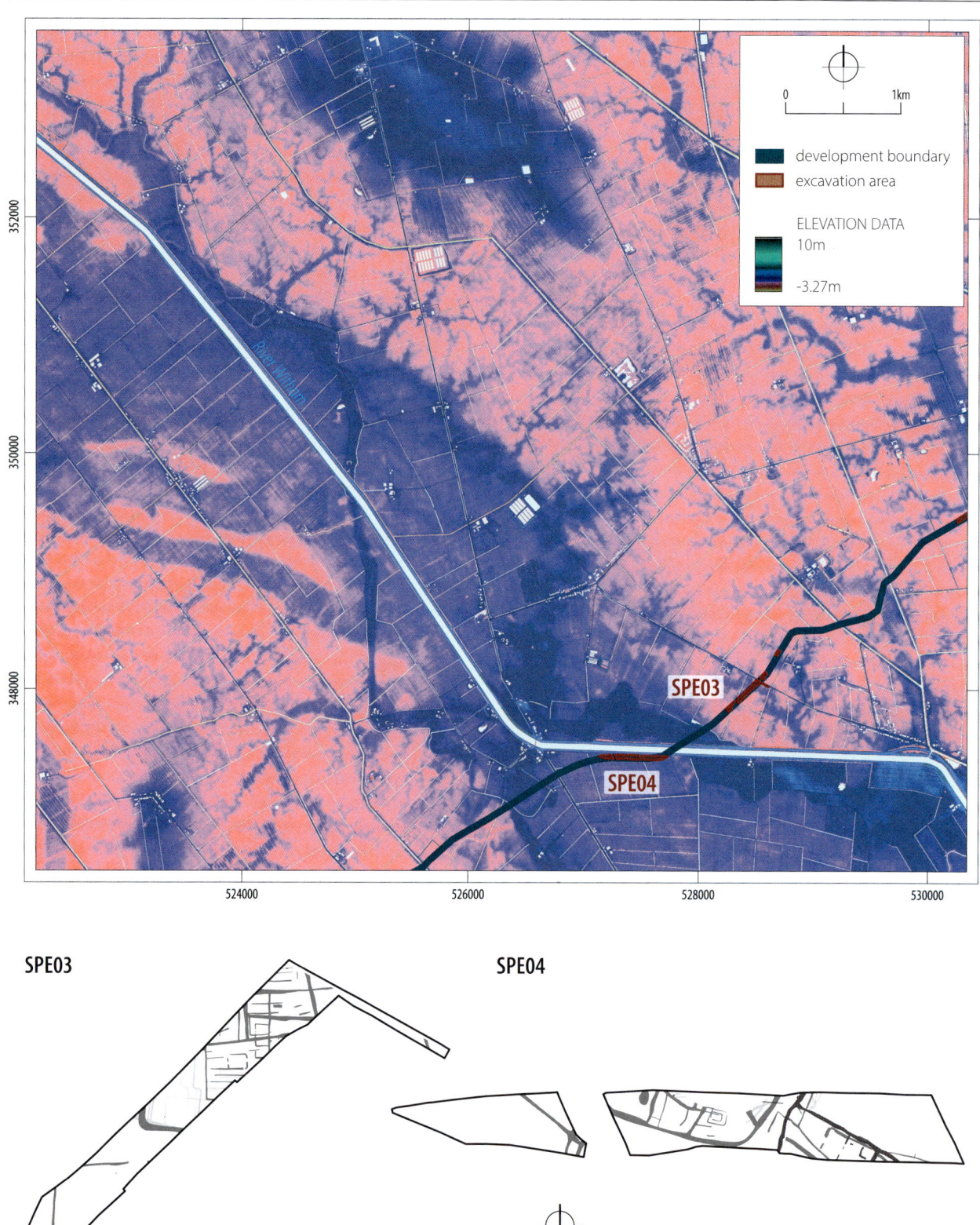

Figure 6.3 Topography and layout of SPE03 and SPE04 (LiDAR background mapping: Environment Agency reproduced under Open Government Licence v3.0; Environment Agency 2024)

secondary products. As highlighted in Chapter 4, pastoral regimes during the Roman period were centred on cattle and sheep with subtle variations in patterns of exploitation. These patterns reflect a range of factors, including the relative value placed on particular products, such as meat or dairy, as well as environmental factors, such as the availability of grazing and feed (Payne 1972). The impact of these factors can be seen across the faunal assemblages with subtle variations in patterns of husbandry across the Scheme. Within the Inland Fen Edge and Fen Edge cattle were dominant, being retained for meat, traction, and dairy, with the latter being particularly dominant at the Inland Fen Edge. Within Lincolnshire Marsh sheep were the primary domesticate, with evidence for on site butchery, whereas joints of beef were brought into site rather than being processed onsite.

The variations in sheep versus cattle husbandry practices are accompanied by subtle differences in butchery practices noted between the Landscape Parcels. Direct evidence for butchery in the form of cut or chop marks was relatively restricted, prohibiting closer scrutiny of the scale and intensity of butchery and whether 'specialist' butchers were operating at any of the sites (see Maltby 2007; 2022). This could be reflective of poor bone preservation or differences in carcass disposal practices. The latter factor is especially pertinent when considering that within larger more complex sites such as SMR01/TAM04 (Inland Fen Edge) there is evidence for the zoning of activities, a pattern also noted at the complex farmstead just to the south at Bicker Fen (Gaunt et al. 2024; Fig. 6.4). It is possible that within these sites butchery waste was being disposed of within the unexcavated elements of the settlement, introducing a possible bias into the data (see Allen and Lodwick 2017).

Notwithstanding the caveats just noted, the data from the Scheme indicate that on site butchery may have been restricted to a handful of sites, with others being in receipt of processed joints of meat. Turning to the evidence for butchery first, the data from the Inland Fen Edge suggest that, during the early Roman period, cattle remains represent kitchen waste, relating to products brought onto site. This pattern changes in the middle and late Roman periods when there is evidence of primary and secondary butchery on site. These shifts correspond with the expansion and development of the enclosures suggesting a growth in the scale of pastoral regimes at the site. Considering what appears to be the relatively low levels of crop processing on site, it may be the case that emphasis was instead being placed on animal husbandry. Alongside cattle, sheep were also

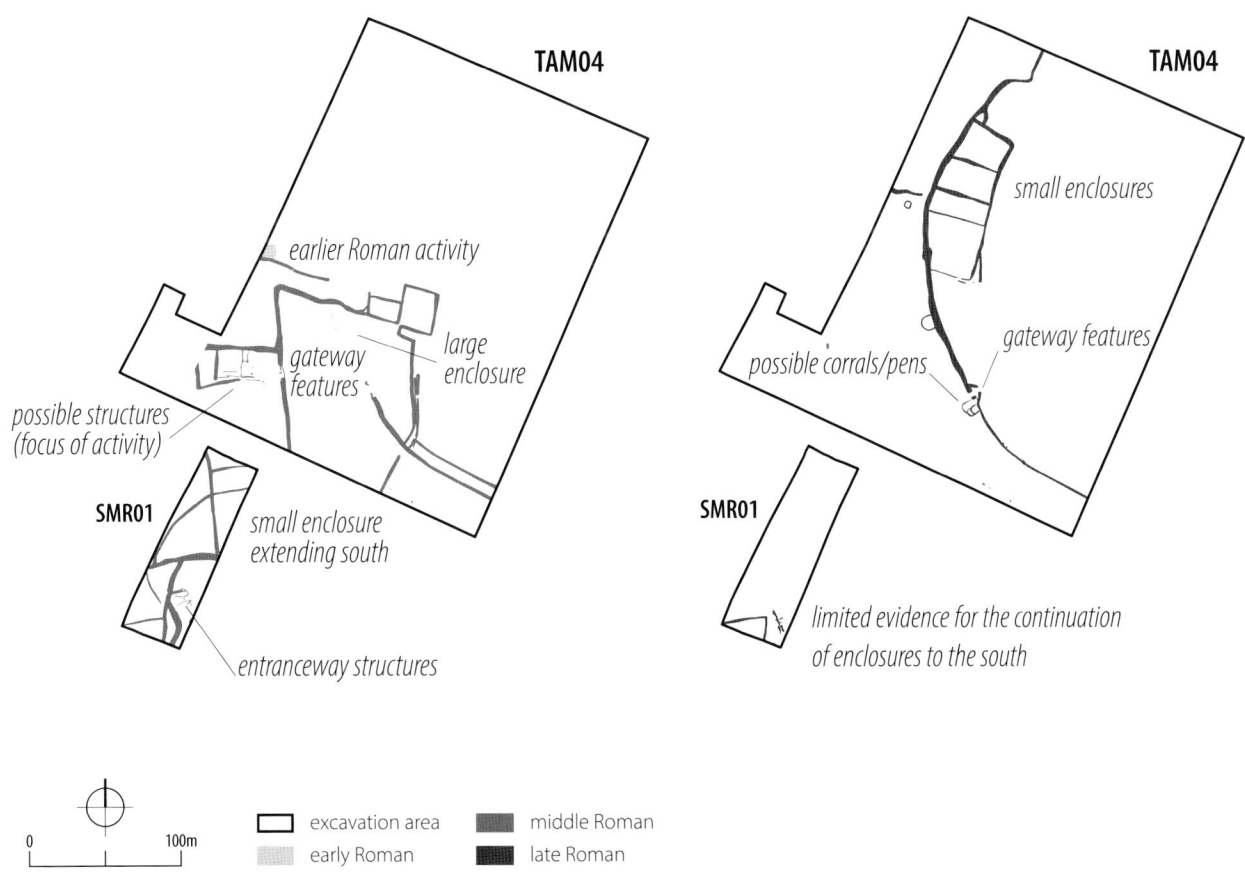

Figure 6.4 Interpretive plan of early–late Roman activity at TAM04/SMR01

butchered on site at the Inland Fen Edge, though the meat-bearing elements appear to have been exported. In contrast, within both the Fen Edge and Lincolnshire Marsh sites, sheep appear to have been fully processed and consumed on site. At the latter, it is possible that while this reflects the provision of meat for daily subsistence, it could also be linked to the culling of ewes in the autumn (McCarthy 2013, table 4.1).

If the Fen Edge and Lincolnshire Marsh sites were being utilised seasonally, this culling could have occurred before the movement of livestock to drier regions prior to winter flooding. This would have reduced the pressure on fodder over the winter as well as provided meat which could be salted and used over the winter months. In the absence of modern refrigeration techniques, most joints of meat would have been salted prior to movement to ensure their preservation. This could involve either dry or wet curing, with the latter involving the immersion of joints into brine (Dobney 2001, 41; Allen 2017, 123). At the roadside settlement at Nantwich, Cheshire, there was evidence for the storage and processing of brine, alongside cattle processing with joints of meat being cured on site (Arrowsmith and Power 2002). The incidence of shoulders of beef and some whole carcasses at SMR06 and SPE02 (Lincolnshire Marsh) could also indicate similar preservation activities although, unlike Nantwich, it is not possible to draw any direct associations between the excavated features and the faunal data.

In addition to meat, cattle and sheep were retained for a range of secondary products, primarily dairy and wool. Evidence for wool and dairy production was widely noted across the Scheme, being evidenced through not only the faunal data but also artefactually. Alongside these, other secondary products such as leather, grease, and bone will have been exploited. The evidence for dairying comprises three key strands of information, the faunal, artefactual, and residue data. The most direct evidence for dairying regimes is usually a high incidence of neonatal cattle, which were culled in their first year, freeing up the milk for human consumption (Allen 2017, 114). Tentative evidence for this is noted at the Fen Edge, where more than half of the cattle remains from the middle Roman period comprised neonates. This could suggest the culling of calves as part of a dairying regime, an impression that is further illustrated by the incidence of lipids within several pottery vessels, which show that dairy products from cattle and sheep were processed (Dunne *et al.* 2023). The degree to which this represents an opportunistic exploitation or a focus on dairying as a primary product is difficult to gauge. Cattle dairying is typically considered to have been of low importance within pastoral regimes, in part due to a lack of references to it by Roman writers (White 1970, 277). However, this likely reflects cultural values within Italy, rather than a view that is applicable to the Empire as a whole (see Dobney 2001, 37). In contrast, sheep/goat milk was consumed, as indicated by comments by Columella (White 1970, 277). Unlike cattle, sheep/goats milk proportionally gives more cheese than other livestock in higher yields (Trow-Smith 1957).

Evidence for residues deriving from the processing of dairy products was noted across the Scheme, with particular concentrations at the Inland Fen Edge and Fen Edge. At both sites residue analysis of several pottery vessels revealed the presence of ruminant adipose deriving from the processing of animal fats during cooking, alongside ruminant dairy indicative of dairy products (see Dunne *et al.* 2023). In total, 11 sherds from the Fen Edge had residues deriving from ruminant dairy, with the remainder containing ruminant adipose; this fairly even split has been documented at other sites including Bicker Fen where dairying seemed to be of less importance (Gaunt *et al.* 2024). The pattern at the Inland Fen Edge is the inverse with a bias towards ruminant dairy, which could suggest the site was more heavily involved in dairying. Jars were the dominant form with evidence of ruminant dairy, but three bowls also showed signs of dairy (*e.g.* IF06; Fig. 6.5). Jars could have been employed for the heating of milk as part of the transformative process, which would have also required salt, probably at a ratio of 1:10 (Keen 1988, 25). Although no ceramic strainers or cheese presses were noted within the Fen Edge, at the Inland Fen Edge, a pierced jar base was recovered from SMR01/TAM04 that had traces of dairy residue, while a fragment of a Nene Valley grey ware cheese press was also recovered (IFE10; Fig. 6.5). Other strainers were probably made of perishable materials (Gerrard 2008, 121). Also of note is a funnel from Lincolnshire Marsh made from salt bleached clay, suggesting it may have been produced on site (LM01; Fig. 6.5). Analysis of residue from this vessel suggests it was used in processing dairy products and could indicate some level of dairy production on site, potentially stimulated by the access to salt. The relative predominance of ruminant dairy residues across the Scheme contrasts with other sites in the region where ruminant carcass products are more common, as at Goxhill and Horton, although this could also be reflective of the better preservation and large scale sampling of residues at Triton Knoll (see Dunne *et al.* 2023). Overall, the Triton Knoll evidence indicates that the site at SMR01/TAM04 may have placed an emphasis on dairying as part of the overall pastoral regimes across the site. Although there was evidence for dairying within other sites this appears to have been occurring on a relatively low scale.

Turning from milk to the evidence for wool, this, like dairy, comprises both faunal and artefactual data. The faunal data from Inland Fen Edge suggest an emphasis on wool, a view that is corroborated by the incidence of several artefacts relating to the manufacture of textiles. These include pin beaters and a possible fragment of a weaving

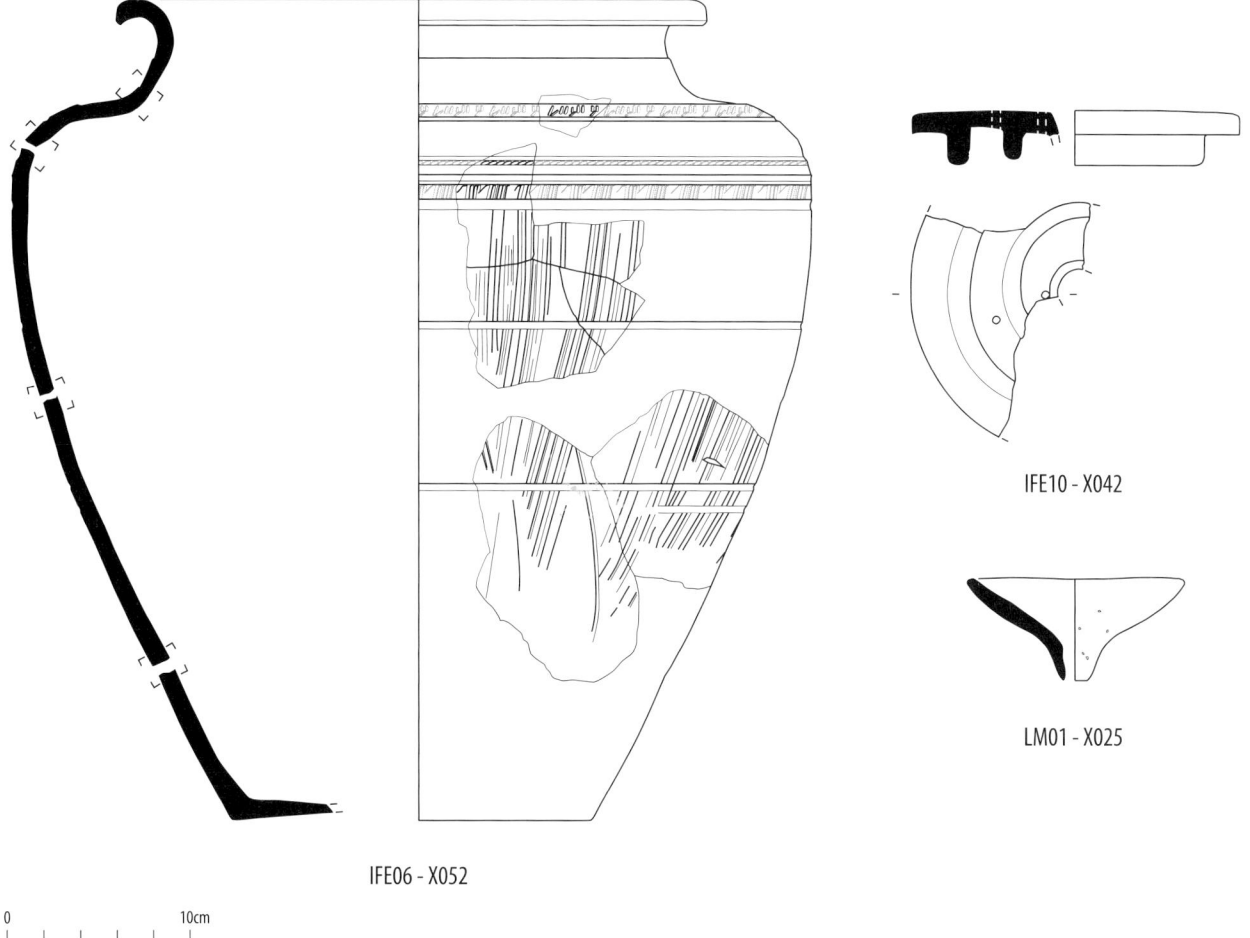

Figure 6.5 Pottery vessels with evidence of dairy residue: IFE06. necked storage jar from TAM04. IFE10. Nene Valley grey ware cheese press or 'wring' lid with pierced holes from TAM04. LM01. handmade funnel from SPE02

tablet (Fig. 6.6). Alongside these items, fragments of loom weights were also recovered, suggestive of the presence of a warp-weighted loom on site. As a whole, this suggests that textile production was taking place within the Inland Fen Edge, rather than the raw product being moved elsewhere for subsequent processing (see Smith 2017). It is unclear whether this evidence represents domestic level production or a larger 'industry'. It is possible that raw wool was also brought onto site from other areas for processing, a trend that is widely documented in the later Roman period, where particular processes such as milling appear to have become increasingly centralised, a notion that is returned to in the final section of this chapter. Taken alongside the evidence for dairying this suggests a pastoral emphasis within the Inland Fen Edge, with secondary products such as dairy and wool playing key roles. Whilst arable cultivation was occurring this does not appear to have been occurring on a scale similar to SPE03 and SPE04, although this could indicate that whilst cereal cultivation occurred at the Inland Fen Edge, cereal products may have been processed elsewhere, perhaps even at SPE03 and SPE04, which as noted may have been home to a mill.

Of pigs and horses

So far, the review of livestock regimes has been focused on the principal domesticates, sheep and cattle, but alongside these pigs and equids were also kept. Pigs were recorded in varying quantities with the bulk being from the Inland Fen Edge and Fen Edge. At the Coastal and Lincolnshire Marsh Landscape Parcels, the evidence suggests that pork was brought onto site, although some breeding may have occurred at Lincolnshire Marsh. It is possible that whole carcasses were also brought into the Fen Edge and Inland Fen Edge, with the identified remains representing table waste. It has been suggested that the consumption of pork is reflective of a 'special' status for the inhabitants (Dobney 2001, 37). The presence of neonate pig remains at the Fen Edge could indicate the consumption of suckling pig, although as noted it is possible these represent animals that did not survive birth or infancy. The consumption of suckling pig has tended

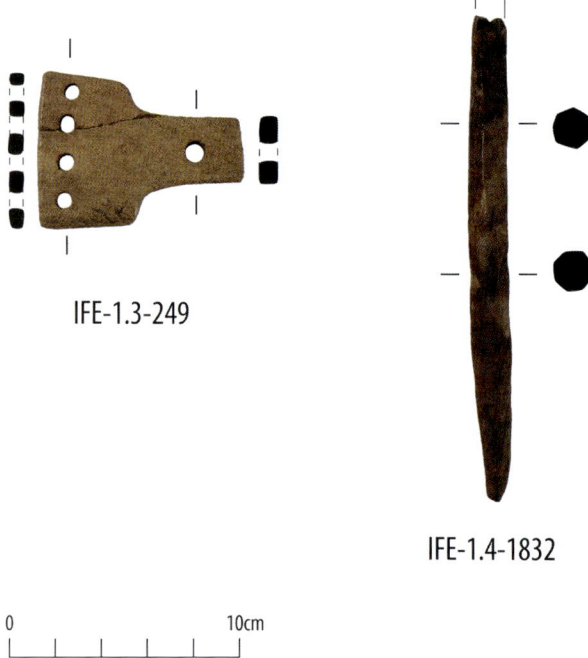

Figure 6.6 Examples of weaving tools from TAM04/SMR01: IFE-1.3-29. possible weaving tablet fragment; IFE-1.4-1832 Bone pin beater

to be associated with high-status consumption (Gerrard 2007), although there is little else from this site to suggest high status activity.

The presence of equids has also been taken as an indicator of high-status activity, being viewed as prestige animals from the Iron Age onwards (see Johnstone 2008; Allen 2017, 126). Equids were noted from middle and late Roman contexts at sites across the Scheme, albeit in relatively low numbers, with the exception of the Inland Fen Edge. Here the age at death suggested a high degree of infant mortality and, when coupled with the presence of adult and elderly animals, could suggest horse breeding (Allen 2017, 127). Horses would have been largely employed for traction and transport, and it is possible that breeding on site was undertaken to meet the growing demand for horses within the Roman period. One key consumer would have been the state itself, which would have required horses for both the army and the *cursus publicus* with estimates suggesting around 128,000 horses in the service of the latter (Johnstone 2008, 130). There was no evidence for the consumption of horse meat across the Scheme, although evidence for this has been noted at other sites including Lincoln (Dobney *et al.* 1996, 46). Instead, it appears that horses were retained for traction and transport, rather than consumption.

Salt of the earth: Saltworking at Triton Knoll

Embedded within the agricultural regime was a range of secondary 'industries' which would have served to provide items required on site as well as products which could be exchanged or sold to supplement the disposable surplus generated by agriculture. The most notable of these products comprises salt, as evidenced within the Lincolnshire Marsh Landscape Parcel. These sites, as outlined in Chapter 5, formed part of a wider distribution of salt production sites, some of which date to the middle–late Iron Age, with a further expansion of saltworking into the early Roman period (Lane and Morris 2001, 247; Fig. 5.1). The data from SPE02 and SMR06 indicate a late Roman phase of saltworking which suggests that, counter to the previously mooted idea of a decline in the industry, it instead persisted into the 3rd and 4th centuries AD. At present it is unclear if SPE02 and SMR06 represent isolated occurrences or if there are further unrecognised examples within the region.

The incidence of late Roman saltworking at SMR06 and SPE02 reflects the continued demand for salt, which was partly driven by the need to preserve agricultural produce, notably joints of meat. A 19th century source suggests a ratio of one pound of salt (0.45 kg) to approximately 14½ pounds (6.5 kg) of beef (Kurlansky 2002, 174), while calculations by Gerrard (2008, 121) suggest that 113 tons of salt would have been needed to preserve the yearly mutton required by the 4th century AD Roman army. Salt was also required in a range of other industries including dairying, leatherworking, dyeing, soapmaking, and medicine, underscoring the importance of this resource (Kinory 2012). The value of salt may have led to production being undertaken under the auspices of the state, although the evidence for this is limited. While state ownership is attested in Italy for some marine salt production sites, it is unclear to what degree this was the norm across the whole Roman world (see Marzano 2024). At Droitwich, Worcestershire, a villa was suggested to be the residence of an official in charge of the local salt industry or of a wealthy contractor (Barfield 2006, 239), though with no firm evidence. At the site of Middleton, Norfolk, the scale of production, formality of the site's layout, and its riverside location facilitating transport out of the Wash has led to the suggestion it fell under the 'military production' mode (Lane and Morris 2001, 398).

As highlighted in Chapter 5 a similar degree of formality can be observed especially in the layout of SPE02, contrasting with earlier saltern sites, suggestive of a greater degree of investment and organisation (Fig. 5.7). This could suggest this activity was undertaken within the context of a larger farmstead as part of a wider agricultural regime, possibly with some connection to state supply networks. The regime as seen at SPE02 and SMR06 included the summer grazing and butchering of sheep alongside the salting of meat products, and possibly dairying. The incidence of fish remains at Lincolnshire Marsh could also hint at one further productive activity. Although these remains could represent material consumed on site, deposits of fish remains were also noted at Stanford Wharf and suggested to be linked to the production of a fish sauce, *garum*, *liquamen*, or more likely, a derivative, *allec*, which was made from fish intestines or blood mixed with salt (Biddulph and Stansbie 2012, 169). In addition, or alternatively, fish could have been – like beef – salted on site for preservation and exported inland.

Building connections: Exchange and community

So far, this chapter has focused on the regional view, considering the data from the individual sites, outlining the nature of the agricultural economy across the Scheme alongside the data pertaining to the salt industry. Emergent from this review is a sense of the inter-connectedness of the various sites across the Scheme as evidenced through the movement of agricultural produce. This includes the movement of chaff for use as fuel as well as the distribution of carcasses and joints of meat. The evidence also hints at some sites placing a particular emphasis on certain activities – salt production and probably curing meat at Lincolnshire Marsh, cereal cultivation and larger scale processing at Fen Edge, and finally livestock husbandry (including horse breeding) at Inland Fen Edge (Table 6.1). In the case of the Lincolnshire Marsh and Fen Edge the evidence points towards increased levels of organisation and possibly greater centralisation of processes during the later Roman period. As noted in the introduction, the relative proximity of the sites both to each other and those within the immediate landscape, may have facilitated this focus. To understand the driving factors behind this shift towards particular products we need to consider the supra-regional networks which the Triton Knoll sites were part of. To this end these final sections review the wider settlement landscape, highlighting the key nodes and providing a broader context for exploring the role of larger settlements as not only consumers, but also as settings for the collection of taxes and the provision of markets.

Beyond Triton Knoll

As highlighted in the introduction, the area to the west of the Scheme is characterised by a higher density of known settlement, which is in part reflective of higher levels of development and archaeological investigation in this region (Fig. 6.7). Of note, just to the west of the Wolds is the major centre at Lincoln (*Colonia Domitiana Lindensium*) *c.* 54 km west of SPE02. From the late 1st century AD, Lincoln was a major civilian centre initially settled by veterans of the Ninth Legion (Jones 2002, 52). Within the walls of the settlement were stone buildings including a forum and a basilica which would have undertaken a range of administrative and commercial functions (Rogers 2011, 75). The settlement within Lincoln extended to the banks of the River Witham, providing access to and from the coast. This route may have been further accentuated through the addition of the Car Dyke, which could have facilitated movement from north to south, although its precise route and date of construction and use is disputed (see Simmons and Cope-Faulkner 2004; Evans *et al.* 2017). In addition, Lincoln was located on the junction of several roads, including Ermine Street, facilitating connections with other settlements in the vicinity including Caistor, located 31 km to the northeast.

Positioned at the northern end of the Wolds, Caistor was occupied from the 1st century AD and was located along a north–south routeway which may have been prehistoric in origin (Willis 2013, 371). This routeway provided access across the Wolds, including to the settlement at Horncastle at the southern end. The settlements at Caistor and Horncastle share a number of aspects in common, including the presence of stone walls. Classed as 'small towns', the origins of both are uncertain, although Horncastle may have developed from the Iron Age (Burnham and Wacher 1990, 240). The enclosure of the settlements possibly took place in the 3rd century AD, echoing the broader trend in the later Roman period for the provisioning of settlements with defences (Smith and Fulford 2019). In the case of Horncastle these defences were located on the outskirts of the early Roman settlement and have been suggested to represent a fort rather than the enclosure of the existing town (Bidwell and Hodgson 2009, 163). The nature of activity within the circuits of both settlements is uncertain and it has been suggested they formed elements of a defensive system, protecting the hinterland (Burnham and Wacher 1990, 245). An alternative scenario is to see these defended settlements as points utilised for the collection and protection of agricultural produce during the later Roman period, an idea that will be returned to below (Smith and Fulford 2019).

A limited number of settlements are noted between Caistor and Horncastle, with the *Roman Rural Settlement Project* cataloguing six sites (Fig. 6.7). Five of these were unclassifiable, whilst the sixth, at Mount Pleasant House, Nettleton, *c.* 4 km south of Caistor, comprised a roadside settlement with extensive evidence of domestic activity alongside a possible shrine (Willis 2013). Approximately 10.5 km south of Nettleton multiple finds and geophysical survey suggest further settlement (*ibid.*, 12). Along the western fringe of the Wolds several villa sites are also known, although these have received little systematic attention, and their overall dating and development is uncertain (Taylor 2006, 146). Movement eastwards across the Wolds was facilitated by a series of east–west roads, including the main road extending east from Lincoln, which bifurcates before the Wolds (Fig. 6.7). The northeast branch extends to the coast, passing through Ludborough, whilst the southeast extension extends to Burgh le Marsh, possibly continuing to the coast. Burgh le Marsh was located alongside this road with the limited excavations and isolated finds suggesting settlement activity during the Roman period (Snee 2000; Malone 2001). The precise function of Burgh le Marsh is uncertain, although it has been suggested that the coastline ran close to the settlement and it has been proposed, but not yet proven,

Table 6.1 Summary of economic activities across the Scheme

Landscape Parcel	Key sites	Summary	Arable	Pastoral	Saltworking	Other economic activity
Coastal	SMR01, SPE01, SMR04	Iron Age & Roman activity	Low arable – chaff prob. imported for fuel	Pork brought onto site	–	–
Lincolnshire Marsh	SMR05, SMR06, SPE02, SMR07	Middle–late Roman salt production sites	Low arable – Chaff prob. imported for fuel	Sheep fully processed & consumed on site – subsistence or culling of ewes before livestock movement – poss. salt preservation of sheep & cattle joints; funnel used in processing dairy products	Main focus of site in mid–late Roman period	Fish remains – poss. fish sauce production alongside salt curing
Fen Edge	SMR09, SMR10, HDD95, SMR12, SMR13, SMR14, SMR17, SPE03, SPE04, SMR16.	Roman farmsteads	SPE03: change to spelt wheat in middle Roman period SPE03 & SPE04: crop processing. Poss. milling at SPE04 in late Roman period, focus of activity poss. shifts from SPE03 to SPE04	Sheep fully processed & consumed on site Half of cattle comprises neonates, suggesting poss. dairying regimes. Residues deriving from processing of dairy products also noted; Pigs in reasonable quantity indicating poss. consumption of suckling pig	–	–
Inland Fen Edge	SMR01 and TAM4	Both sites represent elements of a single Roman farmstead including a multiphase structure	Minimal crop processing – low arable – chaff poss. imported for fodder	Prob. main emphasis was on livestock husbandry – expansion of pastoral over Roman period (primary & secondary butchery) Cattle main but sheep also butchered; residues deriving from processing of dairy products (bias towards ruminant dairy) – jar with pierced base & residue from dairying; emphasis on wool; Pigs in reasonable quantity; evidence for horse breeding	–	–

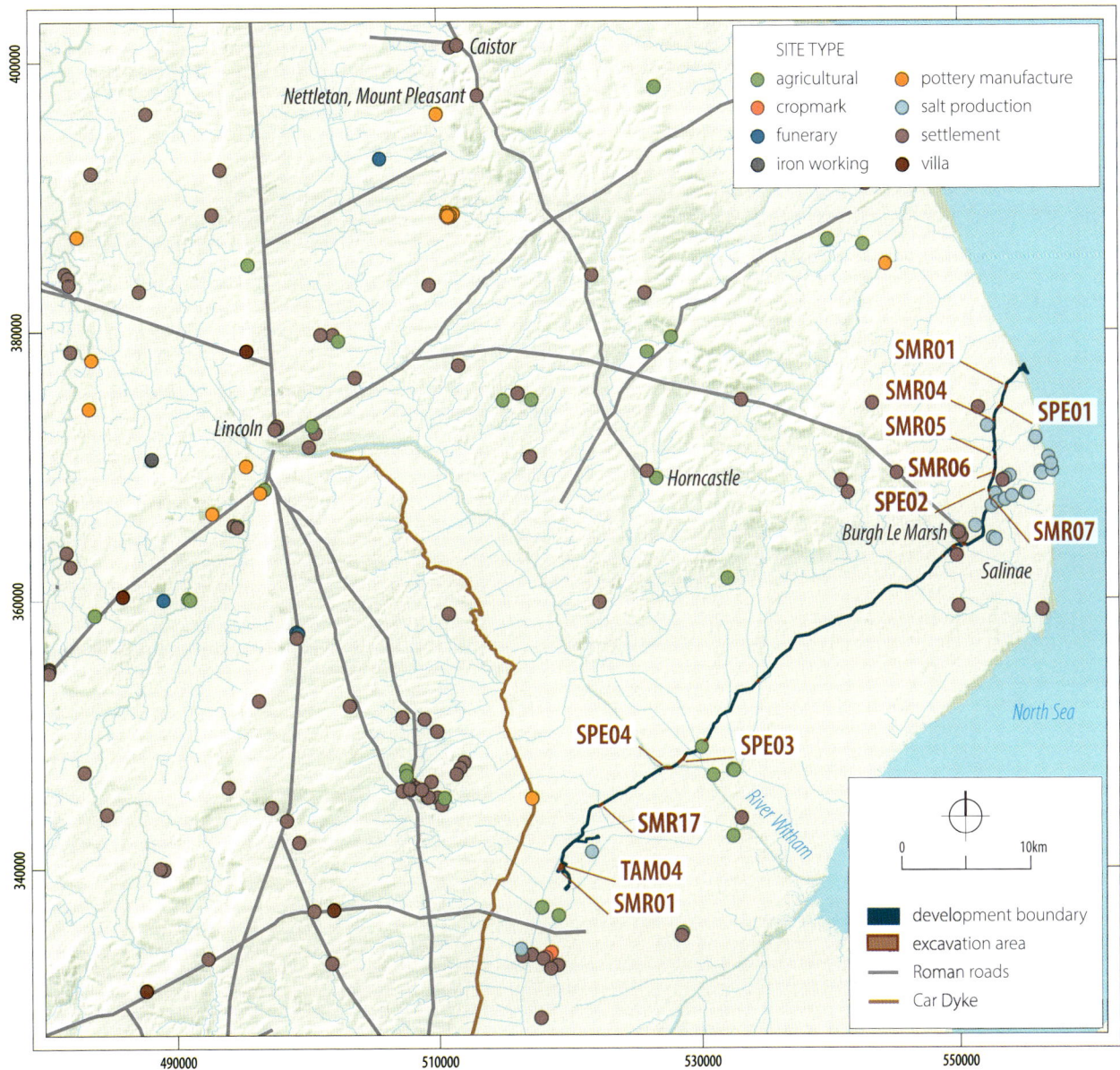

Figure 6.7 The wider Roman context of the Scheme

that it was served by a port (Whitwell 1993). This would have offered an alternative trade route for exporting salt or other produce from the Fen Edge. Further east of Burgh le Marsh, the evidence for settlement is more constrained and is dominated by the evidence for early Roman salt production with few known settlement sites. In contrast the data from the southern end of the Scheme, coupled with that from recent work at Bicker Fen, indicates a potentially denser pattern of settlement than previously realised. At Bicker Fen, 2.3 km to the south of SMR01/TAM04 (Inland Fen Edge), the remains of a complex farmstead were uncovered (Gaunt *et al.* 2024). Approximately 3.5 km to the northwest of Bicker Fen was evidence for further settlement located close to the line of the Car Dyke (MLI90004), suggesting it may have been positioned to take advantage of this arterial route.

More speculative evidence for occupation to the east of Burgh le Marsh includes the possible settlement at *Salinae* (Figs 5.1 and 6.7). This settlement is mentioned by the Roman geographer Ptolemy before AD 122, who described *Salinae* as being near the Wash. Although others have questioned this location in the past, and continue to do so, Alistair Strang's reassessment of the data concluded that '*Salinae* is definitely near Skegness' (Strang 1997, 23). *Salinae* was recognised by Ptolemy possibly as a general area where salt was made, but also possibly as a town/settlement whose name connected it to the local industry or, indeed, it may have been a centre of control for that industry. There is no evidence now of a Roman town or settlement near Skegness, probably due to the considerable erosion that has taken place along that part of the coast (Lane 2018, 110). It is eminently possible that erosion could have accounted for the eradication of a Roman town in this low-lying landscape, as it almost certainly did for an unknown number of salterns. Moreover, John Leland visited Skegness in about 1540 and was told that: 'there was ons an haven and a toune waullid having also a castelle [and that] ... the old toune is clene consumed and eaten up with the se[a]. At low water there appear yet manifest tokens of old buildings' (Robinson 1981, 21).

Whether those old buildings were once a Roman town, or something dating to much later, is now impossible to know. There was, for instance, a severe flood in 1526 when the 'church and the greater part of the parish [of Skegness] was submerged' (Owen 1952, 340).

In summary, there is a general sense that not only the number of settlements but also our understanding of their chronology and function diminishes the further one moves eastwards from Lincoln towards the coast. This is in part reflective of the levels of development across the region, with the area west of the Wolds having seen a greater number of investigations over the years. The data from the southern end of the Scheme suggest the presence of larger more complex farmsteads but the location of these may have been driven by environmental factors. The general absence of settlement within the Lincolnshire Marsh and immediate environs could be similarly reflective of land that was utilised for seasonal occupation, with more permanent occupation sites being located elsewhere, perhaps within centres such as Burgh le Marsh, or within farmsteads on the Wolds. This question and the inter-relationships of the sites to the wider landscape sketched out here are further developed in the final section of this chapter.

Big worlds, little worlds: Creating communities and connections at Triton Knoll

The opening half of the chapter set out the key facets of the agricultural economy alongside the data pertaining to salt production within the Triton Knoll sites. The preceding review has set out the key aspects of the wider landscape. But how did these elements relate to each other? This final section sets out to explore this question by looking at the position of the Triton Knoll sites not only in their broader settlement context but also within their wider socio-economic networks, and how this changed between the middle–late Roman period.

The middle Roman period (*c.* AD 100–250) saw the establishment of the majority of the recorded sites across the Scheme, with all but one being founded *de novo*, with no definite evidence for an Iron Age predecessor (Chapter 4; Table 4.1). This absence of Iron Age precursors in itself is likely reflective of environmental conditions at the time (see Chapter 2). The development of the early Roman sites across Triton Knoll forms part of a broader expansion of settlement across the region with a peak in settlement numbers on the North Lincolnshire coversands and clays to the west of the Scheme (Allen 2016, 248). East of this area comparative data are limited, but the farmsteads at Bicker Fen, 2.3 km south of SMR01/TAM04 and Heckington Fen Energy Park, *c.* 4.6 km to the northeast of SMR01/TAM04 were also established during the 2nd century AD, overlapping with the development of the Fen Edge and Inland Fen Edge sites (Dabill 2022; Gaunt *et al.* 2024). Part of the mechanisms behind this 2nd century AD expansion have in the past been linked to the emergence of an Imperial Estate following the Boudican revolt, which encompassed elements of the Cambridgeshire and Lincolnshire Fens (see Evans *et al.* 2017, 126–130). The veracity of this interpretation is questionable, and there are limited data to support such an interpretation (Malim 2005, 128; Mattingly 2006, 385). While the nascent state would have no doubt impacted regional economies, the degree to which it was directly involved needs to be carefully considered, rather than utilised as a *de facto* explanation. An alternative model is to see parts of the region as *ager publicus*, with the local population being allowed occupancy in exchange for rents and taxes levied in terms of products required by the state (Mattingly 2006, 385). Demand for products would have also been driven by emergent centres such as Lincoln, which may have drawn resources from an extensive hinterland, which could have included the Lincolnshire Coast and Marshes (Allen 2016, 280). Lincoln would have acted not only as a key consumer but also as an important point for regional markets and the collection of taxes. Other settlement sites such as Burgh le Marsh could have acted as local markets or redistribution points but as outlined previously our data for the settlement is too limited to make a definite interpretation of the functional role of the settlement.

This increased demand in the 2nd century AD would have not only included agricultural produce but also other products such as salt, which was required as an additive and preservative. Across the Lincolnshire Coast and Marshes, a large number of early Roman saltern sites are known, although the overall dating of these as noted in Chapter 6, is uncertain. It is possible that some of these sites reflect a continuity of late Iron Age saltworking sites, which may have been a major source of wealth (Elsdon 1997, 5). The data from SMR06 indicate middle Roman saltworking, with six saltern mounds recorded across the site indicative of multiple seasons of saltworking. As discussed earlier, how saltworking was organised during this period is uncertain, with prior interpretations invoking the spectre of state involvement. Instead, it is probable that it was an *ad hoc* activity taking place on a seasonal basis, couched within broader patterns of transhumance (Bradley 1992). There is limited evidence for settlement alongside these production sites and, as a whole, comparative settlement data from across the area around the Lincolnshire Marsh Landscape Parcel are limited, prohibiting more nuanced analysis of wider settlement trends. Scattered incidences of Roman finds across the region could hint at settlement activity but could also be reflective of manure spread material (Fig. 6.8). It could, as was the case in the later Roman period, be that elements of the Lincolnshire Marsh were exploited on a seasonal basis rather than forming a locus for permanent settlement, a trend that appears to persist into the Roman period.

This pattern of land use contrasts with the evidence from the southern end of the Scheme where a denser pattern of occupation is observed (Fig. 6.7). These sites are in general clustered around the edge of the ridge, with saltworking taking place further east, potentially indicating seasonal use of waterlogged elements of the landscape during the early Roman period. The development of these southernmost sites was closely connected to the expansion of agricultural regimes in the early–middle Roman period. This pattern of expansion is also seen at Bicker Fen, which was likely established in the 2nd century AD (Gaunt *et al.* 2024). As at the Inland Fen Edge and the Fen Edge there was evidence at Bicker Fen for the increased use of cattle for traction, indicative of the exploitation of

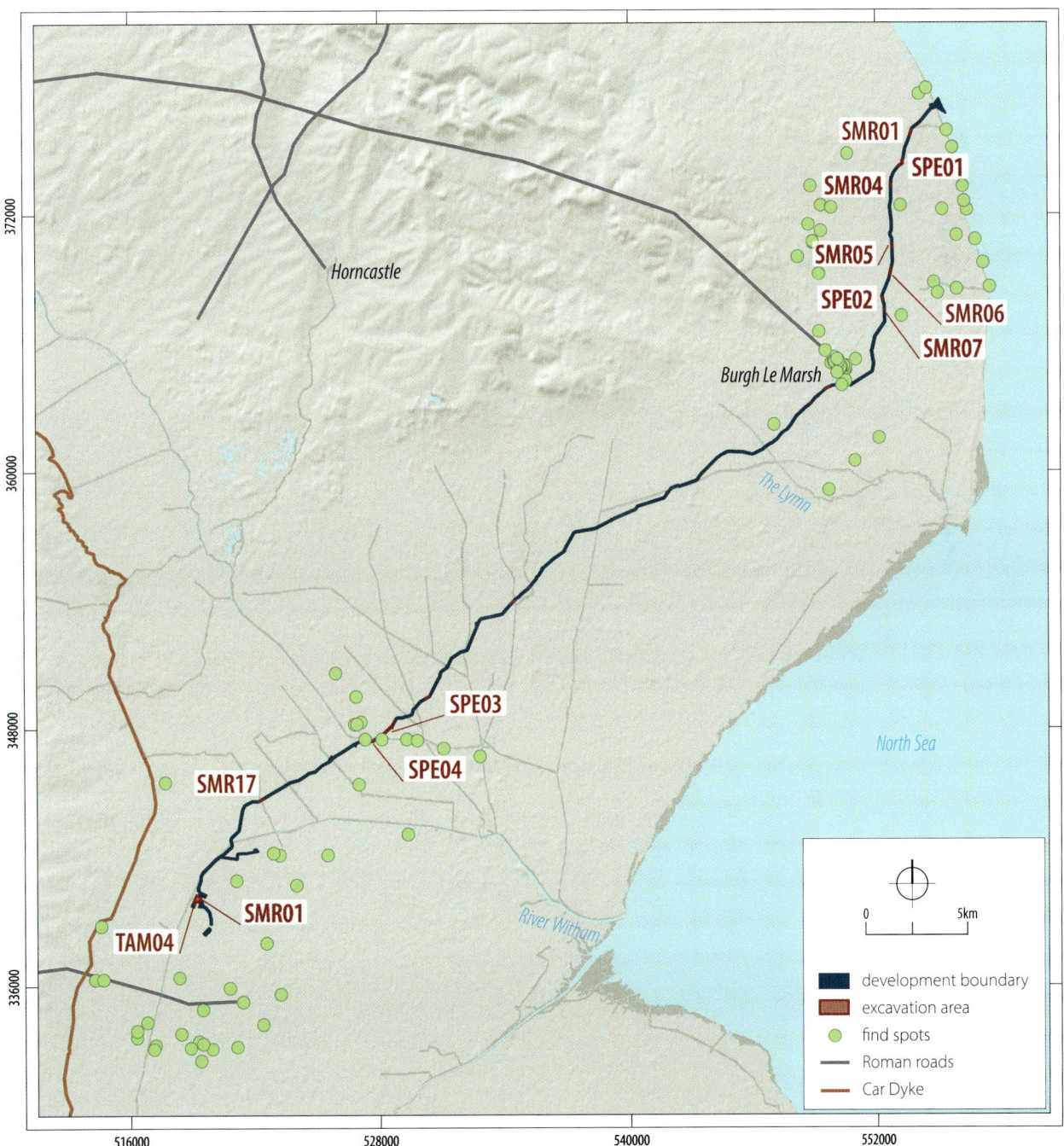

Figure 6.8 Roman find spots identified in the Historic Environment Record (HER) 1 km from the route of the Scheme

heavier clay soils within the vicinity of the sites (*ibid.*). The economy of the southernmost Triton Knoll sites during the 2nd century AD appears to be focused on a range of agricultural products but it is possible to detect certain emphases within this. This includes the Fen Edge where the emphasis appears to have lain on arable produce, whilst at the Inland Fen Edge a greater emphasis was placed on animal products (Table 6.1). In the case of the Fen Edge, the data from SPE04 suggest milling taking place at or near to the site during the later Roman period. This could suggest an increase in the relative scale of cereal processing, contrasting with the earlier household levels of production but, as noted, deducing the precise levels of production is difficult given the small archaeobotanical assemblages. The presence of querns alongside millstones could be indicative of a continued grinding of grain by hand, with the milled products being primarily intended for export (Lodwick 2017, 72). Mills were infrequent until the late Roman period and their expansion during this period has been cited as evidence for increased centralisation of grain processing (Shaffrey 2015, 63, 72; Lodwick 2017, 72).

Milling was not the only activity which became centralised with evidence from across the province for the potential centralisation of other processes such as butchery and textile production (*e.g.* Smith 2017, 228–230). The incidence of textile production at the Inland Fen Edge could, based on parallels with data from other later Roman sites, also be cited as evidence for the concentration of this activity within particular farmsteads (see Smith 2017, 228). It is also possible that butchery was subject to a degree of centralisation, as evidenced through the movement of joints of meat and the relatively low incidence of primary butchery waste, but the data at present is not nuanced enough to allow further comment. Aspects of centralisation can be detected within the Lincolnshire Marsh Landscape Parcel in the late Roman period, with the development of larger complex salt production sites, which finds parallel with other sites such as Middleton and Stanford Wharf. In contrast to the middle Roman phases of SMR06, the late Roman layouts of SPE02 and SMR06 suggest an increased formalisation of saltworking, with the establishment of clearly defined working areas and the investment in water management, aspects which are not clearly present on the middle Roman saltworking sites. The expansion and development of these sites is in part reflective of the continued demand for salt both within the vicinity of Triton Knoll and across the wider region. The pattern of working at these sites may have been much the same as it was in the middle Roman period, but speculatively rather than multiple seasonal saltworking sites, the process was increasingly centralised within more 'formal' sites. Importantly these sites could have been a locus for other salt related activities including meat curing and the production of fish sauce. At present given that the late Roman salt production sites at SPE02 and SMR06 appear to be unique, it is difficult to gauge the full scale of late Roman salt production, and whether these represent part of a wider pattern of late Roman saltworking or an exception. As highlighted in Chapter 5, the shift towards alternative technologies of salt production including the use of lead pans presents a number of difficulties in identifying late Roman salt production sites. Nonetheless, the existence of SMR06 and SPE02 challenges the notion of the salt industry being a purely early Roman phenomenon.

These developments in the late Roman period may reflect wider shifts in the Roman world from the 3rd century AD. Increasing demands by the Roman state for agricultural produce, notably to supply the army, may have led to greater control of the rural populace (Smith and Fulford 2018, 354). This control may have been exercised through a number of ways including increased delegation of authority to elites, or the exertion of direct military control (see Gerrard 2013). The walled settlements at Caistor and Horncastle could be cited as evidence for this more direct involvement. As argued for other walled settlements, the functioning of these may not have been principally defensive, but more certain locales for the control of the movement of products and materials (Smith and Fulford 2019). Again, a lack of detailed information prohibits closer scrutiny of this possible role, but the strategic location of both sites at either end of the ridge would have enabled control over movements east and westwards.

By the later 4th century AD most of the Triton Knoll sites had fallen out of use, at SMR06 and SPE02 there is limited evidence for activity beyond the mid-4th century AD. In the case of the Fen Edge and Inland Fen sites, these appear to have persisted into the 4th century AD (see Chapter 4). It is possible that in some cases this decline was linked to changing environmental factors, with parts of the area subject to flooding (Chapter 2). To the west, across the Lincolnshire coversands and clays, there is a congruent decline in settlement numbers, suggesting a more general contraction in settlements during the period (Allen 2016). While environmental factors were likely a contributing factor, supra-regional aspects including the changes in wider networks and the diminishment of central authority will have likely been contributing factors (see Gerrard 2013).

In summary, the emergent picture from Triton Knoll can be viewed as a tale of two halves. The first, occurring in the middle Roman period, sees a colonisation of areas of land following an episode of marine regression. This pattern of expansion forms part of a wider picture of settlement growth in the 2nd century AD, reflecting the development of the region following the initial conquest phase of the 1st century AD. How this process of 'colonisation' was organised is uncertain, although the creation of the Car Dyke indicates some degree of state investment. This investment can also be seen in the creation of the road network with the development of Ermine Street and several subsidiary roads. To a degree, there may have been some continuity in land ownership or tenancy from the late Iron Age, while in other cases land confiscations or allocations may have occurred. The degree to which the sites at Triton Knoll were the outcome of these processes is at present uncertain. Furthermore, while the sites from Triton Knoll have been treated as independent entities it is also possible that they represent foci within larger estates, but the data are not nuanced enough to examine this further. That said, close inter-connections between the sites can be detected, including the movement of joints of meat across the Scheme. These inter-connections may have enabled sites to place an emphasis on certain products, a trend that persisted into the later Roman period.

During the later Roman period, there was little change in the overall number of settlements, with the exception of the decline of SPE03. Of particular note during this period is the evidence for milling, textile production, dairying, and saltworking. These activities could reflect increased specialisation or the centralising of key processes within particular sites. This shift was in part stimulated by wider factors including increased demands from the state. It is also possible that this reflects the operation of larger estates exerting increased control over the rural populace, with an increasing disparity between the upper and lower social orders (Smith and Fulford 2018, 354). Nevertheless, the impression is one of a productive landscape producing a range of products, with close interconnections between each of the Triton Knoll sites being indicated. The later Roman period appears to reflect the zenith of these sites, implying a relatively prosperous agricultural landscape that was keyed into the wider socio-economic networks of the Roman world.

Romans on the edge: Final thoughts

In the preceding two chapters the Roman archaeology of Triton Knoll has been outlined, with Chapter 4 providing an overview of the evidence for settlement alongside the environmental and finds data. In Chapter 5 the data from the saltworking was further examined, highlighting the late Roman date for aspects of this industry. Here, in Chapter 6, these various threads have been woven together to build a picture of socio-economic practices across the Scheme, and their relationship to other sites. Whilst appearing marginal and peripheral it is evident from these reviews that Roman sites across the Scheme formed parts of wider dynamic landscapes, characterised by a diverse array of agricultural strategies, in part driven by environmental factors and in others by socio-economic choices. The distinctive and dynamic environments recorded across the Scheme would have presented communities with a landscape that could be utilised in several distinct ways, ranging from the reclamation or cultivation of existing land for arable farming to the utilisation of saltmarsh areas for salt production and summer grazing (Bradley 1992; Rippon *et al.* 2000). This includes the utilisation of marginal land for pastoral activity and salt production, whilst the drier sites within the southern section practised a mixed arable and pastoral regime, exploiting a range of soil types. The dynamism of this region continued to impact patterns of settlement in the post-Roman period a topic that is further considered in the following chapter.

7

Medieval and post-medieval rural settlement and industry

Joshua T. Hogue and Maria Stockdale
With contributions from Marina Chorro-Giner, Hannah Russ,
Rebecca Sillwood, and Jane Young

Even very recently it has been claimed that the southern Lincoln Marsh and the Low Grounds along the eastern fen edge lacked medieval settlement entirely, being referred to as 'the great empty area' (Simmons 2022, xxxiv). In part, any perceived emptiness may reflect the lack of environments fit for habitation at times during this period. Towards the end of the Roman period there was a phase of coastal inundation, newly established roddons and creeks transforming the landscape. A number of coastal inlets were formed through the expansion of the intertidal zone and these embayments may have been the focus of activity. For much of the early medieval period, the southern Lincoln Marsh may have been substantially inundated forming a tidal lagoon to the north of All Saints Wainfleet and to the south of the settlement the coastline was likely as far inland as the Low Ground to the west of 'the Tofts' (Simmons 2017; 2022; Green 2023a; Figs 7.1 and 7.2).

In the following centuries the coastline shifted eastwards, with territory periodically claimed from the sea through a process of drain and bank construction. Episodes of high sea levels and the vulnerability of the coast to sea surges and sea floods led to a relatively dynamic landscape, an environment in which settlements were reclaimed by the sea sometimes to be re-established and other times entirely abandoned. By *c.* AD 1500 the east coast was relatively stable but still vulnerable to surges and floods. Rapid seaward advance of the coastline through enclosure and embankment of the marshlands occurred in the late-16th and early-17th centuries and within several decades many of the settlements that had begun this period near the coast were located several kilometres inland (Simmons 2017; 2022; Green 2023a). Few opportunities have been afforded to study the nature of settlement activity in this dynamic environment and consequently archaeological investigations undertaken as part of the Triton Knoll Electrical System provide an opening into the realities of rural settlement during the medieval and post-medieval eras. This chapter provides an overview of medieval and post-medieval activity recorded across the Scheme and situates the findings in the wider landscape setting.

Medieval field systems and landscape evolution

There was no evidence for direct continuity from the Roman period and the early medieval activity observed along the route likely dates no earlier than the start of the 9th century AD, following the first documented Viking incursions into Lincolnshire in AD 841 and during a period in which the system of *wapentakes* likely developed (Stafford 1985, 141–142).

There was also relatively limited evidence for activity in the centuries immediately preceding the Norman Conquest but important insights into the nature of early medieval (Saxon) rural settlement in the vicinity of Burgh le Marsh are provided by excavations at SMR10 and tentatively at SMR09, within the Fen Edge Landscape Parcel (Stockdale *et al.* 2024). From the Coastal Landscape Parcel, at the far north of the Scheme, further evidence of activity during this period is also provided at SPE01, near Mumby (Gaunt and Roberts 2024), although it is restricted to a small number of features dating towards the end of the early medieval period and may be better understood in the context of the proliferation of activity following the conquest.

Evidence of medieval activity following the Norman Conquest is somewhat better reflected across the Scheme. Much of the activity was of similar magnitude and scope to that which immediately preceded the conquest, mostly comprising ditches demarcating and draining the land for use in a range of farming activities. In the Coastal Landscape Parcel evidence of medieval field systems was recorded at SPE01, with broad continuity from the preceding early medieval activity. There was also evidence of subsequent field systems broadly on the same alignment dating to the post-medieval to modern periods, plausibly indicating continuity of land use through until today (Gaunt and Roberts 2024). A field system was also suggested to be of medieval date at SMR01 (*ibid.*) but the lack of any finds and associated dating evidence somewhat limits wider discussion. Much of the evidence of medieval rural activities, however, comes from SMR17, Amber Hill (Swineshead), within the Fen Edge Landscape Parcel. Here, a medieval farmstead with remains of at least two structures was identified suggesting activity during the 13th–14th centuries (Stockdale *et al.* 2024). SMR12 at Westerhouses, Stickney, also produced a pottery assemblage including sherds dating to the 13th–15th centuries, but all were thought to be residual from the excavations; no medieval features were recorded (*ibid.*). Evidence of late medieval and post-medieval brick making likely dating between the 15th and 17th centuries was uncovered at SMR09, but the nature of the activity was distinct and does not fit within the range of rural activities recorded elsewhere (*ibid.*).

Figure 7.1 Distribution of key medieval and post-medieval sites across the Scheme

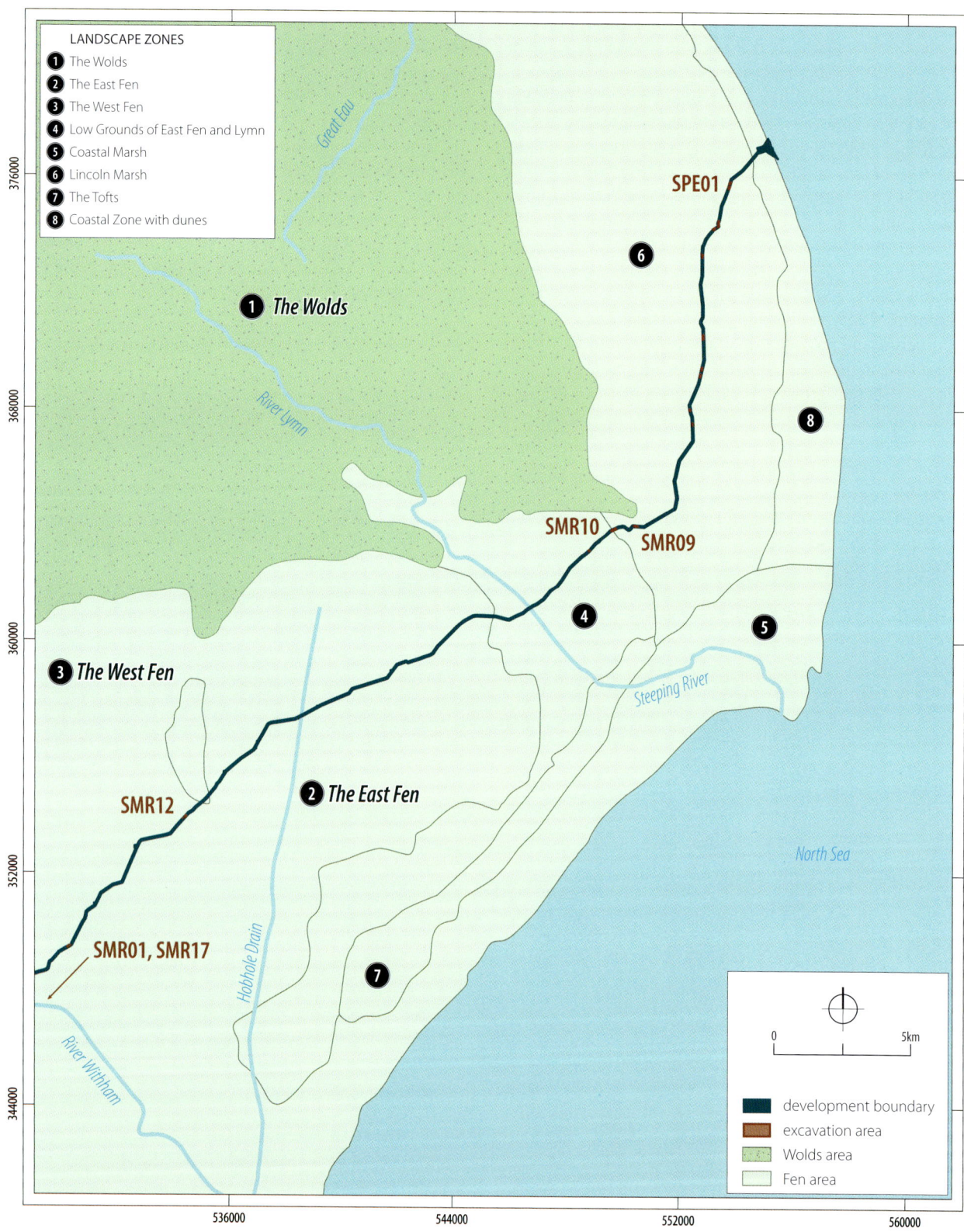

Figure 7.2 Sites in relation to the Landscape Parcels as outlined by Simmons (2022)

As a dataset, the medieval sites can be best understood by grouping the principal sites into geographical zones reflecting similarities in environment, rather than necessarily by their Landscape Parcels. While the Coastal, Fen Edge, Inland Fen Edge, and Marsh Landscape Parcels act as a convenience for grouping sites along the Triton Knoll Electrical System, and the names reflect some approximation of their geographical distribution, a more nuanced division of sites can be established. In terms of ecological zones, the sites might be better divided into those of the Lincoln Marsh, east of the Wolds and north of the Lymn/Steeping River; and those of the Fen (after Simmons 2017; 2022).

Falling within the Lincoln Marsh are the early medieval (Saxon) field systems dating from the 9th–11th centuries at SMR10 and the medieval field systems dating from the 11th–15th centuries at SPE01. Critically, both sites would have been relatively close to the coast in the Saxon and medieval periods, with the areas immediately east of Burgh le Marsh not drained until the 17th and 18th centuries (Bealby 1911). Until very recently it has been claimed that this area lacked medieval settlement entirely (Simmons 2022, xxxiv) and so the available data, albeit relatively scant, provide important insights into the nature of land use in this area from the 9th–15th centuries. In the Fen, a medieval farmstead, likely dated to the 13th–14th centuries, was identified at SMR17. The Fenland Project has provided a much more intensive understanding of settlement of this area and further south (*e.g.* Hayes and Lane 1992; Hall and Coles 1994), but SMR17 nevertheless provides an interesting insight into activity at the southern extremity of the Scheme.

Rural activity in the Lincoln Marsh during the late 9th/10th to late 12th/13th centuries

Little is understood of the evolution of medieval field systems in the Lincoln Marsh. Lincolnshire is often discussed as part of the Midlands, but the extent to which settlement of this area fits into the established 'Midland System' of common-field farming with large and nucleated villages is debatable. The fact that Lincolnshire is the only county in the Midlands with a coastline, all others being landlocked, may advise against the use of models principally derived for the gently rolling countryside for the description of settlement in the wetlands to the east of the Wolds (Jones and Lewis 2012). Models for the enclosure of the Lincolnshire Fens, but also the Norfolk and Cambridge Fens (*e.g.* Hall and Coles 1994; Oosthuizen 2017), may serve as better models for the Lincoln Marsh, with the closer similarities in environment. Further afield, studies of the colonisation and drainage of the coastal marshes of the Severn Estuary (Rippon 2002), may also be relevant. A major theme in medieval settlement studies is the timing and process by which settlements became nucleated – dispersed farms and hamlets clustered into villages – and, though it was likely to have occurred at different times in different places, it is generally thought to have been a protracted process beginning in the 8th century and becoming more widely established in the 11th–12th (Rippon 2004; Oosthuizen 2010; Jones and Lewis 2012). In the case of the Lincolnshire Fen, it has been argued that many of the settlements may have become nucleated from as early as the 7th century (Hayes 1988; Hayes and Lane 1992).

Both major localities within the Lincoln Marsh (SMR10 and SPE01) seemingly relate to larger field systems inferred from consideration of the cartographic sources and LiDAR information (Figs 7.3 and 7.4), albeit any inferred settlement patterns are problematic due to the inherent issues of historic landscape reconstruction. In both instances, the sites are within field systems restricted to higher ground within the marsh, following variation in the underlying geology, and created through a series of ditches that reinforce the natural topography and afford protection from flooding. SMR10 is located at Croft End, near Burgh le Marsh, though relatively imperceptibly to the eye, this area sits slightly above the surrounding marsh on a peninsula of Devensian till surrounded by mud flat deposits (NERC 2024), the western margins reinforced through a series of a meandering drains, including Cowcroft Drain, and the eastern edge formed by drainage running along Low Lane (Fig. 7.3). SPE01, near Mumby, is slightly raised above the surrounding landscape in an enclosure formed by a series of irregular land parcels largely bounded by drainage ditches (Fig. 7.4), the form in part owing itself to the underlying natural geology, recorded through an auger survey as being that of an island within saltmarsh with a tidal creek scouring the edge of the site (Gaunt and Roberts 2024).

Neither of the Lincoln Marsh sites seems to have been the focus of major settlement activity, with the evidence indicating that the sites were principally agricultural in nature. However, the extent to which they reflect agricultural activity related to dispersed farmsteads rather than peripheral activities at the margins of a village core, consistent with nucleated settlement, is difficult to determine. There is no reasonable way of determining the nature of medieval field systems on the archaeological evidence alone, only documentary evidence can clarify these issues with certainty (Taylor 1981; Oosthuizen 2010). However, evidence of more intensive manuring – in the form of higher densities of pottery derived from middens – may indicate an area of core arable 'infield' land, whilst lower densities may be taken to indicate less intensive 'outfield' activities, such as land used for grazing (Oosthuizen 2010, 128). Albeit any such distinction may be somewhat arbitrary in this instance anyway.

In terms of documentary sources, the Domesday Book (Open Domesday 2024) may provide some evidence for greater settlement dispersion in southeast Lincolnshire before the Norman Conquest, as reflected in the fact that vills – small administrative units broadly equivalent to parishes – during this time were more often divided among numerous landowners (Simmons 2022, 16–17). For instance, SMR10, Croft End, is located near the borders of Burgh le Marsh and Croft, which shows an incredible diversity of potential owners before the conquest. Burgh le Marsh was held by Earl Ralph the Constable, Ulf (Fenman), Godric, Godwin, Toki (of Burgh), Grimkel, Klak, and Swartbrand (son of Ulf). It was also relatively large and affluent comprising 64 households, including 24 villagers, 34 freemen, and ten smallholders. It covered over 14 ploughlands, with over 11 plough teams (one

Figure 7.3. SMR09 and SMR10 in their landscape and historical context (LiDAR background mapping: Environment Agency reproduced under Open Government Licence v3.0 (Environment Agency 2024). Historic Farms data from Lake and Partington 2015)

belonging to the lord and ten to the men), with 615 acres (*c.* 249 ha) of meadow and one church. Croft was held by Othenkar (son of Alnoth) in 1066, and had a population of 15 households, comprising three villagers, nine freeman, and three smallholders. Its resources included more than two ploughlands, supported by two lord's plough teams and three men's plough teams, as well as 120 acres (*c.* 48.5 ha) of meadow and, notably, a salthouse. The closest location in Domesday to SPE01 was Mumby, which was similarly held by numerous lords; Ernwin (the priest), Svavi (father of Swein), Alric, Ormketill, Holmketill, Sifrith, Swein (son of Svavi), Tonni (of Lusby), and Godwin. It was also relatively large, with 97 households, consisting of 64 villagers, four freemen, and 29 smallholders, and its resources comprised almost 18 ploughlands, worked by six lord's plough teams and almost nine men's plough teams, additionally, there were 630 acres (*c.* 255 ha) of meadow.

Regarding the specific activities that occurred on site, some insights into the function of the field system are provided by the pottery at SMR10. Here, most of the sherds were relatively abraded and small, indicating secondary deposition (Young 2024a), plausibly the movement of materials through repeated ploughing and/or as a result of manuring. Of a similar origin may have been the numerous highly fragmentary fired clay fragments of uncertain function (Tomlinson 2024). It is an interesting note, that according to antiquarian sources the name Croft may be

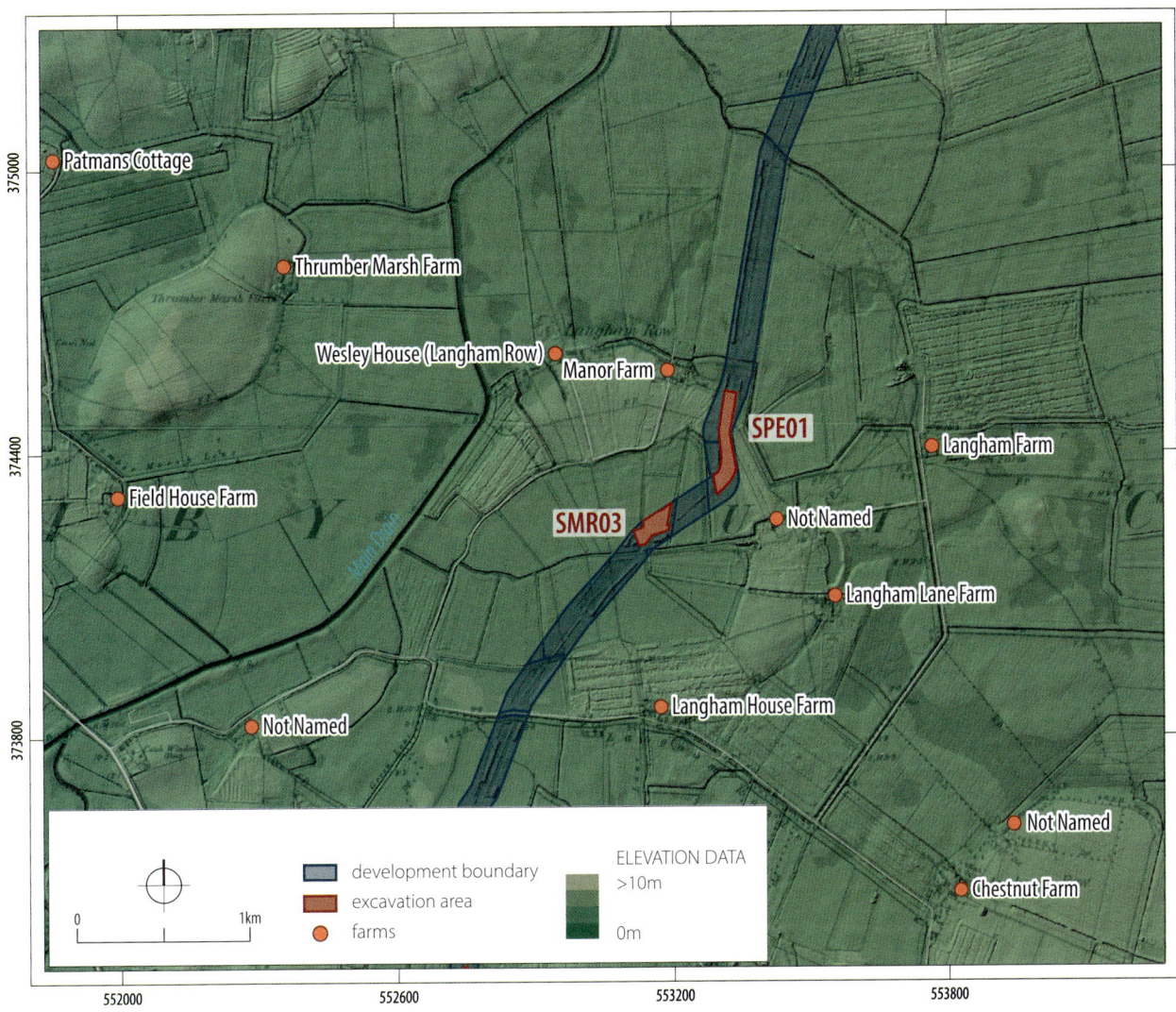

Figure 7.4. SPE01 in its landscape and historical context. (LiDAR background mapping: Environment Agency reproduced under Open Government Licence v3.0 (Environment Agency 2024). Historic Farms data from Lake and Partington 2015)

a corruption of the Old England *Creafe*, signifying handicraft and '… applied to such grounds, as were principally manured and extraordinarily dressed by the labour and skill of the owner.' (Oldfield 1829, 134)

A range of animal bones was recovered, albeit the majority of the assemblage was not closely identifiable. No clear dominance of a single domestic mammal was noted (Chorro-Giner 2024c), although plough animals (cow and horse) were more common than other stock animals (sheep/goat and pig). Furthermore, age of death data indicate the use of equids as traction and transport animals, as well as possibly some of the cattle, while the other mammals were primarily used for meat exploitation. It is difficult to draw any definite conclusions based on the size of the identifiable assemblage (n=66) (*ibid.*) but tentatively they may indicate a focus on arable land use.

A bronze object, possibly a stylus, and an iron key, possibly for a chest or box, were associated with the Saxon activity at SMR10. These may indicate connections with *monasteria* sites but certainly represent more 'high-status' activities than identified through the other finds; it is tempting to imagine a scenario in which they may have been introduced during the appraisal of the lands, but any such suggestion is purely speculative. It may be that these finds were introduced from a nearby manor and other finds may have similarly been introduced from a domestic setting.

A possible square enclosure was identified through geophysical survey immediately to the west of the site, less than 100 m away (Harrison 2012). A subsequent trial trench evaluation carried out in September 2012 confirmed the existence of the enclosure, revealing several ditches and pits. A small number of medieval pottery sherds were also discovered, dated to between the 11th and early/mid-13th century, although a sherd from a sandy ware spouted vessel of uncertain age may point to an earlier date. A significant collection of animal bones was found in the medieval layers, including remains of

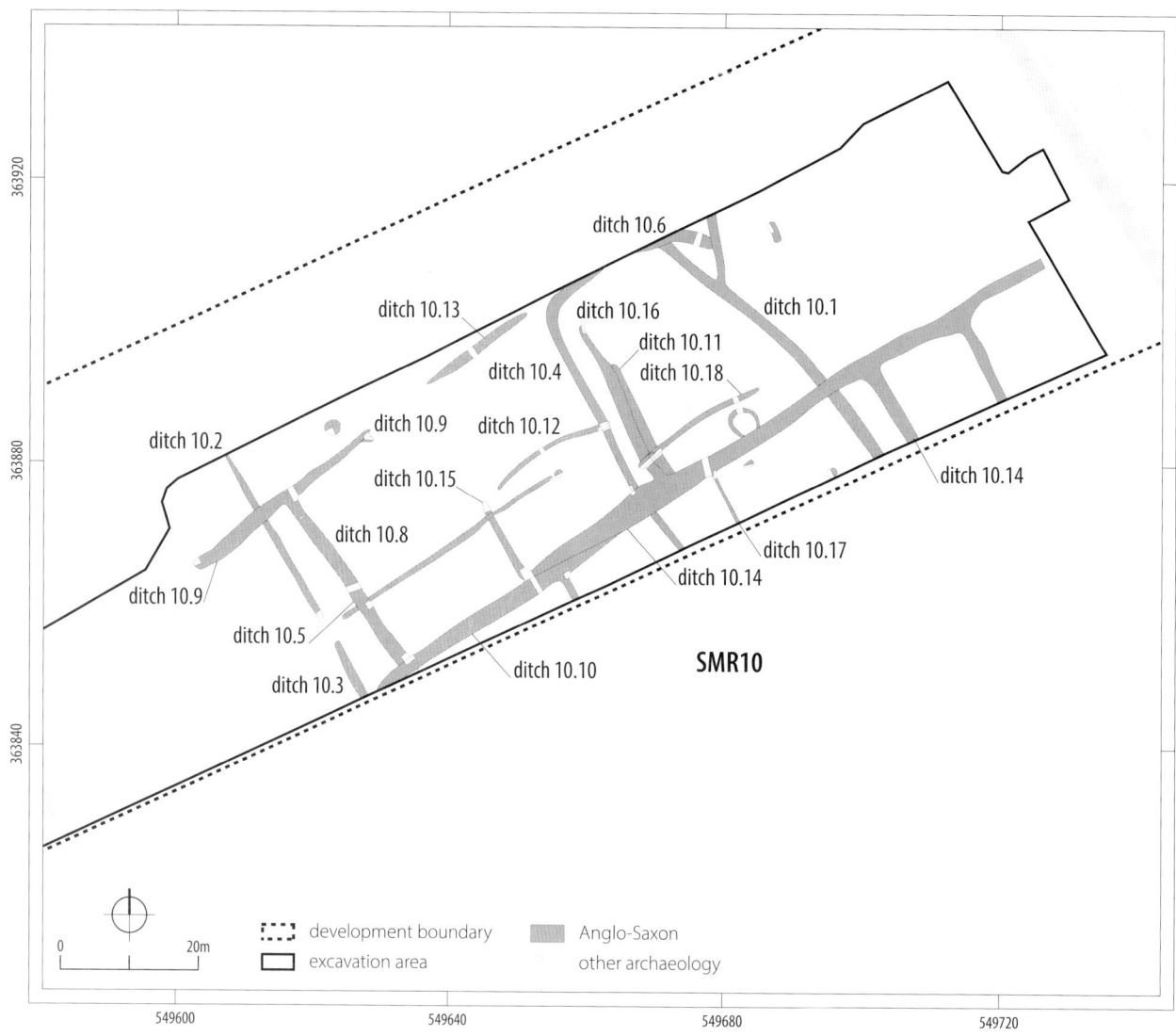

Figure 7.5. Early medieval (Saxon) archaeological features and other activity at SMR10, Croft End

cattle, horse, pig, sheep, dog, and chicken (MLI87788; Harrison 2013). It is certainly plausible that the activity here has earlier origins and was related to that at SMR10.

Further evidence of activity in the area may be inferred by later records but the extent to which these sources of information can extend our understanding of settlement back through time is arguable. Nearby farms, identified as part of the *Greater Lincolnshire Farmstead Project*, may have earlier origins, such as County Acres (MLI120238), 0.12 km north, and Croft House (MLI120239), 0.32 km southwest, dating from at least the 19th century on mapping (Lake and Partington 2015). Beehive Cottage, located less than 100 m southeast, may also be a reasonable candidate for earlier settlement. It is included in the 1846 tithe apportionment (IR 29/20/07) at which time it was owned by William Cook Esq. Notably, the property is surrounded by a broadly square ditched enclosure, measuring *c.* 50 × 40 m, which may plausibly be that of a medieval moated manor. However, these typically date from slightly later (*c.* 1150–1550; Aberg 1978) than the activity at SMR10.

Not only does the pottery suggest a slightly later date of the focus of activity at SPE01 to that of SMR10 but also that the sites may have differed in use. Pre-conquest activity is poorly reflected in the pottery at SPE01, but the 12th–13th century assemblage is in relatively good condition and a number of vessels indicate at least some primary deposition associated with the field system (Young 2024b, 14), plausibly indicating that the site was within relatively close proximity to any settlement activity (rather than a result of much spreading). Most of the vessels were domestic kitchen wares and/or related to dairy (*ibid.*, 13) and look likely to have been locally produced, regionally imported vessels being extremely rare. Further evidence for domestic activity nearby may also be inferred by the animal bone assemblage, with increases in the volume of surviving bone during this era plausibly reflecting greater settlement intensity and/

Figure 7.6. Early medieval (Saxon) field boundary at SMR10, Croft End

or the relative significance of livestock, with the ditches reflecting control of livestock between nearby low-lying marsh that would have provided valuable seasonal grazing (Gaunt and Roberts 2024, 25). A fragment of a millstone, possibly part of a four-armed medieval chase, was recovered, although due to the intensity of earlier Roman activity it was considered residual (Hayward and Shaffrey 2024c, 24). If it is indeed medieval, as finds of this type would be more commonly dated, it would again add to the impression that settlement activity was within close proximity to the field system.

No archaeological sites have been excavated within the immediate area, so any further inferences regarding the nature of activity must be drawn from more recent sources. Wesley House, Langham Row (MLI118843), Langham Lane Farm (MLI118841), Langham House Farm (ML118852), Manor Farm (MLI118842), and an unnamed farmstead (MLI118840), interestingly are all situated on the same ring of relatively high ground on which this site resides, both of the latter farms being less than 100 m away. All these farms were identified as part of the *Greater Lincolnshire Farmsteads Project* (Lake and Partington 2015), all are recorded on the late 19th–early 20th century mapping, but ultimately any could have had earlier origins. It is interesting that the farmstead of Manor Farm is the closest and the term 'manor', derived from the Latin *manerium*, refers to landed estates in the Domesday Book, albeit it is also spuriously used by later houseowners to add value to their property (Wright 2021). Notably, the name 'Langham', that is reflected in three of the farmsteads and lends its name to a nearby road, provides some indication as to the nature of the settlement. The name Langham may come from the OE *lang* or Old Norse *langr*, meaning 'long', and OE *hamm* or *hām*, referring to water 'land hemmed in by water or marsh' or *hām* meaning 'a village', possibly referring to a long homestead or enclosure, hemmed in by water (Mills 1998; Watts 2007).

While settlement of the Lincoln Marsh was likely more complex and nuanced than reflected in the available data and much remains uncertain regarding the activity undertaken during the early medieval (Saxon) and medieval eras, the findings from the Triton Knoll Scheme provide important insights, offering rare glimpses into the agricultural practices and settlement patterns that have been largely unrecorded for the region. Notably, the available data challenge existing models, suggesting land use in these areas have been more dispersed and adapted to the marshland environment, with settlements established using existing topographical features that were then embellished through the excavation of drainage features

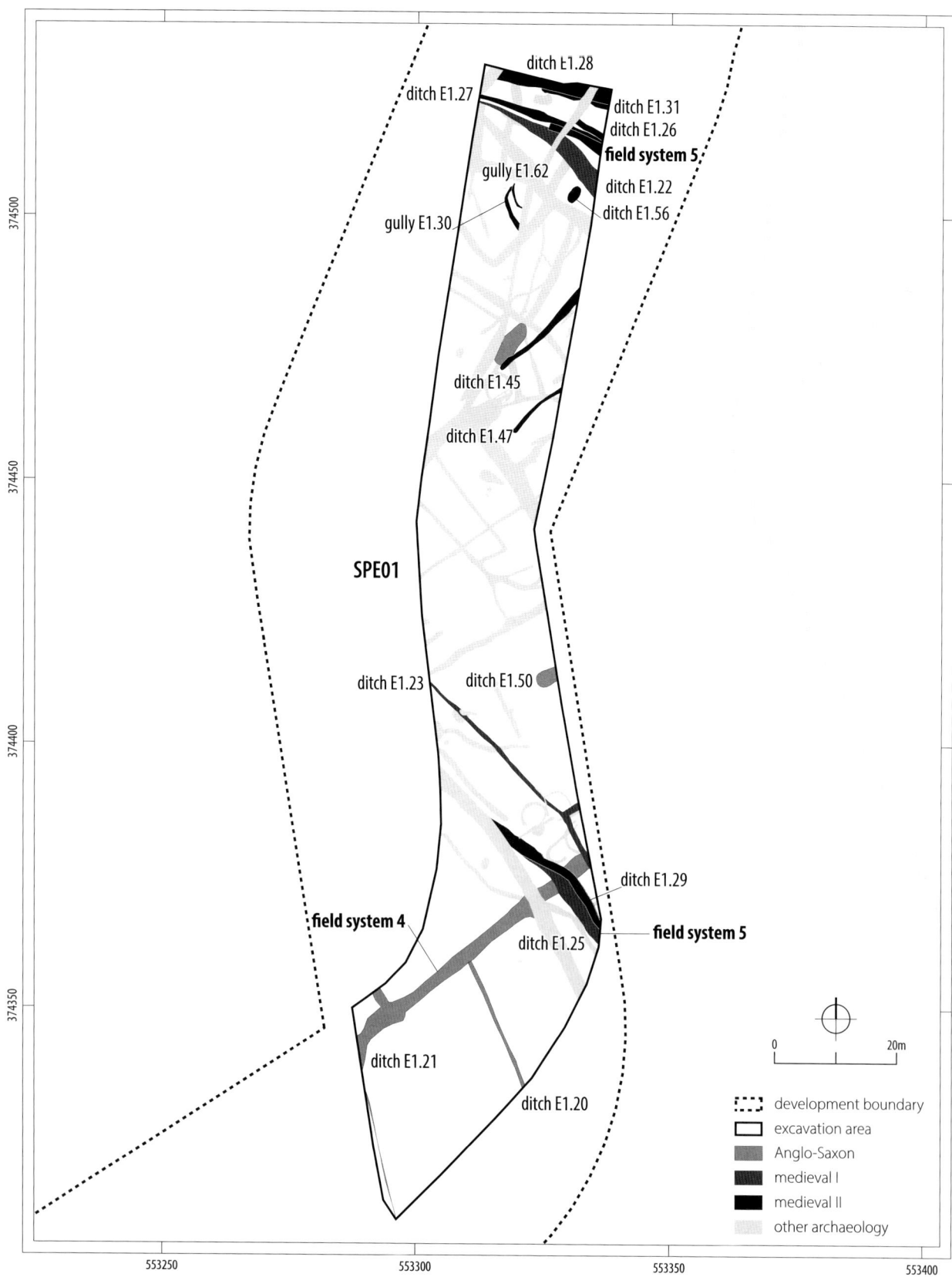

Figure 7.7 Early medieval (Saxon) and medieval archaeological features at SPE01, near Mumby

and may have survived as relatively isolated settlements, while others become nucleated.

A 13th–14th century farmstead in the Fen

Adaption to differing local conditions is further exemplified by the varied nature of settlement uncovered at the extreme southern end of the Scheme. Located in the Lincolnshire Fens, SMR17 in Amberhill (Swineshead) (Figs 7.8 and 7.9), was occupied broadly at the same time as later activity at SPE01 in the 13th–14th century, albeit with *c.* 45 km separating the two locations. SMR17, consequently, provides a glimpse into activity within a different environment to the other sites associated with medieval activity.

A 13th–14th century farmstead was established at SMR17 after a long hiatus following the Roman period (see Chapter 4; Stockdale *et al.* 2024). SMR17 is unique for the area in providing evidence for structures dating to the medieval era. At least two rectangular structures were recorded, one as a series of segmented beam slots (Structure 1), plausibly with gaps indicating the location of entranceways, another as a rectangular ditch with no observable entrance (Structure 2), and the corner of potentially two other structures, recorded as L-shaped sections of ditch (17.6) or beam slots (17.2). Both the better-preserved examples were relatively similar in form and measured *c.* 13–14 m long by 6–7 m wide and had interior measurements of *c.* 75 m². It is plausible that these structures reflected different phases of activity (Stockdale *et al.* 2024, 68-73), but the lack of intercutting features and limited resolution of associated finds does not preclude the structures from being contemporaneous. A large pit or backfilled watering hole (17.7) and a substantial ditch (17.5), containing cross-joining pottery, were likely dated to subsequent medieval activity.

No internal features were recorded within the structures. Most finds were recovered from the infilling of structural elements (*e.g.* beam slots) or later medieval features, although the overall finds assemblage gives us some impression of the activities that took place. Most of the pottery, due to its small size and abraded nature, is consistent with redeposition (Young 2024a, 58). Most the vessels date between the late 13th and mid-14th century, principally comprising vessels from potting industries at Bourne and Toynton All Saints. A reliance on these industries distinguishes the site from contemporary assemblages at the northern end of the Scheme (SMR09 and SMR10) that seem to be dominated by a multitude of minor, short-lived, and localised industries (*ibid.*). A large millstone, deliberately repurposed as a secondary whetstone, was recovered from a medieval feature, along with two hand quern fragments, although all were typologically dated to the Roman era (Hayward and Shaffrey 2024a, 90). A relatively substantial animal bone assemblage was recovered. Cattle were dominant, followed by moderate numbers of horse, and much smaller frequencies of sheep/goat and pig. Even though none of the bones identifiable to family bears cut marks, there is some tentative evidence for primary butchery based on skeletal part representation (Chorro-Giner 2024c). None of the finds provides clear evidence to the use of the site, with perhaps the low density of finds indicating that it was only a relatively minor and short-lived smallholding.

No archaeological evidence for contemporary activity has been identified within the immediate vicinity. Documentary sources referring to the area at the time of its settlement are not available. In the Domesday Book, the nearest settlement (now deserted) is that of Steyning, located *c.* 4 km south of SMR17. In 1086 this was in the lordship of Geoffrey (of) Tournai and Robert of Vessey, with a meagre population of nine households, all villagers, but with notable resources including almost four ploughlands (two lord's plough teams and half a men's plough team), 68 acres (*c.* 27.5 ha) of meadow, significantly a fishery and eight salthouses. It is plausible that the land was once part of the vill, albeit it may equally have been part of South Kyme, *c.* 7 km northwest, or any of the other settlements in the surrounding area.

Skerth Drain runs immediately to the west of the site. Not much is recorded regarding the history of the dyke albeit it may reflect canalisation of an earlier river course, its irregular form being consistent with an earlier date. It was certainly redug and extended during the 19th century and was potentially originally part of the original course of Car Dyke (MLI12598) – a Roman canalised water course linking Peterborough to Lincoln (MLI60706). If it is the case, it may have served as a watercourse between the settlements of South Kyme and Steyning/Swinesheads, SMR17 being notably broadly equidistant between these settlements, as well as providing onwards travel to settlements further afield. No nearby farms have been recorded that might indicate a settlement focus, the nearest being College Farm (MLI122401), *c.* 0.35 km to the west of Skerth Drain, and an unnamed farmstead (MLI122394), identified a similar distance to the east. Neither is known to have existed before the 19th century (Lake and Partington 1995) but could be the location of earlier manors.

In contrast to the Lincoln Marsh sites (SMR10 and SPE01) it is unclear if the natural geology formed the basis of why the settlement was established in the area. No natural topographical features are immediately evident that may have led to the settlement of this area although former roddons may be observable from the LiDAR (Fig. 7.8) and there is some tentative evidence that the buildings were situated on these at a relatively high elevation (Stockdale *et al.* 2024, 74).

Late medieval and post-medieval industry

Even though most activity revealed across the Scheme related to farming, there was evidence for small scale

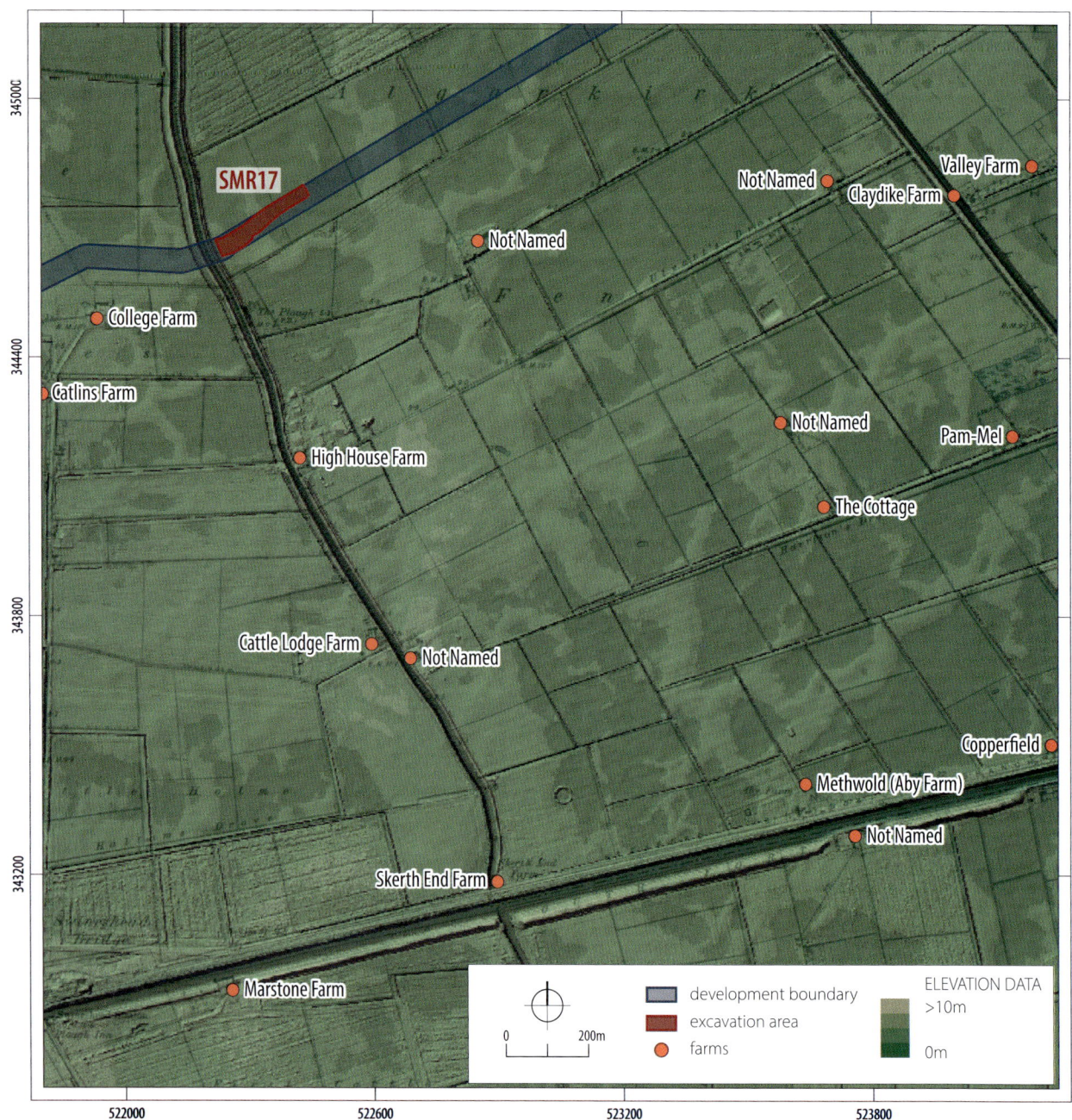

Figure 7.8 SMR17 in its landscape context and historic setting (LiDAR background mapping: Environment Agency reproduced under Open Government Licence v3.0 (Environment Agency 2024). Historic Farms data from Lake and Partington 2015)

industrial activity at SMR09 to the south of Burgh le Marsh (Figs 7.1 and 7.10). Evidence for brick manufacture was recorded in the form of pits, primarily for clay extraction, associated ditches, remnants of a cobbled path, brick structures such a drying shed, and of brick clamps/ kilns, likely used in the manufacture of bricks and related activities between the mid-15th and 17th centuries (Stockdale *et al.* 2024). In the following, a description of the evidence for brick manufacture in the mid-15th century is provided before delving into the evidence assigned to the post-medieval period.

Early brick manufacture?

Most of the surviving late medieval activity (Industry 1) was principally related to clay extraction, with a group of 21 pits recorded. Many of the pits likely served a secondary function to that of clay extraction, given the variation in how they were infilled. A few contained clay fills, possibly waste from processing, while others had evidence of intentional backfilling with debris, plausibly resulting from their subsequent use as refuse pits and/or deliberate closure (Stockdale *et al.* 2024). A statute dating to AD 477 indicates that clay was typically extracted in the

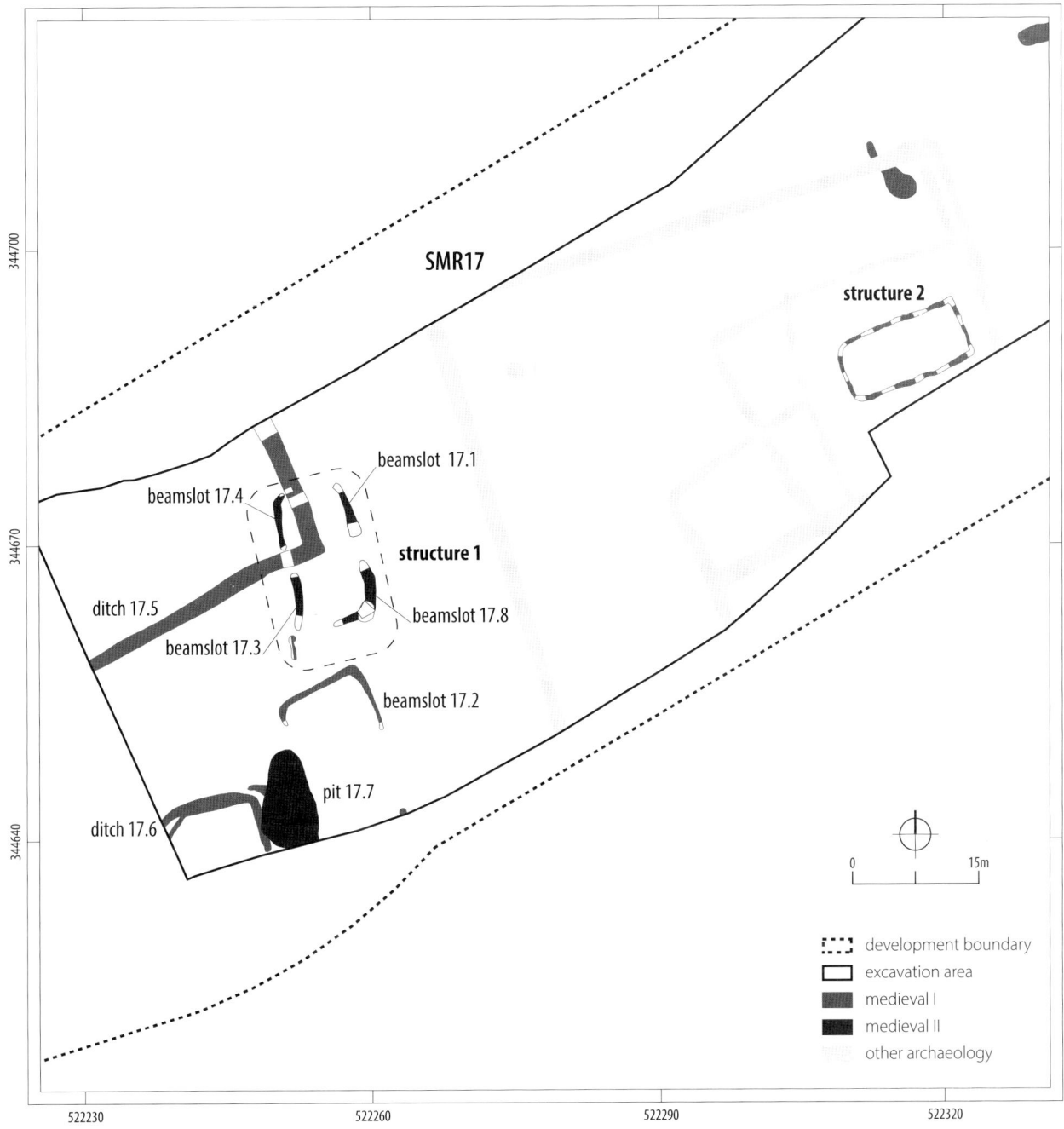

Figure 7.9 Plan of medieval features at SMR17

autumn (Drury 1981), then dug, sifted, and left to weather over the winter to prevent shrinking and warping during firing (Dobson 1850; Clifton-Taylor 1972; White 1982; Steane 1984). In Norfolk, 'washing pits' were used to soak clay in water during tempering (Hearne 2011; Crawley 2013), a practice possibly followed at this site. Tempering involved mixing the clay with water using feet, horses, spades, or later, a pugmill, to remove stones that could cause cracking (Clifton-Taylor 1972).

Most of the later medieval pits were surrounded by ditches, likely marking the main clay extraction and processing area (Stockdale *et al.* 2024, 12). These ditches may also have provided a water source and served as a boundary between the wet clay processing works and the forming, drying, and firing of bricks, which appeared to take place to the east. Separating these activities was essential to keep unfired bricks dry, as moisture could hinder the firing process (Proctor *et al.* 2000).

A single layer of brick bedded in clay (Brick Ramp 9.5) was identified east of the main clay extraction area. Based on stratigraphy, it was linked to the late medieval

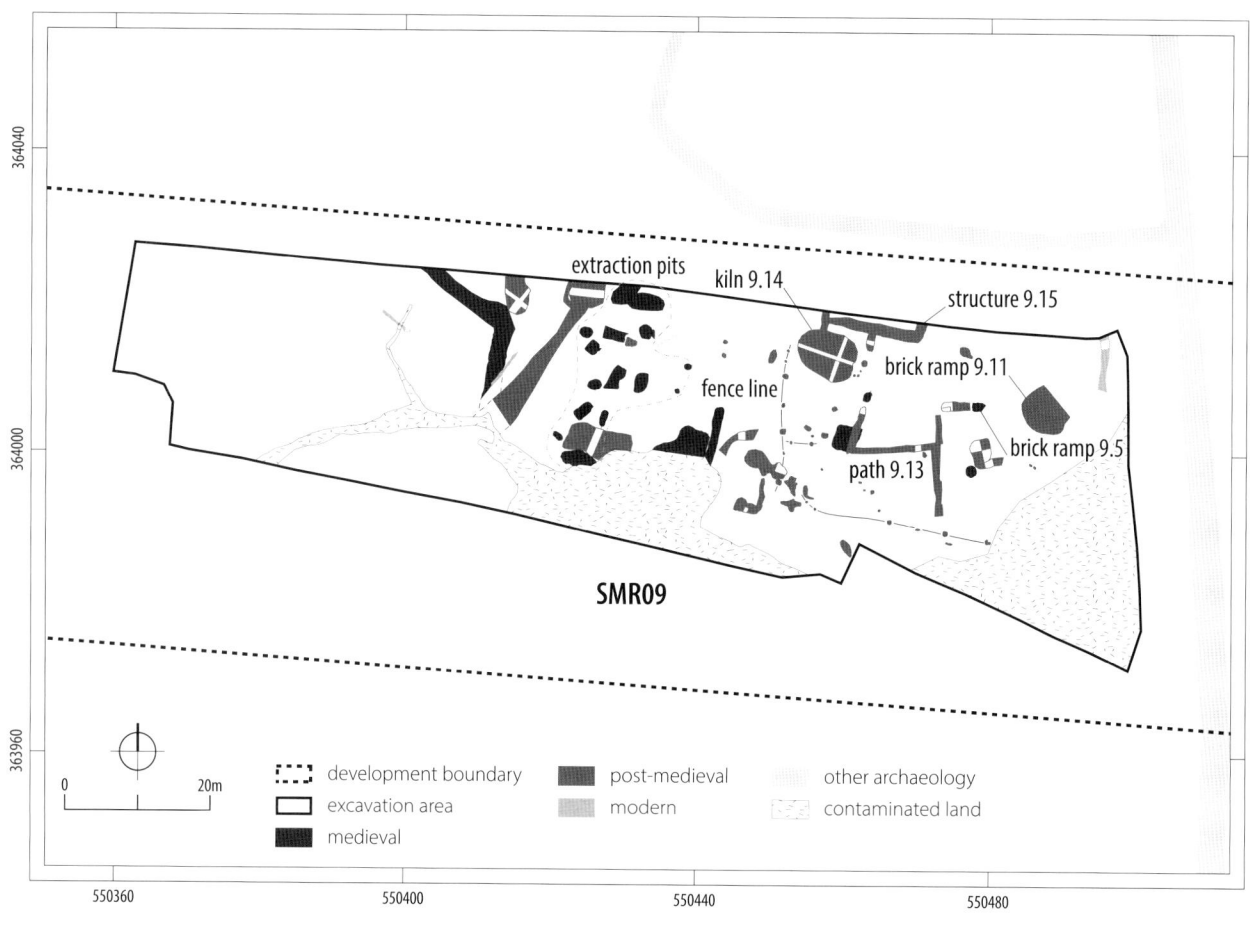

Figure 7.10 Plan of all features at SMR09

activity (Stockdale *et al.* 2024, 14). This feature may have been part of a brick clamp, a temporary structure for firing bricks, constructed by stacking unfired bricks with spacing for flues on a foundation of previously fired bricks. Brick clamps were advantageous over kilns as they were cheaper, quicker, and easier to construct. They could be built near raw materials or construction sites, reducing transportation costs (Dobson 1850). Although no bricks from the structure were analysed, a small number of heavily fired tiles, formless fired clay pieces, and abraded handmade brick fragments, were recovered from the associated features and dated tentatively to the late medieval period (Tomlinson 2024).

Medieval brick production in the area is inferred primarily from surviving buildings and historical sources discussing local brick manufacture. Brickmaking was known in Lincolnshire by the early 15th century, with earlier bricks likely imported from further afield. Immigration may have brought the essential skills for local brick manufacture to the country from the 13th century, with the import of so-called 'Flander tiles' via the coastal ports in Lincolnshire, who mainly dealt with the Netherlands and Baltic countries, providing brick but also a source of skills in the 13th and 14th centuries. North of the Humber, local brick manufacture dates from the early 14th century (Evans 2006), and it is plausible that production also occurred in North Lincolnshire, as evidenced by materials in secular buildings like Thornton Abbey (Oswald *et al.* 2010). In southern Lincolnshire, notable brick-built structures include Tattershall Castle, dated to the 15th century, associated with brick kilns at Edlington Moor, Stixwould (Simpson 1960, 42). The chancel of St Lawrence's Church in Bardney, built in AD 1434, also used locally manufactured bricks, likely from Tile House Beck (Everson *et al.* 1991; MLI51147). Magdalen College School, Wainsfleet, built in *c.* 1484, also survives from this era (White 1982; HE List Entry No. 1004931), approximately 5 km south of the site. However, archaeological evidence of late medieval/early post-medieval brick manufacture and associated clay extraction in the region is limited.

A brick assemblage, many in poor condition and likely intended for use in a kiln or its flooring, was found at Mareham le Fen, plausibly indicating brick production in the village from at least the 15th century, possibly as early as the mid-14th (Archaeological Project Services 2005). Large rectangular pits, thought to be for clay extraction, and a brick surface made of tile and brick waste, used for small scale local manufacture, were discovered during trial trenching at Meadow Lane, North Hykeham (Clay 2002; MLI83030). Archaeomagnetic dating of the associated clamp kiln suggested its last firing occurred around AD 1505 (Karloukovski and Hounslow 2005). Heat-affected sediments and scatters of brick and rubble, possibly from brick manufacture, were uncovered along with clay pits during trenching for the A16 Spalding Bypass, south of Tointons Farm; based on the size of bricks recovered these were thought to have been 17th century in date (Field and George 1994). Two possible brick kilns/clamps were identified off Low Road, Spalding, though they may date slightly later (Snee 2004). Handmade brick wasters recovered from Cowbit, near Spalding, were thought to indicate the presence of a later medieval brick clamp, though further evidence is scarce (Archaeological Project Services 2002; MLI81606). Clay pits and a scatter of early post-medieval pottery and bricks, alongside possible brick kilns, was noted near Tattershall Thorpe, East Lindsey (MLI40143). Even though much of the archaeological evidence is tentative, the locations of the sites at Mareham le Fen, Tattershall Thorpe, and now Burgh le Marsh provide an interesting distribution of sites which appear to follow a broadly linear route connecting the villages between the market towns of Sleaford and Burgh le Marsh.

A proliferation of brickmaking

Most of the activity on the site was associated with activities linked to the manufacture of brick and tile (Industry 2) during the post-medieval era. An eastern working area was demarcated by fence lines observed as a series of evenly spaced post-holes. Inside this area was evidence that the ground had been levelled (sealing the earlier medieval brick layer) with bedding material and stone, finds from this layer dated to the 15th–16th centuries (Stockdale *et al.* 2024).

A heavily truncated layer of brick (Kiln 9.14), covering c. 3.6 × 1.6 m, sat within a wide construction cut lined with sterile sand-rich bedding, in the northwestern corner of the work yard. Immediately adjacent to this was a series of linear cuts infilled with the same sterile material (*ibid.*, 19), suggesting they were contemporaneous. Rather than these being a discrete structure, the configuration of the cuts may plausibly suggest a related use to that of the brick surface, seemingly representing flue cuts of a brick clamp kiln, as observed elsewhere (Proctor *et al.* 2000), albeit the remains were only poorly surviving. The proposed brick clamp was constructed on the layers of bedding material and stone that levelled the site, plausibly reflecting earlier working surfaces, but also possibly related to immediate ground preparation in advance of the kiln. An account of the construction of such kilns mentions that:

> The ground on which the clamp was to be constructed was first prepared by levelling, draining and compacting. It was important that the chosen plot of land was adequately drained to prevent the unfired bricks from becoming wet, thus making firing difficult. Discarded bricks, if available from previous firings, could be used to level the ground and facilitate drainage. Channels in the prepared floor formed flues which extended through the entire thickness of the clamp. Bricks were placed on the floor between the flues to form platforms onto which the unfired or 'green' bricks were stacked. (Proctor *et al.* 2000, 189)

Exact dating of this activity is unclear. Excluding any residual pottery, most of the vessels associated with the work yard dated to the 16th to mid-17th centuries. A small number of sherds were dated to the 18th or 19th centuries, but these were not thought to represent primary discard and may have been introduced through later agricultural activity (Young 2024a, 54), plough lines truncating the archaeology (Stockdale *et al.* 2024, 18). Most of the ceramic building materials recorded, unfortunately, were only broadly dated. Bricks recovered from the layer were typical calcareous fabric from the area, handmade and sand moulded with an average size of 250–260 mm length, 130 mm width, and 60–65 mm thickness (Tomlinson 2024, 104). This brick size is broadly equivalent to the 10 × 5 × 2½ inch brick size standard stipulated in York in AD 1585 and longer, wider, and thinner than later brick specifications (Dobson 1850), albeit there was a lack of standardisation into the early-20th century (Rivingtons 1919).

In the centre of the yard were sections of tightly packed cobbles, interpreted as remains of former pathways (Path 9.13) (Stockdale *et al.* 2024; Fig. 7.10). They were cut through by subsequent pitting and the later agricultural activity but the original form of the cobble surfaces was thought to have been H-shaped. It is plausible that the surfaces functioned as paths for movements of traffic around the site, especially during the wetter seasons (*ibid.*, 18). Cobbled paths have been identified in association with brick manufacture of broadly contemporary date (*e.g.* New Cross, London: Proctor *et al.* 2000, and Ellough, Suffolk: Boulter 1997), but alternative uses have also been suggested, such as processing of wet clays (*e.g.* Newfound Farm, Cringleford, Norfolk: OA 2022), and for drying bricks, a critical part of the manufacturing process (Steane 1984).

East of the cobbled surfaces was a substantial and relatively well-surviving brick structure (Brick Ramp 9.11). It survived as three gently sloping brick surfaces set in a fan-shaped or radiating arrangement (Stockdale *et al.* 2024). Each surface was made of a single course of handmade bricks set in a bedding layer, stretcher side up and header to header. A stepped appearance was created through the slight offsetting of bricks but this did not appear to be consistent and the presence of brick tumble, alongside earlier pits underlying the structure, seems to indicate that the sloped and stepped appearance of the brick surfaces was due to subsequent subsidence, rather than having been originally constructed that way. All bricks appeared to have been fired with no apparent green stock among them and some were fused together suggesting they had been exposed to high temperatures and positioned close to the heat source. The fusing of the bricks must have happened *in situ*, but any evidence of the presumably overlying heat source did not survive. All examples sent for analysis were of a similar type of brick, some with evidence of being sintered, and the overall typology was considered consistent with industrial use, plausibly brick manufacture (Tomlinson 2024). Brick dimensions were c. 230 mm long, 105–110 mm wide, and 60 mm thick, broadly equivalent to 9 1/16 × 4 1/8 × 2 1/16 inch, placing them broadly in the size range of bricks manufactured from the mid-16th century–19th century.

From the associated levelling material, a small assemblage of bowls was recovered, including sherds identified as from mid-16th to mid-17th century Toynton/Bolingbroke bowls and a Glazed Red Earthenware bowl. These provide a *terminus post quem* for the construction (Young 2024a). From the infill came sherds from a mix of vessels, the latest being of 18th century date, including a Nottingham Stoneware cup, decorated Slipware press-moulded dishes, and a sherd of late 17th–18th century Brown-glazed Earthenware (*ibid.*). A small assemblage of glass was also recovered (Sillwood 2024, 87), notably including sherds from a mallet wine bottle dated to 1730–1770 (after Dumbrell 1983) and likely provide a *terminus ante quem* for the end of the industrial activity.

The function of the 'ramped' brick structure remains unclear. It was initially suggested that it may have been a brick clamp (Stockdale *et al.* 2024, 23), although these are typically recorded as rectangular brick platforms with a series of orthogonal flues (*e.g.* New Cross, London: Proctor *et al.* 2000). A similar construction was identified as a brick causeway 'garden feature' in Great Horkesley (Essex) in association with 16th–17th century brick kilns, although no evidence of fusing of bricks was observed (Clarke and Haskins 2021). At least superficially, the circular nature and observable tapering of the brick surfaces resemble the stepped ramps surrounding the entrance of a lime 'pot' kiln, as described by Chapman (2008). However, no evidence of any kiln structure at the centre of the brick surfaces or for lime processing was recorded here. The brick surfaces may perhaps be best likened to that laid at the base of a round tile oven or Cupola as described by Dobson (1850, 40), who portrays a circular kiln consisting of a floor made of stacks of bricks arranged in a wedge-shaped pattern, with surrounding walls and a domed roof. The benefit of this form was for creating particularly high temperatures, and the presence of fused bricks would attest to particularly high temperatures at Burgh le Marsh. Importantly, Dobson (1850, 38) states that there are 'many ways of constructing kilns, and scarcely any two are exactly alike' and consequently we should not expect the proposed brick kilns/clamps to conform to any pre-arranged schema at SMR09, near Burgh le Marsh. Nor is the relatively elaborate and more formalised manufacturing industry of the 19th century necessarily a good comparator for the brickworks of earlier centuries.

It is likely that the observed brick manufacture was relatively local in scale, with brick not transported any great distance prior to the construction of 19th century railways (Trinder 2013) and, as noted above, early brickworks were often sited adjacent to the raw material sources and immediately within the vicinity of any planned building as a means by which to reduce costs. No contemporary brick structures have been identified within the close proximity of the site, but it is notable that the site is situated on sizeable land parcel known as 'Old House Ground' at the time of the 1841 tithe apportionment of Burgh le Marsh. There is limited evidence, beyond the domestic objects recovered, for any such property. Medieval to post-medieval roof tiles were also retrieved from the backfill of a post-medieval extraction pit and it has been suggested that the tile may have come from a single structure (Tomlinson 2024). However, given the relatively narrow window of intervention that is not necessarily surprising. It may be that the early brickworks were originally set up for the embellishment of earlier stone-built structures, such as through the introduction of brick chimneys, and subsequently brick manufacture re-established at the site for the maintenance of the house, or even the erection of an entirely new building. Any brick manufacture at the site had certainly ceased by the 1841 tithe apportionment of Burgh le Marsh. No evidence for brickworks at the site is identifiable on the 1888 Ordnance Survey, nor of any associated house. Evidence of brickworks and plausibly mineral extraction for the production of brick, however, is recorded in the wider region in the 19th century. In fact, in Lincolnshire there was a tripling of brickworks in the early part of the century and at its zenith in *c.* 1880, 187 were recorded in the region, by 1969 this number was just 16 (Robinson 1993).

Artefactual evidence
Post-Roman pottery
Jane Young

A total of 2043 sherds of post-Roman or presumed post-Roman type, representing 1351 vessels, were recovered from the evaluation and excavation phases of the Scheme. The identifiable pottery ranges in type from the middle Saxon to early modern periods (Tables 7.1–7.3) with most of the recovered vessels being of medieval and late medieval type. Despite having several known major pottery industries, Lincolnshire has a complex ceramic sequence, especially between the post-conquest 11th and mid-14th centuries. A proliferation of small, usually localised and often short lived, industries is found across much of Lincolnshire during this period. Many of these small centres produced pottery in the style of the main industries found in Lincoln, Bourne, and Toynton All Saints, while others manufactured types previously unknown in the county; although these may have been influenced by wares from the eight surrounding counties or other regional imports brought in by coastal or river trade. The Scheme crosses the two Lincolnshire divisions of East Lindsey to the north and Holland to the south and covers 13 parishes in five medieval *Wapentakes* (Roffe

1993). Initial work suggested that in some areas it is these *Wapentakes* that may influence distribution of the minor ware types, however, a major research programme integrating multiple datasets across the region would be needed to explore this further (Knight *et al.* 2012, 99, 104). The pottery is discussed below by ceramic periods which, although mainly corresponding to actual dates do not always follow them. For instance, pottery of 12th century date may fall into Saxo-Norman, early medieval, and medieval traditions, while some medieval types extend into the 16th century and some coarse late post-medieval earthenwares overlap with industrially produced early modern fine wares. Furthermore, the nomenclature for ceramic periods does not have direct equivalence with the terminology used to distinguish periods as derived from the East Midlands Research Framework. For instance, the 'Early Medieval' pottery spans the post-conquest 11th and early/mid-13th centuries, but the period 'early medieval' refer to sites dating to AD 410–1066.

The pottery under discussion here was mainly recovered from cut features such as pits, ditches, field boundaries, gullies, and post-holes. This is fairly typical of post-Roman pottery assemblages recovered from rural sites in Lincolnshire, where it is rare to find well-stratified sequences. Unfortunately, this has limited interpretation of the interaction of different types and their close dating, although it has not hampered the main aim of the project in defining post-Roman types in use in the area.

The post-Roman pottery was recorded at the initial stages of the project (Young 2018, 2019; Young and Daubney 2020), with further work undertaken during the analysis phase of the project. The full methodology and results by site can be found in the Landscape Parcel reports, which are available in the ADS archive along with the database that includes detailed attribute data, such as decoration, condition, and usage. During this stage, it was possible to compare directly at a microscopic level (using a ×20 binocular microscope) several of the previously loosely defined types with more recently available excavated material from some of the surrounding parishes and refine their attribution. This subsequent work on the assemblage has enabled several new types and fabrics to be added to the known range of post-Roman wares previously recovered from the areas under investigation.

Results

A total of 2043 sherds representing 1351 vessels of post-Roman or presumed post-Roman type recovered from the Scheme were examined. The identified material ranges in date from the middle Saxon to early modern periods, although most vessels are of medieval to late medieval type (Tables 7.1 and 7.2) and represents eighty identified post-Roman ware types (Table 7.3). Recovered wares include local, regional, and continental types, although the vast majority of the assemblage was produced within Lincolnshire. The pottery types are summarised here by ceramic period with any individual site-based fabric descriptions available in the archive.

MIDDLE SAXON

Two vessels recovered from SMR10 in the Fen Edge Landscape Parcel are of middle Saxon type, although both may be late in the sequence (Stockdale *et al.* 2024). A single sherd from a large jar is of Ipswich type (IPST). The sherd does not have a typical Ipswich ware fabric as defined by Blinkhorn (2012, 25). Blinkhorn's survey concluded that the type was solely made in Ipswich and that he found no evidence for production elsewhere but more recently a kiln producing Ipswich-type vessels of potential 8th–10th century date has been discovered at Wrenningham in Norfolk (Sudds 2016). A non-Ipswich source for this vessel has been confirmed by thin-section analysis (Wood 2024). A small number of similar vessels have been encountered in the county, most notably

Table 7.1 Pottery from all sites summarised by sherd count, vessel count, weight, and Rim Estimated Vessel Equivalence (REVE)

Ceramic Period	Total sherds	Total vessels	Total weight (g)	REVE
Uncertain date	51	37	46	
Middle Saxon	9	2	1395	0.36
Late Saxon	66	31	1524	1.15
Saxo-Norman	42	24	338	0.34
Early medieval	15	9	201	0
Medieval	938	524	20,313	5.64
Late medieval	508	432	12,942	3.99
Post-medieval	325	235	15,405	8.38
Early modern	89	57	1053	1.09
Total	2043	1351	53,217	20.95

Table 7.2 Pottery summarised by Landscape Parcel and ceramic period with vessel count

Ceramic period	Coastal	Fen Edge	Inland Fen Edge	Lincolnshire Marsh	U/S	Total
Uncertain date	31	6	0	0	0	37
Middle Saxon	0	2	0	0	0	2
Late Saxon	6	25	0	0	0	31
Saxo-Norman	7	16	0	1	0	24
Early medieval	4	5	0	0	0	9
Medieval	144	378	0	2	0	524
Late medieval	11	420	0	1	0	432
Post-medieval	21	203	5	4	2	235
Early modern	9	21	11	15	1	57
Total	233	1076	16	23	3	1351

Table 7.3 Pottery summarised by Codename with full name and date range by sherd count, vessel count, weight, and REVE

Ceramic codename	Full name	Earliest date	Latest date	Total sherds	Total vessels	Total weight (g)	REVE
BERTH	Brown glazed earthenware	1550	1950	22	7	1268	0.20
BEVO1T	Beverley Orange-type ware Fabric 1	1100	1230	1	1	3	0
BEVO2	Beverley Orange ware Fabric 2	1230	1350	4	4	22	0
BL	Black-glazed wares	1550	1950	13	9	176	0.20
BOLF	Fine Bolingbroke-type	1650	1720	1	1	27	0.06
BOU	Bourne D ware	1350	1650	6	6	51	
BOUA	Bourne-type medieval Fabrics A to G	1150	1400	57	24	1022	0
CELEMG	Coastal East Lincolnshire Early Medieval Glazed	1150	1230	5	1	149	0
CELMG	Coastal East Lindsey Medieval Glazed ware	1180	1350	29	16	366	0.21
CIST	Cistercian-type ware	1480	1650	6	5	28	0
CREA	Creamware	1770	1830	29	15	204	8
ELDOXU	East Lincolnshire Dull Oxidised Unglazed	1200	1450	3	3	34	0.02
ELEFS	East Lincolnshire Early Fine shelled	800	1020	8	1	1351	0.36
ELGSG	East Lincolnshire Greensand Quartz Shell & Grog	1050	1200	2	1	29	0.13
ELLSLG	East Lindsey Late Saxon Lincoln-type Greyware	900	1030	5	2	48	0
ELLSLLG	East Lindsey Late Saxon Lincoln-type Light-firing Greyware	980	1030	25	2	1162	1.05
ELMAS	East Lincolnshire Medieval Abundant Shelly	1180	1300	57	18	974	0.25
ELMLRFE	East Lincolnshire Medieval Light Reduced with Iron	1200	1350	2	2	18	0

(Continued)

Table 7.3 Pottery summarised by Codename with full name and date range by sherd count, vessel count, weight, and REVE (Continued)

Ceramic codename	Full name	Earliest date	Latest date	Total sherds	Total vessels	Total weight (g)	REVE
ELMWTS	East Lincolnshire Medieval Wheel-thrown Shelly	1180	1350	106	8	4163	1.23
ELSNCQC	East Lincolnshire Saxo-Norman Coarse Quartz and Chalk	950	1200	18	6	122	0
ELSNFQ	East Lincolnshire Saxo-Norman Fine Sandy ware	950	1100	2	2	37	0
ELSNQ	East Lincolnshire Saxo-Norman Sandy ware	950	1200	2	1	11	0
EMHM	Early Medieval Handmade ware	1100	1250	3	2	12	0
ENGS	Unspecified English Stoneware	1750	1900	4	4	54	0
ENPO	English Porcelain	1743	2000	1	1	1	0
FREC	Frechen stoneware	1530	1680	2	2	50	0.45
GRE	Glazed Red Earthenware	1500	1650	83	71	2970	2.33
GRIM	Grimston ware	1200	1550	2	2	62	0
GSS	Greensand and shell	1050	1250	3	3	43	0
HUM	Humberware	1250	1550	3	3	55	0
IPST	Ipswich-type ware	750	850	1	1	44	0
LANG	Langerwehe stoneware	1350	1500	3	2	35	0
LBLAK	Late Blackware (modern)	1700	1930	3	1	13	0.04
LEMS	Lincolnshire Early Medieval Shelly	1130	1230	2	2	7	0
LERTH	Late earthenwares	1750	1900	1	1	27	0
LFS	Lincolnshire Fine-shelled ware	970	1200	1	1	5	0
LKT	Lincoln kiln-type shelly ware	850	1000	9	7	89	0
LMLOC	Late Medieval local fabrics	1350	1550	2	2	72	0
LMX	Late Medieval Non-local fabrics	1350	1550	1	1	11	0
LSWV	Lincoln Sandy ware variant	1150	1500	5	4	106	0
MARTIII	Martincamp red earthenware	1600	1750	1	1	6	0
MEDLOC	Medieval local fabrics	1150	1450	24	16	645	0.45
MEDX	Non Local Medieval Fabrics	1150	1450	13	7	276	0
MISC	Unidentified types	400	1900	50	36	38	0
MLBSL	Midlands Light-bodied Slipware	1680	1800	8	4	72	0
MVAL	Mature Valencian Lustreware	1430	1500	1	1	2	0
NCBW	19th-century Buff ware	1800	1900	7	4	422	0.22
NOTS	Nottingham stoneware	1690	1900	3	3	32	0.17
PEARL	Pearlware	1770	1900	10	9	54	0.13
PGE	Pale Glazed Earthenware	1600	1750	40	19	2891	1.70
POTT	Potterhanworth-type Ware	1250	1500	32	21	951	0.32
RAER	Raeren stoneware	1450	1600	3	3	68	0.30

(Continued)

Table 7.3 Pottery summarised by Codename with full name and date range by sherd count, vessel count, weight, and REVE (Continued)

Ceramic codename	Full name	Earliest date	Latest date	Total sherds	Total vessels	Total weight (g)	REVE
REFR	Refined Red Earthenware	1730	1800	1	1	18	0
RGRE	Reduced glazed red earthenware	1600	1850	6	5	108	6
RMED	Roman or medieval	40	1500	1	1	8	0
SCAR	Scarborough ware	1150	1350	1	1	7	0
SLIP	Unidentified slipware	1650	1750	5	5	164	0.03
SLQS	South Lincolnshire Quartz and shell (generic)	1180	1500	1	1	5	0
SLSHCW	South Lincolnshire Shell-tempered coarseware (generic)	1100	1400	32	14	126	0
SLSNT	South Lincolnshire St Neots-type	980	1100	3	3	19	0.08
SLSQ	South Lincolnshire Shell and Quartz (generic)	1200	1500	3	2	28	
SLST	South Lincolnshire Shell Tempered ware	1150	1350	77	31	1795	0.04
SNLOC	Local Saxo-Norman fabrics	870	1150	1	1	9	0.05
ST	Stamford Ware	970	1200	5	4	24	0.08
STMO	Staffordshire/Bristol mottled-glazed	1690	1800	5	4	69	0
STSL	Staffordshire/Bristol slipware	1680	1800	14	8	98	0.02
SWSG	Staffordshire White Salt-glazed stoneware	1700	1770	2	2	4	0
TB	Toynton/Bolingbroke wares	1450	1750	122	96	7495	3.33
TGW	Tin-glazed ware	1640	1770	2	2	8	0
THETT	Thetford-type fabrics	880	1150	5	2	39	0
TORKT	Torksey-type ware	850	1100	3	2	16	0.03
TOY	Toynton medieval Ware	1250	1450	481	341	9447	2.86
TOYBT	Toynton Bourne-type	1300	1500	1	1	5	0.26
TOYCALC	Calcareous Toynton-type	1250	1350	5	5	206	0
TOYII	Toynton Late medieval ware	1450	1550	486	412	12675	3.69
TPW	Transfer printed ware	1770	1900	24	12	207	0.45
UNGS	Unglazed Greensand-tempered fabrics	950	1250	1	1	8	0
WEMS	Wheel-thrown Early Medieval Shell-tempered	1050	1220	3	2	22	0
WEST	Westerwald stoneware	1600	1800	1	1	3	0
WHITE	Modern Whiteware	1850	1900	4	4	17	0
WLSS	Wheel-thrown Late Saxon Shell-tempered	900	1030	12	8	110	0.07
WLSSFE	Wheel-thrown Late Saxon Shell and Iron-tempered (Lincoln Type)	900	1030	4	4	44	0
WLSSQ	Wheel-thrown Late Saxon Shell & Quartz-tempered (Lincoln Type)	900	1030	8	6	55	0
Total				2043	1351	53217	10.88

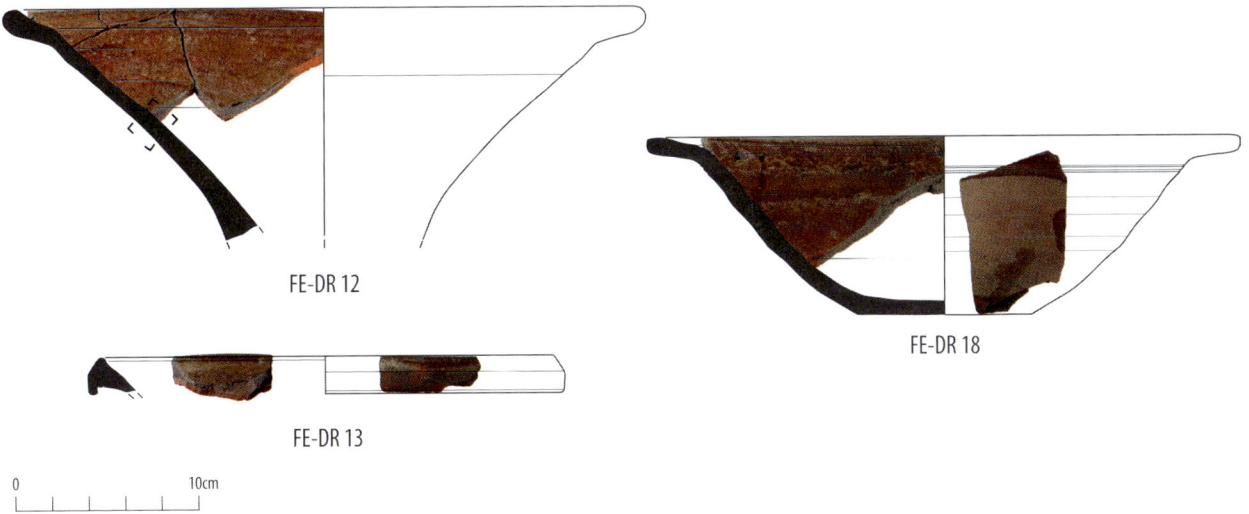

Figure 7.11 Selected examples of medieval and post-medieval pottery from SMR09

a sherd from the coastal parish of Hutoft was recovered with newly defined late Saxon wheelthrown types (Young 2023a). It is not unreasonable to think that there may have been other centres producing similar vessels, perhaps in Lincolnshire, as the vessel recovered from Croft (SMR10) has a more typically Lincolnshire-looking fabric.

This site also produced a number of sherds from a large, shallow, cylindrical bowl in a newly defined handmade shell-tempered ware type (ELEFS). Similar vessels in a central Lincolnshire early fine-shelled ware (ELFS) date to the period between the 9th and mid-10th centuries spanning the handmade middle Saxon and wheelthrown late Saxon traditions (Young *et al.* 2005, 37; Young and Vince 2009, 356–357). These vessels are found on several sites in central and northern Lincolnshire with some textural, firing colour, and manufacturing differences occurring, perhaps suggesting dispersed production or as yet undetectable chronological differences. Thin-section analysis of the vessel from Croft (SMR10) suggests that this vessel is comparable to ELFS as found in Lincoln despite visual differences in fabric, form, and manufacture (Wood 2024). As the type first occurs in deposits of potential late 8th–early 9th century date (Young and Vince 2009, 356–357) but is also found in secure assemblages of late 9th–early 10th century date in Lincoln (Young *et al.* 2005, 37) it is not unsurprising that such differences are to be expected.

Late Saxon

A total of 66 sherds representing 31 wheelthrown vessels are of late Saxon type with the majority recovered from the Fen Edge Landscape Parcel and most being found on site SMR10 (13 vessels). Six vessels were recovered from site SPE01 in the Coastal Landscape Parcel. Vessels tempered with fossil shell (25 vessels) outnumber those in reduced quartz-tempered fabrics (six vessels). The reduced sandy ware vessels include four in two newly defined ware types (Wood 2024)

A total of nine sherds from seven shell-tempered vessels recovered during evaluation (Trench 270 in the Sibsey parish) are of Lincoln Kiln-type (LKT). This competently potted ware was produced in Lincoln between the mid/late 9th and late 10th centuries (Gilmour 1988; Young 1989; Young *et al.* 2005, 47–56). The recovered vessels include three large bowls, two jars, and two vessels of unknown form. The bowls all have in-turned rims, two of which are of early/mid- to late 10th century type and one dates more specifically to between the early and early/mid-10th century. This site also produced two sherds from Lincoln-type wheelthrown shell and quartz-tempered jars (WLSSQ) of probable late 9th to 10th century date. Further sherds from jars or bowls of potential late 9th to early/mid-11th century date were recovered from two other sites in the Fen Edge Landscape Parcel (SMR10 and SMR17) and one (SPE01) in the Coastal Landscape Parcel. The 12 shell-tempered sherds not containing additional quartz grains (WLSS) are from eight jars or bowls. All the vessels were found in the parish of Croft on the SMR10 site in the Fen Edge Landscape Parcel. Most sherds are typologically of 10th–early 11th century type but an in-turned rim bowl likely dates to the earlier half of the 10th century. Three other shell-tempered jars and a jar or bowl with the addition of iron-rich grains in the fabric (WLSSFE) are of probable 10th–early 11th century date. Three of these vessels were recovered from site SMR10 but a small jar was found on site SMR09 in Burgh le Marsh. All the shell-tempered vessels are of Lincoln-type and form part of what is becoming evident as a widespread tradition across eastern Lincolnshire for the use of finely potted shell-tempered vessels not paralleled by the main Lincoln types.

The fabric group also contained 33 reduced quartz-tempered sherds from six vessels. Two sherds from a small jar (SMR10) and an in-turned rim bowl (SPE01) (TORKT), although visually similar to Torksey ware, do not match known productions there (Barley 1964; 1981; Hadley *et al.* 2023), but this does not preclude manufacture there. Typologically the vessels are of 10th and early/mid-10th–early/mid-11th century type. The other 30 quartz-tempered sherds recovered from site SPE01 at Mumby on the coast are from four vessels in two newly defined Lincoln-type productions.

A group of 24 sherds in a very poor condition have tentatively been identified as an East Lindsey Lincoln-type Late Saxon Light-firing Greyware (ELLSLLG) of potential late 10th–early/mid-11th century date. The sherds are from a large shallow bowl with a clubbed rim recovered from SPE01, Ditch E1.21 (0057). Thin-section analysis of this vessel shows an Ooid Ironstone fabric and suggests a potential local source (Wood 2024). This fabric is designated as Group 1 within the database.

The same ditch, E1.21, in SPE01, produced a light-firing sherd from a large bowl decorated with spaced thumb-pressings around the outer rim edge. A similar vessel was recovered from Goxhill in north Lincolnshire (Young 2023d). Microscopic examination of these vessels by the author showed a visually different fabric (Group 2) to that of the shallow bowl and this was confirmed by thin-section analysis which indicates the source of the fabric to be a Sandy Sandstone with shale (Wood 2024). Light firing late Saxon fabrics are not unknown in Lincoln but their presence is confined to the period of the mid/late 9th and early 10th centuries, and all are highly fired and of a much finer production than these vessels. Also in this ditch group is a basal sherd from a small jar in a higher-fired grey ware also of Lincoln-type (ELLSLG). A further sherd from a medium-sized jar was recovered from the site. These vessels are of probable late 10th to early/mid-11th century date. The medium-sized jar was examined by thin-section analysis and found to fall into a similar Sandy Sandstone with shale fabric to that of the decorated bowl. These two grey wares are part of a growing number of new late Saxon wheelthrown types found in eastern Lincolnshire and may represent previously unencountered Lincoln fabrics or daughter industries set up by Lincoln potters (Wood 2024).

SAXO-NORMAN

A total of 42 sherds from 24 vessels in ten ware types are of Saxo-Norman type, recovered from SMR06, SMR09, Trench 320, 262, 017, TAM09, and predominantly SMR10 and SPE01. Several of these industries are of long-lived type with only two (ST and THETT) representing known industrial centres. The majority of sherds come from handmade jars or bowls in quartz, shell, or mixed inclusion fabrics most probably made in east Lincolnshire. The three wheelthrown ware types include three small shell-tempered South Lincolnshire St Neots-type jars (SLSNT) of probable 10th to mid-11th century date, four glazed Stamford ware (ST) jars or pitchers of peri- or post-conquest type (Kilmurry 1980), and two Thetford-type ware vessels of which one appears to have been manufactured in Lincolnshire.

A single body sherd found in Burgh le Marsh (site TAM09) is from a small Lincolnshire Fine-shelled ware (LFS) jar of 11th or 12th century date. This is often the most common Saxo-Norman shell-tempered tradition to be found in central and northern Lincolnshire and may have been manufactured in the Lincoln area (Young *et al.* 2005, 88). Three sherds from small and medium-sized jars in Greensand quartz and shell-tempered fabrics (GSS) represent a tradition not uncommonly found in eastern Lincolnshire. The quartz-tempered fabric suggests a Lincolnshire Wolds source. The vessels have a potential mid-11th to mid-13th century date span but are most commonly found associated with mid-11th to late 12th century groups.

The remaining 25 sherds are from 11, mainly quartz-tempered, vessels of which most are identifiable as small and medium sized jars. With one exception, the vessels appear to be either completely handmade or possibly finished on a turntable. The only completely wheelthrown vessel is a collared jar in a reduced quartz-tempered fabric (SNLOC) recovered from SMR06. This jar is of probable mid-11th to mid-12th century date as similar, although not identical, wheelthrown reduced, quartz-tempered jars are known from groups of this date in Goltho (Young *et al.* 2005, fig. 73) and north Lincolnshire (Boyle *et al.* 2011). The other vessels are all probably of East Lindsey and possibly fairly local production. These four recently defined primarily quartz-tempered types contain a range of quartz sands and chalk grains that suggest that they were certainly made within eastern Lincolnshire with two types (ELGSG and ELSNCQC) probably being manufactured within the area of the Lincolnshire Wolds. Unfortunately, close dating is not yet possible, although general manufacture suggests a 10th or 11th century date for most vessels; apart from the only ELGSG sherd in the group, which is of possible post-conquest type.

EARLY MEDIEVAL

Little pottery of ceramic early medieval tradition was recovered from the Scheme (15 sherds from nine vessels). These wares span the period between the post-conquest 11th and early/mid-13th centuries. Except for a single sherd from an East Yorkshire Beverley 1 jug or jar (BEVO1) from SPE01 and a 'splash-glazed' jug in a newly defined Coastal East Lindsey fabric (CELEMG), also SPE01, all the pottery of this period is from shell- or quartz-tempered coarsewares. The convex basal sherd representing the CELEMG jug is quite distinctive and has knife-trimming around the basal edge. The jug appears to be of Lincoln 'early shouldered'type (Young *et al.* 2005, 647–648, 650, fig. 92). Thin-section analysis indicates a Basic Igneous temper and the possibility of fairly local production (Wood 2024).

The two Early Medieval Handmade ware vessels (EMHM) recovered from SPE01 are the only coarseware vessels likely to have been produced outside of Lincolnshire. The small jar, and jar or bowl, are likely to have been made in East Anglia between the 12th and early/mid-13th centuries.

The base from a small Lincolnshire Early Medieval Shelly ware jar (LEMS) from TAM09 and a jar or bowl body sherd from SMR09 can be dated to between the mid-12th and early/mid-13th centuries. A body sherd from a Wheelthrown Early Medieval Shell-tempered ware (WEMS) jar in Fabric B found in Burgh le Marsh (TAM09) is of 12th century date. Initially this type was thought to be restricted to the area of the Bain Valley however an increasing number of vessels are being found along the east coast possibly suggesting more than one area of production for the type. A single sherd from an unglazed Greensand quartz-tempered jar with a slightly ridged shoulder is likely to be of 12th century date.

Medieval

A large group of medieval pottery (938 sherds from 524 vessels) was recovered from the various interventions with the majority of the pottery coming from the Fen Edge Landscape Parcel (378 vessels) and being of late 13th–15th century Medieval Toynton-type (TOY). A total of 21 ware types were identified of which the vast majority were produced within Lincolnshire. A small number of identifiable regional imports are from Norfolk (GRIM) and Yorkshire (BEVO2, HUM, and SCAR). The form assemblage is fairly typical for rural sites with examples of large bowl, small jug, and undecorated medium sized jugs being the most common forms identified. Few specialised or unusual forms were recovered but these include examples of drinking jugs, a dripping dish, a pipkin, and a small lamp saucer or internally glazed dish.

The bulk of the pottery recovered from the Scheme is of Medieval Toynton-type (TOY) which was recovered from most of the sites producing medieval pottery (Fig. 7.11). This type is one of the three major medieval Lincolnshire productions centred in Bourne, Lincoln, and Toynton All Saints. Production of pottery at the villages of Toynton All Saints and Toynton St Peters in the south of Lincolnshire has been studied for more than 70 years (Healey 1975; 1984; Field 1996). This medieval pottery type was widely marketed within Lincolnshire and was also traded to other areas both in England and on the continent. The only excavated medieval kiln, Kiln 1 (The Roses) is thought to have been in use during the late 13th and early 14th centuries (Aitken and Hawley 1966, 190–191). Numerous finds of misfired and waster sherds suggest other production sites across Lincolnshire. Production of late medieval and post-medieval types continued in the local area until the late 16th or early 17th centuries (see below).

There had been no conclusive evidence for production prior to the late 13th century until recently and secure groups found elsewhere in the county seemed to support this. Finds of Toynton-type vessels in Boston associated with pottery groups of mid/late 13th century date are of slightly different character and are in variant fabrics. These vessels included misfired sherds and suggested earlier production perhaps in Boston itself. More recently excavations in Toynton All Saints itself have produced waste of early medieval and early to mid-13th century date although these vessels are more typical of Lincoln production (Young in prep.).

A few decorated jugs are of definite late 13th–14th century type but only one potential example of a decorated late 13th–early/mid-14th century Roses-type jug occurs in the recovered material. This jug is decorated with applied brown iron-rich pellets on an amber glaze background. The other jugs are decorated with applied iron-rich or self-coloured strips with two small jugs evidencing part of a complex pattern. Most sherds however are from utilitarian large bowls or small to large plain jugs. All the large bowls identified are of the typical sloping Toynton-type with narrow bases. These bowls are identified in documentary references as 'milk pans' (Le Patourel 1968) and, unlike the Bourne-type examples, have no evidence for external soot residues. Single examples of a pipkin, a dripping dish, and the possible saucer of a pedestal lamp are the only identifiable unusual forms although a large basal sherd found on site SMR09 is certainly from a most unusual but unidentifiable form.

It is extremely difficult to date the small and mainly undiagnostic body and basal sherds of this industry, although there is a general trend towards higher-fired vessels, especially jugs, from the late 14th century onwards. Fifteen of the recovered vessels, however, can be dated stylistically to the late 13th–mid-14th centuries, 42 are of late 13th–14th century type and eight are of a potential mid/late 13th–mid-14th century production similar to that found in Boston. Other vessels are identifiable as being of mid-14th–15th century date (20 vessels) or 15th–mid-16th century type (12 examples) but realistically most vessels can only be dated to a late 13th–15th century date range.

Five sherds are from jugs or jars of mid- or late 13th to mid-14th century date and are in Calcareous Toynton-type fabrics (TOYCALC). One of the jugs is decorated with applied, wide, vertical, iron-rich strips. A few misfired sherds have been found in Toynton All Saints but it is also possible that the type was made elsewhere in Lincolnshire. A single sherd of Toynton-Bourne-type (TOYBT) from a small jug or drinking jug was recovered from site SMR09. The type appears have a mix of Medieval Toynton ware and Late Medieval Bourne ware characteristics and probably dates to the 14th or 15th centuries.

Medieval Bourne ware (BOUA) was recovered from a single investigated site (SMR17) at Amber Hill in the Holland district of Lincolnshire. The post-Roman potting industry in Bourne was established by at least the late 12th century with production centring on the area known as Eastgate towards the east of the modern town. The main medieval products were jugs, jars, and bowls in Fabrics A, B, and C. These fabrics were first identified by Healey in the late 1960s (1969, 108–109) and have remained the main types to be recovered throughout Lincolnshire, although in essence most fabrics are typically a hybrid of more than one of Healey's types as it is rare to recover a sherd in a pure Fabric A or Fabric B. Further fabrics have been added (Fabrics E, F, and G) but none of these was recovered. Vessels in a similar tradition and fabrics appear to have also been made at Baston, a village 6.4 km south of Bourne (Le Patourel 1968), and Hall Farm where wasters of several Baston-type wares have also been recovered (Precious *et al.* 2003, 21; Young 2008). Other known centres producing similar pottery include Colne in Cambridgeshire (Healey *et al.* 1998).

The 57 Medieval Bourne ware sherds recovered from site SMR17 represent 24 vessels in several fabric combinations of which none is dominant but 13 of the vessels have a high iron-rich content suggesting a similar source for the vessels. This could potentially represent production outside of Bourne itself but, as little scientific work has been done on the waste recovered from the town and the fabrics seen by this author are very mixed and certainly include some iron-rich examples, a Bourne source is more likely. Most of the sherds can be identified as coming from small, medium, or large jars with ridged shoulders of which at least two have a pulled pouring line. Seven of these jars have internal glazes, most of which are not fully matured. The four large sloping bowls are typical of Bourne-type production and the presence of external soot deposits on three of these suggests their use for cooking. Typologically there is little change in vessel form throughout the medieval production in Bourne and the recovered vessels can only be dated to the 13th–mid-14th centuries.

Lincoln Glazed wares (Young *et al.* 2005) were in production from the early part of the 12th into the 16th century. No Lincoln-produced wares were recovered from the Scheme but four Lincoln-type jugs, the earliest of which has a 'splashed-type' glaze, were recovered. These jugs were produced by potters directly copying form and decorative techniques used by the Lincoln potters. Their visual closeness to actual Lincoln products may suggest potters moving out of Lincoln to work elsewhere between the mid-12th and 14th centuries. The only jug to be recovered from the Coastal Landscape Parcel (site SPE01) is of small size and has a 'splashed-type', glaze and potentially dates to between the mid-12th and early/mid-13th centuries. The other three jugs were recovered from the Fen Edge Landscape Parcel (SMR09 and TKOW Trench 280). Two of the jugs, one of which has a misfired glaze, are of 13th century type whilst the other, thicker glazed, jug could date to the 13th or 14th centuries. Two other finely potted and Lincoln-influenced sherds found at Burgh le Marsh (SMR09) are in a light firing iron-rich fabric (ELMLRFE). These jugs are of potential 13th–mid-14th century date but most probably belong to a 13th century production.

A group of 29 glazed sherds representing 16 vessels recovered from the Coastal (SPE01) and Fen Edge Landscape Parcels (SMR09) are of recently defined Coastal East Lindsey Medieval Glazed ware-type (CELMG). The sherds mainly come from small and medium-sized jugs, but a large internally glazed bowl and a jar were also identified. Firing of three of the vessels was at quite a low temperature resulting in one of the glazes not fully maturing. Glazing is of mixed 'splashed' and suspension type and this together with early decorative motifs indicates a late 12th–early/mid-13th century date for this group. A corrugated bulging neck together with a cuffed rim on one of the jugs suggests that they are of Lincoln-type form. Decoration includes the use of applied vertical iron-painted and notched strips, plain applied notched strips, and applied scales. This type was thought by the author to potentially represent a fairly localised East Lindsey coastal production. The two samples submitted for thin-section analysis show a similar Basic Igneous fabric and confirm that the vessels may have been quite locally produced.

The SMR09 site at Burgh le Marsh produced three unusual unglazed sherds from bowls with cut flat-topped rims similar to those found on early–middle Saxon Maxey-type wares. The quartz temper found in these vessels is similar to that found in some Medieval Toynton ware vessels but these bowls are possibly handmade and are in a low-fired, dull oxidised fabric now defined as East Lincolnshire Dull Oxidised Unglazed ware (ELDOXU). Only one of the three bowls was recovered from a stratified deposit being associated with a large Medieval Toynton ware bowl of 14th or 15th century date that appears to have been crushed *in situ*. It is likely that these bowls are of medieval date and fulfilled a specific domestic or industrial purpose.

A small number of vessels (24 sherds from 16 vessels) are in fabrics suggestive of a Lincolnshire source (MEDLOC). The 12 vessels recovered from the Coastal Landscape Parcel (site SPE01) are all of Toynton-type manufacture but with atypical fabrics. Most of the sherds are from jugs or jars but one sherd is from a bowl with a misfired internal glaze. Three of the other four vessels recovered from the Fen Edge Landscape Parcel were found in Burgh le Marsh (SMR09 and TKOW Trench 233). These three jugs include one with small applied and stamped pads. The other jug recovered from within the bounds of site SPE03 (TKOW Trench 125) is in a finer sandy fabric and has prominent internal finger pressings and a smooth external surface. None of these vessels can be closely dated but by association most appear to be of 13th or 14th century date.

The large group of primarily shell-tempered medieval coarsewares recovered (308 sherds from 95 vessels) is quite diverse with seven ware groupings. There is no evidence for any forms typical of post-mid-14th century production. The form emphasis in the shell-tempered wares is on large jars or bowls, with most, but not all, having evidence for use over an open flame suggesting their use as cooking vessels. There is a complete lack in the shell-tempered assemblage of specialised forms such as curfews, dripping dishes, fish smokers, or industrial vessels. These vessels are certainly produced at Potterhanworth and in the south Lincolnshire industry (SLST).

Three main coarse fossil shell-tempered traditions occur across the county, although only two of them were recovered from sites under consideration here. The only known production site for medieval shell-tempered vessels is at the village of Potterhanworth c. 10 km southeast of Lincoln. The type (POTT) was in production from the 13th century until at least the end of the 15th (Young et al. 2005, 163–170). Vessels in this ware are found throughout Lincolnshire and Nottinghamshire with examples also occurring in Norfolk, Cambridgeshire, and Yorkshire. The second main production group of South Lincolnshire vessels (SLST) possibly started earlier than the Potterhanworth industry at some point in the late 12th century and appears to have ceased production by the mid-14th century. Potterhanworth ware (32 sherds from 21 vessels) was only recovered from the Coastal Landscape Parcel while the South Lincolnshire Shell-tempered-type (77 sherds from 31 vessels) was also found in the Fen Edge Landscape Parcel. Recovered vessels in the two types are mainly large jars or large bowls. Fourteen further coarsely shell-tempered vessels have been grouped together as South Lincolnshire Shell-tempered Coarseware (SLSHCW). This very loose grouping covers vessels probably made within south Lincolnshire but not fitting into the SLST definition. The presence of other medieval shell-tempered wares in eastern Lincolnshire, including a number of unclassified types, has long been known, although finds have been isolated and the recovered sherds have often been leached of their shell-temper. Only with the larger group from SPE01, where sizeable sherds still retain the fossil shell-temper and identifiable forms were recovered, has it been possible to define two new types (ELMAS and ELMWTS) with any certainty. At the time of the assessment these types had previously not been noted in the county although subsequent excavations in East Lindsey have shown them to be present in other parishes as far north as Maidenwell (Young 2023b) and as far south as Surfleet (Young 2023c).

The 18 East Lincolnshire Abundant Shelly ware (ELMAS) vessels were mainly recovered from the Coastal Landscape Parcel (site SPE01) but four jars or bowls were found at Burgh le Marsh (site SMR09). The presence of an abundant fine fossil shell temper remarkably similar to that found in some middle Saxon and Saxo-Norman types may have resulted in a difficulty to previously characterise this mainly coil-built ware type. Larger sherds recovered from site SPE01 show that although coil-built with readily visible finger pressed coils at least some of the vessels appear to have been finished on a turntable or wheel. A late 12th–13th century date is proposed for the type. The presence of a primarily wheelthrown medieval shell-tempered industry in the early medieval period on sites in eastern Lincolnshire has long been noted, but until recently, there has been no evidence for an extension into the medieval period. The newly defined East Lincolnshire Medieval Wheelthrown Shelly ware (ELMWTS) is in a coarse shell-tempered fabric similar to that used for other medieval shell-tempered types. Four of the eight vessels recovered from the SPE01 site are large jars with sharp everted rims and two are large bowls. One of the large jars has a heavily ridged shoulder. Vessels of this type recovered from elsewhere in East Lindsey (Young and Gray 2023) show a slight bead to the base; this trait is unusual in shell-tempered medieval vessels in Lincolnshire although it has occasionally been noted elsewhere on quartz-tempered vessels. A date for this type in the late 12th and 13th centuries is preferred but until further well-stratified groups are recovered a late 12th to potential mid-14th century date should be considered. Thin-section analysis on these two visually different shell-tempered types shows a similar fabric grouping of shelly fabrics derived from a Biosparite limestone (Wood 2024). Further work outside of this project is needed to determine a source for these fabrics but it is notable that so far all noted vessels have been recovered from within East Lindsey.

Three sherds from a jar and a thin-walled unknown form are of South Lincolnshire Shell and Quartz-tempered type (SLSQ). These two vessels are likely to be of 13th or 14th century date as is a similar but more heavily quartz-tempered small jar (SLQS).

Considering the coastal position of most of the sites investigated, no continental imports and surprisingly few regional imports were recovered from the Scheme. Three of the identified types (BEVO2, HUM, and SCAR) are Yorkshire-produced. Beverley 2 (BEVO2) and Humberware (HUM) are quite commonly found along the eastern edge of Lincolnshire with both being major types in Grimsby (Young 2014). Two of the four, 13th– early/mid-14th century, Beverley 2 vessels are internally glazed jars or bowls and one thin-walled sherd appears to be from a miniature vessel. Two of the three Humberware sherds are from jugs while the other sherd could be from a jug or jar of late 14th–15th century date. The 13th century Scarborough ware sherd recovered from site SMR09 is from a jug with applied and notched vertical strip and scale decoration. Two sherds from Grimston ware jugs (GRIM), one of which has complex applied strip decoration, date to the 13th–mid-14th centuries.

Thirteen sherds from seven vessels are regional imports from unknown centres. At least three of the vessels are jugs in light firing fabrics with one recovered from Burgh le Marsh (TAM09) being visually similar to vessels produced in Brandsby, Yorkshire (Brookes 1987, 153–154; Mainman and Jenner 2013). A fossil shell and quartz-tempered jar and large bowl are likely to be products of 12th–14th century kilns in the East Midlands.

Late medieval

A large group (508 sherds from 432 vessels) of late medieval–early post-medieval pottery was recovered from the Scheme. Almost all the pottery was found on the SMR09 site (401 vessels) within the Burgh le Marsh parish in the Fen Edge Landscape Parcel. The vast majority of these vessels (486 sherds from 412 vessels) are of mid-15th to mid-16th century Late Medieval Toynton-type (TOYII, example shown in Fig. 7.11) and are consistent with products associated with Kiln 3 (Healey 1975) at Toynton All Saints. The type is most commonly found in Lincolnshire in early to early/mid-16th century deposits surviving into Dissolution deposits but is rarely found in good post-deposition groups. This industry is fairly standardised mainly producing a range of undecorated jugs, jars, bunghole vessels, and large 'pancheon-type' sloping bowls. As is typical for rural sites the assemblage is dominated by large bowls and undecorated jugs for domestic and dairy use, although a drinking jug and a dripping dish were also recovered.

Six sherds, each representing a separate vessel of mid-15th–16th century date, are of late medieval–post-medieval Bourne-type (BOU). Vessel forms are jars or jugs. This ware is sporadically found in most of Lincolnshire in 16th century deposits and is quite common in Lincoln in the late medieval period being at its height in the early and mid-16th century (Young et al. 2005, 231) but rarely occurs as the most common late medieval type on rural sites except in the south of Lincolnshire. Two sherds from an internally glazed bowl and a large jug of mid-15th–16th century type are in local fabrics (LMLOC). Their similarity to Toynton and Bolingbroke products suggests that they may be from kilns in that area.

Six undecorated Cistercian ware sherds (CIST) are from five cups likely to be of mid-15th–16th century date. These are regional imports from Ticknall in Derbyshire (Spavold and Brown 2005) or Wrenthorpe in Yorkshire (Moorhouse and Slowikowski 1992). An internally and externally glazed sherd found on site TAM01 at Anderby on the coast is from a regionally imported jug or jar of mid-15th to mid-16th century type (LMX). The vessel is similar but cannot be directly paralleled to some late medieval vessels produced in Yorkshire.

The seven imported late medieval sherds recovered from the Scheme were all found on the SMR09 site in Burgh le Marsh in the Fen Edge Landscape Parcel. This may be a reflection of the status of the original owners or the importance of the town itself in the late medieval period. Three sherds are from two plain Langerwehe drinking jugs of potential mid-14th–15th century date. Two of the three imported, plain, mid-15th–16th century Raeren-type German stoneware drinking jugs found on the site are not an unusual find for the area but a highly decorated panel jug of late 16th century date (Hurst et al. 1986, 203–206) is a less common find. However, a sherd from a small Mature Valencian Lustre ware bowl (ibid., 42–48) with external lustre decoration of parallel oblique lines above a horizontal line and internal curved lines possibly representing tendrils, gives an indication of some status. Previous finds of this type in the county include examples from Lincoln and Boston (Hurst 1991; Young et al. 2005, 229–230).

Post-medieval

A sizeable group of post-medieval pottery (325 sherds from 235 vessels) was recovered from the Scheme with most of the vessels coming from the Fen Edge Landscape Parcel (203 vessels). The majority of vessels are of 16th–17th century date and were produced within Lincolnshire (at least 173 vessels). The most common of these Lincolnshire-produced wares (122 sherds from 96 vessels) is Toynton/Bolingbroke ware (TB) produced at a number of centres, notably Toynton All Saints and Bolingbroke (Healey 1975). This type is an extension of the late medieval tradition (TOYII) and appears to have declined by the mid-17th century, although a finer version of the ware continued in production in Bolingbroke into the 18th century. Production of the type appears to have started in the mid-15th century but does not become common until into the 16th century. The type was produced at several centres including Kiln 2 at Toynton All Saints, Toynton St Peters, Coningsby, Bolingbroke, and Ingoldmells. It overlaps with the production of both medieval types (TOY) and late medieval types (TOYII) at Toynton. Vessels are typically of early post-medieval types and reflect the changes in taste for higher-fired, darker colours and new forms such as chafing dishes. Most of the recovered sherds come from large sloping bowls with a small number of undecorated jars (usually of large size) and jugs also occurring. The only unusual form is a large footed pipkin of probable mid-16th to early/mid-17th century date. Few vessels are closely datable but examples of mid-15th–16th century and late-16th to mid-17th century date are present A single example of the later finer Bolingbroke fabric (BOLF) was found on site SMR09 in Burgh le Marsh. The sherd is from a large bowl with stamped lettering around the rim flange. The two visible letters appear to be 'AN', probably part of 'Robert Stanney' a potter from a Bolingbroke potting dynasty (White 1982; 1989). A previous find from the town is more readily readable. White argues for a c. 1650–1690 date for these bowls.

The Glazed Red Earthenware vessels recovered (83 sherds from 71 vessels) encompass those of earlier (mid-16th to mid-17th) and later (mid-17th–18th century) production, although most are of mid- or late 16th–17th century type. Known manufacturing sites in Lincolnshire include Boston, Grimsby, Toynton St Peter and Bolingbroke. The vessels are almost entirely utilitarian comprising mainly large bowls or dishes. Other identifiable forms include large cylindrical jars, small and medium-sized jars, small and medium-sized bowls, and a single cup. At least three vessels are likely to date into the 18th century. Six Reduced Glazed ware (RGRE) sherds from four large bowls and a large jar of mid-16th–17th century date are likely to have been produced at the same centres as the more oxidised GRE. Most of the 19 light-firing earthenwares (PGE) are also likely to have been produced in the county, probably at Bolingbroke. The type is commonly found in the county in groups of 17th–mid-18th century date but the form of some bowls may suggest production possibly outside of Lincolnshire into the 19th century. Almost all the recovered sherds come from large internally-glazed bowls.

Thirty-five sherds from 16 vessels are in black (BL) or brown (BERTH) iron-glazed earthenwares. The earliest of these vessels dates to between the mid-16th and mid-17th centuries whilst the latest vessels are of 19th–mid-20th century type. Most of the sherds come from utilitarian bowls or jars but a few sherds are from finer drinking vessels, which include two early black-glazed mugs and a cup of mid-16th to early/mid-17th century type and a brown-glazed cup of mid-17th–18th century Staffordshire/Derbyshire-type.

A small number of slipware vessels (21 vessels) of mixed date and type were recovered. Fourteen sherds are from eight Staffordshire-type Slipware (STSL) vessels including slip-decorated press-moulded dishes, cups, and a small cup or honey pot. Most of the vessels are of general mid- or late 17th–18th century type but the largest press-moulded dish is of more certain 18th century date. Five further Staffordshire-type vessels with manganese mottle glazes (STMO) are from four 18th century drinking vessels including two mugs. Five other slipware sherds (SLIP) are from press-moulded or thrown dishes of 18th or 18th–19th century type. Two of these vessels with manganese mottling on an internal yellow glaze are likely to be products of kilns in West Yorkshire or Sunderland. The eight recovered Midlands Light-bodied Slipware sherds (MLBSL) are from two large bowls and two jars or bowls of mid- or late 17th–18th century date. These vessels are fairly low-fired and have poorly fitting internal black glazes.

Two small sherds found on site SMR09 are from lead-backed early Tin-glazed Earthenware plates (TGW) with internal blue and yellow painted decoration. These plates are of potential mid-15th to mid-16th century date and could be of English or continental production. A small unstratified sherd is from a Martincamp Type III flask (MARTIII) of probable 17th century date. Only three imported German stoneware sherds of this period were recovered. The two Frechen-type sherds (FREC) are from drinking jugs of which the narrow-necked jug can be dated to the mid/late 16th–early/mid-17th centuries. The single Westerwald-type sherd (WEST) is a handle from a drinking jug of 17th or 18th century date.

EARLY MODERN

Early modern sherds (89 sherds from 57 vessels) were recovered from many of the sites investigated with most vessels being found in the Fen Edge and Lincolnshire Marsh Landscape Parcels. Most of the sherds come from industrial finewares (CREA, ENPO, PEARL, SWSG, TPW, and WHITE) with plates being the most common form identified. A small number of quality vessels include three decorated tea bowls of variable early/mid-18th – early 19th century date (CREA, PEARL, and SWSG), while other sherds are from more utilitarian forms such as chamber pots. Other utilitarian earthenware forms include a teapot (LBLAK) and dishes and jars for the kitchen (NCBW) whilst the seven stoneware vessels (ENGS and NOTS) include bottles, a small cylindrical ribbed 'jam jar', and an oval baking dish. The earliest vessels are of early/mid–late 18th century date while the latest are of late 19th–mid-20th century type.

Discussion

The large group of post-Roman pottery recovered from the Triton Knoll interventions is quite diverse in date and ware content. The most northerly sites lie within the parish of Anderby, at a coastal point in East Lindsey, whilst the most southerly sites are in Bicker, approximately 10 km west of Boston in the Holland division of Lincolnshire. At the time of the assessment report, many of the parishes explored had either produced little or no post-Roman pottery to provide an outline for ceramic use in the area. The ceramic profile of the East Lindsey coastal area and hinterland is only just beginning to be understood. There is more evidence for the Boston area as a large number of excavations have taken place in the town over a number of years, however even there the ceramic sequence is incomplete and is complex as is to be expected at a major medieval port. Between the 10th and 14th centuries the area within the northern Fen Edge and Coastal Landscape Parcels appears to have had a divergent ceramic sequence. The evidence from the Scheme, together with more recent excavations in the area, suggest a multitude of minor, short-lived, and possibly fairly local industries (Wood 2024). Further investigation at the analysis stage has resulted in new late Saxon and medieval fabrics being identified. The classification of these types together with those identified at the assessment stage and their inclusion into the Lincolnshire Fabric Type Series should enable their further identification when found elsewhere in the region. The study of regional post-conquest ceramics and their characterisation and distribution was one of the key aims set out within the initial East Midlands Research Agenda (Cooper 2006, 214–215). Systematic recording of types within a region can in the future, with a large enough sample, lead to a greater understanding of not only potential modes of distribution of production centres themselves but also wider questions of communication infrastructures and the role of local markets, fairs, and ports within a region (Knight *et al.* 2012, 99, 104).

The potential interpretation of the recovered assemblages is somewhat restricted by the small size of most excavated groups and lack of securely stratified sequential and primary assemblages. The Scheme has, however, provided a broader spectrum of types than had been previously envisioned in most of the parishes and provided ceramic evidence for pre-conquest occupation in parishes where it was not previously known. With perhaps the exception of the three unusual bowls found at Burgh le Marsh (SMR09) the recovered assemblage is entirely domestic in nature and fairly typical of material recovered from rural sites in the county with an emphasis on large bowls, large jars, and a range of jugs.

Only two atypical vessels of middle Saxon type were recovered from site SMR10 in Croft village. One vessel is in a newly defined shell-tempered fabric (ELEFS) while the other is of visual Ipswich-type (IPST) but appears to have been produced in Lincolnshire (Wood 2024). A slightly larger group of late Saxon pottery, also mainly recovered from the village of Croft in the Fen Edge Landscape Parcel (SMR10), has also provided further new wheelthrown quartz- and shell-tempered Lincoln types. Classification of the Late Saxon pottery from Flaxengate in Lincoln (Gilmour 1988; Young 1989; Young *et al.* 2005) showed that, although most of the assemblage could be attributed to production within Lincoln itself or other established Lincolnshire or regional centres, a small percentage of vessels (numbering more than 1000) remained un-sourced. The characterisation and identification of any potential new industries is critical for our understanding of many aspects of pre-conquest marketing and production within Lincolnshire. Certainly, the types recovered from SPE01 differ from those recovered from the Hutoft parish just to the north, where five new late Saxon ware types were defined during assessment of the Zone 1 Viking Link pottery (Young and Gray 2023). This may to some extent be a chronological phenomenon as the recovered pottery from Hutoft is stylistically more of late 9th–mid-10th century type whereas the two diagnostic rims from SPE01 suggest a more likely late 10th to early/mid-11th century dating. It does however add to the growing evidence of usage and possible production of late Saxon types other than the standard Torksey ware, Stamford ware, or Lincoln shell- or Greyware-types along Lincolnshire's east coast. The SMR10 site also produced a small number of new Saxo-Norman fabrics. The sample of Saxon pottery types recovered was too small and unrelated to explore any chronological interaction of the types but hopefully future finds will help answer this question.

The largest single ceramic period group of pottery to be recovered is of medieval type. Much of this assemblage is dominated by the late 13th–15th century Medieval Toynton ware products in the two Landscape Parcels producing medieval pottery (Table 7.3). The recovered assemblages however do seem to suggest that prior to the mid-14th century, there were significant differences in the use of pottery types between the parishes in the Coastal and northern Fen Edge Landscape Parcels and those in the southern Fen Edge Landscape Parcel. The assemblage found within the Coastal Landscape Parcel (SPE01) mainly comprises sherds from a range of large medieval shell-tempered jars and bowls. Two of the shell-tempered ware types present (ELMAS and ELMWTS) had, at the time of the assessment not previously been noted in the county, although subsequent excavations in East Lindsey have shown them to be present in other parishes as far north as Maidenwell (Young 2023a) and as far south as Surfleet (Young 2023b). Definition and characterisation of new medieval shell-tempered wares should lead to a better identification and understanding of 13th century shell-tempered coarsewares and their distribution within the county. They are often overlooked in favour of the glazed finewares but have much to offer in our understanding of local markets and cultural identity as distribution may be more restricted. There are also glazed quartz-tempered wares in Lincoln glazed ware (CELMG) and Medieval Toynton ware (MEDLOC) style. Thin-section analysis suggests a potential fairly local source for the CELMG vessels (Wood 2024). A similar pattern was found in the northern part of the Fen Edge Landscape Parcel in Burgh le Marsh (SMR09) whereas in Amber Hill, to the south of the Landscape Parcel (SMR17), these wares are absent and there seems to be less reliance on shell-tempered coarsewares. At Amber Hill there appears to be a different pattern of ceramic use with this being the only site to produce Medieval Bourne ware vessels. Medieval Bourne ware dates to between the late 12th–14th centuries whilst Medieval Toynton ware is generally of late 13th–15th century date. Unfortunately, the site sequence at SMR17 was too unrelated and groups were too small to completely answer the question of chronological and functional usage of the two overlapping types, although the groups do suggest that Bourne might be the preferred type until into the early part of the 14th century.

Production at both centres is conservative with manufacturing techniques and basic form shapes changing little over time. The types represent totally different traditions with Medieval Bourne ware representing a dispersed production (Spoerry 2008; 2016) whereas, although misfired and wasted sherds suggest some production elsewhere, Medieval Toynton ware is more centralised.

The pre-mid-16th century late medieval to early post-medieval pottery recovered (especially from the Fen Edge Landscape Parcel sites of SMR09 and SMR12) is dominated by Late Toynton ware with a few early Toynton/Bolingbroke vessels also identified as belonging to this period. By the mid-16th century post-medieval Toynton/Bolingbroke vessels are the main pottery type in use with Glazed Red Earthenwares probably made in Boston or Grimsby increasing in number from the early 17th century (White 1989). By the mid-17th century lighter-bodied earthenwares (PGE) also seem to be in common use on the SMR09 site. This pattern of mid-15th to mid-17th century ceramic use is fairly typical for much of Lincolnshire during the post-medieval period differing only in the south where Late Medieval to Post-medieval Bourne ware and post-late 16th century Glazed Red Earthenwares are preferred to the later Toynton/Bolingbroke vessels and to the north where Late Humberware makes a significant impact.

The assessment phase (Young 2018; 2019; Young and Daubney 2020) identified several key research aims that have been advanced by further work on the key assemblages (SPE01, SMR09, SMR10, and SMR17). Despite the disadvantages of small individual groups, the contribution made by a linear Scheme such as this cannot be under-estimated. The ability to be able to compare and contrast assemblages over the length of a route along the eastern edge of Lincolnshire that transected some parishes that had previously not produced ceramic evidence for the pre-early modern periods has given an opportunity to test previous theories and define new ceramic types.

One of the main East Midlands ceramic research aims has been highlighted by Cooper (2006):

Systematic regional study of the distribution of post-Conquest ceramics, including those produced in the region and those imported into it, could elucidate the modes of distribution and spheres of exchange of rural and urban production centres. (Cooper 2006, 214–215)

Without a systematic approach to fabric identification, ensuring that pottery types are recorded using local and regional Type Series and defining new types, it will be impossible to further other broader key local and regional research aims, such as our understanding of the impact of the Danelaw and the impact of early ceramic production and distribution (Cooper 2006, 214) or regional communications infrastructures (Knight *et al.* 2012).

Small finds
Rebecca Sillwood

A total of 74 small finds were recovered from post-Roman features, or classified as post-Roman types, from the excavation phases of the Triton Knoll Scheme. The small finds were mainly recovered from eight excavation areas spread across the Coastal, Inland Fen, Fen Edge, and Lincolnshire Marsh Landscape Parcels. The full description of the finds by site can be found in the associated Landscape Parcel reports, available on the ADS. A summary of the key finds is provided here.

EARLY MEDIEVAL

Only three small finds were associated with phased features of early medieval (late Saxon) date; an iron nail, an iron key (Fig. 7.12A), and a copper alloy awl or stylus (Fig. 7.12B). All were recovered from Field System 2 at SMR10 (Croft End), within the Fen Edge Landscape Parcel. Disregarding the nail, the other objects are unusual and ambiguous of classification.

Of the object described as a copper alloy awl or stylus, the most likely possibility seems to be that of a stylus; a pen-like item used to scratch letters into wax-filled tablets. It does not fully resemble most Anglo-Saxon styli, but a similar item has been catalogued on the Portable Antiquities Scheme (PAS) database (Rogerson 2022). There are differences: the PAS object is decorated with ring and dot pattern whereas the Triton Knoll example is plain and much pitted. Most Anglo-Saxon styli are circular sectioned, have a large flared 'eraser' at one end, and are usually decorative. If indeed the object is a stylus, it is evidence of literacy on the site that is not commonly found. Flixborough in north Lincolnshire yielded at least 20 styli (Pestell 2009, 123), a 'remarkable' quantity, and Pestell states (*ibid.*, 125) that many styli are found on known *monasteria* sites or those known as 'productive' sites. Alternatively, the object bears some similarities to a Bronze Age awl and may be much earlier in date. It is plausible that it was disturbed from an earlier context during the excavation of ditches for the creation of the field system in the early medieval period, although no other finds or features were found to support an earlier age.

The second object was a complete iron key. Many things about this key are unusual, from the angled oval bow, the solid flattened profiled shank, to the bifurcated bit, with each tine bent a different way. The likelihood is that this key is a type used in conjunction with a barrel padlock and that it is simply of unusual form to fit a particular lock. The presence of this key points to there being something on the site worth locking away. The key is fairly small and so perhaps was not used for a door but rather a casket or box.

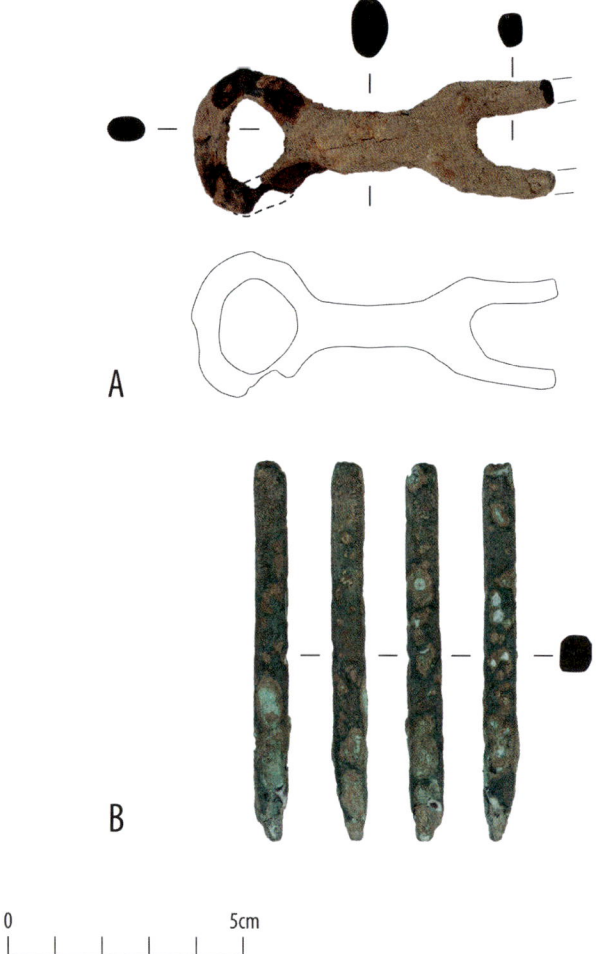

Figure 7.12 a) Iron key b) Copper alloy awl or stylus

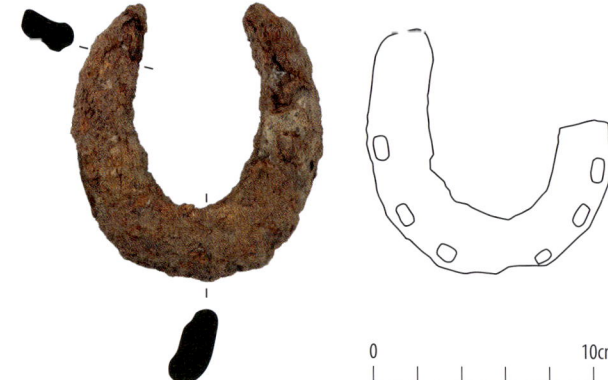

Figure 7.13 Iron Horseshoe

MEDIEVAL

A total of 16 small finds were associated with medieval activity, 13 from SMR09 and three from SMR17 (both in the Fen Edge Landscape Parcel). All medieval finds recovered from SMR09 were associated with extraction pits and ditches associated with Industry 1, broadly dated to the 13th–15th centuries. Most of the finds are iron nails (n=10), all of which are not closely datable and could reflect a variety of purposes. The other finds include an iron horseshoe (Fig. 7.13), which is fortunately complete and identifiable to type, dating to the 14th–15th centuries. An undiagnostic iron spike and a copper alloy chape/ferrule made up the remainder of the small finds, and both continue the theme of industrial type finds from the site.

From SMR17, the medieval finds include two iron nails and a staple for use in affixing to timber. The metalwork that was found may point to some structural activity but not of any intensity nor can the type of settlement here be determined from the small finds. The presence here of a small medieval farmstead is not obvious from the small finds.

POST-MEDIEVAL

A total of 55 small finds were associated with post-medieval activity. Most of these were associated with the proliferation of industrial activity observed at SMR09 (n=49). Almost half of the items are iron nails (n=22). Many of the other items point to carpentry, including a chisel, a spoon bit used for boring holes in wood, a possible file, and at least four knives (Fig. 7.14). There were also numerous items inferring the presence of a building, perhaps a barn or workshop, including hooks and looped spikes, staples, a strap hinge, and miscellaneous structural fittings. The use of horses was also attested through the recovery of a horseshoe nail, harness buckle, and spurs, including rowel spur more closely dated to the 17th century. Further demonstrating the industrial nature of the assemblage was the lack of personal possessions or domestic items, with only a single drawn wire pin recovered.

All other finds dating to the post-medieval era were found in isolated contexts, often unstratified, and provide limited information about the use of the sites where they were recovered. From the Fen Edge Landscape Parcel, a 17th–19th century crotal bell, likely worn around the neck of an animal, was recovered from topsoil at TAM14, and a William III halfpenny was collected from the surface at TAM16. An 18th century horseshoe and a copper-alloy harness decoration were found in subsoil at SPE01 and a nail was recovered from a ditch at SMR02, both within the Coastal Landscape Parcel. A nail recovered from a field boundary at SPE02 was the only small find possibly dating from the post-medieval era in the Lincolnshire Marsh Landscape Parcel, although it may have been residual, dating from earlier Roman activity.

Environmental evidence

A variety of environmental data was collected, including cereal assemblages and faunal material, offering valuable insights into agricultural practices throughout the medieval and post-medieval eras. The key aspects of this data are discussed in the following section, beginning with

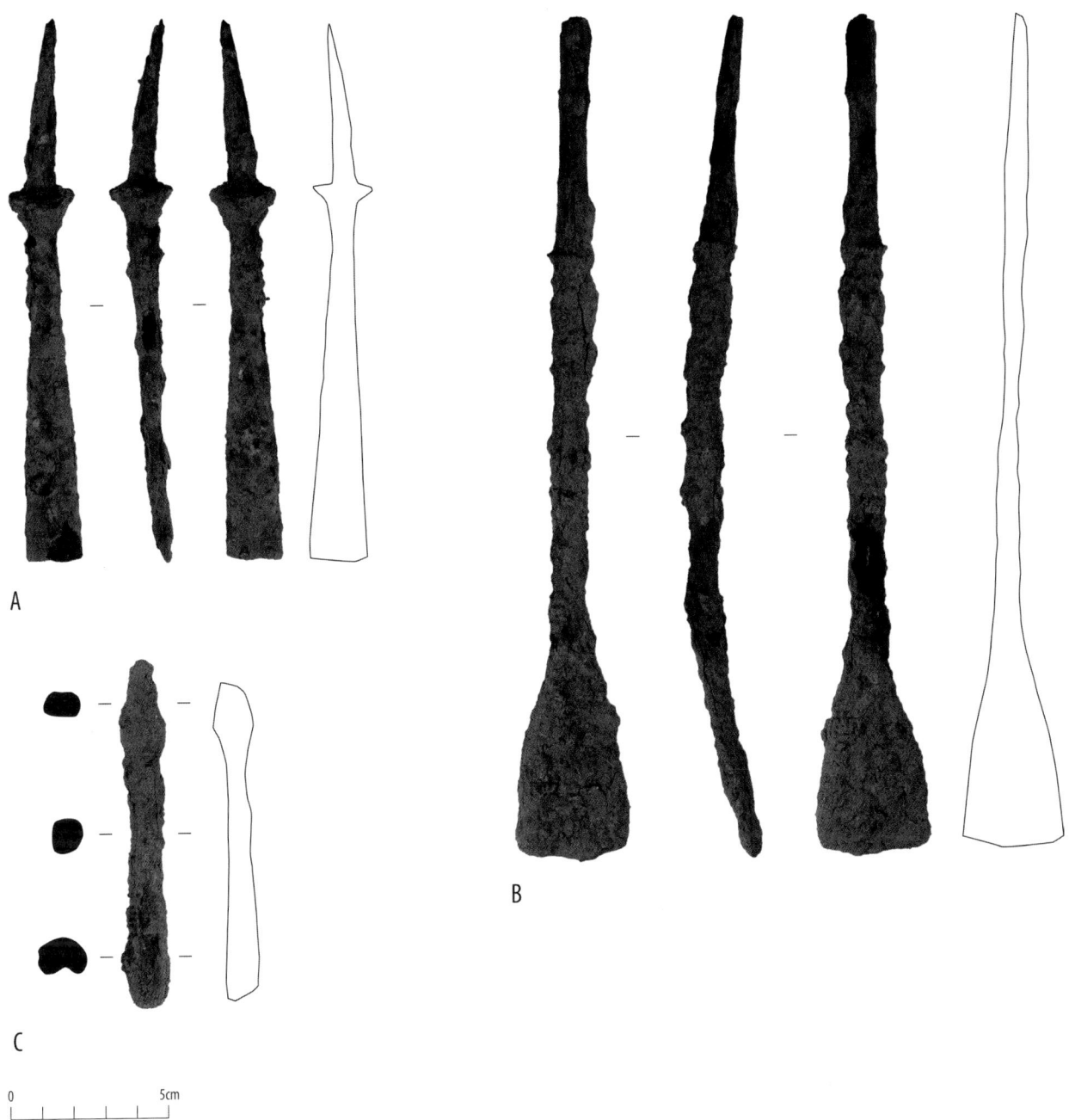

Figure 7.14 Small finds from SMR10: A. Iron chisel SF113; B. Iron chisel; C. Iron spoon bit SF118

an overview of the environmental findings, followed by an examination of the faunal evidence. This information contributes to the broader discussion of settlement and farming practices discussed above.

Plant remains

The only cereal remains found in association with early medieval activity were recovered from SMR10. A poorly surviving assemblage of cereal, including barley, oats, bread/club wheat, and indeterminate glume wheat was recovered (Walker and Kriti 2020, 103) but all in insufficient quantity to merit further analysis.

More substantial botanical assemblages were recovered in association with later medieval activity, including at SPE01 and SMR09. None of the late Saxon features was subjected to environmental analyses from SPE01 but the post-conquest botanical assemblages from the site included an abundance of barley and numerous indeterminate cereals, as well as a small number of legumes, including peas and broad beans (Fryer and Bailey 2024, 35–41). As discussed in previous chapters, barley is well suited to highly saline environments (Murphy 2001a) and is commonly found in plant assemblages from sites in the southern fenland, closer to the Wash (Murphy

2001c, 380; Rayner 2003). A variety of arable weeds such as stinking chamomile and wild radish were also recorded. Stinking chamomile is a common weed of arable land and waste places (Clapham *et al.* 1962) that frequently occurs in heavier soils (Stace 1997, 733) and was likely incidentally harvested with the cereal crops. Its abundance would imply that harvesting took place at a medium height with some straw retained (Lodwick 2017, 47). In the fenland environments straw may have been a particularly valuable commodity, plausibly imported for thatch, building material, fodder, and/or fuel. Locally available wetland taxa may have been utilised for a similar range of purposes with the samples also containing spikerushes, sedges, knotweeds, and mixed grasses (Poaceae). Alongside these wetland taxa, aquatic species such as duckweeds and crowfoot were also recorded, which suggest that some features were waterfilled. None of the plant assemblages associated with medieval activity at SMR09 was subjected to further analyses but initial assessment (Walter and Kriti 2020) provided a similar assemblage with cereals including grains of spelt, indeterminate glume wheat, barley, oats, bread/club wheat, and indeterminate cereals, as well as legumes, such as peas, broad bean, and possible lentil. As with those from SPE01, wetland taxa such as rushes and hairy buttercup (*Ranunculus sardous*) and an abundance of aquatic taxa, including duckweeds, crowfoot, and horned pondweed (*Zannichellia palustris*), suggest wet conditions. The environmental assemblages from these sites, albeit relatively limited in scope, provide glimpses into the importance of wetland habitats.

Activity dated to the post-medieval period was more prolific, albeit much of the evidence was restricted to that of field boundaries and did not warrant further environmental investigation. Following assessment during the initial stage of works, samples derived from post-medieval deposits were subsequently analysed from SMR06, SMR09, and SMR12. The presence of spelt wheat, largely replaced by hulled wheats by the early medieval era, suggests significant reworking of material from earlier contexts at SMR06 (Fryer and Turner 2024, 84), but the samples analysed from SMR09 and SMR12 provided some interesting insights into the shifting nature of activity in the post-medieval era (Wallace and Fryer 2024). Both samples included pulses like common pea and broad bean, as well as oats, but also featured more unusual crops for the region, such as durum wheat and barley. Durum wheat, found in the SMR09 sample, is uncommon for medieval Britain and more typical in southern regions (Moffett 2006). Its presence here, though rare, may be under-represented due to the difficulty in recognising durum wheat archaeobotanically (Roushannafas and McKerracher 2023).

Wheat, particularly bread wheat, dominated the SMR09 sample, indicated by the substantial number of rachis internodes – an uncommon find for post-medieval sites in the Midlands (Carruthers and Hunter Dowse 2019).

In contrast, the SMR12 sample was primarily composed of barley grains. The use of barley, while common, may again suggest the cultivation of saline soils (Murphy 2001c; Newman and Newman 2006). In addition to the staple crops, food additives were found in both samples, though only in small quantities. The presence of mint and medicinal plants such as henbane and hemlock were noted but their numbers were too few to indicate deliberate collection or widespread use.

Animal bone
Marina Chorro-Giner, Hannah Russ, and Joshua T. Hogue

A total of 3503 fragments of animal bone were recovered from activity dated to the early medieval (7.1% by count, n=247), medieval (28.0% by count, n=982), and post-medieval (64.9% by count, n=2274) eras. Most of the material came from the Fen Edge Landscape Parcel (*e.g.* SMR09, SMR10, SMR12) (90% by count, n=3151), animal bone from the other three Landscape Parcels being minimal and, as such, the former Landscape Parcel forms the focus of discussion. Furthermore, the total assemblage was skewed to a few sites, with more than half of the faunal remains recovered from SMR09 (53.1% by count, n=1859), modest frequencies from SMR12 (18.6% by count, n=651) and SMR17 (13.0%, n=457), and only minimal quantities from the other sites (Table 7.4). A comparison of the assemblages, however, provides opportunity to glean some insights into the similarities and differences in animal husbandry and exploitation across the Scheme and situate the work in a wider setting. Further methodological information and a full dataset is available as part of the Landscape Parcel reports, which are available from the ADS.

Mammals

Most of the animal remains recovered for the early medieval (Saxon) period were that of mammals, but the total assemblage size was relatively small and many were poorly preserved, in contrast to the later eras. Of the 81 fragments from SPE01, only two fragments were identified as pig (*Sus domesticus*) and two as sheep/goat bones (*Ovis aries/Capra hircus*), the remainder representing a range of different sized mammals that could not be more closely identified. More information is available for the material from SMR10 at Croft End (in the Fen Edge Landscape Parcel), with 66 of the 156 mammal bones (~40%) being identified to at least family level. The identifiable taxa included domesticated cattle (*Bos taurus*), equids (*Equus* sp.: horse/donkey/mule), pig, sheep/goat, as well as small species, such as European mole (*Talpa europaea*) and mouse/small vole (*Mus* sp./*Apodemus* sp./*Myodes* sp./*Microtus* sp.).

Many more mammal remains were associated with medieval activity (n=964); mostly these were recovered

Table 7.4 Quantification of the animal bone assemblages (according to fragment count by class) by site and period

Site	Mammal		Bird		Fish		Amphibian		Unclassified/ other		Total
	n	%	n	%	n	%	n	%	n	%	
Early medieval											
SMR10*	156	94.5	1	0.6	2	1.2	2	1.2	4	2.4	165
SPE01†	81	98.8	0	0.0	1	1.2	0	0.0	0	0.0	82
Subtotal	237	96.0	1	0.4	3	1.2	2	0.8	4	1.6	247
Medieval											
HDD37‡	1	100.0	0	0.0	0	0.0	0	0.0	0	0.0	1
HDD44*	13	100.0	0	0.0	0	0.0	0	0.0	0	0.0	13
SMR01†	53	100.0	0	0.0	0	0.0	0	0.0	0	0.0	53
SMR09*	350	99.2	3	0.8	0	0.0	0	0.0	0	0.0	353
SMR17*	453	99.1	4	0.9	0	0.0	0	0.0	0	0.0	457
SPE01†	93	89.4	4	3.8	5	4.8	2	1.9	0	0.0	104
TAM1†	1	100.0	0	0.0	0	0.0	0	0.0	0	0.0	1
Subtotal	964	98.2	11	1.1	5	0.5	2	0.2	0	0.0	982
Post-medieval											
SMR06‡	21	95.5	0	0.0	0	0.0	0	0.0	0	0.0	22
SMR07‡	2	100.0	0	0.0	0	0.0	0	0.0	0	0.0	2
SMR09*	1343	89.2	60	4.0	45	3.0	58	3.9	0	0.0	1506
SMR12*	566	86.9	43	6.6	28	4.3	11	1.7	3	0.6	651
SMR13*	2	100.0	0	0.0	0	0.0	0	0.0	0	0.0	2
SPE01†	64	100.0	0	0.0	0	0.0	0	0.0	0	0.0	64
SPE02‡	20	100.0	0	0.0	0	0.0	0	0.0	0	0.0	20
TAM17*	2	100.0	0	0.0	0	0.0	0	0.0	0	0.0	2
TAM18*	1	50.0	0	0.0	0	0.0	0	0.0	0	0.0	2
TAM21§	1	100.0	0	0.0	0	0.0	0	0.0	0	0.0	1
TAM22§	2	100.0	0	0.0	0	0.0	0	0.0	0	0.0	2
Subtotal	2024	89.0	103	4.5	73	3.2	69	3.0	3	0.0	2274
Total	3225	92.1	115	3.3	81	2.3	73	2.1	7	0.1	3503

* Fen Edge, † Coastal, ‡ Lincolnshire Marsh, ‡ Inland Fen Edge Landscape Parcel sites

from SMR09 (36.3% of the mammal remains, n=350), just outside Burgh le Marsh, and SMR17 (47.0% of the mammal remains, n=453), near Swineshead (both within Fen Edge Landscape Parcel). At SMR09, the identifiable species included, in diminishing numbers, sheep, cattle, and pig (all with evidence of butchery and/or burning), as well as small numbers of equids, dog family remains (Canidae – likely dog, *Canis familiaris*, or red fox, *Vulpes vulpes*), cat (*Felis catus*), and hare (*Lepus europaeus*). At SMR17, cattle were most dominant, followed by moderate numbers of horse, and much smaller frequencies of sheep/goat and pig (no butchery marks were recorded on any of the bones identifiable to family). No other mammals were identified. A relatively substantial assemblage was also recovered from SPE01 at Mumby (in the Coastal Landscape Parcel) (n=93) and it included the same range and relative frequency of mammals as SMR17, but direct evidence of animal butchery was recorded as chop marks on cattle bones

Most mammal remains were associated with post-medieval activity at SMR09 (n=1343) and at SMR12 (n=566) (both in the Fen Edge Landscape Parcel), all the other sites yielded comparatively little in the way of animal bone for this period. SMR09 yielded the same range of domesticates as recorded in association with the medieval activity at the site, but rather than sheep being dominant they were found in similar frequencies to cattle, followed by smaller numbers of pig and equids. A fragment of possible cervid – red (*Cervus elaphus*) or fallow (*Dama dama*) deer was also recovered alongside the larger mammals. Additionally, the assemblage included black/brown rat (*Rattus rattus/R. norvegicus*), mole, wood/house mouse, field/bank vole (*Myodes glarelous/Microtus agrestis*), and shrew (*Sorex* sp.). SMR12 had the same domesticates, but with sheep most dominant, followed by small frequencies of cattle, pig (including a butchered phalanx), and equid.

Higher frequencies of cattle and equids in the early medieval sites are consistent with their use as traction animals, which is suggested at several other sites, notably in Northamptonshire, such as at Burystead and Langham Road, (Davis 1992), West Cotton (Albarella and Davis 1994), and Kings Meadow Lane (Albarella and Johnstone 2000). It is plausible that some of the cattle were bred for meat production with the age profiles indicating that the cattle slaughtered were relatively young, but the numbers are too small to be conclusive. Even if used primarily for traction, their use for meat and milk would presumably also have been important. Horses were likely primarily kept for traction, although the consumption of older animals is plausible, as observed at Maxley, Northamptonshire (Seddon *et al.* 1965) and West Cotton (Albarella and Johnstone 2000).

Cattle also dominated at both the principal rural settlements dated to the medieval era (SPE01 and SMR17), plausibly indicating the continued use of plough animals into this era. The increasing age of cattle may indicate that meat exploitation was less common during this period. This is suggested at other sites, where juveniles are less prevalent (*e.g.* Norwich: Albarella *et al.* 2009). Notably, horse is more prevalent, although still less common than cattle in the medieval period. An increasing frequency of horses was noted at Burystead and Langham Road (Davis 1992), as well as West Cotton (Albarella and Davis 1994), and is suggested to be part of the increasing importance of horses in agriculture and their substitution for cattle as traction/draught animals (Albarella 1997).

Cattle and equids were notably less common in both the medieval and post-medieval phases at the industrial site of SMR09. This is presumably due to the fewer requirements for traction animals at the site. Sheep and pigs were more prevalent, a fact likely linked to their consumption. Sheep were more common in general due to the expansion of the wool trade from the medieval period, but neonate infant mortality is relatively high at the site suggesting food exploitation. The mortality profiles of the pigs also supports the consumption of suckling pigs, with fusion and dental recording indicating slaughter at 1–2 years old. Notably, it appears in other areas that, by the post-medieval era, pigs were being slaughtered at even younger ages, for instance in Exeter (Maltby 1979), Lincoln (Dobney *et al.* 1996), and at Castle Mall, Norwich (Albarella *et al.* 1997). The presence of dogs at the site may imply lower-status sites (Albarella 1997) and certainly the industrial context of most of the canid remains may be consistent with this suggestion. The presence of vermin (*e.g.* rats, mice), recorded most numerously at the site, may have required dogs for ratting. Cats, also recorded at the site, may have served a similar purpose. The remains of both taxa have been recorded at other sites from the early medieval to post-medieval eras, such as Maxley (Seddon *et al.* 1965), Burystead and Langham Road (Davis 1992), Park Street in Towcester, Northmaptonshire (Payne 1980), and Kings Meadow Lane (Albarella and Johnstone 2000).

Sheep were most dominant during post-medieval activity, notably at the principal agricultural sites (*e.g.* SMR12). This seems to be part of a wider trend in sheep exploitation, with an increasing number of sheep observed more generally in many areas of Britain from the medievalperiod, likely reflecting the rise of the wool trade (Albarella 1997). The age of individuals seems to have increased during the post-medieval period, with fewer young animals and the slaughtering of older individuals. A similar trend is considered to reflect the increasing importance of sheep for wool exploitation at, for instance St Peter's Lane and Little Lane, Leicester (Gidney 1991a; 1991b; 1991c; 1992), Colchester, Essex (Luff 1993), and Launceston Castle in Lincoln (Dobney *et al.* 1996).

A few other mammals provided some important information. The presence of hares in small frequencies was likely linked to their exploitation for food and/or pelts, as has been noted since their introduction in the Roman period (Morley and Gurney 1997; Fairnell 2003); during the 14th–15th centuries they formed part of an important fur trade (Serjeantson 1989). The presence of possible red or fallow deer at SMR09 is also of some interest, as from the early medieval period onwards, very strict hunting laws were in place and deer parks were strictly controlled. Thus, they are usually unrelated to diet and are very common in assemblages from high-status sites of this period, such as Burystead and Langham Road (Davis 1992), West Cotton (Albarella and Davis 1994), and Kings Meadow Lane (Albarella and Johnstone 2000). The general scarcity of deer and other game animals across the Scheme may indicate that most of the sites were of lower status, without access to hunting rights or lands.

BIRDS

Use of avian resources is attested throughout each period, albeit in a relatively minor way (3.3% of total assemblage; n=115). Bird specimens were recorded in slightly increasing frequencies in early medieval (0.4% by period, n=1), medieval (1.1% by period, n=11), and post-medieval (4.5% by period, n=103) contexts, plausibly indicating increasing use of fowl, wildfowl, and other bird species.

An indeterminate bird bone was the only specimen recovered in association with early medieval (Saxon) activity (from SMR10 at Croft End). The identifiable species associated with medieval activity included goose (*Anser* sp.), mallard duck (*Anas platyrhynchos*), domestic fowl/chicken (*Gallus gallus domesticus*), and carrion crow (*Corvus corone*). Individual specimens of goose were recovered from SPE01 near Manor Farm and SMR17 in Swineshead, the former also providing a fragment of duck bone. Two domestic fowl/chicken bones (including one with butchery cut marks) and a crow bone came from SMR09 at Burgh le Marsh.

A much larger bird assemblage was recorded in association with the post-medieval activity at SMR09 (n=60). All the above families were identified, the assemblage comprising geese, including specimens of duck, waterfowl (Anatidae), chicken, landfowl (Galliformes), carrion crow, and jackdaw (*Corvus monedula*). A substantial bird assemblage was also recorded in association with the post-medieval activity at SMR12 (n=43), including a similar range of domestic and wild birds, but also notably grey heron (*Ardea cinerea*). Three goose humerii, a duck carpometacarpus, and a waterfowl skull had evidence of butchery in the form of cut or chop marks.

All the assemblages seem to show the importance of geese, ducks, and chicken; it is difficult to distinguish the remains of domestic and wild geese and ducks but the recovery of these remains alongside other animal bones suggests that they were likely intentionally introduced to the sites rather than natural occurrences. All these species may have been particularly important sources of meat, eggs, and, in the case of goose, feathers as well (Albarella 1997). Evidence of butchery on all three of these taxa, as well as on waterfowl, indicates the use of these species for meat but other uses are likely, though less easily observed archaeologically. More substantial animal bone assemblages have been recorded indicating the value of these bird species from the early medieval period, such as Kings Meadow Lane (Albarella and Johnstone 2000), West Cotton (Albarella and Davis 1994), Burystead and Langham Road (Davis 1992), and Park Street, Towcester (Payne 1980). Notably, geese, duck, and chicken were recorded alongside corvid remains at all the mentioned sites; it is unlikely that corvids represented food waste but instead may have been naturally occurring, accidentally introduced as a scavenging species (Albarella and Thomas 2002, 33).

Notably, the assemblages seem to suggest a slight increase in frequencies of bird species, and plausibly also an increase in the number of wild bird species – as evidenced most markedly by the occurrence of heron. This fits with analyses that show the largest frequencies of wild birds in archaeological assemblages between the 14th to early 16th centuries, slightly reduced numbers, albeit still relatively high, in the 16th–17th centuries, but fewer than half the wild birds in assemblages dating to the 9th–14th centuries (Albarella and Thomas 2002). Even though large birds like swan, crane and heron, may not have been particularly appetising, their consumption is documented and probably reflects methods by which to demonstrate social status – as aristocratic table dressing. Certainly, by the late medieval period these species were controlled and closely managed (MacGregor 1989; Woolgar 1999, 14; Albarella and Thomas 2002, 34), and the occurrence of heron at SMR12, dated to the 16th century, provides an interesting anecdote.

FISH

Fish played a minor role in human diet (2.3% of total assemblage; n=81) across all periods. Absolute and relative frequencies of fish were similar among the early medieval (1.2% by period, n=3) and medieval (0.5% by period, n=5) assemblages and more common in the post-medieval assemblages (3.2% by period, n=73), plausibly indicating an increasing role of fish in the diet, albeit still small.

Early medieval assemblages provided evidence of flatfish (Pleuronectidae; SMR10). Medieval fish remains included three-spined stickleback (*Glasterosteus aculeatus*), along with the remains of larger fish that were unidentifiable to family (SPE01). Diversity or lack of diversity of the fish species during these periods is likely a reflection of small assemblage sizes, rather than reflecting dietary considerations. Many more fish remains were recovered from features dated to the post-medieval era – albeit from a single assemblage – and reflect a greater range of taxa, including marine species: Atlantic cod (*Gadus morhua*), haddock (*Melanogrammus aeglefinus*), pollack/saithe (*Pollachius* sp.), flatfish, Atlantic herring (*Clupea harengus*), and skate/ray (Rajidae); freshwater pike (*Esox lucius*), perch (*Perca fluviatilis*), carp family (Cyprinidae), and migratory the species European eel (*Anguilla anguilla*), at SMR09. All the species recorded are typical of those that could be sourced locally within freshwater environments or from the sea off the east coast of England. Few fish assemblages have been recorded, often as a consequence of recovery strategies, but a mixture of marine, freshwater, and migratory fish being exploited and sourced locally has been recorded at other sites such as Kings Meadow Lane (Albarella and Johnstone 2000), West Cotton (Albarella and Davis 1994), and Burystead and Langham Road (Davis 1992).

AMPHIBIANS

Amphibians were recorded in small frequencies in all phases (2.1% of the total assemblage, n = 73). Few remains were associated with early medieval (0.8% by period, n = 2) and medieval (0.2% by period, n = 2) activity, but were slightly more prevalent during the post-medieval era (3.0% by period, n = 69). Common frog (*Rana temporaria*) and more generally the order of Anura (frog/toad) were recorded across all periods, with newt (Pleurodelinae) also being present within the samples from SMR09. The amphibian remains are indicative of relatively humid environments in the vicinity and were likely naturally introduced.

Conclusion

The excavation and analysis of the medieval and post-medieval landscape along the Scheme provides key insights into the development and adaptation of settlements in the dynamic environment of southeast Lincolnshire. Despite previous assumptions of the region's lack of medieval settlement, evidence recovered from along the route demonstrates that rural activity and settlements were present, even if scattered. The evolving landscape, influenced by coastal inundation, drainage, and reclamation efforts, played a significant role in shaping both settlement patterns and agricultural practices from the medieval through the post-medieval period. These findings help to illuminate the region's transformation from a largely unsettled, marshy landscape into a more stable agricultural zone. While evidence of more concentrated settlement remains were limited, the archaeological data contribute to a broader understanding of rural life, land use, and industry in Lincolnshire.

8

Ebbs and flows: The archaeology of Triton Knoll

Owain Scholma-Mason, Joshua T. Hogue, and Claire Christie

The chapters in this volume have traversed a dynamic landscape, both in terms of its natural and human aspects, highlighting the diverse character of the region and the multitude of ways the landscape was utilised by people from prehistory through to the modern period. Throughout, the complex interplay between human and natural aspects has been highlighted and attention drawn to the myriad of interactions that once took place across the Scheme. The works along the Scheme, extending from Anderby Creek to Bicker Fen, have provided important insights into a range of topics, enhancing our understanding of an area that has seen limited sustained archaeological work previously but has recently become the focus of a variety of large infrastructure projects.

The earliest recorded activity across the Scheme, as outlined in Chapter 3, dated to the Mesolithic (9500–4000 BC). The evidence for this period consisted of *ex situ* scatters of worked flints. An exception to this was the recovery of Mesolithic/early Neolithic worked flints from a pit at SPE01, in the Coastal Landscape Parcel at the northernmost end of the Scheme (Fig. 3.1). Further finds of Neolithic date (4000–2200 BC) are noted within the Historic Environment Record (HER) (Fig. 3.2), with the location of these in part reflecting the nature of the landscape during this period (see Chapters 2 and 3). Marine transgression during this period pushed the coast westward, with much of the area of the Scheme consequently being inundated (see Chapter 2, Fig. 2.4). The evidence is indicative of seasonal movements across this landscape, a viewpoint that is further illustrated when considering the wider distribution of finds from across this area (Fig. 3.2). Neolithic to early Bronze Age activity (4000–1500 BC) was noted in SMR09, within the northern half of the Scheme. This, like the earlier Mesolithic/early Neolithic finds from SPE01, comprised an assemblage of finds recovered from a pit fill. Among these were sherds of pottery and worked lithics, with the lithics dating to the later Neolithic–early Bronze Age and the pottery to the 2nd millennium BC, suggesting the deposition of curated material.

From around 1700 BC there was a phase of marine regression, followed by an episode of marine flooding in the middle Bronze Age *c.* 1400 BC. In the context of the Scheme there is evidence for peat growth during the early Bronze Age (2200–1500 BC), succeeded by the development of saltmarshes and a further phase of peat growth in the middle Bronze Age (1500–1150 BC) (see Chapter 2). It is into this dynamic environment that the enigmatic timber structure at HDD95, was constructed to the north of the village of Northlands (Figs 3.5 and 3.6). This structure comprised two parallel rows of oak timber posts, samples of which were dated to the 2nd millennium BC. A late Bronze Age awl and socketed axe were recovered from SMR10 and TAM14 respectively.

Features dating to the late Bronze Age–Iron Age were recorded within SPE01 and include the first evidence within the Scheme for salt production (Fig. 3.12). These represent a comparatively rare example of a later prehistoric salt production site on the Lindsey Marshes, with most of the recorded examples being located further to the south (see Lane 2018). It is possible that further examples remain undiscovered under later alluvial deposits (*e.g.* Cowbit: Lane and Morris 2001, 91). The presence of the saltworking site, alongside that at Tetney to the north (Palmer-Brown 1994), suggests that the overall distribution of saltworking sites during this period remains to be fully determined. Further bias is introduced by the relative lack of dating evidence recovered from these sites, with most of the salterns within the vicinity of the Scheme having seen little excavation or being identified primarily on the basis of spreads of briquetage (see Chapter 5). Outside of the principal excavation areas, further saltern sites were identified in several of the direct drilling sites and were in general dated to the late Iron Age–early Roman period (Table 5.1). Other Iron Age remains included several middle Iron Age features at SPE03 in the Fen Edge Landscape Parcel, from which sherds of Iron Age pottery were recovered.

The presence of late La Tène style pottery alongside early Roman sherds at TAM04 and SPE03 suggests that these farmsteads were established in the post-conquest period. They formed part of a wider pattern of settlement expansion in the early Roman period (AD 43–100), with an increase in settlement numbers from the middle Roman period onwards (AD 100–250) (Table 4.1). This period, as outlined in Chapter 4, saw the establishment of farmsteads at SPE04 and SMR01, alongside the continued use of SPE03 and TAM04. The expansion of Roman sites was in part facilitated by a phase of marine regression which probably started in the later Iron Age (see Chapter 2). Notably, the recorded farmsteads were restricted to the southern end of the Scheme, although a limited suite of agricultural remains were recorded in the Coastal Landscape Parcel (Fig. 4.1). The expansion of Roman farmsteads in this period, as highlighted in Chapter 6, forms part of a wider pattern of agricultural expansion in the early–middle Roman period. Crucially, the data from the Scheme provide key insights into the nature of this expansion to the east of the Wolds.

Of note within the recorded farmsteads from the Scheme was the evidence for timber buildings, providing valuable insights into rural structures within this region. These include the moated post-built structure at TAM04, which was remodeled on at least three occasions during the early Roman period (Fig. 4.17). Other structures include the beam slot buildings at SPE03, which recall similar structures at Colne Fen in Cambridgeshire (Evans 2013). The economic data from each of these farmsteads, as elaborated in Chapter 6, suggest a mixed agricultural regime, but some sites appear to have placed an emphasis on particular products. This appears to become more pronounced in the late Roman period (AD 250–410), with evidence for the possible centralisation of certain processes, such as milling, textile production, and dairying.

The development of the salt production sites at SPE02 and SMR06 in the later Roman period can be interpreted in a similar vein. Hitherto, most salt production sites within the region have been dated to the Iron Age–early Roman period, with the 'industry' generally seen as having declined by the mid-2nd century AD (Hallam 1970, 70; Lane 2018, 128–129). The data from the Triton Knoll sites, in particular SPE02, suggests a later Roman episode of saltworking which was associated with a high degree of organisation. The layout of SPE02, as outlined in Chapter 5, echoes those at other known late Roman saltworking sites and could be indicative of a degree of centralisation (Fig. 5.7). In the absence of other comparative sites within the vicinity of the Triton Electrical Scheme it is difficult to gauge the extent of this later episode of saltworking and whether it was on the scale of other known late Roman saltworkings such as at Middleton, Norfolk and London Gateway, Essex (Crowson 2001; Biddulph and Stansbie 2012; Biddulph 2017), or reflected a small-scale operation that sought to make use of marginal land at the time. Nevertheless, the presence of late Roman saltworking challenges the perceived model of decline across the region. This highlights the need for further radiocarbon dating of such features to build a more robust chronology for them.

During the post-Roman period there was a period of inundation and for much of the early medieval period the southern Lincolnshire Marsh may have been inundated, forming a tidal lagoon to the north of All Saints Wainfleet, while to the south of the village, the coastline was likely to have been as far inland as the low ground west of 'the Tofts' (Fig. 2.4). Over the subsequent centuries this coastline shifted to the east, with various programmes of land reclamation also taking place. This dynamic environmental picture in part accounts for the relatively limited pattern of activity in the immediate post-Roman period, although there was evidence for early medieval rural settlement at SMR10 and SMR09 in the vicinity of Burgh le Marsh, in the Fen Edge Landscape Parcel, and at SPE01 within the Coastal Landscape Parcel. The field systems within SMR10 and SPE01 appear to relate to larger field systems recorded in LiDAR data and cartographic sources, which are restricted to higher ground within the marsh. These field systems did not appear to be associated with settlement activity, although at SPE01 it is possible that the post-conquest elements were located close to a settlement. The period following the Norman Conquest in general witnessed an uptake in activity, with a focus recorded within the Fen at SMR17, broadly contemporaneous with the continued activity at SPE01. These medieval datasets, like their Roman counterparts, fill in important gaps in our understanding of wider patterns of medieval settlement (Simmons 2022). The farmstead at SMR17 was established in the 13th–14th centuries and included evidence for medieval structures (Fig. 7.9). The finds from the farmstead suggest that it was probably a relatively minor and short-lived smallholding.

Moving into the later medieval period, there was evidence for possible brick manufacture at SMR09, chiefly comprising a series of extraction pits, some of which may have been used for a variety of secondary activities, such as 'washing pits' and/or refuse (Fig. 7.10). These features were outlined by an enclosure ditch, demarcating the area between the wet clay processing and the forming, drying, and firing of bricks, which appeared to take place to the east. A single brick ramp in this area probably relates to these activities and may represent a temporary structure for firing bricks. Brickworking continued at SMR09 into the post-medieval period, with evidence for a range of structures and features associated with brick manufacture. These included further possible brick clamps, cobbled surfaces, and a brick structure formed of a series of brick ramps. The precise function of the latter is uncertain but could have been associated with the firing of bricks.

Our understanding of the broad landscape and settlement changes taking place across the Scheme have been furthered by a suite of specialist environmental and artefactual studies. The full results of these are all presented within the ADS archive (https://doi.org/10.5284/1125918). This work has included a series of scientific analyses, including the application of isotopic techniques to faunal and botanical remains from the Scheme, as well as detailed residue analysis of pottery (Dunne *et al.* 2023). As emphasised throughout this monograph, this package of works provides a significant body of data highlighting a range of aspects. The data from the residue analysis, for example, provide insights into the multiple ways pots were used for a range of activities from cooking to the production of cheese or other dairy products. The isotope data, whilst limited, highlight the potentially varied conditions in which crops were grown, as well as illuminating probable patterns of movement. This notion is reinforced in the botanical data where several sites during the Roman period appeared to be utilising cereal waste that was brought to site for use as fuel. In the case of the Lincolnshire Marsh sites this may have been linked to the need for fuel for the salt ovens. These sites also showed evidence for the importation of animal products, both for consumption and salt curing, highlighting the multifarious connections between different sites of the period. These inter-connections can also be observed in the post-Roman periods with the sites drawing on local resources and satisfying local demand for materials.

Throughout the 10,000 years of occupation across the Scheme, it is evident that the region underwent a series of shifts, both in terms of its natural and its human aspects. These ebbs and flows in activity themselves reflect on the dynamics of this region, which has acted as the setting for a range of activities from Mesolithic hunter-gatherers and later prehistoric and Roman saltworking, through to medieval and post-medieval agriculture and brickmaking. It is clear from the Triton Knoll data that there is much yet to be gleaned from this rich and unique region and the project provides a formative basis for future work.

Bibliography

Aberg, F.A. (1978). *Medieval Moated Sites*. London: Council for British Archaeology Research Reports 17. Available at: Archaeological Data Service https://doi.org/10.5284/1000332.

Aitken, M.J. and Hawley, H.N. (1966). Magnetic dating 3: Further archaeomagnetic measurements in Britain. *Archaeometry* 9, 190–1.

Albarella, U. (1997). Size, power, wool and veal: Zooarchaeological evidence for late medieval innovations. *Environment and Subsistence in Medieval Europe* 9, 19–31.

Albarella, U. (2019). *Review of Animal Bone Evidence from Central England*. Swindon: Historic England Research Report Series 61-2019.

Albarella, U. and Davis, S. (1994). *The Saxon and Medieval Animal Bones Excavated 1985–1989 from West Cotton, Northamptonshire*. London: English Heritage Ancient Monuments Laboratory Report 1717/94.

Albarella, U. and Johnstone, C. (2000). *The Early to Late Saxon Animal Bones Excavated in 1995 from Kings Meadow Lane, Higham Ferrers, Northamptonshire*. London: Historic Building and Monuments Commission for England Ancient Monument Laboratory Report 79/2000.

Albarella, U. and Mulville, J.A. (2001). Animal bone. In Lane and Morris (eds), 383–385.

Albarella, U. and Thomas, R. (2002). They dined on crane: Bird consumption, wild fowling and status in medieval England. *Acta zoological cracoviensia* 45, 23–38.

Albarella, U., Beech, M.J. and Mulville, J. (1997). *The Saxon, Medieval and Post-Medieval Mammal and Bird Bones Excavated 1989–91 from Castle Mall, Norwich, Norfolk*. London: Historic Building and Monuments Commission for England Ancient Monuments Laboratory Report 72/97.

Albarella, U., Beech, M., Curl, J., Locker, A., Moreno Garcia, M. and Mulville, J. (2009). *Norwich Castle: Excavations and historical surveys 1987–98. Part III: A zooarchaeological Study*. Norwich: East Anglian Archaeology Occasional Paper 22.

Allason-Jones, L. (2011). *Jet, Shale and other allied materials by Linday Allason-Jones*. York: Roman Finds Group Datasheet 2.

Allen Archaeology (2018a). *Archaeological Non-Intrusive Survey Report: Metal detector survey for the Triton Knoll Offshore Wind Farm – Onshore Electrical Connection*. Cambridge: Allen Archaeology Limited unpublished report.

Allen Archaeology (2018b). *Archaeological Non-Intrusive Survey Report: Geophysical survey by magnetometry for the Triton Knoll Offshore Wind Farm – Onshore Electrical Connection*. Cambridge: Allen Archaeology Limited unpublished report.

Allen Archaeology (2018c). *Geoarchaeological Desk-Top Report: Triton Knoll Wind Farm, Onshore Cable Route*. Cambridge: Allen Archaeology Limited unpublished report.

Allen Archaeology (2018d). *Archaeological Evaluation Report: Triton Knoll Electrical System (TKES), Lincolnshire*. Cambridge: Allen Archaeology Limited unpublished report.

Allen Archaeology (2019). *Archaeological Auger Survey for Triton Knoll Offshore Windfarm onshore electrical system cable route and substation, Lincolnshire for the Triton Knoll Electrical System*. Cambridge: Allen Archaeology Limited: unpublished report.

Allen Archaeology (2020). *Geoarchaeology Stage 4 Coring Report: For the Triton Knoll Electrical System*. Cambridge: Allen Archaeology Limited unpublished report.

Allen Archaeology (2021a). *Archaeological Assessment Report and Updated Project Design: E1 package of works for the onshore cable system, Triton Knoll Electrical System (TKES), Lincolnshire* Volume 1. Cambridge: Allen Archaeology Limited: unpublished report AAL202104.

Allen Archaeology (2021b). *Archaeological Assessment Report and Updated Project Design: E3 package of works for the onshore cable system, Triton Knoll Electrical System (TKES), Lincolnshire*. Cambridge: Allen Archaeology Limited unpublished report.

Allen Archaeology (2022a). *Archaeological Assessment Report and Updated Project Design: E1 package of works for the onshore cable system, Triton Knoll Electrical System (TKES), Lincolnshire*. Cambridge: Allen Archaeology Limited unpublished report

Allen Archaeology (2022b). *Archaeological Evaluation Report: Geophysical survey by magnetometry on land at Mill House, Sea Lane Hogsthorpe, Skegness, Lincolnshire*. Cambridge: Allen Archaeology Limited unpublished report AAL2022091.

Allen, J.R.L. (2014). *Whetstones from Roman Silchester (Calleva Atrebatum), North Hampshire, Character, Manufacture, Provenance and Use 'Putting and edge on it'*. Oxford: British Archaeological Report 597.

Allen, M. (2016). The North-East. In Smith *et al.* (eds) 2016, 242–281.

Allen, M. (2017). Pastoral farming. In M. Allen, L. Lodwick, T. Brindle, M. Fulford and A. Smith (eds), *The rural economy of Roman Britain, New visions of the countryside of Roman Britain. Volume 2,* 85–141. London: Britannia Monograph 30.

Allen, M. and Lodwick, L. (2017). Agricultural strategies in Roman Britain. In M. Allen, L. Lodwick, T. Brindle, M. Fulford and A. Smith (eds), *New Visions of the Countryside of Roman Britain. Volume 2: The rural economy of Roman Britain,* 142–177. London: Britannia Monograph 30.

Allen, M. and Smith, A. (2016). Rural settlement in Roman Britain: Morphological classification and overview. In Smith *et al.* (eds) 2016, 17–43.

Allison, E. (2024). Insects. In Headland Archaeology and Allen Archaeology 2024c, 205–213.

Andersen, S.T. (1970). *The Relative Pollen Productivity and Pollen Representation of North European Trees and Correction Factors for Tree Pollen Spectra*. Copenhagen: Danmarks Geologiske Undersøgelse II 96.

Andersen, S.T. (1973). The differential pollen productivity of trees and its significance for the interpretation of a pollen diagram from a forested region. In H.J.B. Birks and R.G. West (eds), *Quaternary Plant Ecology*, 109–115. Oxford: Blackwell.

Araus, J., Febrero, A., Buxó, R., Rodríguez-Ariza, M., Molina, F., Camalich, M., Martín, D. and Voltas, J. (1997). Identification of ancient irrigation practices based on the carbon isotope discrimination of plant seeds: A case study from the South-East Iberian Peninsula. *Journal of Archaeological Science* 24, 729–740.

Archaeological Project Services. (2002). *Land at Curlew Drive, Cowbit, Lincolnshire. Archaeological Evaluation*. Sleaford: Archaeological Project Services unpublished report.

Archaeological Project Services. (2005). *Land at Fieldside, Mareham le Fen, Lincolnshire. Archaeological Excavation*. Sleaford: Archaeological Project Services unpublished report.

Archaeological Project Services (2006). *Archaeological Evaluation at 'Noss Mayo', 2 High Street Burgh le Marsh Lincolnshire*. Sleaford: Archaeological Project Services unpublished report.

Bacon, J.K.F. and Fitzpatrick, A.P. (2001). Copper alloy objects. In Chowne *et al.* 2001, 21–23.

Baker, T. (1960). The Iron Age salt industry in Lincolnshire. *Lincolnshire Architectural and Archaeological Society Reports and Papers* 8, 26–34.

Bakels, C. (2019). Baselines for $\delta^{15}N$ values of cereals retrieved from archaeological excavations. *Archaeometry* 61, 470–477.

Bamforth, M. (2024). Waterlogged and worked wood. In Headland Archaeology and Allen Archaeology 2024c, 122–128.

Bang, P.F. (2008). *The Roman Bazaar: A comparative study of trade and markets in a tributary empire*. Cambridge: Cambridge University Press.

Barfield, L. (2006). Bays Meadow villa, Droitwich: excavations 1967–77. In D. Hurst (ed.), *Roman Droitwich: Dodderhill Fort, Bays Meadow Villa and Roadside Settlement*, 78–242. York: Council for British Archaeology Research Report 146.

Barford, P.M., Elsdon, S.M., May, J., Waddington, T., and Wild, P. (1996). Fired Clay Artefacts other than Pottery. In May 1996, 327–344.

Barley, M.W. (1964). The medieval borough of Torksey: excavations 1960–62. *Antiquaries Journal* 44, 164–187.

Barley, M.W. (1981). The medieval borough of Torksey: excavations 1963–8. *Antiquaries Journal* 61, 263–291.

Barton, B.M. (2011). John Rennie and the drainage of the Witham Fens, Lincolnshire, UK. *Proceedings of the Institution of Civil Engineers – Engineering History and Heritage* 164(3), 175–187.

Batey, C. (2005). From raw material to finished product: Resources and resourcefulness in the North Atlantic. In H. Luik, A.M. Choyke, C. Batey and L. Lougas (eds), *From Hooves to Horns, from Mollusc to Mammoth: Manufacture and Use of Bone Artefacts from Prehistoric Times to the Present*, 351–358. Tallinn: Ajaloo Instituut.

Baxter, I.L. (2006). A dwarf hound skeleton from a Romano-British grave at York Road, Leicester, England, UK., with a discussion of other Roman small dog types and speculation regarding their respective aetiologies. In L.M. Snyder and E.A. Moore (eds), *Dogs and People in Social, Working, Economic or Symbolic Interaction*, 12–23. Oxford: Oxbow Books.

Baxter, I.L. (2010). Small Roman dogs. *Alexandria Archive* 901, 1–9.

Bealby, J.T. (1911). Fens. *Encyclopaedia Britannica* 10, 256–258.

Beamish, M. (1990). *Excavations at Scalford Brook, Melton Mowbray*. Leicester: Leicestershire Archaeological Unit unpublished report.

Beamish, M. (1997). *Wing to Whatborough Trunk Main. Interim Report and Post-Excavation Assessment and Project Design*. Leicester: Leicestershire Archaeological Unit unpublished report.

Bellis, L. (2020). A Dog's Life: An Interdisciplinary Study of Human–Animal Relationships in Roman Britain. Unpublished PhD Thesis, University of Leicester.

Bennett, D. and Timm, R.M. (2016). The dogs of Roman Vindolanda, Part II: Time stratigraphic occurrence, ethnographic comparisons, and biotype reconstruction. *Archaeofauna* 25, 107–126.

Bennett, D., Campbell, G. and Timm, R.M. (2016). The dogs of Roman Vindolanda, Part I: Morphometric techniques useful in differentiating domestic and wild canids. *Archaeofauna* 25, 79–106.

Biddulph, E. (2017). The Roman salt industry in south-eastern Britain. In D. Bird (ed.), *Agriculture and Industry in South-eastern Roman Britain*, 210–235. Oxford: Oxbow Books.

Biddulph, E. and Stansbie, D. (2012). The salt industry expands – the later Roman period. In E. Biddulph, S. Foreman, E. Stafford, D. Stansbie and R. Nicholson (eds), *London Gateway Iron Age and Roman salt making in the Thames Estuary. Excavaiton at Stanford Wharf Nature Reserve, Essex*, 105–176. Oxford: Oxford Archaeology Monograph 18.

Bidwell, P. and Hodgson, N. (2006). *The Roman Army in Northern England*. Newcastle Upon Tyne: Arbeia Society.

Birks, J.B. (1989). Holocene isochrone maps and patterns of tree-spreading in the British Isles. *Journal of Biogeography* 16, 503–540.

Birley, B. (2012). *Roman Beads*. York: Roman Finds Group Datasheet 3.

Blinkhorn, P. (2012). *The Ipswich Ware Project: Ceramics, Trade and Society in Middle Saxon England*. London: Medieval Pottery Research Group Occasional Paper 7: The Ipswich Ware Project.

Bocherens, H. and Drucker, D. (2003). Trophic level isotopic enrichment of carbon and nitrogen in bone collagen: Case studies from recent and ancient terrestrial ecosystems. *International Journal of Osteoarchaeology* 13, 46–53.

Bogaard, A., Fraser, R., Heaton, T.H.E., Wallace, M., Vaiglova, P., Charles, M., Jones, G., Evershed, R.P., Styring, A.K., Andersen, N.H., Arbogast, R.-M., Bartosiewicz, L., Gardeisen, A., Kanstrup, M., Maier, U., Marinova, E., Ninov, L., Schäfer, M. and Stephan, E. (2013). Crop manuring and intensive land management by Europe's first farmers. *Proceedings of the National Academy of Sciences of the United States of America* 110, 12589–12594.

Boulter, S. (1997). *Bernard Matthews plc site, south of Benacre Road, Ellough. Airfield Record of Archaeological Evaluation and Excavation*. Bury St Edmunds: Suffolk County Council Archaeological Service unpublished report.

Boyle, A. (2024). Osteological analysis. In Headland Archaeology and Allen Archaeology 2024b, 123–126.

Boyle, A., Didsbury, P., Vince, A. and Young, J. (2011). The medieval pottery. In H.E.M. Cool and M. Bell (eds), *Excavations at St Peters Church, Barton upon Humber*. English Heritage, 1051–1055. Available at: https://doi.org/10.5284/1000389.

Bradley, R. (1975). Salt and settlement in the Hampshire Sussex borderland. In K.W. de Brisay and K.A. Evans (eds), *Salt: The study of an ancient industry.* Colchester: Colchester Archaeological Group.

Bradley, R. (1992). Roman salt production in Chichester harbour: Rescue excavations at Chidham, West Sussex. *Britannia* 23, 27–44.

Bradley, R. (2007). *The Prehistory of Britain and Ireland*. Cambridge: Cambridge University Press.

Bradley-Lovekin, T. and Kitch, J (2006). *Archaeological Evaluation at 'Noss Mayo', 2 High Street, Burgh Le Marsh, Lincolnshire (BMHS06)*. Sleaford: Archaeological Project Services unpublished report.

Branch, N. and Lowe, J. (1996). *Market Deeping Bypass (Lincolnshire) Assessment Report*. Keckington: ArchaeoScape Consulting: unpublished.

Brennand, M. and Taylor, M. (2003). The survey and excavation of a Bronze Age timber circle at Holme-next-the-sea, Norfolk 1998–9. *Proceedings of the Prehistoric Society* 69, 1–84.

Brew, D.S., Holt, T., Pye, K. and Newsham, R. (2000). Holocene sedimentary evolution and palaeocoastlines of the Fenland embayment, eastern England. *Geological Society of London Special Publications* 166(1), 253–273.

Brew, D.S., Horton, B.P., Evans, G., Innes, J.B. and Shennan I. (2015). Holocene sea-level history and coastal evolution of the north-western Fenland, eastern England. *Proceedings of the Geologists' Association* 126(1), 72–85.

British Geological Survey (BGS) (1995). Geological Survey of England and Wales 1:50 000 Provisional series. Sheet 115. *Horncastle. Solid and Drift Geology*. https://largeimages.bgs.ac.uk/iip/mapsportal.html?id=1001607 [last accessed November 2024].

Britton, K., Müldner, G. and Bell, M. (2008). Stable isotope evidence for salt-marsh grazing in the Bronze Age Severn Estuary, UK: implications for palaeodietary analysis at coastal sites. *Journal of Archaeological Science* 35, 2111–2118.

Brookes, C.M. (1987). *Medieval and Later Pottery from Aldwark and Other Sites.* London: The Archaeology of York: Fascicule 16/3, Pottery.

Bronk Ramsey, C. (2021) Bayesian analysis of radiocarbon dates. *Radiocarbon* 51, 337–360.

Brown, T. (2013). Divisions of floodplain space and sites on riverine 'islands': function, ritual, social or liminal places. *Journal of Wetland Archaeology* 3, 3–15.

Brown, W.V. (1960). A cytological difference between the Eupanicoideae and the Chloridoideae (Gramineae). *Southwestern Naturalist* 5(1), 7–11.

Browning, J. (2015). Animal bone. In M. Luke, B. Barker and J. Barker, *A Romano-British Farmstead at Stretton Road, Great Glen, Leicestershire*, 65–67. Albion Archaeology Monograph 2.

Brück, J. (2000). Settlement, Landscape and Social Identity: The Early-Middle Bronze Age Transition in Wessex, Sussex and the Thames Valley. *Oxford Journal of Archaeology* 19, 273–300.

Brück, J. (2019). *Personifying Prehistory: Relational ontologies in Bronze Age Britain and Ireland*. Oxford: Oxford University Press.

Brunning, R. (2007). Structural Wood in Prehistoric England and Wales. Unpublished PhD Thesis, University of Exeter.

Burnham, B.C. and Wacher, J. (1990). *The 'Small Towns' of Roman Britain*. London: Batsford.

Butler, C. (2000). *Saxon Settlement and Earlier Remains at Friar's Oak, West Sussex*. Oxford: British Archaeological Report 295.

Butterworth, C.A. and Lobb, S.J. (1992). *Excavations in the Burghfield Area, Berkshire: Developments in the Bronze Age and Saxon landscapes*. Salisbury: Wessex Archaeology Report 1.

Cappers, R.T.J. and Raemaekers, D.C. (2008). Cereal cultivation at Swifterbant? Neolithic wetland farming on the North European plain. *Current Anthropology* 49(3), 385–402.

Carruthers, W.J. and Hunter-Dowse, K.L. (2019). *A Review of Macroscopic Plant Remains from the Midland Counties*. Swindon: Historic England Research Department Report Series 47/2019. https://historicengland.org.uk/research/results/reports/8484/AReviewofMacroscopicPlantRemainsfromtheMidlandCounties.

Challis, A. and Harding, D. (1975). *Later Prehistory from the Trent to the Tyne*. Oxford: British Archaeological Report 20.

Chambers, L.G., Steinmuller, H.E. and Breithaupt, J.L. (2019). Toward a mechanistic understanding of 'peat collapse' and its potential contribution to coastal wetland loss. *Ecology* 100(7): e02720. doi: 10.1002/ecy.2720.

Chapman, P. (2008). Reporting on brick and tile in commercial archaeology. *British Brick Society* 108, 6–11.

Chenery, C., Müldner, G., Evans, J., Eckardt, H. and Lewis, M. (2010). Strontium and stable isotope evidence for diet and mobility in Roman Gloucester, UK. *Journal of Archaeological Science* 37, 150–163.

Chisholm, M. (2012). Water management in the Fens before the introduction of pumps. *Landscape History* 33(1), 45–68.

Chorro-Giner, M. (2024a). Animal bone and shell. In Headland Archaeology and Allen Archaeology 2024a, 42–62.

Chorro-Giner, M. (2024b). Animal bone and shell. In Headland Archaeology and Allen Archaeology 2024b, 95–122.

Chorro-Giner, M. (2024c). Animal bone and shell. In Headland Archaeology and Allen Archaeology 2024c, 150–204.

Chowne, P. (2024). Prehistoric pottery. In Headland Archaeology and Allen Archaeology 2024c, 13–16.

Chowne, P., Healy, F. and Bradley, R. (1993). *The Excavation of a Neolithic Settlement at Tattershall Thorpe, Lincolnshire*. Sleaford: East Anglian Archaeology 57.

Chowne, P., Cleal, M. J., Fitzpatrick, A. P. and Andrews, P. (2001). *Excavations at Billingborough, Lincolnshire, 1975–8: A Bronze–Iron Age Settlement and Salt-working Site*. Sleaford; East Anglian Archaeology 94.

Christie, C. (2024). Conspicuous by its absence: Middle–Late Bronze Age settlement on the A14. In E. West, C. Christie, O. Scholma-Mason, L. Billington, M. Brudenell, D. Moretti, J. Franklin and A. Smith, *Time Travellers Tales, Essays from the A14 Cambridge to Huntingdon Archaeological Excavations*. London: Museum of London Archaeology.

Clapham, A.R., Tutin, T.G. and Warburg, E.F. (1962). *Flora of the British Isles*. Cambridge: Cambridge University Press.

Clarke, G. and Haskins, A. (2021). *Early Medieval Charcoal Pits and Early Post-medieval Brick Kilns at Nayland Road, Great Horkesley, Essex*. Cambrdige: Oxford Archaeology East unpublished report.

Clay, C. (2002). *Meadow Lane, North Hykeham, Lincolnshire*. London: Pre-Construct Archaeology Ltd unpublished report.

Clay, P. (2022). *Neolithic and Early to Middle Bronze Age*. East Midlands Archaeological Research Framework. Available at: https://researchframeworks.org/emherf/regional-overview/neolithic-and-early-to-middle-bronze-age/.

Clifton-Taylor, A. (1972). *The Pattern of English Building*. London: Faber and Faber.

Cloern, J.E., Canuel, E.A. and Harris, D. (2002). Stable carbon and nitrogen isotope composition of aquatic and terrestrial plants of the San Francisco Bay estuarine system. *Limnology and Oceanography* 47, 713–729.

Coles, J.M. and Hall, D. (1998). *Changing Landscapes: The ancient Fenland*. Cambridge: Cambridgeshire County Council, Wetland Archaeology Research Project.

Cool, H.E.M. (2006). *Eating and Drinking in Roman Britain*. Cambridge: Cambridge University Press.

Coombe, P.C., Grew, F., Hayward, K.M.J. and Henig, M. (2015). *Corpus Signorum Imperiii Romani Great Britain 1.10 Roman Sculpture from London and the South-East*. Oxford: Oxford University Press.

Coombe, P.C., Hayward, K.M.J., Henig, M., with Crosby, V., Lowerre, A., Neal, D.S. and Paynter, S. (2021). The sculptured and architectural stonework from Stanwick Roman Villa, Northamptonshire. *Britannia* 52, 227–275.

Cooper, J.H., Stewart, J.R. and Serjeantson, D. (2022). The birds of ancient Britain: First recommendations for Category F of the British List. *Ibis* 164, 911–923.

Cooper, N.J. (2006). *The Archaeology of the East Midlands: An archaeological resource assessment and research agenda*. Leicester: Leicester Archaeology Monograph 13.

Cope-Faulkner, P. (2006). *Archaeological Watching Brief and Earthwork Survey Along the Route of the Northern Bypass Addlethorpe, Lincolnshire*. Sleaford: Archaeological Project Services unpublished report.

Corder, P. (1961). *The Roman Town and Villa at Great Casterton, Rutland: Third Report for the Years 1954–1958*. Nottingham: University of Nottingham.

Crawley, P. (2013). *Archaeological Trial Trenching Evaluation at Newfound Farm, Cringleford, Norfolk*. Norwich: Norfolk Archaeological unit. Available at: https://doi.org/10.5284/1050618.

Critchley, S. (2005). Stone objects. In R. Atkins (eds), *Partney Bypass, Lincolnshire. Post Excavation Assessment and Updated Project Design. Volume 1*, 34. Cambridge: Cambridgeshire County Council Archaeological Field Unit Report 788.

Cromarty, A.M., Barclay, A., Lambrick, G. and Robinson, M. (2006). *Late Bronze Age Ritual and Habitation on a Thames Eyot at Whitecross Farm, Wallingford: The archaeology of the Wallingford Bypass 1986–92*. Oxford: Thames Valley Landscapes Monograph 22.

Crowson, A. (2001). Excavations at Middleton. In Lane and Morris (eds) 2001, 162–238.

Crowson, A., Lane, T. and Reeve, J. (2000). *Fenland Management Project Excavation 1991–1995*. Sleaford: Lincolnshire Archaeology and Heritage Reports Series 3.

Crummy, N. (1983). *Colchester Archaeological Report 2: The Roman small finds from excavations in Colchester 1971–85*. fig. 72, no. 2006, 68. Colchester: Colchester Archaeological Trust.

Cummings, C. (2009). Meat consumption in Roman Britain: The evidence from stable isotopes. In M. Driessen, S. Heeren, J. Hendriks, F. Kemmers and R. Visser (eds), *TRAC 2008: Proceedings of the Eighteenth Annual Theoretical Roman Archaeology Conference, Amsterdam 2008*, 73–83. Oxford: Oxbow Books.

Dabill, H. (2022). *Heckington Fen Energy Park, Lincolnshire: Archaeological Evaluation*. Salisbury: Wessex Archaeology unpublished report.

Dabill, H. (2023). *Heckington Fen Energy Park Lincolnshire. Archaeological Evaluation. 267010.02*. Sheffield: Wessex Archaeology unpublished report.

Daniel, P. and Halldórsdóttir V. (2023). *Viking Link, Lincolnshire, Zones 2 and 3. Post-excavation Assessment Volume 1: Main Text and Figures. 218714.01*. Sheffield: Wessex Archaeology unpublished report.

Darling, M.J. (1977). *A Group of Late Roman Pottery from Lincoln*. London Council for British Archaeology/Lincoln Archaeological Trust Monograph 16:1.

Darling, M.J. (2007). *Report 251 on Pottery from Excavations at Wygate Park, Spalding, Lincolnshire, SWP05*. Sleaford: Archaeological Project Services unpublished report.

Darling, M.J. (2009). Pottery and the fired clay items. In P. Boyer, J. Proctor and R. Taylor-Wilson (eds), *On the Boundaries of Occupation: Excavations at Burringham Road Scunthorpe and Baldwin Avenue Bottesford, North Lincolnshire*. London: Pre-Construct Archaeological Monograph 9.

Darling, M.J. and Precious, B. (2001). A saltern at Gold Dyke Bank, Wrangle, Lincolnshire. In Lane and Morris (eds) 2001, 424–246.

Darling, M.J. and Precious, B.J. (2014). *Corpus of Roman Pottery from Lincoln*. Oxford: Lincoln Archaeological Studies 6.

Darling, M., Rowlandson I.M. and Fiske, H.G., Wild, F.C. and Monteil, G. (2020). Roman pottery. In R. Atkins, J. Burke, L. Field and A. Yates (eds), *Middle Bronze Age and Roman*

Settlement at Manor Pit, Baston, Lincolnshire: Excavations 2002–2014., Oxford: Archaeopress.

Davey, P.J. (1973). Bronze age metalwork from Lincolnshire. *Archaeologia* 104, 51–127.

Davis, S.J. (1992). *Saxon and Medieval Animal Bones from Burystead and Langham Road, Northants; 1984–1987 Excavations*. London: Historic Building and Monuments Commission for England Ancient Monuments Laboratory Report 71/92.

Davis, S.J.M. (1997). *Animal Bones from the Roman Site Redlands Farm, Stanwick, Northamptonshire, 1990 Excavations*. London: Historic Building and Monuments Commission for England Ancient Monuments Laboratory Report 106/97.

Department for Environment, Food and Rural Affairs (DEFRA) (2023). *Lowland Agricultural Peat Task Force Chair's Report* https://assets.publishing.service.gov.uk/media/649d6fe1bb13d-c0012b2e349/lowland-agricultural-peat-task-force-chairs-report.pdf [last accessed September 2024].

Devaney, R. (2021). *Lincoln Eastern Bypass (LEB16), The Flint.* Lincoln: Network Archaeology unpublished report.

Dobney, K. (2001). A place at the table: The role of vertebrate zooarchaeology within a Roman research agenda. In S. James and M. Millett (eds), *Britons and Romans: Advancing an archaeological agenda*, 36–46. York: Council British Archaeology Research Report 125.

Dobney, K, Jaques, S.D. and Irving, B.G. (1996). *Of Butchers & Breeds: Report on vertebrate remains from various sites in the City of Lincoln*. Lincoln: City of Lincoln Archaeology Unit.

Dobson, E. (1850). *A Rudimentary Treatise on the Manufacture of Bricks and Tiles: Containing an outline of the principles of brickmaking, and detailed accounts of the various processes employed in the making of bricks and tiles in different parts of England*. London: Weale.

Drury, D. and Allen, T. (2020). *New Work on Long Barrows in Lincolnshire*. In A. Barclay, D. Field and J. Leary (eds), *Houses of the Dead?* Oxford.: Neolithic Studies Group Seminar Papers 17.

Drury, P.J. (1981). The production of brick and tile in medieval England. *Medieval Industry* 40, 126–142.

Dugdale, W. (1662). *The History of Imbanking and Drayning of Divers Fenns and Marshes, both in Forein Parts and in this Kingdom, and of the Improvements Thereby Extracted from Records, Manuscripts, and other Authentick Testimonies*. London: Alice Warren.

Dumbrell, R. (1983). *Understanding Antique Wine Bottles*. Woodbridge: Antique Collectors Club.

Dunne, J. and Evershed, P. (2018a). *Organic Residue Analysis of Pottery from the A160/A180 Port of Immingham Improvement Scheme*. Bristol: University of Bristol School of Chemistry for Network Archaeology unpublished report.

Dunne, J. and Evershed, P. (2018b). *Organic Residue Analysis of Pottery from Goxhill Feeder 9 Project*. Bristol: University of Bristol School of Chemistry for Oxford Archaeology North unpublished report.

Dunne, J., Haberfield G. and Evershed R.P. (2023). *Organic Residue Analysis of Romano-British Pottery from Triton Knoll, Lincolnshire*. Bristol: University of Bristol School of Chemistry unpublished report.

Eaton, R.A. and Hale, M.D.C. (1993). *Wood: Decay, pests and protection*. London: Chapman and Hall.

Ellis, S., Fenwick, H., Lillie, M., and Van de Noort, R. (2001). *Wetland Heritage of the Lincolnshire Marsh*, Kingston upon Hull: Humber Wetlands Project.

Elsdon, S. (1996). *Iron Age Pottery in the East Midlands. A Handbook*. Nottingham: University of Nottingham.

Elsdon, S.M. (1997). *Old Sleaford revealed: a Lincolnshire settlement in Iron Age, Roman, Saxon and medieval times: excavations 1882–1995*. Oxbow Monograph 78. Oxford: Oxbow Books.

Environment Agency. (2024). *Survey Data Service*. https://environment.data.gov.uk/survey [last accessed November 2024].

Erdkamp, P. (2015). Agriculture, division of labour, and the paths to economic growth. In P. Erdkamp, K. Verboven and A. Zuiderhoek (eds), *Ownership and Exploitation of Land and Natural Resources in the Roman World*. Oxford: Oxford University Press.

Evans, C. (2013). *Process and History. Romano-British Communities at Colne Fen, Earith: An Inland Port and Supply Farm*. Cambridge: Cambridge Archaeological Unit Landscape Archive Series: The Archaeology of the Lower Ouse Valley 2.

Evans, D.H. (2006). Crafts and industries in Beverley and Hull from 1200–1700. In M. Gläser (eds), *Lübecker Kolloquium zur Stadtarchäologie im Hanseraum V: Das Handwerk*. Lübeck: Schmidt-Römhild.

Evans, D.J., Roberts, D.H., Bateman, M.D., Ely, J., Medialdea, A., Burke, M.J., Chiverrell, R.C., Clark, C.D. and Fabel, D. (2019). A chronology for North Sea Lobe advance and recession on the Lincolnshire and Norfolk coasts during MIS 2 and 6. *Proceedings of the Geologists' Association* 130(5), 523–540.

Evans, J., Macaulay, S. and Mills, P. (2017). *The Horningsea Roman Pottery Industry in Context*. Bar Hill: East Anglian Archaeology 162.

Everson, P.L., Taylor C.C. and Dunn D.J. (1991). *Changes and Continuity: Rural settlement in North-West Lincolnshire*. London: Royal Commission on the Historic Monuments (England) & HMSO.

Fairnell, E.H. (2003). The Utilisation of Fur-bearing Animals in the British Isles. Unpublished MSc Dissertation, University of York.

Farquhar, G. and Richards, R. (1984). Isotopic composition of plant carbon correlates with water-use efficiency of wheat genotypes. *Australian Journal of Plant Physiology* 11, 539–552.

Ferrio, J., Araus, J., Buxo, R., Voltas, J. and Bort, J. (2005). Water management practices and climate in ancient agriculture: inferences from the stable isotope composition of archaeobotanical remains. *Veg Hist Archaeobot* 14, 510–517.

Ferrio, J., Voltas, J., Alonso, N. and Araus, J. (2007). Reconstruction of climatic and crop conditions in the past based on the isotope signature of archaeobotanical remains. *Terrestrial Ecology* 1, 319–332.

Field, D. (2006). *Earthen Long Barrows: The earliest monuments in the British Isles*. Stroud: Tempus.

Field, F.N. (1996). *Proposed Residential Development, Main Street, Toynton-All-Saints*. Sheffield: Lindsey Archaeological Services unpublished report 213.

Field, F.N. and George, I. (1994). Archaeology in Lincolnshire. *Lincolnshire History and Archaeology* 29, 45–57.

Field, N. and Pearson, P.M. (2003). *Fiskerton. An Iron Age Timber Causeway with Iron Age and Roman Votive Offerings*. Oxford: Oxbow Books.

Fiorentino, G., Ferrio, J.P., Bogaard, A., Araus, J.L. and S. Riehl. (2015). Stable isotopes in archaeobotanical research. *Vegetation History and Archaeobotany* 24, 215–227.

Fiske, H.G., Rowlandson, I.M. with Monteil, G. (2023). A late Roman colour-coated ware kiln site beside the River Witham at Lincoln in 2009. *Journal of Roman Pottery Studies* 20, 93–129.

Fraser, R., Bogaard, A., Schäfer, M., Arbogast, R. and Heaton, T.H.E. (2013). Integrating botanical, faunal and human stable carbon and nitrogen isotope values to reconstruct land use and palaeodiet at LBK Vaihingen an der Enz, Baden-Württemberg. *World Archaeology* 45, 492–517.

Fraser, R., Bogaard, A., Heaton, T., Charles, M., Jones, G., Christensen, B.T., Halstead, P., Merbach, I., Poulton, P.R., Sparkes, D. and Styring, A.K. (2011). Manuring and stable nitrogen isotope ratios in cereals and pulses: Towards a new archaeobotanical approach to the inference of land use and dietary practices. *Journal of Archaeological Science* 38, 2790–2804.

French, C.A.I. (2000). Dewatering, desiccation and erosion: An appraisal of water and peat in the Fenlands. In A. Crowson, T. Lane and J. Reeve (eds), *Fenland Management Project Excavations 1991–1995*, 00–00. Sleaford: Lincolnshire Archaeology and Heritage Reports Series 3.

Fryer, V. and Bailey, L. (2024). Archaeobotanical. In Headland Archaeology and Allen Archaeology 2024d, 56–61.

Fryer, V. and Turner, K. (2024). Archaeobotanical. In Headland Archaeology and Allen Archaeology 2024b, 70–94.

Gale, R. (2001). The derivation and uses of some plant-based fuels. In Lane and Morris (eds) 2001, 456–459.

Gale, R. and Cutler, D. (2000). *Plants in Archaeology: Identification manual of artefacts of plant origin from Europe and the Mediterranean*. Otley: Westbury Academic and Scientific.

Galloway, J. A. (2013). Coastal flooding and socioeconomic change in eastern England in the later Middle Ages. *Environment and History* 19(2), 173–207.

Gardiner, M. (2021). A landscape of medieval common peat fens: The lower Witham valley and Wildmoor, Lincolnshire UK. *Landscapes* 22(2), 173–190.

Garnsey, P. and Saller, R. (2014). *The Roman Empire: Economy, society and culture*. London: Bloomsbury.

Garrow, D. (2007). Placing pits: Landscape occupation and depositional practice during the Neolithic in East Anglia. *Proceedings of the Prehistoric Society* 73, 1–24.

Gaunt, K. and Roberts, M. (2024). *Triton Knoll Electrical System: Coastal Landscape Analysis Report*. Headland Archaeology (UK) Limited and Allen Archaeology Limited unpublished report in project archive. Available at: Archaeological Data Service: https://doi.org/10.5284/1125918.

Gaunt, K., van Tongeren, T. and Christie, C. (2024). Fenland fields: Evolving Settlement and agriculture on the Roddon at Viking Link Substation, Bicker Fen, Lincolnshire. *Internet Archaeology* 67. https://doi.org/10.11141/ia.67.10.

Gearey, B., Chapman, H. and Howard, A.J. (2016). *down by the river: archaeological, paleoenvironmental and geoarchaeological investigations of the Suffolk River Valleys*. Oxford: Oxbow Books.

Gearey, B.R., Chapman, H.P., Howard, A.J., Krawiec, K., Bamforth, M., Fletcher, W.G., Hill, T.C.B., Marshall, P., Tetlow, E. and Tyers, I. (2011). The Beccles triple post-alignment, Beccles Marshes, Suffolk: Excavation and paleoenvironmental analyses of an Iron Age wetland site. *Proceedings of the Prehistoric Society* 77, 231–250.

Gerrard, J. (2007). Rethinking the small pig horizon at York Minster. *Oxford Journal Archaeology* 26, 303–307.

Gerrard, J. (2008). Feeding the army from Dorset: Pottery, salt and the Roman state. In S. Stallibrass and R. Thomas (eds), *Feeding the Roman Army: The archaeology of production and supply in NW Europe*. Oxford: Oxbow Books.

Gerrard, J. (2013). *The Ruin of Roman Britain: An archaeological perspective*. Cambridge: Cambridge University Press.

Gidney, L.J. (1991a). *Leicester, The Shires 1988 Excavations: The animal bones from the medieval deposits at Little Lane*. London: Historic Building and Monuments Commission for England Ancient Monuments Laboratory Report 57/91.

Gidney, L.J. (1991b). *Leicester, The Shires 1988 Excavations: The animal bones from the medieval deposits at St Peters Lane*. London: Historic Building and Monuments Commission for England Ancient Monuments Laboratory Report 116/91.

Gidney, L.J. (1991c). *Leicester, The Shires 1988 Excavations: The animal bones from the post-medieval deposits at St Peters Lane*. London: Historic Building and Monuments Commission for England Ancient Monuments Laboratory Report 131/91.

Gidney, L.J. (1992). *Leicester, The Shires 1988 Excavations: The animal bones from the post-medieval deposits at St Peters Lane*. London: Historic Building and Monuments Commission for England Ancient Monuments Laboratory Report 24/92.

Gilmour, L.A. (1988). *Early Medieval Pottery from Flaxengate, Lincoln*. London: The Archaeology of Lincoln Vol. 17:2.

Giorgi, J.A. (1998). *The Charred Plant Remains. An Archaeological Excavation on land South of Bourne Road, Spalding, Lincolnshire*. Newark: John Samuels Archaeological Consultants unpublished report.

Giorgi, J.A. (2000). *The Charred Plant Remains. Archaeological Evaluation Excavation at Holland Park, Horseshoe Road, Spalding*. Newark: John Samuels Archaeological Consultants unpublished report.

Godwin, H. (1978). *Fen: Its ancient past and uncertain future*. Cambridge: Cambridge University Press.

Green, C.R. (2023a). *Land on the Edge: The landscape evolution of the Lincolnshire Coastline*. Louth: Historic England.

Green, C.R. (2023b). *Land on the Edge. Headline Stories*. https://business.visitlincolnshire.com/wp-content/uploads/sites/2/2023/09/Coastal-Headline-Stories-1.pdf.

Greig, J. (1984). The palaeoecology of some British hay meadow types. In W. van Zeist and W.A. Casparie (eds), *Plants and Ancient Man: Studies in palaeoethnobotany*, 213–226. Rotterdam: AA Balkena.

Gurney, D.A. (1978). Iron Age and Romano-British Salt-making on the Essex Coast. Unpublished dissertation, University of Durham.

Hadley, D.M., Richards, J.D., Craig-Atkins, E. and Perry, G. (2023). Torksey after the Vikings: Urban origins in England. *Antiquaries Journal* 103, 1–33.

Hall, D. and Coles, J. (1994). *Fenland Survey: An essay in landscape and persistence*. London: English Heritage Archaeological Monograph. Available at: https://doi.org/10.5284/1028203.

Hallam, S.J. (1970). Settlement around the Wash. In P. Salway, S.J. Hallam, T.J.I.A. Bromwich, D.M. Churchill and C.W. Phillips (eds), *The Fenland in Roman Times: Studies of a major area of peasant colonization with a gazetteer covering all known sites and finds*, 22–113. London: Royal Geographical Society Research Series 5.

Handley, L.L., Azcón, R., Ruiz Lozano, J.M. and Scrimgeour, C.M. (1999). Plant $\delta^{15}N$ associated with arbuscular mycorrhization, drought and nitrogen deficiency. *Rapid Communications in MassSpectrometry* 13, 1320–1324.

Harman, J.H. (1976). The animal bones. In J. Williams, Excavations on a Roman Site at Overstone near Northampton. *Northamptonshire Archaeology*, 100–133. https://doi.org/10.5284/1083036.

Harman, M. (1996). Animal remains. In May (ed.) 2001, 141–171.

Harrison, D. (2013). *The Hollies Solar Park, Burgh-le-Marsh Lincolnshire*. Leeds: Archaeological Services WYAS unpublished report.

Hayes, P.P. (1988). Roman to Saxon in the South Lincolnshire Fens. *Antiquity* 62, 321–326.

Hayes, P.P. and Lane, T.W. (1992). *The Fenland Project Number 5: Lincolnshire Survey, The South-West Fens.* East Anglian Archaeology 55.

Hayes, P.P. and Lane, T. (1993). *The Fenland Project Number 8: Lincolnshire Survey, The Northern Fen-Edge.* East Anglian Archaeology 66.

Hayward, K.M.J. (2015). Types and sources of stone. In Coombe et al. 2015, 35–46.

Hayward, K.M.J. (2023a). *The Worked and Unworked Stone, Thorpebury, Leicestershire X.48.2021.* Museum of London Archaeology (MOLA) - Northants: unpublished.

Hayward, K.M.J, (2023b). *The worked and unworked stone, Site 15 (A developed Romano-British Complex Fields 64 and 65). A428 Black Cat to Caxton Gibbet Improvement Scheme, Bedfordshire ECB6876.* Northampton: Museum of London Archaeology unpublished report.

Hayward, K.M.J. and Meckseper, C. (2022). Crystal Park, Bottisham. The constructions materials of a roman villa complex – a Cambridgeshire case study. *Britannia* 53, 295–322.

Hayward, K.M.J. and Shaffrey, R. (2024a). Worked stone. In Headland Archaeology and Allen Archaeology 2024c, 92–97.

Hayward, K. and Shaffrey, R. (2024b). Worked stone. In Headland Archaeology and Allen Archaeology 2024d, 39–44.

Hayward, K. and Shaffrey, R. (2024c). Worked stone. In Headland Archaeology and Allen Archaeology 2024a, 24–25.

Headland Archaeology (2020). *Triton Knoll Electrical System: Lot 1 and Lot 2 (SMR14, 15 & 16) Mitigation. Post-excavation Assessment.* Silsoe: Headland Archaeology unpublished report.

Headland Archaeology (2023). *Scheme Wide Updated Project Design: E1 and E3 Packages of Work. Triton Knoll Electrical System Edinburgh.* Edinburgh: Headland Archaeology unpublished report.

Headland Archaeology and Allen Archaeology (2024a). *Triton Knoll Electrical System: Coastal Landscape Analysis Report. Volume 2: Specialist reports.* Silsoe/Cambridge: Headland Archaeology (UK) Ltd/Allen Archaeology Ltd unpublished report in project archive. Available at Archaeological Data Service: https://doi.org/10.5284/1125918.

Headland Archaeology and Allen Archaeology (2024b). *Triton Knoll Electrical System: Lincolnshire Marsh Landscape Analysis Report. Volume 2: Specialist reports.* Silsoe/Cambridge: Headland Archaeology (UK) Ltd/Allen Archaeology Ltd unpublished report in project archive. Available at Archaeological Data Service: https://doi.org/10.5284/1125918.

Headland Archaeology and Allen Archaeology (2024c). *Triton Knoll Electrical System: Fen Edge Landscape Analysis Report. Volume 2: Specialist reports.* Silsoe/Cambridge: Headland Archaeology (UK) Ltd/Allen Archaeology Ltd unpublished report in project archive. Available at Archaeological Data Service: https://doi.org/10.5284/1125918.

Headland Archaeology and Allen Archaeology (2024d). *Triton Knoll Electrical System: Inland Fen Edge Landscape Analysis Report. Volume 2: Specialist reports.* Silsoe/Cambridge: Headland Archaeology (UK) Ltd/Allen Archaeology Ltd unpublished report in project archive. Available at Archaeological Data Service: https://doi.org/10.5284/1125918.

Healey, R.H. (1969). Bourne Ware. *Lincolnshire History and Archaeology* 4, 108–109.

Healey, R.H. (1975). Medieval and Sub-Medieval Pottery in Lincolnshire. Unpublished MPhil thesis, University of Nottingham.

Healey, R.H. (1984). Toynton All Saints: Decorated jugs from the Roses kiln. In F.N. Field and A.J. White (eds), *A Prospect of Lincolnshire. Collected Articles on the History and Traditions of Lincolnshire in Honour of Ethel H Rudkin*, 73–8. Lincoln: privately published.

Healey, R.H., Malim, M. and Watson, K. (1998). A medieval kiln at Colne, Cambridgeshire. *Proceedings of the Cambridge Antiquarian Society* 87, 49–58.

Hearne, J. (2011). *Brickmaking in Bunwell*. Bunwell: Bunwell Heritage Group 1.

Heaton, T. (1987). The $^{15}N/^{14}N$ ratios of plants in South Africa and Namibia: Relationship to climate and coastal/saline environments. *Oecologia* 74, 236–246.

Heaton, T. (1999). Spatial, species, and temporal variations in the $^{13}C/^{12}C$ ratios of C_3 plants: Implications for palaeodiet studies. *Journal of Arkeological Science* 26, 637–649.

Heaton, T., Jones, G., Halstead, P.and Tsipropoulos, T. (2009). Variations in the $^{13}C/^{12}C$ ratios of modern wheat grain, and implications for interpreting data from Bronze Age Assiros Toumba, Greece. *Journal of Arkeological Science* 36, 2224–2233.

Hedges, R.E.M. and Reynard, L.M. (2007). Nitrogen isotopes and the trophic level of humans in archaeology. *Journal of Arkeological Science* 34, 1240–1251.

Hey, G., Bell, C., Dennis, C. and Robinson, M. (2016). *Yarnton: Neolithic and Bronze Age settlement and Landscape, Results of Excavations 1990-98*. Oxford: Thames Valley,Landscapes Monograph 39.

Hill, J.D. (1995). *Ritual and Rubbish in the Iron Age of Wessex: A study of the formation of a specific archaeological record*. Oxford: British Archaeological Report 242.

Hinman, M. and Zant, J. (2018). *Conquering the Claylands: Excavations at Love's Farm, St Neots, Cambridgeshire*. Cambridge: East Anglian Archaeology 165.

Hodgson, J.G., Halstead, P., Wilson, P.J. and Davis, S. (1999). Vegetation history and archaeobotany functional interpretation of archaeobotanical data: Making hay in the archaeological record. *Plant Ecology* 8, 261–271.

Hoover, H.C. and Hoover, L.H. (1950) (trans.). *Georgius Agricola: De Re Metallica* (facsimile reprint of 1912 edition). New York: Dover Publications.

Hopkinson, D. (2014). *Archaeological Post-excavation Assessment & Updated Project Design Report. Land West of 34 Havant Road, Horndean, Hampshire*. London: Archaeology South-East unpublished report.

Horton, B.P. and Shennan, I. (2009). Compaction of Holocene strata and the implications for relative sea level change on the east coast of England. *Geology* 37(12), 1083–1086.

Hunt, L. (2011). *Excavations at Great Casterton Primary School, Pickworth Road, Great Casterton, Rutland, Leicester*. Leicester: University of Leicester Archaeological Services unpublished report.

Hurst, J.G. (1991). Medieval and post-medieval pottery imported into Lincolnshire. In D. Tyszka, K. Miller and G.G. Bryant (eds), *Land, People and Landscapes*, 49–65. Lincoln: Lincolnshire Books.

Hurst, J.G., Neal, D.S. and van Beuningen, H.J.E. (1986). *Pottery Produced and Traded in North-West Europe 1350-1650*. Rotterdam: Rotterdam Papers VI.

Hutton, J. (2007). *Excavations at Langtoft, Lincolnshire. Areas F to H. The Blubell Land*. Cambridge: Cambridgeshire Archaeological Unit unpublished report.

Iorga, A., Gosden, C., Lock, G. and Schulting, R. (2021). Stable carbon and nitrogen isotope analysis and Romano-British animal management along the Ridgeway, Oxfordshire. *Journal of Archaeological Science* 40A, 103254. https://doi.org/10.1016/j.jasrep.2021.103254.

Johnstone, C. (2008). Commodities or logistics? The role of equids in Roman supply networks. In S. Stallibrass and R. Thomas (eds), *Feeding the Roman Army: the archaeology of production and supply in NW Europe*, 128–145. Oxford: Oxbow Books.

Jones, M. (1985). Archaeobotany beyond subsistence reconstruction. In G. Barker and C. Gamble (eds), *Beyond domestication in prehistoric Europe*, 102–128. London: Academic Press.

Jones, M. (2002). *Roman Lincoln. Conquest, Colony, Capital*. Stroud: History Press.

Jones, R. (1978). Appendix II. The animal bones. In D.A. Jackson, T.M. Ambrose, A.L. Pacitto, P.J. Woods, R. Jenkins, R. Goodburn and J.R B. Arthur (eds), Excavations at Wakerley, Northants, 1972–75. *Britannia* 9, 115–242.

Jones, R. and Lewis, C. (2012). The Midlands: Medieval settlements and landscapes. In N. Christie and P. Stamper (eds), *Medieval Rural Settlement: Britain and Ireland, AD 800–166*, 186–205. Oxford: Oxbow Books.

Jones, R.T., Levitan, B.M., Malim, T. and Stevens, P.M. (1985). *Vertebrate Remains from Clay Lane, Northamptonshire*. London: Historic Building and Monuments Commission for England Ancient Monuments Laboratory Report 4811.

Kane, N. (2011). Twelve honest and lawful men in the land of mist and malaria: Jury regulation of common rights in the English Fens in the time of enclosure. *New York University School of Law Environmental Law Journal* 19, 554–590.

Karloukovski, V. and Hounslow, M.W. (2005). *Report on the Archaeomagnetic Dating of a Brick-built Kiln, Meadow Lane, North Hykeham, Lincolnshire*. Sleaford: Archaeological Project Services unpublished report.

Keen, L. (1988). Medieval salt working in Dorset. *Proceedings of the Dorset Archaeological and Natural History Society* 109, 25–28.

Kilmurry, K. (1980). *The Pottery Industry of Stamford, Lincolnshire c. 900–1250*. Oxford: British Archaeological Report 84.

King, A. (1999). Diet in the Roman world: A regional inter-site comparison of the mammal bones. *Journal of Roman Archaeology* 12, 168–202.

Kinory, J. (2012). *Salt Production, Distribution and Use in the British Iron Age*. Oxford: British Archaeological Report 559.

Knight, D. (1994). Late Bronze Age/Early Iron Age pottery from Tetney. In Palmer-Brown 1994, Specialist Report 9.4.

Knight, D. (2002). A Regional ceramic sequence: Pottery of the first millennium BC between the Humber and the Nene. In A. Woodward and J.D. Hill (eds), *Prehistoric Britain: The ceramic basis*, 119–142. Oxford: Prehistoric Ceramics Research Group Occasional Publication 3.

Knight, D. (2010). The Iron Age pottery. In Lane and Trimble (eds) 2010, 82–147.

Knight, D., Vyner, B. and Allen, C. (2012). *An Updated Research Agenda and Strategy for the Historic Environment of the East Midlands*. Nottingham: Nottingham Archaeological Monograph 6.

Knight, M., Ballantyne, R., Brudenell, M., Cooper, A., Gibson, D. and Zeki, R. (2024). *Must Farm Pile Dwelling Settlement. Volume 1. Landscape, Architecture and Occupation*. Cambridge: Cambridge Archaeological Unit Must Farm/Flag Fen Basin Depth and Time Series 2.

Kurlansky, M. (2002). *Salt. A World History*. London: Jonathan Cape.

Lake. J. and Partington, A. (2015). *Building the Evidence Base for Historic Farmsteads in Greater Lincolnshire*. York: Archaeology Data Service https://doi.org/10.5284/1035172.

Lambeck, K. (1993). Glacial rebound of the British Isles – I. Preliminary model results. *Geophysical Journal International* 115, 941–959.

Lane, T. (1993). *The Fenland Project Number 8: Lincolnshire Survey, the Northern Fen-edge*. Sleaford: East Anglian Archaeology 66.

Lane, T. (2007). Until the seas boil dry: Landscape and salt in Bronze Age Lincolnshire. In J. Howard and D. Start (eds), *All Things Lincolnshire*, 121–131. Lincoln: Society for Lincolnshire History and Archaeology.

Lane, T. (2017). Impacts of past climate and environmental change: The effects on prehistoric and Roman coastal salt-making in Lincolnshire, UK. *Historic Environment Policy & Practice* 8(2), 157–169.

Lane, T. (2018). *Mineral from the Marshes: Coastal salt-making in Lincolnshire*. Heckington: Lincolnshire Archaeology and Heritage Reports Series 12.

Lane, T. (2024a). Briquetage. In Headland Archaeology and Allen Archaeology 2024a, 32–34.

Lane, T. (2024b). Three millennia of salt production: Briquetage and salt structure on the east coast of Lincolnshire, England. *Quaternary Science Reviews* 334, 108702. https://doi.org/10.1016/j.quascirev.2024.108702

Lane, T. (2024c). Briquetage. In Headland Archaeology and Allen Archaeology 2024b, 51–62.

Lane, T. and Morris, E.L. (2001). *A Millennium of Saltmaking. Prehistoric and Romano-British salt production in the Fenland*. Heckington: Lincolnshire Archaeology and Heritage Reports Series 4.

Lane, T. and Trimble, D. (2010). Fluid Landscapes and Human Adaptation: Excavations on prehistoric sites on the Lincolnshire fen Edge 1991–1994. Heckington: Lincolnshire Archaeology and Heritage Reports Series 9.

Last, J. and Willis, S. (2023). *Lincolnshire Wolds Landscape Network. Archaeology, Community and Landscape*. Portsmouth: Historic England Research Report Series 53/2023.

Leary, R.S. (2013). *Iron Age and Romano-British pottery from The Hollies Solar Park, Burgh-le-Marsh*. Leeds: Archaeological Services WYAS unpublished report.

Le Patourel, H.E.J. (1968). Documentary evidence and the medieval pottery industry. *Medieval Archaeology* 12(1), 101–126.

Lincolnshire County Council (2024). Lincolnshire Heritage Explorer. https://heritage-explorer.lincolnshire.gov.uk/map [last accessed November 2024].

Lodwick, L. (2017). Arable farming, plant foods and resources. In M. Allen, L. Lodwick, T. Brindle, M. Fulford and A. Smith (eds), *The Rural Economy of Roman Britain: New visions of the countryside of Roman Britain*, 11–85. Volume 2. London: *Britannia* Monograph Series 30.

Lodwick, L. (2023). Cultivating villa economies: Archaeobotanical and isotopic evidence for Iron Age to Roman agricultural practices on the chalk downlands of southern Britain. *European Journal of Archaeology* 26(4), 445–466.

Lodwick, L. Campbell, G. Crosby, V. and Müldner, G. (2021). Isotopic evidence for changes in cereal production strategies in Iron Age and Roman Britain. *Environmental Archaeology* 26, 13–28.

Long, A.J., Scaife, R.G. and Edwards, R.J. (2000). Stratigraphic architecture, relative sea-level, and models of estuary development in southern England: new data from Southampton Water. *Geological Society of London Special Publications* 175(1), 253–279.

Loughlin, N. (1977). Dales Ware: A contribution to the study of Roman coarse pottery. In D.P.S. Peacock (eds), *Pottery and Early Commerce: Characterisation and Trade in Roman and Later Ceramics*, 85–146. London: Academic Press.

Luff, R. (1993). *Animal Bones from Excavations in Colchester 1971–85*. Colchester: Colchester Archaeology Report 12.

Luke, M. and Preece, T. (2011). *Farm and Forge: Late Iron Age/Romano-British farmsteads at Marsh Leys, Kempston, Bedfordshire*. Bedford: East Anglian Archaeology 138.

MacGregor A. (1989). Animals and the early Stuarts: Hunting and hawking at the court of James I and Charles I. *Archives of Natural History* 16, 305–318.

Mainman, A. and Jenner, A. (2013). *Medieval Pottery from York*. York: The Archaeology of York 16:9: The Pottery.

Malim, T. (2005). *Stonea and the Roman Fens*. Stroud: Tempus.

Malone, S. (2001). *Archaeological Evaluation at Hall Lane, Burgh Le Marsh, Lincolnshire*. Sleaford: Archaeological Project Services unpublished report.

Maltby, M. (1979). *Faunal Studies on Urban Sites: Animal bones from Exeter, 1971–75*. Sheffield: University of Sheffield.

Maltby, M. (2007). Chop and change: Specialist cattle carcass processing in Roman Britain. In B. Croxford, N. Ray, R. Roth and N. White (eds), *TRAC 2006*, 56–76. Oxford: Oxbow Books.

Maltby, M. (2022). Animal bone. In D. Ingham (ed.), *Land South of Cambridge Road and the former Dairy Crest Site, Fenstanton, Cambridgeshire*, 94–128. Bedford: Albion Archaeology unpublished report.

Manning, W.H. (1985). *Catalogue of the Romano-British Iron Tools, Fittings and Weapons in the British Museum*. London: British Museum.

Marzano, A. (2024). Marine salt production in the Roman world: The salinae and their ownership. *Quaternary Science Reviews* 335, 108776. DOI:10.1016/j.quascirev.2024.108776.

Mattingly, D. (2006). *An Imperial Possession, Britain in the Roman Empire*. London: Penguin Books.

Maudson, G.S. (1904). Ancient pottery sites. *Lincolnshire Notes and Queries* 8, 33–38.

May, J. (1996). *Dragonby: Report on excavations at Iron Age and Romano-British settlement in North Lincolnshire*. Oxford: Oxbow Books.

McCarthy, M. (2013). *The Romano-British Peasant*. Oxford: Windgather Press.

McConnell, G.A. and Mustchin, A. (2012). *Land Adjacent to Great Casterton Primary School, Pickworth Road, Great Casterton, Rutland: Research Archive Report*. Sheffield; Archaeological Solutions unpublished report.

McConnell, D., Grassam, A. and Mustchin, A. (2012). *Land Adjacent to Great Casterton Primary School, Pickworth Road, Great Casterton, Rutland: Research Archive Report*. Sheffield: Archaeological Solutions unpublished report.

Membery, S. (2000). *An archaeological resource assessment of the Neolithic and early Bronze Age in Lincolnshire*. East Midlands Archaeological Research Framework: Resource Assessment of Neolithic and Early Bronze Age Lincolnshire https://researchframeworks.org/emherf/wp-content/uploads/sites/6/2018/11/3.-NeoEarlyBronzeLincs.pdf.

Miles, W.D. (1965). *A History of Deeping Fen and Pode Hole Pumping Station*. Spalding: Deeping Fen, Spalding and Pinchbeck Internal Drainage Board. Available at: https://www.heritagesouthholland.co.uk/wp-content/uploads/2014/07/A0S-P-0279-History-of-Deeping-Fen-and-Pode-Hole-Pumping-Station.pdf.

Mills, D. (1998). *A Dictionary of British Place Names*. Oxford: Oxford University Press.

Moffett, L. (2006). The archaeology of medieval plant foods. In C. Woolgar, D. Serjeantson and T. Waldron (eds), *Food in Medieval England: Diet and Nutrition*, 41–55. Oxford: Oxford University Press.

Monckton, A. (1997). The charred plant remains. In M. Hewson and R. White (eds), *Archaeological Excavations at Stamford Road, Oakham, Leicestershire*, 10–11. Birmingham: Birmingham University Field Archaeology Unit unpublished report.

Moore, J. Ostrum, B. Rogers, B. Wallace, M. and Montgomery, J. (2023). *Multi isotope analysis of charred grains from the A14 Cambridge to Huntingdon Road development scheme*. Durham: Department of Archaeology Durham University unpublished report prepared for MOLA-Headland Archaeology.

Moorhouse, S. and Slowikowski, A. (1992). The pottery. In S. Moorhouse and I. Roberts, *Wrenthorpe potteries: Excavations of 16th and 17th-century Potting Tenements*

Near Wakefield, 1983–86, 89–149. Leeds: Yorkshire Archaeology 2.

Morgan, J. E. (2017). The micro-politics of water management in early modern England: regulation and representation in Commissions of Sewers. *Environment and History* 23(3), 409–430.

Morley, B. and Gurney, D. (1997). *Castle Rising Castle, Norfolk*. East Dereham: East Anglian Archaeology 81.

Morris, E.L. (2001). Briquetage. In Lane and Morris (eds) 2001, 351–376.

Morris, E.L. (2007). Making magic: Later prehistoric and Early Roman salt production in the Lincolnshire Fenland. In C. Haselgrove and T. Moore (eds), *The Later Iron Age in Britain and Beyond*, 430–443. Oxford: Oxbow Books.

Morris, E.L. and Percival, S. (2001). The Fenland Survey: A reassessment. In Lane and Morris (eds) 2001, 325–341.

Mudd, A., Hart, J. and Rippon, S. (2024). *The Archaeology of Hinkley Point C Nuclear Power Station, Somerset. Excavations in 2012–16*. Andover: Cotswold Archaeology Monograph 18.

Müldner, G. (2013). Stable isotopes and diet: their contribution to Romano-British research. *Antiquity* 87, 137–149.

Müldner, G., Britton, K. and Ervynck, A. (2014). Inferring animal husbandry strategies in coastal zones through stable isotope analysis: New evidence from the Flemish coastal plain (Belgium, 1st–15th century AD). *Journal of Archaeological Science* 41, 322–332.

Murphy, P. (2001a). Environmental summary. In Lane and Morris (eds) 2001, 156

Murphy, P. (2001b). Impressions and other plant material in briquetage from saltern sites at Cowbit, Middleton and Morton saltern. In Lane and Morris (eds) 2001, 376–377.

Murphy, P. (2001c). Environmental studies: A general discussion. In Lane and Morris, 377–383.

Murphy, P. (2003). Charred mollusc shells as indicators of industrial activities. In P. Murphy and P. Wiltshire (eds), *The Environmental Archaeology of Industry*, 135–140. Oxford: Oxbow Books.

Natural Environment Research Council (NERC) (2024). *British Geological Survey*. http://www.bgs.ac.uk/ [Accessed: 30 August 2024].

Needham, S. (1991). *Excavation and Salvage at Runnymede Bridge, 1978: The Late Bronze Age waterfront site*. London: British Museum Press.

Network Archaeology. (1999). *Hatton to Silk Willoughby 1050mm Natural Gas Pipeline. Archaeological evaluation, Excavation and Watching Brief 1998*. Lincoln: Network Archaeology unpublished report.

Newman, C. and Newman, R. (2006). A brief history of barley foods. *Cereal Foods World* 51(1), 4–7.

Oldfield, E. (1829). *A Topographical and Historical Account of Wainfleet and the Wapentake of Candleshoe*. London: Longman.

Oosthuizen, S. (2010). Medieval field systems and settlement nucleation: common or separate origin. In N.J. Higham (ed.), *Landscapes Archaeology of Anglo-Saxon England*, 107–132. Wadebridge: Boydell & Brewer.

Oosthuizen, S. (2017). *The Anglo-Saxon Fenland*. Oxford: Windgather Press.

Open Domesday (2024). *Map: England II 1086* https://opendomesday.org/map/ [last accessed August 2024).

Oswald, A., Goodall, J., Payne, A. and Sutcliffe, T-J. (2010). *Thronton Abbey, North Lincolnshire. Historical, Archaeological and Architectural Investigations*. London: English Heritage Research Department Report Series 100–2010.

Owen, A.E.B. (1952). Coastal erosion in east Lincolnshire. *Lincolnshire Historian* 9, 330–341.

Palmer-Brown, C.P.H. (1993). Bronze Age salt production at Tetney. *Current Archaeology* 12(4), 143–145.

Palmer-Brown, C.P.H. (1994). *Salt Processing in the Late Bronze Age at Tetney, Lincolnshire*. Sheffield: Lindsey Archaeological Services unpublished report.

Pawley, S. (1984). Lincolnshire Coastal Villages and the sea c.1300–1600: Economy and society. Unpublished PhD Thesis, University of Leicester. Available at: https://hdl.handle.net/2381/29309.

Payne, S. (1972). Kill-off patterns in sheep and goats: The mandibles from Aşvan Kale. *Anatolian Studies* 23, 281–303.

Payne, S. (1980). The animal bones. In G. Lambrick (ed.), Excavations in Park Street, Towcester. *Northamptonshire Archaeology* 15, 35–118.

Peacock, D. (2013). *The Stone of life. Querns, mills, and flour production in Europe up to* c. *AD 500*. Cambridge: Cambridge University Press.

Perrin, J.R. (ed.), (1999). Roman pottery from excavations at and near to the Roman small town of *Durobrivae*, Water

Pestell, T. (2009). The syli. In D.H. Evans and C. Loveluck (eds), *Life and Economy at Early Medieval Flixborough c. AD 600–1000: The artefact evidence*, 123–137. Oxford: Oxbow Books.

Phillips, C.W. (1970). *The Fenland in Roman Times*. London: Royal Geographical Society Research Series 5.

Philpott, R. (1991). *Burial Practices in Roman Britain: A survey of grave treatment and furnishing AD 43–410*. Oxford: British Archaeological Report 219.

Precious, B. and Rowlandson, I. (2008). *A Report on the Roman Pottery and Fired Clay from Burgh le Marsh Primary School, Burgh le Marsh, East Lindsey, Lincolnshire (BLMS07)*. Lincoln: M & M Archaeological Services unpublished report.

Precious, B., O'Neill, J. and Young, J. (2003). The pottery. In G. Taylor (eds), Hall Farm, Baston, Lincolnshire: Investigation of a Late Saxon village and medieval manorial complex. *Lincolnshire History and Archaeology* 32, 21–24.

Proctor, J. Sabel, K. and Meddens M. (2000). Post-medieval brick clamps at New Cross in London. *Post-Medieval Archaeology* 34, 187–202.

Pryor, F.M.M. (2001). *The Flag Fen Basin: Archaeology and environment of a Fenland landscape*. London: English Heritage Archaeological Monograph. Available at: https://doi.org/10.5284/1028203.

Pryor, F.M.M. and Bamforth, M. (2010). *Flag Fen, Peterborough, Excavation and Research 1995–2007*. Oxford: Oxbow Books.

Rackham, J. (2013). Animal bones. In S. Willis (ed.), *The Roman Roadside Settlement and Multi-Period Ritual Complex at Nettleton and Rothwell, Lincolnshire Volume 1*, 321–35. London: Pre-Construct Archaeology and University of Kent.

Rackham, J. (2018). *Geoarchaeological Desk-Top Report: Triton Knoll Wind Farm, onshore cable Route*. Cambridge: Allen Archaeology Limited: unpublished report in project archive. Available at Archaeological Data Service: https://doi.org/10.5284/1125918.

Rackham, J. (2019). *Geoarchaeology stage 3 auger survey: For the Triton Knoll Electrical System*. Allen Archaeology Limited: unpublished report in project archive. Available at Archaeological Data Service: https://doi.org/10.5284/1125918.

Rackham, J. (2020). *Geoarchaeology Stage 4 Coring Report: For the Triton Knoll Electrical System*. Cambridge: Allen Archaeology Limited unpublished report. Available at: https://doi.org/10.5284/1125918.

Rackham, J., Scaife, R. and Langdon, C. (2021). *Geoarchaeological Stage 4 Analysis Report: For the Triton Knoll Electrical Scheme*. Cambridge: Allen Archaeology Limited: unpublished report in project archive. Available at Archaeological Data Service: https://doi.org/10.5284/1125918.

Rayner, T. (2003). *Land at Backgate, Cowbit, Lincolnshire. Archaeological Evaluation*. Sleaford: Archaeological Project Services unpublished report 78/03. Available at: https://doi.org/10.5284/1014947.

Redfern, R.C. Hamlin, C. and Athfield, N.B. (2010). Temporal changes in diet: a stable isotope analysis of late Iron Age and Roman Dorset, Britain. *Journal of Archaeological Science* 37, 1149–1160.

Reed, K. and Wallace, M. (2024). To pretreat, or not to pretreat, that is the question. The value of pretreatment protocols in the stable carbon and nitrogen isotope analysis of archaeobotanical cereal grains from Croatia and Serbia, STAR. *Science & Technology of Archaeological Research* 10(1), 1–17.

Reimer, P.J., Austin, W.E.N., Bard, E., Bayliss, A., Blackwell, P.G., Ramsey, C.B., Butzin, M., Cheng, H., Edwards, R.L., Friedrich, M., Grootes, P.M., Guilderson, T.P., Hajdas, I., Heaton, T.J., Hogg, A.G., Hughen, K.A., Kromer, B., Manning, S.W., Muscheler, R., Palmer, J.G., Pearson, C., Plicht, J.V.D., Reimer, R.W., Richards, D.A., Scott, E.M., Southon, J.R., Turney, C.S.M., Wacker, L., Adolphi, F., Büntgen, U., Capano, M., Fahrni, S.M., Fogtmann-Schulz, A., Friedrich, R., Köhler, P., Kudsk, S., Miyake, F., Olsen, J., Reinig, F., Sakamoto, M., Sookdeo, A. and Talamo, S. (2020). The IntCal20 Northern Hemisphere Radiocarbon Age Calibration Curve (0–55 cal kBP). *Radiocarbon* 62, 725–757.

Reynardson, J.B. (1850). *Catalogue of Antiquities, Memoirs illustrative of the History and Antiquities of the County and City of Lincoln, communicated to the Annual meeting of the Archaeological Institute of Great Britain and Ireland, held in Lincoln, July 1848*. Lincoln: Proceedings of the Annual Meeting of the Archaeological Institute 1845.

Richards, M. and Hedges, R.E.M. (1999). A Neolithic revolution? New evidence of diet in the British Neolithic. *Antiquity* 73, 891–897.

Rippon, S. (2002). Infield and outfield: The early stages of marshland colonisation and the evolution of medieval field systems. In T. Lane and J. Coles (eds), *Through Wet and Dry; Essays in honour of David Hall*, 54–70. Sleaford and Exeter: Lincolnshire Archaeology and Heritage Report Series 5/WARP Occasional Paper 17.

Rippon, S. (2004). *Historic Landscape Analysis: Deciphering the countryside*. Council for British Archaeology Practical Handbook 16.

Rippon, S., Albersberg. G., Allen, J.R.L., Allen, S., Cameron, N., Gleed-Owen, C., Davis, P., Hamilton-Dyer, S., Haslett, S., Heathcote, J., Jones, J., Margetts, A., Richards, D., Shiel, N., Smith, D., Smith, J., Timby, J., Tinsley, H. and Williams, H. (2000). The Romano-British exploitation of coastal wetlands: Survey and excavation on the north Somerset Levels, 1993–7. *Britannia* 31, 69–200.

Rivingtons (1919). *Rivingtons Notes on Building Construction Part III. Materials. Seventh Edition*. London: Longmans, Green and Co.

Robinson, D.N. (1981). *The Book of the Lincolnshire Seaside: The Story of the Coastline from the Humber to the Wash*. London: Barracuda Books.

Robinson, D. (1993) Brick and tile making. In S. Bennett and N. Bennett (eds), *An Historical Atlas of Lincolnshire*, 116–117. Hull: University of Hull Press.

Robinson, Z.I., Bamforth, M., Challinor, D., Hazell, Z. and Knight, M. (2024). Structural wood. In R. Ballantyne, A. Cooper, D. Gibson, M. Knight and I. Robinson Zeki (eds), *Must Farm Pile-dwelling Settlement: Volume 2. Specialist Reports*, 235–246. Cambridge: McDonald Institute for Archaeological Research

Robson, J.D. (1985). *Soils of Lincolnshire IV: Sheet TF45 (Friskney)*. Rothamsted: Soil Survey Record 88.

Rodwell, W.J. (1976). Coinage, *oppida* and the rise of Belgic power in southeastern Britain. In B. Cunliffe and T. Rowley (eds), *Oppida: The Beginnings of Urbanisation in Barbarian Europe*, 181–367. Oxford: British Archaeological Reports International Series 11.

Roffe, D. (1993). Medieval administration. In S. Bennett and N. Bennett (eds), *An Historical Atlas of Lincolnshire*, 34–43. Hull: University of Hull Press.

Rogers, A. (2011). *Late Roman Towns in Britain: Rethinking change and decline*. Cambridge: Cambridge University Press.

Rogerson, L. (2022). KENT-7FBD56. An early medieval stylus. Portable Antiquities Scheme. Available at: https://finds.org.uk/database/artefacts/record/id/1074856 [last accessed September 2023].

Roushannafas, T. and McKerracher, M. (2023). Diversity of free-threshing wheat in early medieval England supported by geometric morphometric analysis of grains. *Environmental Archaeology* 1–18. https://doi.org/10.1080/14614103.2023.2223406.

Rowlandson, I.M. (2011a). The Roman pottery. In N. Field and M. McDaid, *Biomass Generating Station, Hobson Way, Stallingborough, North-East Lincolnshire Archaeological Excavation*. Sleaford: Naomi Field Archaeological Consultancy unpublished report.

Rowlandson, I.M. (2011b). The Roman pottery. In C. Palmer-Brown and J. Rylatt, *How Times Change: Navenby Unearthed*, 73–101. Lincoln: Pre-Construct Archaeological Services Monograph 2.

Rowlandson, I.M. (2013). *An Assessment of the Prehistoric and Roman Ceramics from Trial Trenching at The Old School House, Orby Lane, Burgh-le-Marsh, Lincolnshire, OSBE13, TF 49952 65192*. Lincoln: Pre-Construct Archaeological Services unpublished report.

Rowlandson, I.M. (2014a). *The Roman Pottery from Land Adjacent to the A16 and Tytton Lane, Boston, Lincolnshire (SNPB10, Accn. 2010.61, TF 3390 4362)*. Lincoln: Pre-Construct Archaeological Services unpublished report.

Rowlandson, I.M. (2014b). *The Roman Pottery Archive-Burgh le Marsh – MRMBY14*. Unpublished report for Marc Berger.

Rowlandson, I.M. and Fiske, H.G. (2016). *The Prehistoric and Roman Pottery from the A160/A180 Port of Immingham Improvement (IMM26)*. Lincoln: Network Archaeology unpublished report.

Rowlandson, I.M. and Fiske, H.G. (2018). *The Other Roman Pottery from Triton Knoll Offshore Wind Farm, Onshore Electrical Connection, Lincolnshire [TKOW17]*. Cambridge: Allen Archaeology Limited unpublished report.

Rowlandson, I.M. and Fiske, H.G. (2019a). The Iron Age and Roman pottery. In N.A Cavanagh (ed.), *Becoming Roman in North East Lincolnshire. Excavation and Survey along the A160/A180 Port of Immingham Improvement Scheme*, 47–100. Oxford: British Archaeology Report 685.

Rowlandson, I.M. and Fiske, H.G. (2019b). *The Other Roman Pottery from Evaluation and Excavation of Land Either Side of the A16, South of Tytton Lane East, Boston, Lincolnshire (BTLE13 & BTLX15)*. Lincoln: Pre-Construct Archaeological Services unpublished report.

Rowlandson, I.M. and Fiske, H.G. (2019c). The other Roman pottery from Hatcliffe Top. In Willis 2019, 171–204.

Rowlandson, I.M. and Fiske, H.G. (2020). *An Assessment of the Iron Age and Roman Pottery from the Goxhill Feeder 9 scheme*. Lancaster: Oxford Archaeology North unpublished report.

Rowlandson, I.M. and Fiske, H.G. (2021). *Lincoln Eastern Bypass Project, Lincolnshire (LEB16): The Iron Age and Roman pottery assessment, version 1*. Lincoln: Network Archaeology unpublished report.

Rowlandson, I.M. and Fiske, H.G. (2022). A second century mortarium and colour-coated ware production site in the Newport suburb of Lincoln. *Journal of Roman Pottery Studies* 19, 200–234.

Rowlandson, I.M. and Fiske, H.G. (2023a). *The Prehistoric and Roman Pottery from Phases 2 and 3 of the Viking Link scheme, Lincolnshire (218713–5)*. Wessex Archaeology Limited: unpublished.

Rowlandson, I.M. and Fiske, H.G. (2023b). *The Prehistoric and Roman Pottery from Phase 1 of the Viking Link scheme, Lincolnshire (218716)*. Salisbury: Wessex Archaeology unpublished report.

Rowlandson, I.M. and Fiske, H.G. (2023c). Iron Age and Romano-British Pottery. In Tuck 2023, 127–192.

Rowlandson, I.M. and Fiske, H.G. (2024a). Iron Age and Roman pottery. In Headland Archaeology and Allen Archaeology 2024a, 1–8.

Rowlandson, I.M., and Fiske, H.G. (2024b). Iron Age and Roman pottery. In Headland Archaeology and Allen Archaeology 2024c, 17–44.

Rowlandson, I.M. and Fiske, H.G. (2024c). Iron Age and Roman pottery. In Headland Archaeology and Allen Archaeology 2024b, 1–23.

Rowlandson, I.M. and Monteil, G. (2014). *The Iron Age and Roman Pottery from Excavations at Solar Park Limited, Coronation Farm, Skegness, (COFS14)*. Glasgow: Neo Environmental unpublished report.

Rowlandson, I.M., Darling, M.J. and Monteil, G. (2011). The Roman pottery. In C. Palmer-Brown and J. Rylatt. *How Times Change: Navenby Unearthed*, 73–101. Lincoln: Pre-Construct Archaeological Services Monograph 2

Rowlandson, I.M. Fiske, H.G. and Monteil, G. (2017). *An Assessment of the Prehistoric and Roman Pottery from the Able Marine Energy Park scheme, North Killingholme, North Lincolnshire (NKAM13)*. Cambridge: Allen Archaeology Limited unpublished report.

Rowlandson, I.M. Fiske, H.G. and Monteil, G. (2020). *The Roman Pottery from Excavations at Clay Lake Bank, Spalding, Lincolnshire (CLSL18)*. Newark: Pre-Construct Archaeology unpublished report.

Rowlandson, I.M. with Hartley, K.F. and Monteil, G. (2015). *The Roman Pottery from Newport, Lincoln (LINP13)*. Cambridge: Allen Archaeology Limited unpublished report.

Rowlandson, I.M., Darling, M.J., Monteil, G., Tomlin, R. and Williams, D.F. (2014). *The Roman Pottery from Excavations at Bishop's Palace, Lincoln, (LIBI11)*. Cambridge: Allen Archaeology Limited unpublished report.

RSK (2015). *Triton Knoll Offshore Wind Farm Limited: Triton Knoll Electrical System Environmental Statement (Volume 3: Chapter 8 – Historic Environment)*. Helsby: RSK unpublished report.

Samuels, J. (1983). The Production of Roman Pottery in the East Midlands. Unpublished PhD Thesis, Nottingham University.

Schoch, W., Heller, I., Schweingruber, F.H. and Kienast, F. (2004). *Wood Anatomy of Central European Species*. www.woodanatomy.ch.

Scholma-Mason, O. (2024). *Triton Knoll Electrical System: Lincolnshire Marsh Landscape Analysis Report*. Silsoe/Cambridge: Headland Archaeology (UK) Limited and Allen Archaeology Limited unpublished report in project archive. Available at Archaeological Data Service: https://doi.org/10.5284/1125918.

Scott, E. (1993). *A Gazetteer of Roman Villas in Britain*. Leicester: Leicester Archaeology Monograph 1.

Seddon, D., Calvocoressi, D., Cooper, C. and Higgs, E.S. (1965). A Dark-Age settlement at Maxey, Northants. *Medieval Archaeology* 8, 20–73.

Serjeantson, D. (1989). Animal remains and the tanning trade. In D. Serjeantson and T. Waldron (eds), *Diet and Crafts in Towns: The evidence of animal remains from the Roman to the post-medieval periods*, 129–146. Oxford: British Archaeological Report 199.

Shaffrey, R. (2015). Intensive milling practices in the Romano-British landscape of southern England. Using newly established criteria for distinguishing millstones from rotary querns. *Britannia* 46, 55–92.

Shaffrey, R. (2024). The worked stone. In Gaunt *et al.* 2024.

Shennan, I. (1988). UK – England – Lincolnshire. In H.J. Walker (eds), *Artificial Structures and Shorelines*, 145–154. Dordrecht: GeoJournal Library 10.

Shennan, I. (1994a). Models of coastal sequences. In Waller 1994, 35–36.

Shennan, I. (1994b). Clastic sedimentary environments. In Waller 1994, 36–38.

Shennan, I. and Andrews, J.E. (eds), (2000). *Holocene Land-Ocean Interaction and Environmental Change around the North Sea*. London: Geological Society Special Publication 166.

Shennan, I., Lambeck, K., Flather, R., Horton, B., McArthur, J., Lloyd, J., Rutherford, M. and Wingfield, R. (2000). Modelling western North Sea palaeogeographies and tidal changes during the Holocene. In Shennan and Andrews (eds) 2000, 299–319.

Sidell, J. and Haughey, F. (2007). *Neolithic Archaeology in the Intertidal Zone*. Oxford: Neolithic Studies Group Seminar Papers 8.

Sidell, J., Cotton, J., Rayner, L. and Wheeler, L. (2002). *The Prehistory and Topography of Southwark and Lambeth*. London: Museum of London Monograph 14.

Sillwood, R. (2024). Small finds. In Headland Archaeology and Allen Archaeology 2024c, 71–88.

Simmons, B. (1979). The Lincolnshire Car Dyke: Navigation or drainage? *Britannia* 10, 183–196.

Simmons, B. (1993). Iron Age and Roman coasts around the Wash II: Archaeology. In S. Bennett and N. Bennett (eds), *An Historical Atlas of Lincolnshire*, 20–21. Hull: University of Hull Press.

Simmons, B. (2010). Late Roman coastal defence around the Wash. In S. Malone and M. Williams, (eds), *Rumours of Roman Finds. Recent work on Roman Lincolnshire*, 47–52. Sleaford: Heritage Trust of Lincolnshire.

Simmons, B. and Cope-Faulkner, P. (2004). *The Car Dyke Past Work, Current State and Future Possibilities.* Sleaford: (Lincolnshire Archaeology and Heritage Reports Series 8.

Simmons, I.G. (2017). Fen and sea: Medieval and early modern landscape evolution in south-east Lincolnshire before 1700. *Landscapes* 18(1), 37–54.

Simmons, I.G. (2022). *Fen and Sea: The landscapes of southeast Lincolnshire AD 500–1700*. Oxford: Windgather Press.

Simmons, I.G. and Foster, M.R. (2023). Both 'firmer'and 'queachy': drainage of the lands along the Lincolnshire Wash in the seventeenth century. *Water History* 15(3), 315–335.

Simpson, W.D. (1960). *The Building Accounts of Tattershall Castle 1434–72*. Lincoln: Lincoln Record Society 55.

Sirianni, M.J., Comas, C., Mount, G.J., Pierce, S., Coronado-Molina, C. and Rudnick, D. (2023). Understanding peat soil deformation and mechanisms of peat collapse across a salinity gradient in the southwestern Everglades. *Water Resources Research* 59(1) https://doi.org/10.1029/2021WR029683.

Smith, A. (2016). Buildings in the countryside. In Smith *et al.* (eds) 2016, 44–74.

Smith, A. (2017). Rural crafts and industry. In M. Allen, L. Lodwick, T. Brindle, M. Fulford and A. Smith (eds), *The Rural Economy of Roman Britain. New Visions of the Countryside of Roman Britain*, Volume 2, 78–234. London: *Britannia* Monograph Series 30.

Smith, A. (2018). Death in the countryside: Rural burial practices. In M. Allen, L. Lodwick, T. Brindle, M. Fulford and A. Smith (eds), *Life and Death in the Countryside of Roman Britain* Volume 3, 205–280. London: *Britannia* Monograph Series 31.

Smith, A. and Fulford, M. (2018). Conclusions. In M. Allen, L. Lodwick, T. Brindle, M. Fulford and A. Smith (eds), *Life and Death in the Countryside of Roman Britain* Volume 3, 346–357. London: *Britannia* Monograph Series 31.

Smith, A. and Fulford, M. (2019). The defended Vici of Roman Britain: Recent research and new agendas. *Britannia* 50, 109–47.

Smith, A., Allen, M., Brindle, T. and Fulford, M. (2016). *The Rural Settlement of Roman Britain, New Visions of the Countryside of Roman Britain* Volume 1. London: *Britannia* Monograph Series 29.

Smith, D.M., Zalasiewicz, J.A., Williams, M., Wilkinson, I.P., Redding, M. and Begg, C. (2010). Holocene drainage systems of the English Fenland: Roddons and their environmental significance. *Proceedings of the Geologists' Association* 121, 256–269.

Snee, J. (2000). *Archaeological Watching Brief of Development at Hall Lane, Burgh Le Marsh, Lincolnshire.* Sleaford: Archaeological Project Services unpublished report.

Snee, J. (2004). *Archaeological Excavation on Land at Low Road, Spalding, Lincolnshire (SLR02).* Sleaford: Archaeological Project Services unpublished report.

Spavold, J. and Brown, S. (2005). *Ticknall Pots and Potters.* Ashbourne: Landmark Publishing.

Spence, C. (2009). *Interim Report on Archaeological Excavations at Sudbrooke (Roman Villa) Lincolnshire (SUD08: July–August 2008.* Lincoln: Department of Culture and Environment Bishop Grosseteste University College https://www.academia.edu/911036/Interim_Report_on_Archaeological_Excavations_at_Sudbrooke_Roman_Villa_Lincolnshire.

Spoerry, P. (2008). *Ely Wares*. Cambridge: East Anglian Archaeology Report 122.

Spoerry, P. (2016). *The Production and Distribution of Medieval Pottery in Cambridgeshire.* Cambrdige: East Anglian Archaeology 159.

Stace, C. (1997). *New flora of the British Isles*. Cambridge: Cambridge University Press.

Stafford, E. (2012). *Landscape and Prehistory of the East London Wetlands Investigations along the A13 DBFO Roadscheme, Tower Hamlets, Newham and Barking and Dagenham, 2000– 2003.* Oxford: Oxford Archaeology Monograph 17.

Stafford, P. (1985). *The East Midlands in the Early Middle Ages*. Leicester: Leicester University Press.

Steane, J.M. (1984). *The Archaeology of Medieval England and Wales*. Athens GA: University of Georgia Press.

Stevens, C. (2003). An investigation of agricultural consumption and production models for Prehistoric and Roman Britain. *Environmental Archaeology* 8, 61–76.

Stockdale, M., Gaunt, K. and Roberts, M. (2024). *Triton Knoll Electrical System: Fen Edge Landscape Analysis Report.* Headland Archaeology (UK) Limited and Allen Archaeology Limited unpublished report in project archive. Available at Archaeological Data Service: https://doi.org/10.5284/1125918.

Strang, A. (1997). Explaining Ptolemy's Roman Britain. *Britannia* 28, 1–30.

Stroud, E. (2022). Understanding early medieval crop and animal husbandry through isotopic analysis. In M. McKerracher and H. Hamerow (eds), *New Perspectives on the Medieval 'Agricultural Revolution': Crop, stock and furrow*, 41–60. Liverpool: Liverpool University Press.

Styring, A.K., Vaiglova, P., Bogaard, A., Church, M.J., Gröcke, D.R., Larsson, M., Liu, X., Stroud, E., Szpak, P. and Wallace, M.P. (2024). Recommendations for stable isotope analysis of charred archaeological crop remains. *Frontiers Environmental Archaeology* 3, 1470375. https://doi.org/10.3389/fearc.2024.1470375.

Sudds, B. (2016). The pottery. In C. Jackson, *Land North of Church Road, Wreningham, Norfolk.* Cambridge: Pre-Construct Archaeology Limited unpublished report 12683.

Swan, V.G. (1984). *The Pottery Kilns of Roman Britain*. London: Royal Commission on the Historic Monuments (England) and HMSO Supplementary Series 5.

Swinnerton, H.H. (1932). The Prehistoric pottery sites of the Lincolnshire Coast. *Antiquaries Journal* 12, 239–253.

Szpak, P. (2022). Why zooarchaeology needs stable isotope analysis. In A. Sharpe and J. Krigbaum (eds), *Applications of Isotope Research in Zooarchaeology*, 248–270. Gainesville FL: University Press of Florida.

Tabor, J. and Phillips, T. (2024). *Cattle, Community and Place. The Archaeology of the Cambridge Biomedical Campus.* Cambridge: McDonald Institute for Archaeological Research.

Taylor, C.C. (1981). Archaeology and the origins of open-field agriculture. In T. Rowley (ed.), *The Origins of Open Field Agriculture*. London: Routledge Library Editions: The Medieval World.

Taylor, J. (2006). The Roman period. In Cooper (ed.), 2006, 137–159.

Taylor, J. (2007). *An Atlas of Roman Rural Settlement in England*. York: Council for British Archaeology Research Report 151.

Taylor, M. (1998). Wood and bark from the enclosure ditch. In F.M.M. Pryor (ed.), *Etton: Excavations at a Neolithic causewayed enclosure near Maxey, Cambridgeshire*. London: English Heritage Archaeological Monograph. Available at: https://doi.org/10.5284/1028203.

Taylor, M. (2001). The wood. In Pryor (ed.) 2001, 167–228.

Taylor, M. (2010). Big Trees and monumental timbers. In Pryor and Bamforth (eds) 2010, 90–97.

Telford, A. and Stockdale, M. (2024). *Triton Knoll Electrical System: Inland Fen Edge Landscape Analysis Report*. Silsoe/Cambridge: Headland Archaeology (UK) Limited and Allen Archaeology Limited unpublished report in project archive. Available at Archaeological Data Service: https://doi.org/10.5284/1125918.

Thomas, R. and Stallibrass, S. (2008). For starters: Producing and supplying food to the army in the Roman north-west provinces. In S. Stallibrass and R. Thomas (eds), *Feeding the Roman Army: The archaeology of production and supply in north-west Europe*, 1–17. Oxford: Oxbow Books.

Tomlinson, Z. (2019). *An Assessment Report on the Fired Clay from Land on the West of the A16, South of Tytton Lane East, Boston, Lincolnshire. Site Code: BTLX15*. Cambridge: Allen Archaeology Limited unpublished report.

Tomlinson, Z. (2024). Ceramic building material. In Headland Archaeology and Allen Archaeology 2024c, 101–118.

Trimble, D. (2001). Excavation of an early Roman saltern in Morton Fen, Lincolnshire. In Lane and Morris (eds) 2001, 99–161.

Trinder, B. (2013). *Britain's Industrial Revolution. The Making of Manufacturing People, 1700–1870*. Lancaster: Carnegie Publishing.

Trow-Smith, R. (1957). *A History of British Livestock Husbandry to 1700*. London: Routledge.

Tuck, A. (2023). *The Archaeology of the Hornsea Project One Offshore Windfarm Cable Route. Agriculture, settlement, moats and saltworking in the Lincolnshire Marshes*. Salisbury: Wessex Archaeology Report 41.

Tyers, I. (2024). Dendrochronology. In Headland Archaeology and Allen Archaeology 2024c, 129–134.

Tyrrell, R. (2015). Ceramic loom weights. In M. Atkinson and S.J. Preston Heybridge (eds), *A Late Iron Age and Roman Settlement, Excavations at Elms Farm 1993–5*. Volume 2. Internet Archaeology 40. https://doi.org/10.11141/ia.40.1.

Upex, S.G. (2018). *Iron Age and Roman Settlement: Rescue excavations at Lynch Farm 2, Orton Longueville*. Peterborough: East Anglian Archaeology 163.

Van de Noort, R. (2004). *The Humber Wetlands: The archaeology of a dynamic landscape*. Macclesfield: Windgather Press.

Van de Noort, R. and Davies, P. (1993). *Wetland Heritage: An archaeological assessment of the Humber Wetlands*. Hull: University of Hull Press.

Van de Noort, R., Ellis, S., Taylor, M. and Weir, D. (1999). Preservation of Archaeological sites. In M. Van der Veen, The economic value of chaff and straw in arid and temperate zones. *Vegetation History and Archaeobotany* 8(3), 211–244.

Van der Veen, M. (2014). Arable farming, horticulture, and food: expansion, innovation, and diversity in Roman Britain. In M. Millett, L. Revell and A. Moore (eds), *The Oxford Handbook of Roman Britain*, 807–833. Oxford: Oxford University Press.

Van der Veen, M. and Jones, G. (2007). The production and consumption of cereals a question of scale. In C. Haselgrove and T. Moore (eds), *The later Iron Age in Britain and Beyond*, 419–429. Oxford: Oxbow Books.

Van der Veen, M. and O'Connor, T. (1998). The expansion of agricultural production in late Iron Age and Roman Britain. In J. Bayley (eds), *Science in Archaeology: An agenda for the future*, 217–228. London: England Heritage.

Vujovic, M. (2007). Clay slingshots from the Roman fort Novae at Čezava (Serbia). In A.W. Busch and H.J. Schalles (eds), *Waffen in Aktion, Akten der 16. Internationalen Roman Military Equipment Conference*, 249–256. Mainz am Rhein: von Zabern.

Wacher, J. (1974). *The Towns of Roman Britain*. London: Book Club Associates.

Walker, A. and Kriti, A. (2020). *Environmental Assessment: Charred, uncharred and waterlogged plant remains. Headland Archaeology Triton knoll Electrical system Lot 1 and Lot 2 (SMR14, 15 & 16) Mitigation. Volume 2: Environmental and Artefact Assessment*. Silsoe: Headland Archaeology Limited unpublished report.

Walker, J., Gaffney, V., Fitch, S., Muru, M., Fraser, A., Bates, M. and Bates, R. (2020). A great wave: The Storegga tsunami and the end of Doggerland? *Antiquity* 94(378), 1409–1425.

Wallace, M. and Fryer, V. (2024). Archaeobotanical analysis. In Headland Archaeology and Allen Archaeology 2024c, 135–149.

Wallace, M.P., Jones, G., Charles, M., Fraser, R., Heaton, T.H.E. and Bogaard, A. (2015). Stable Carbon Isotope Evidence for Neolithic and Bronze Age Crop Water Management in the Eastern Mediterranean and Southwest Asia. *PLoS ONE* 10(6), e0127085.

Wallace, M., Jones, G., Charles, M., Fraser, R., Halstead, P., Heaton, T.H.E. and Bogaard, A. (2013). Stable carbon isotope analysis as a direct means of inferring crop water status and water management practices. *World Archaeology* 45, 388–409.

Wallace, M., Montgomery, J., Rogers, B., Moore, J., Nowell, G., Bowsher, D. and Smith, A. (2024). Revealing continuity and sustainability through stable isotope analysis on the A14 project, Cambridgeshire, UK. *Quaternary Science Reviews* 346, 109059.

Waller, M. (1994). *The Fenland Project, Number 9: Flandrian environmental change in Fenland*. Cambridge: East Anglian Archaeology 70.

Waller, M. and Grant, M. J. (2012). Holocene pollen assemblages from coastal wetlands: Differentiating natural and anthropogenic causes of change in the Thames estuary, UK. *Journal of Quaternary Science* 27(5), 461–474.

Wardle, A. (1981). Musical Instruments in the Roman World. Volume I & II. Unpublished PhD thesis, University of London.

Watts, S. (2014). *The Life and Death of Querns: The deposition and use contexts of querns in southwestern England from the Neolithic to the Iron Age*. Southampton: Highfield Press.

Watts, V. (2007). *The Cambridge Dictionary of English Place-Names: Based on the collections of the English Place-Name Society.* Cambridge: Cambridge University Press.

Webley, L. (2006). *A Fen-edge Landscape at Parnwell Peterborough: Prehistoric, Roman and Post-Roman occupation.* Cambridge: Oxford Archaeology unpublished report.

Wessex Archaeology. (2023). *Viking Link, Lincolnshire. Zones 2 and 3 Post-excavation Assessment.* Salisbury: Wessex Archaeology unpublished report.

Wheeler, E., Baas, P and Gasson, P. (1989). IAWA list of microscopic features for hardwood identification. *International Association of Wood Anatomists Bulletin* 10(3), 219–332.

Whitaker, W. and Jukes-Brown, A.J. (1899). *Geology of the Border of the Wash: Including Boston and Hunstatnton: an explanation of Sheet 69 (old series).* London: Memoir of the Geological Survey of Great Britain: England and Wales Sheet 69.

White, A. (1982). *Early Brick Buildings in Lincolnshire: A guide.* Lincoln: Lincolnshire Museums.

White, A.J. (1989). Post Medieval Pottery in Lincolnshire 1450–1850. Unpublished PhD thesis University of Nottingham.

White, K.D. (1970). *Roman Farming.* London: Thames & Hudson.

Whitwell, J.B. (1993). *History of Lincolnshire, Volume 2: Roman Lincolnshire Lincoln.* Lincoln: History of Lincolnshire Committee.

Williams, B. (1977). Salt in Prehistory. Unpublished BA thesis, University of Sheffield.

Williams, D. (2010). *Newbridge Quarry Extension, Pickering, North Yorkshire. Archaeological Excavation: Phase 1. Interim Report.* Leeds: Archaeological Services WYAS unpublished report.

Willis, S. (2013). *The Roman Roadside Settlement and Multi-Period Ritual Complex at Nettleton and Rothwell. The Central Lincolnshire Wolds Research Project Volume 1. Lincolnshire.* Cambridge: Pre-Construct Archaeology Limited with the University of Kent, Kent.

Willis, S. (2019). *The Waithe Valley through Time. 1. The Archaeology of the valley and excavation and survey in the Hatcliffe Area. The Central Lincolnshire Wolds Research Project. Volume 2.* London: Pre-Construct Archaeology.

Wilson, K. and White, D.J.B. (1986). *The Anatomy of Wood.* London: Stobart.

Wood, I. (2024). *The Thin-section Analysis of the Post-Roman Pottery from the Triton Knoll Project.* In Headland Archaeology (UK) Limited and Allen Archaeology Limited: unpublished report in project archive. Available at Archaeological Data Service: https://doi.org/10.5284/1125918.

Woolgar, C.M. (1999). *The Great Household in Late Medieval England.* New Haven CO: Yale University Press.

Wright, A. (2021). *Raising the Dead. England's unique treasure.* San José CA: Matador.

Wymer, J.J. and Straw, A. (1977). Hand-axes from beneath glacial till at Walton-le-Wold, Lincolnshire and the distribution of palaeoliths in Britain. *Proceedings of the Prehistoric Society* 43, 355–360.

Young, J. (1989). The pottery. In P. Miles, J. Young, and J. Wacher (eds), *A Late Saxon Kiln-Site at Silver Street, Lincoln 203–221.* London: The Archaeology of Lincoln 17:3.

Young, J. (2008). The pottery. In D. Hounsell (eds), *Land at Millstone Lane, Barnack, Cambridgeshire: Post-excavation assessment and updated project design,* 39–87. Cambridge: Oxford Archaeology East unpublished report 972.

Young, J. (2010). *A report on the Daub and Fired Clay from St. Nicholas C of E Primary School, Boston, Lincolnshire (snpb 10).* Cambridge: Allen Archaeology Limited unpublished report.

Young, J. (2014). *Post-Roman Pottery Report for Cartergate, Grimsby, Lincolnshire (CGNL09 and CGRM09).* London: Pre-Construct Archaeology unpublished report.

Young, J. (2018). *The Post-Roman pottery from Triton Knoll Offshore Wind Farm, Onshore Electrical Connection, Lincolnshire, TKOW17.* Cambridge: Allen Archaeology Limited unpublished report.

Young, J. (2019). *The Post-Roman pottery from Triton Knoll Offshore Wind Farm, Onshore Electrical Connection, Lincolnshire, TKML17.* Silsoe: Headland Archaeology unpublished report.

Young, J. (2023a). *Assessment of the Post-Roman Pottery from Viking Link Zones 2 and 3.* Salisbury: Wessex Archaeology unpublished report.

Young, J. (2023b). *The Post-Roman Pottery from Archaeological Investigations at Maidenwell Manor House, Maidenwell, Lincolnshire (MMHM21).* London Pre-Construct Archaeology Limited, unpublished report.

Young, J. (2023c). *The Post-Roman Pottery from an Archaeological Investigation at Sunny Dale Close, Surfleet, Lincolnshire (SUSC22).* Sleaford: Archaeological Project Services unpublished report.

Young, J. (2023d). *The Post-Roman Pottery from Goxhill Feeder 9, North Lincolnshire.* Cambridge: Oxford Archaeology Limited unpublished report.

Young, J. (2024a). Post-Roman pottery. In Headland Archaeology and Allen Archaeology 2024c, 51–70.

Young, J. (2024b). Post-Roman pottery. In Headland Archaeology and Allen Archaeology 2024a, 10–20.

Young, J. and Daubney, A. (2020). *The Post-Roman pottery from Triton Knoll Offshore Wind Farm, Onshore Electrical Connection, Lincolnshire, TRKN18.* Cambridge: Allen Archaeology Limited unpublished report.

Young, J. and Gray, J. (2023). *The Post-Roman Pottery from Zone 1 of the Viking Link, Lincolnshire (VIK19).* Sleaford: Archaeological Project Services unpublished report.

Young, J. and Vince A. (2009). The Anglo-Saxon pottery. In D. Evans and C. Loveluck, *Life and Economy at Early Medieval Flixborough,* c *AD 600–1000: The artefact evidence. Excavations at Flixborough, Volume 2,* 339–397. Oxford: Oxbow Books.

Young, J., Vince, A.G. and Nailor, V. (2005). *A Corpus of Anglo-Saxon and Medieval Pottery from Lincoln.* Oxford: Lincoln Archaeology Studies 7.